The
Apocalyptic
Premise

ERNEST W. LEFEVER received a B.D. and a Ph.D. in Christian ethics from Yale University. He has been a foreign policy researcher at the Library of Congress, the Institute for Defense Analyses, the Brookings Institution, and the Johns Hopkins University School of Advanced International Studies. He has taught at American, Maryland, and Georgetown universities. Among the fourteen books he has written or edited are *Ethics and United States Foreign Policy* (1957), *Arms and Arms Control* (1962), *Uncertain Mandate: Politics of the U.N. Congo Operation* (1967), *Ethics and World Politics* (1972), and *Nuclear Arms in the Third World: U.S. Policy Dilemma* (1979).

E. STEPHEN HUNT has an M.A. from the American University School of International Service and a Ph.D. in political science and higher education from the University of Virginia. He has done research in international relations and education, has been a staff consultant to the Board of Higher Education and Ministry, United Methodist Church, and has been a staff associate of the Division of Education and Ministry, National Council of Churches.

The Apocalyptic Premise

Nuclear Arms Debated

Thirty-one Essays by Statesmen, Scholars,
Religious Leaders, and Journalists

Edited by Ernest W. Lefever
and E. Stephen Hunt

Ethics and Public Policy Center
Washington, D.C.

Library of Congress Cataloging in Publication Data
Main entry under title:
The Apocalyptic premise.
   Includes index.
   1. Atomic warfare—Moral and ethical aspects—
Addresses, essays, lectures.   2. Atomic warfare—
Religious aspects—Addresses, essays, lectures.
3. Antinuclear movement—Addresses, essays, lectures.
4. United States—Military policy—Addresses, essays,
lectures.   5. Europe—Defenses—Addresses, essays,
lectures.   I. Lefever, Ernest W.   II. Hunt, E. Stephen,
1948-   .   III. Ethics and Public Policy Center
(Washington, D.C.)
UF767.A528   1982   172'.42   82-18315
ISBN 0-89633-062-1
ISBN 0-89633-063-X (pbk.)

$14 cloth, $9 paper   Second printing 1983

Contents

Nuclear Arms and the Uses of Fear

FEW GREAT DEBATES are truly great. No matter how vital the issue, the public discussion is usually trivialized by ignorance, naïveté, deception, demagoguery, self-righteous posturing, and exaggerated hopes and fears. Truth, reason, realism, and even patriotism are sometimes overwhelmed by less noble human passions.

Although all this was strikingly true of the nuclear arms debate that in 1982 gained momentum in secular and religious circles on both sides of the Atlantic, the debate has been more than a babble of tongues. Thoughtful voices have not been completely smothered by simplistic slogans, apocalyptic visions, misplaced fears, distorted statistics, and the beguiling doubletalk of those with hidden agendas.

We believe and hope that the quality of discourse can be improved, and that this collection of thirty-one essays, selected from a wide variety of sources reflecting diverse views, will play a small part in bringing this to pass.

For those of us who share the rich Judeo-Christian heritage, identifying the ends we seek is not the central moral and political problem in the nuclear debate. Prime Minister Margaret Thatcher put it succinctly in her 1982 address at the United Nations: we are striving for "peace with freedom and justice." The most perplexing problem in ethics and politics is to find the best ways of moving toward these high goals. Ideas play an important role in determining the means we choose. Some ideas obscure desirable ends and confuse the means for reaching them. As a result, we fix our gaze on short-term objectives or adopt measures that betray the cause of peace and freedom.

One such influential idea is "the apocalyptic premise," which has always flourished in times of trouble and uncertainty. Both the Old Testament and the New Testament have vivid apocalyptic passages portraying how the world will end for both the righteous and the unrighteous. These prophetic visions, properly understood, lend perspective to faithful Jews and Christians, who believe there is a dimension beyond history that gives meaning to the here and now.

But in current secular usage, an apocalyptic event is one that spells doom for a nation, a civilization, or the human race itself. Therefore the apocalyptic premise lacks the hope of the biblical vision of "a new heaven and a new earth." In the nuclear era some secular apocalyptic prophets proclaim that the world will be destroyed by fire and brimstone unless their particular prescriptions for avoiding catastrophe are adopted. One example is Jonathan Schell, whose 1982 book *The Fate of the Earth* made the best-seller lists. Schell's apocalyptic vision is simple and frightening: the splitting of the atom made nuclear weapons inevitable, nuclear weapons make nuclear war inevitable, and nuclear war means the end of the human race; therefore we must eliminate nuclear weapons before they eliminate us.

Since Schell's "solution" to the nuclear threat requires a drastic reconstruction of human nature, he is both an apocalyptic and a utopian. But neither Apocalypse nor Utopia has ever served as a reliable guide to wise statesmanship. Schell calls for the abolition of violence, the state, sovereignty, and the idea of "external enemies"; we must, he says, "reinvent the world." Few readers are likely to enlist in Schell's ultimate crusade, but his call for an immediate "freeze on the further deployment of nuclear weapons" as a minimal first step has given impetus to the freeze movement.

A freeze on both Soviet and American nuclear arms is an attractive idea that avoids the stigma attached to unilateral disarmament. "A Nuclear Freeze Now" has a ring of balance and simplicity. But freeze proponents, motivated by a vague concept of "overkill," ignore hard and verifiable facts about the actual nuclear forces on both sides of the Iron Curtain. They also tend to overlook profound differences in the power, purposes, and behavior of the Soviet Union and the United States during the past three decades. Moral reasoning and political calculation require the actor, whether citizen or statesman, to draw precisely these distinctions of fact and analysis, which may make the difference between war and peace, tyranny and freedom.

The political leaders, theologians, journalists, professors, and strategic analysts who wrote the essays in this volume disagree on the nature of the primary threat. Some regard the Soviet Union as the chief threat, while others see the United States in that role. Still others believe that technology—the bomb itself—is the threat, that somehow technology has a dynamism of its own and man has lost control.

One's view of the threat is always closely related to fear, that powerful human emotion that can be harnessed for good or manipulated for ill. Reasoned fear based on real dangers is essential for survival. Unreasoning fear based on myths or highly unlikely dangers can lead to unwise and destructive behavior. The nuclear debate provides examples of both.

On the positive side, it is reasonable and prudent for the people of Western Europe to fear a conventional invasion or a nuclear attack by the Soviet Union. Neither is likely at the moment, but given Moscow's massive conventional forces and its 315 deployed SS-20 missiles (which to quote one of our writers could in minutes "obliterate every sizable city from Oslo to Lisbon, from Glasgow to Istanbul"), fear of the Soviet Union is justified—all the more so because current NATO forces have no such intermediate-range missiles to counter the SS-20s.

In this highly unsymmetrical and unstable situation, the United States plans to deploy Pershing II missiles to deter a Soviet strike. Many nuclear freeze proponents show greater anxiety over the not-yet-deployed Pershing IIs than over the already deployed Soviet SS-20s. Fear of a future possibility over a present reality, especially given the Soviet record of expansion and conquest, is the kind of unreasoning fear that may lead to policies that further endanger peace and freedom. In contrast, reasoned fear can lead to prudent policies calculated to deter nuclear war and nuclear blackmail.

The peace movements in Western Europe and the United States have had a significant but unquantifiable effect on the decisions of Western statesmen. The authors in this volume differ widely on the influence the Soviet Union has had on these movements. Part Two includes three major essays on the question of Soviet involvement, one by a seasoned journalist, one by two scholars, and one by a distinguished Soviet émigré. The arguments of pro-freeze and anti-freeze proponents should, of course, be judged on their merits, not their sources. As St. Augustine said, "Truth by whomever spoken is of God." The central question to ask is, Will the freeze proposal if adopted promote the cause of peace and freedom or have the opposite effect? At the same time, no responsible citizen should ignore the connections and hidden agendas of persons and organizations influential in this vital debate.

A theme that is usually implicit rather than explicit in the essays is that of the "just war." Virtually all the authors hold that wars of self-defense are just, but they define self-defense in various ways. Soviet spokesmen and their supporters appear to believe that it is just for the Soviet Union to develop, deploy, and threaten to use nuclear arms, but that it is unjust for "capitalist" states to deploy them, even for deterrence and defense.

Moscow has encouraged the concept of "nuclear pacifism" in the West (though it does not, of course, tolerate the idea within its own realm). Some "nuclear pacifists" insist that the very production of nuclear arms is unjust; others, that the nuclear era has rendered all war unjust. Nuclear pacifism rests on the assumption that nuclear weapons are radically different from conventional weapons and that this difference makes traditional moral arguments about war obsolete. Of course, large nuclear bombs are far more destructive than conventional ones, but if the focus is on human beings and their fundamental right to life and freedom, the technology of war becomes a secondary consideration. Since the end of World War II there have been some 140 conflicts in which perhaps ten million people have been killed, none by nuclear arms. During the same period, hundreds of millions have lost their freedom, none by the threat of nuclear weapons.

Each of the essays in this collection is preceded by a brief introduction, called *Focus,* that points out main themes and relates both complementary and opposing contributors to one another. Other elements that we hope readers will find useful are a chart showing the comparative strength of NATO and Warsaw Pact forces in Europe (p. xii) and a bibliography (p. 401), whose five parts correspond to the text.

We are grateful to the authors and publishers represented here for their permission to reprint the essays, many with new titles and subheads and in excerpted form to avoid excessive overlapping. The editors alone are responsible for the selection of essays and for the introductions.

We offer this book on a timely and fateful issue with the hope that it will stimulate thoughtful discussion on both sides of the Atlantic and in both religious and secular circles. We believe that a vigorous and rational public debate will enable Western political leaders to make wiser and more responsible decisions as they struggle to maintain the bastions of freedom in an increasingly dangerous world.

ERNEST W. LEFEVER
President

E. STEPHEN HUNT
Senior Research Associate

Ethics and Public Policy Center
Washington, D.C.
November 15, 1982

NATO AND WARSAW PACT FORCE COMPARISON
(In Place in Europe, 1982)

NATO Countries

Warsaw Pact Countries

SOURCE: NATO Headquarters, Brussels.

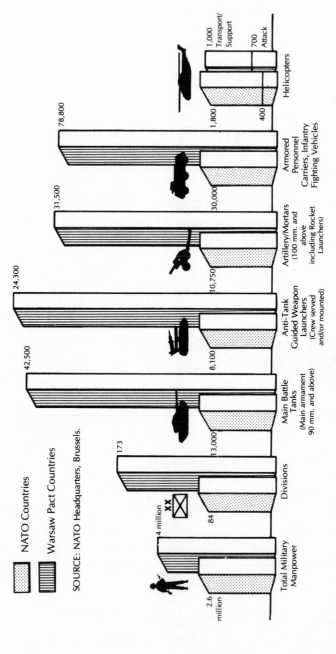

Total Military Manpower	4 million / 2.6 million	
Divisions	173 / 84	
Main Battle Tanks (Main armament 90 mm. and above)	42,500 / 13,000	
Anti-Tank Guided Weapon Launchers (Crew served and/or mounted)	24,300 / 8,100	
Artillery/Mortars (100 mm. and above including Rocket Launchers)	31,500 / 10,750	
Armored Personnel Carriers, Infantry Fighting Vehicles	78,800 / 30,000	
Helicopters	1,000 Transport/Support, 700 Attack / 1,800, 400	

NOTES:

1. Warsaw Pact divisions normally consist of fewer personnel than many NATO divisions but contain more tanks and artillery, thereby obtaining similar combat power.

2. Forces in place in NATO Europe, Warsaw Pact forces as far east as but excluding the three western military districts in western Russia (Moscow, Volga, and Ural).

PART ONE

Arms Control Issues

1. Nuclear Weapons and the Atlantic Alliance

By McGeorge Bundy, George F. Kennan,
Robert S. McNamara, Gerard K. Smith

Focus Declaring that NATO nuclear policy is obsolete and in disarray, these four Americans—who all have served in high posts in recent administrations—call for new approaches to defend Western Europe and to make nuclear war less likely. They refer to "a fantastic proliferation of weapons and delivery systems" on both sides and insist that no "use of nuclear weapons, even on the smallest scale, could reliably be expected to remain limited."

They recommend that the United States adopt a no-first-use policy for nuclear arms. Recognizing that this might tempt the Soviet Union to launch a massive conventional attack across the north German plain, however, they call for a substantial conventional build-up in the West. "No one should underestimate the difficulty or the importance of the shift in military attitudes implied by a no-first-use policy," they warn.

The authors maintain that a no-first-use policy would serve as an effective deterrent, simplify strategic planning, "reduce the risk of conventional aggression," and go a long way toward meeting the "anxieties that underlie much of the new interest in nuclear disarmament" here and in Europe. Also, they hold, such a declaration by NATO would "help in our relations with the Soviet Union" and facilitate "serious reduction of nuclear armaments on both sides." Four West German leaders reply to this proposal in selection 2.

This essay received considerable favorable attention in the American prestige media when it appeared in *Foreign Affairs* early in 1982. Three of its authors were awarded the $50,000 Albert Einstein International Peace Prize in September 1982 (the fourth, George Kennan, was ineligible because he had won the prize the year before).

McGeorge Bundy was special assistant to the president for national security affairs under Presidents Kennedy and Johnson, and has had an extensive academic career as a historian. **George F. Kennan** was a career Foreign Service officer who served as U.S. ambassador to the U.S.S.R. (1952) and to Yugoslavia (1961-63). He has been a member of the Princeton Institute for Advanced Studies since 1953. **Robert S. McNamara** was secretary of defense under Presidents Kennedy and Johnson, 1961-68, and president of the World Bank 1968-81. **Gerard K. Smith** was chief of the U.S. delegation to the Strategic Arms Limitation Talks (SALT) from 1969 to 1972, under President Nixon.

W E ARE FOUR AMERICANS who have been concerned over many years with the relation between nuclear weapons and the peace and freedom of the members of the Atlantic Alliance. Having learned that each of us separately has been coming to hold new views on this hard but vital question, we decided to see how far our thoughts and the lessons of our varied experiences could be put together. The essay that follows is the result. It argues that a new policy can bring great benefits, but it aims to start a discussion, not to end it.

For thirty-three years now, the Atlantic Alliance has relied on the asserted readiness of the United States to use nuclear weapons if necessary to repel aggression from the East. Initially, indeed, it was widely thought (notably by such great and different men as Winston Churchill and Niels Bohr) that the basic military balance in Europe was between American atomic bombs and the massive conventional forces of the Soviet Union. But the first Soviet explosion, in August 1949, ended the American monopoly only one month after the Senate approved the North Atlantic Treaty, and in 1950 Communist aggression in Korea produced new Allied attention to the defense of Europe.

The "crude" atomic bombs of the 1940s have been followed in both countries by a fantastic proliferation of weapons and delivery systems, so that today the two parts of a still-divided Europe are targeted by many thousands of warheads both in the area and outside it. Within the Alliance, France and Britain have developed thermonuclear forces which are enormous compared to what the United States had at the beginning, although small by comparison with the present deployments of the superpowers. Doctrine has succeeded doctrine, from "balanced collective forces" to "massive retaliation" to "mutual assured destruction" to "flexible response" and the "seamless web." Throughout these transforma-

Reprinted by permission from the Spring 1982 issue of *Foreign Affairs* (© 1982 by the Council on Foreign Relations, Incorporated).

tions, most of them occasioned at least in part by changes in the Western view of Soviet capabilities, both deployments and doctrines have been intended to deter Soviet aggression and keep the peace by maintaining a credible connection between any large-scale assault, whether conventional or nuclear, and the engagement of the strategic nuclear forces of the United States.

A major element in every doctrine has been that the United States has asserted its willingness to be the first—has indeed made plans to be the first if necessary—to use nuclear weapons to defend against aggression in Europe. It is this element that needs reexamination now. Both its cost to the coherence of the Alliance and its threat to the safety of the world are rising while its deterrent credibility declines.

This policy was first established when the American nuclear advantage was overwhelming, but that advantage has long since gone and cannot be recaptured. As early as the 1950s it was recognized by both Prime Minister Churchill and President Eisenhower that the nuclear strength of both sides was becoming so great that a nuclear war would be a ghastly catastrophe for all concerned. The following decades have only confirmed and intensified that reality. The time has come for careful study of the ways and means of moving to a new Alliance policy and doctrine: that nuclear weapons will not be used unless an aggressor should use them first.

New NATO Nuclear Policy Needed

The disarray that currently besets the nuclear policy and practices of the Alliance is obvious. Governments and their representatives have maintained an appearance of unity as they persist in their support of the two-track decision of December 1979, under which 572 new American missiles of intermediate range are to be placed in Europe unless a satisfactory agreement on the limitation of such weapons can be reached in the negotiations between the United States and the Soviet Union that began last November. But behind this united front there are divisive debates, especially in countries where the new weapons are to be deployed.

The arguments put forward by advocates of these deployments contain troubling variations. The simplest and, intuitively, the most persuasive claim is that these new weapons are needed as a counter to the new Soviet SS-20 missiles; it may be a recognition of the surface attractiveness of this position that underlies President Reagan's striking—but probably not negotiable—proposal that if all the SS-20s are dismantled the planned deployments will be canceled. Other officials have a quite different argument, that without new and survivable American weapons which can reach Russia from Western Europe there can be no confidence that the strategic forces of the United States will remain committed to the defense of Western Europe. On this argument the new missiles are needed to make it more likely that any war in Europe would bring nuclear warheads on the Soviet Union and thus deter the aggressor in the first place. This argument is logically distinct from any concern about the Soviet SS-20s, and it probably explains the ill-concealed hope of some planners that the Reagan proposal will be rejected. Such varied justifications cast considerable doubt on the real purpose of the proposed deployment.

An equally disturbing phenomenon is the gradual shift in the balance of argument that has occurred since the need to address the problem was first asserted in 1977. Then the expression of need was European, and in the first instance German; the emerging parity of long-range strategic systems was asserted to create a need for a balance at less than intercontinental levels. The American interest developed relatively slowly, but because these were to be American missiles, American planners took the lead as the proposal was worked out. It has also served Soviet purposes to concentrate on the American role. A similar focus has been chosen by many leaders of the new movement for nuclear disarmament in Europe. And now there are American voices, some in the executive branch, talking as if European acceptance of these new missiles were some sort of test of European loyalty to the Alliance. Meanwhile some of those in Europe who remain publicly committed to both tracks of the 1979 agreement are clearly hoping that the day of deployment will never arrive. When the very origins of a new proposal become the source of irritated argument among allies—"You started it!"—something is badly wrong in our common understanding.

A still more severe instance of disarray, one which has occurred under both President Carter and President Reagan, relates to the so-called neutron bomb, a weapon designed to meet the threat of Soviet tanks. American military planners, authorized by doctrine to think in terms of early battlefield use of nuclear weapons, naturally want more "up-to-date" weapons than those they have now; it is known that thousands of the aging short-range nuclear weapons now in Europe are hard to use effectively. Yet to a great many Europeans the neutron bomb suggests, however unfairly, that the Americans are preparing to fight a "limited" nuclear war on their soil. Moreover, neither weapons designers nor the Pentagon officials they have persuaded seem to have understood the intense and special revulsion that is associated with killing by "enhanced radiation."

All these recent distempers have a deeper cause. They are rooted in the fact that the evolution of essentially equivalent and enormously excessive nuclear weapons systems both in the Soviet Union and in the Atlantic Alliance has aroused new concern about the dangers of all forms of nuclear war. The profusion of these systems on both sides has made it more difficult than ever to construct rational plans for any first use of these weapons by anyone.

This problem is more acute than before, but it is not new. Even in the 1950s, a time that is often mistakenly perceived as one of effortless American superiority, the prospect of any actual use of tactical weapons was properly terrifying to Europeans and to more than a few Americans. Military plans for such use remained both deeply secret and highly hypothetical; the coherence of the Alliance was maintained by general neglect of such scenarios, not by sedulous public discussion. In the 1960s there was a prolonged and stressful effort to address the problem of theater-range weapons, but agreement on new forces and plans for their use proved elusive. Eventually the proposal for a multilateral force (MLF) was replaced by the assignment of American Polaris submarines to NATO, and by the creation in Brussels of an inter-allied Nuclear

Planning Group. Little else was accomplished. In both decades the Alliance kept itself together more by mutual political confidence than by plausible nuclear war-fighting plans.

Although the first years of the 1970s produced a welcome if oversold détente, complacency soon began to fade. The Nixon administration, rather quietly, raised the question about the long-run credibility of the American nuclear deterrent that was to be elaborated by Henry Kissinger in 1979 at a meeting in Brussels. Further impetus to both new doctrine and new deployments came during the Ford and Carter administrations, but each public statement, however careful and qualified, only increased European apprehensions. The purpose of both administrations was to reinforce deterrence, but the result has been to increase fear of nuclear war, and even of Americans as its possible initiators. Intended as contributions to both rationality and credibility, these excursions into the theory of limited nuclear war have been counterproductive in Europe.

Yet it was not wrong to raise these matters. Questions that were answered largely by silence in the 1950s and 1960s cannot be so handled in the 1980s. The problem was not in the fact that the questions were raised, but in the way they seemed to be answered.

It is time to recognize that no one has ever succeeded in advancing any persuasive reason to believe that any use of nuclear weapons, even on the smallest scale, could reliably be expected to remain limited. Every serious analysis and every military exercise, for over twenty-five years, has demonstrated that even the most restrained battlefield use would be enormously destructive to civilian life and property. There is no way for anyone to have any confidence that such a nuclear action will not lead to further and more devastating exchanges. Any use of nuclear weapons in Europe, by the Alliance or against it, carries with it a high and inescapable risk of escalation into the general nuclear war which would bring ruin to all and victory to none.

The one clearly definable firebreak against the worldwide disaster of general nuclear war is the one that stands between all other kinds of conflict and any use whatsoever of nuclear weapons. To keep that firebreak wide and strong is in the deepest interest of all mankind. In retrospect, indeed, it is remarkable that this country has not responded to this reality more quickly. Given the appalling consequences of even the most limited use of nuclear weapons and the total impossibility for both sides of any guarantee against unlimited escalation, there must be the gravest doubt about the wisdom of a policy which asserts the effectiveness of any first use of nuclear weapons by either side. So it seems timely to consider the possibilities, the requirements, the difficulties, and the advantages of a policy of no-first-use.

Policy Change Requires German Input

The largest question presented by any proposal for an Allied policy of no-first-use is that of its impact on the effectiveness of NATO's deterrent posture on the central front. In spite of the doubts that are created by any honest look at the probable consequences of resort to a first nuclear strike of any kind, it should be remembered that there were strong reasons for the creation of the American nuclear umbrella over NATO. The original American pledge, expressed in Article 5 of the Treaty, was understood to be a nuclear guarantee. It was extended at a time when only a conventional Soviet threat existed, so a readiness for first use was plainly implied from the beginning. To modify that guarantee now, even in the light of all that has happened since, would be a major change in the assumptions of the Alliance, and no such change should be made without the most careful exploration of its implications.

In such an exploration the role of the Federal Republic of Germany must be central. Americans too easily forget what the people of the Federal Republic never can: that their position is triply exposed in a fashion unique among the large industrial democracies. They do not have nuclear weapons; they share a long common boundary with the Soviet empire; in any conflict on the central front their land would be the first battleground. None of these conditions can be changed, and together they present a formidable challenge.

Having decisively rejected a policy of neutrality, the Federal Republic has necessarily relied on the nuclear protection of the

United States, and we Americans should recognize that this relationship is not a favor we are doing our German friends, but the best available solution of a common problem. Both nations believe that the Federal Republic must be defended; both believe that the Federal Republic must not have nuclear weapons of its own; both believe that nuclear guarantees *of some sort* are essential; and both believe that only the United States can provide those guarantees in persuasively deterrent peacekeeping form.

The uniqueness of the West German position can be readily demonstrated by comparing it with those of France and the United Kingdom. These two nations have distance, and in one case water, between them and the armies of the Soviet Union; they also have nuclear weapons. While those weapons may contribute something to the common strength of the Alliance, their main role is to underpin a residual national self-reliance, expressed in different ways at different times by different governments, which sets both Britain and France apart from the Federal Republic. They are set apart from the United States, too, in that no other nation depends on them to use their nuclear weapons otherwise than in their own ultimate self-defense.

The quite special character of the nuclear relationship between the Federal Republic and the United States is a most powerful reason for defining that relationship with great care. It is rare for one major nation to depend entirely on another for a form of strength that is vital to its survival. It is unprecedented for any nation, however powerful, to pledge itself to a course of action in defense of another that might entail its own nuclear devastation. A policy of no-first-use would not and should not imply an abandonment of this extraordinary guarantee—only its redefinition. It would still be necessary to be ready to reply with American nuclear weapons to any nuclear attack on the Federal Republic, and this commitment would in itself be sufficiently demanding to constitute a powerful demonstration that a policy of no-first-use would represent no abandonment of our German ally.

The German right to a voice in this question is not merely a matter of location, or even of dependence on an American nuclear guarantee. The people of the Federal Republic have demonstrated a steadfast dedication to peace, to collective defense, and to domestic political decency. The study here proposed should be responsive to their basic desires. It seems probable that they are like the rest of us in wishing most of all to have no war of any kind, but also to be able to defend the peace by forces that do not require the dreadful choice of nuclear escalation.

No-First-Use Implies Conventional Upgrading

While we believe that careful study will lead to a firm conclusion that it is time to move decisively toward a policy of no-first-use, it is obvious that any such policy would require a strengthened confidence in the adequacy of the conventional forces of the Alliance, above all the forces in place on the central front and those available for prompt reinforcement. It seems clear that the nations of the Alliance together can provide whatever forces are needed, and within realistic budgetary constraints, but it is a quite different question whether they can summon the necessary political will. Evidence from the history of the Alliance is mixed. There has been great progress in the conventional defenses of NATO in the thirty years since the 1952 Lisbon communiqué, but there have also been failures to meet force goals all along the way.

In each of the four nations which account for more than 90 per cent of NATO's collective defense and a still higher proportion of its strength on the central front, there remain major unresolved political issues that critically affect contributions to conventional deterrence: for example, it can be asked what priority the United Kingdom gives to the British Army of the Rhine, what level of NATO-connected deployment can be accepted by France, what degree of German relative strength is acceptable to the Allies and fair to the Federal Republic itself, and whether we Americans have a durable and effective answer to our military manpower needs in the present all-volunteer active and reserve forces. These are the kinds of questions—and there are many more—that would require review and resolution in the course of reaching any final decision to move to a responsible policy of no-first-use.

There should also be an examination of the ways in which the concept of early use of nuclear weapons may have been built into existing forces, tactics, and general military expectations. To the degree that this has happened, there could be a dangerous gap right now between real capabilities and those which political leaders might wish to have in a time of crisis. Conversely, there should be careful study of what a policy of no-first-use would require in those same terms. It seems more than likely that once the military leaders of the Alliance have learned to think and act steadily on this "conventional" assumption, their forces will be better instruments for stability in crises and for general deterrence, as well as for the maintenance of the nuclear firebreak so vital to us all.

No one should underestimate either the difficulty or the importance of the shift in military attitudes implied by a no-first-use policy. Although military commanders are well aware of the terrible dangers in any exchange of nuclear weapons, it is a strong military tradition to maintain that aggressive war, not the use of any one weapon, is the central evil. Many officers will be initially unenthusiastic about any formal policy that puts limits on their recourse to a weapon of apparently decisive power. Yet the basic argument for a no-first-use policy can be stated in strictly military terms: that any other course involves unacceptable risks to the national life that military forces exist to defend. The military officers of the Alliance can be expected to understand the force of this proposition, even if many of them do not initially agree with it. Moreover, there is every reason for confidence that they will loyally accept any policy that has the support of their governments and the peoples behind them, just as they have fully accepted the present arrangements under which the use of nuclear weapons, even in retaliation for a nuclear attack, requires advance and specific approval by the head of government.

An Allied posture of no-first-use would have one special effect that can be set forth in advance: it would draw new attention to the importance of maintaining and improving the specifically American conventional forces in Europe. The principal political difficulty in a policy of no-first-use is that it may be taken in Europe, and especially in the Federal Republic, as evidence of a reduced American interest in the Alliance and in effective overall deterrence. The argument here is exactly the opposite: that such a policy is the best one available for keeping the Alliance united and effective. Nonetheless, the psychological realities of the relation between the Federal Republic and the United States are such that the only way to prevent corrosive German suspicion of American intentions under a no-first-use regime will be for Americans to accept for themselves an appropriate share in any new level of conventional effort that the policy may require.

Yet it would be wrong to make any hasty judgment that those new levels of effort must be excessively high. The subject is complex, and the more so because both technology and politics are changing. Precision-guided munitions, in technology, and the visible weakening of the military solidity of the Warsaw Pact, in politics, are only two examples of changes working to the advantage of the Alliance. Moreover, there has been some tendency, over many years, to exaggerate the relative conventional strength of the U.S.S.R. and to underestimate Soviet awareness of the enormous costs and risks of any form of aggression against NATO.

Today there is literally no one who really knows what would be needed. Most of the measures routinely used in both official and private analyses are static and fragmentary. An especially arbitrary, if obviously convenient, measure of progress is that of spending levels. But it is political will, not budgetary pressure, that will be decisive. The value of greater safety from both nuclear and conventional danger is so great that even if careful analysis showed that the necessary conventional posture would require funding larger than the 3 per cent real increase that has been the common target of recent years, it would be the best bargain ever offered to the members of the Alliance.

Yet there is no need for crash programs, which always bring extra costs. The direction of the Allied effort will be more important than its velocity. The final establishment of a firm policy of no-first-use, in any case, will obviously require time. What is important today is to begin to move in this direction.

The concept of renouncing any first use of nuclear weapons should also be tested by careful review of the value of existing NATO plans for selective and limited use of nuclear weapons. While many scenarios for nuclear war-fighting are nonsensical, it must be recognized that cautious and sober senior officers have found it prudent to ask themselves what alternatives to defeat they could propose to their civilian superiors if a massive conventional Soviet attack seemed about to make a decisive breakthrough. This question has generated contingency plans for battlefield uses of small numbers of nuclear weapons which might prevent that particular disaster. It is hard to see how any such action could be taken without the most enormous risk of rapid and catastrophic escalation, but it is a fair challenge to a policy of no-first-use that it should be accompanied by a level of conventional strength that would make such plans unnecessary.

In the light of this difficulty it would be prudent to consider whether there is any acceptable policy short of no-first-use. One possible example is what might be called "no-*early*-first-use"; such a policy might leave open the option of some limited nuclear action to fend off a final large-scale conventional defeat, and, by renunciation of any immediate first use and increased emphasis on conventional capabilities, it might be thought to help somewhat in reducing current fears.

But the value of a clear and simple position would be great, especially in its effect on ourselves and our Allies. One trouble with exceptions is that they easily become rules. It seems much better that even the most responsible choice of even the most limited nuclear actions to prevent even the most imminent conventional disaster should be left out of authorized policy. What the Alliance needs most today is not the refinement of its nuclear options, but a clear-cut decision to avoid them as long as others do.

Private and Civilian Advice Should Be Respected

Who should make the examination here proposed? The present American administration has so far shown little interest in questions of this sort, and indeed a seeming callousness in some quarters in Washington toward nuclear dangers may be partly responsible for some of the recent unrest in Europe. But each of the four of us has served in administrations which revised their early thoughts on nuclear weapons policy. James Byrnes learned the need to seek international control; John Foster Dulles stepped back somewhat from his early belief in massive retaliation; Dwight Eisenhower came to believe in the effort to ban nuclear tests, which he at first thought dangerous; the administration of John F. Kennedy (in which we all served) modified its early views on targeting doctrine; Lyndon Johnson shelved the proposed MLF when he decided it was causing more trouble than it was worth; and Richard Nixon agreed to narrow limits on anti-ballistic missiles whose large-scale deployment he had once thought indispensable. There were changes also in the Ford and Carter administrations, and President Reagan has already adjusted his views on the usefulness of early arms control negotiations, even though we remain in a time of general stress between Washington and Moscow. No administration should be held, and none should hold itself, to inflexible first positions on these extraordinarily difficult matters.

Nor does this question need to wait upon governments for study. The day is long past when public awe and governmental secrecy made nuclear policy a matter for only the most private executive determination. The questions presented by a policy of no-first-use must indeed be decided by governments, but they can and should be considered by citizens. In recent months strong private voices have been raised on both sides of the Atlantic on behalf of strengthened conventional forces. When this cause is argued by such men as Christoph Bertram, Field Marshal Lord Carver, Admiral Noel Gayler, Professor Michael Howard, Henry Kissinger, François de Rose, Theo Sommer, and General Maxwell Taylor, to name only a few, it is fair to conclude that, at least in its general direction, the present argument is not outside the mainstream of thinking within the Alliance. Indeed, there is evidence of renewed concern for conventional forces in governments, too.

What should be added, in both public and private sectors, is a fresh, sustained, and careful consideration of the requirements and the benefits of deciding that the policy of the Atlantic Alliance should be to keep its nuclear weapons unused as long as others do the same. Our own belief, though we do not here assert it as proven, is that when this possibility is fully explored it will be evident that the advantages of the policy far outweigh its costs, and that this demonstration will help the peoples and governments of the Alliance to find the political will to move in this direction. In this spirit, we go on to sketch the benefits that could come from such a change.

No-First-Use Would Aid Strategic Planning

The first possible advantage of a policy of no-first-use is in the management of the nuclear deterrent forces that would still be necessary. Once we escape from the need to plan for a first use that is credible, we can escape also from many of the complex arguments that have led to assertions that all sorts of new nuclear capabilities are necessary to create or restore a capability for something called "escalation dominance"—a capability to fight and "win" a nuclear war at any level. What would be needed under no-first-use is a set of capabilities we already have in overflowing measure—capabilities for appropriate retaliation to any kind of Soviet nuclear attack which would leave the Soviet Union in no doubt that it too should adhere to a policy of no-first-use. The Soviet government is already aware of the awful risk inherent in any use of these weapons, and there is no current or prospective Soviet "superiority" that would tempt anyone in Moscow toward nuclear adventurism. (All four of us are wholly unpersuaded by the argument advanced in recent years that the Soviet Union could ever rationally expect to gain from such a wild effort as a massive first strike on land-based American strategic missiles.)

Once it is clear that the only nuclear need of the Alliance is for adequately survivable and varied *second strike* forces, requirements for the modernization of major nuclear systems will become more modest than has been assumed. In particular, we can escape from the notion that we must somehow match everything the rocket commanders in the Soviet Union extract from their government. It seems doubtful, also, that under such a policy it would be necessary or desirable to deploy neutron bombs. The savings permitted by more modest programs could go toward meeting the financial costs of our contribution to conventional forces.

It is important to avoid misunderstanding here. In the conditions of the 1980s, and in the absence of agreement on both sides to proceed to very large-scale reductions in nuclear forces, it is clear that large, varied, and survivable nuclear forces will still be necessary for nuclear deterrence. The point is not that we Americans should move unilaterally to some "minimum" force of a few tens or even hundreds of missiles, but rather that once we escape from the pressure to seem willing and able to use these weapons first, we shall find that our requirements are much less massive than is now widely supposed.

A posture of no-first-use should also go far to meet the understandable anxieties that underlie much of the new interest in nuclear disarmament, both in Europe and in our own country. Some of the proposals generated by this new interest may lack practicability for the present. For example, proposals to make "all" of Europe—from Portugal to Poland—a nuclear-free zone do not seem to take full account of the reality that thousands of long-range weapons deep in the Soviet Union will still be able to target Western Europe. But a policy of no-first-use, with its accompaniment of a reduced requirement for new Allied nuclear systems, should allow a considerable reduction in fears of all sorts. Certainly such a new policy would neutralize the highly disruptive argument currently put about in Europe: that plans for theater nuclear modernization reflect an American hope to fight a nuclear war limited to Europe. Such modernization might or might not be needed under a policy of no-first-use; that question, given the size and versatility of other existing and prospective American forces, would be a matter primarily for European decision (as it is today).

An effective policy of no-first-use will also reduce the risk of conventional aggression in Europe. That risk has never been as great as prophets of doom have claimed and has always lain primarily in the possibility that Soviet leaders might think they could achieve some quick and limited gain that would be accepted because no defense or reply could be concerted. That temptation has been much reduced by the Allied conventional deployments achieved in the last twenty years, and it would be reduced still further by the additional shift in the balance of Allied effort that a no-first-use policy would both permit and require. The risk that an adventurist Soviet leader might take the terrible gamble of conventional aggression was greater in the past than it is today, and is greater today than it would be under no-first-use backed up by an effective conventional defense.

Political Advantages of No-First-Use

We have been discussing a problem of military policy, but our interest is also political. The principal immediate danger in the current military posture of the Alliance is not that it will lead to large-scale war, conventional or nuclear. The balance of terror and the caution of both sides appear strong enough today to prevent such a catastrophe, at least in the absence of some deeply destabilizing political change which might lead to panic or adventurism on either side. But the present unbalanced reliance on nuclear weapons, if long continued, might produce exactly such political change. The events of the last year have shown that differing perceptions of the role of nuclear weapons can lead to destructive recriminations, and when these differences are compounded by understandable disagreements on other matters such as Poland and the Middle East, the possibilities for trouble among Allies are evident.

The political coherence of the Alliance, especially in times of stress, is at least as important as the military strength required to maintain credible deterrence. Indeed, the political requirement has, if anything, an even higher priority. Soviet leaders would be most pleased to help the Alliance fall into total disarray, and would much prefer such a development to the inescapable uncertainties of open conflict. Conversely, if consensus is re-established on a military policy that the peoples and governments of the Alliance can believe in, both political will and deterrent credibility will be reinforced. Plenty of hard questions will remain, but both fear and mistrust will be reduced, and they are the most immediate enemies.

There remains one underlying reality which could not be removed by even the most explicit declaratory policy of no-first-use. Even if the nuclear powers of the Alliance should join, with the support of other Allies, in a policy of no-first-use, and even if that decision should lead to a common declaration of such policy by these powers and the Soviet Union, no one on either side could guarantee beyond all possible doubt that if conventional warfare broke out on a large scale there would in fact be no use of nuclear weapons. We could not make that assumption about the Soviet Union, and we must recognize that Soviet leaders could not make it about us. As long as the weapons themselves exist, the possibility of their use will remain.

But this inescapable reality does not undercut the value of a no-first-use policy. That value is first of all for the internal health of the Western alliance itself. A posture of effective conventional balance and survivable second-strike nuclear strength is vastly better for our own peoples and governments, in a deep sense more civilized, than one that forces the serious contemplation of "limited" nuclear scenarios that are at once terrifying and implausible.

There is strong reason to believe that no-first-use can also help in our relations with the Soviet Union. The Soviet government has repeatedly offered to join the West in declaring such a policy, and while such declarations may have only limited reliability, it would be wrong to disregard the real value to both sides of a jointly declared adherence to this policy. To renounce the first use of nuclear weapons is to accept an enormous burden of responsibility for any later violation. The existence of such a clearly declared common pledge would increase the cost and risk of any sudden use of nuclear weapons by either side and correspondingly reduce the political force of spoken or unspoken threats of such use.

A posture and policy of no-first-use also could help to open the path toward serious reduction of nuclear armaments on both sides. The nuclear decades have shown how hard it is to get agreements that really do constrain these weapons, and no one can say with assurance that any one step can make a decisive difference. But just as a policy of no-first-use should reduce the pressures on our side for massive new nuclear forces, it should help to increase the international incentives for the Soviet Union to show some restraint of its own. It is important not to exaggerate here, and certainly Soviet policies on procurement are not merely delayed mirror-images of ours. Nonetheless, there are connections between what is said and what is done even in the Soviet Union, and there are incentives for moderation, even there, that could be strengthened by a jointly declared policy of renouncing first use. At a minimum, such a declaration would give both sides additional reason to seek for agreements that would prevent a vastly expensive and potentially destabilizing contest for some kind of strategic advantage in outer space.

Finally, and in sum, we think a policy of no-first-use, especially if shared with the Soviet Union, would bring new hope to everyone in every country whose life is shadowed by the hideous possibility of a third great twentieth-century conflict in Europe—conventional or nuclear. It seems timely and even urgent to begin the careful study of a policy that could help to sweep this threat clean off the board of international affairs.

We recognize that we have only opened this large question, that we have exhausted no aspect of it, and that we may have omitted important elements. We know that NATO is much more than its four strongest military members; we know that a policy of no-first-use in the Alliance would at once raise questions about America's stance in Korea and indeed other parts of Asia. We have chosen deliberately to focus on the central front of our central alliance, believing that a right choice there can only help toward right choices elsewhere.

What we dare to hope for is the kind of new and widespread consideration of the policy we have outlined that helped us fifteen years ago toward SALT I, twenty-five years ago toward the Limited Test Ban, and thirty-five years ago toward the Alliance itself. Such consideration can be made all the more earnest and hopeful by keeping in mind one simple and frequently neglected reality: there has been no first use of nuclear weapons since 1945, and no one in any country regrets that fact. The right way to maintain this record is to recognize that in the age of massive thermonuclear overkill it no longer makes sense—if it ever did—to hold these weapons for any other purpose than the prevention of their use.

2. Nuclear Weapons and the Preservation of Peace

By KARL KAISER, GEORG LEBER, ALOIS MERTES, FRANZ-JOSEF SCHULZE

Focus These four West German political leaders take strong exception to the no-first-use proposal made by the four Americans in the Spring 1982 issue of *Foreign Affairs* (see selection 1) and published simultaneously in *Europa-Archiv* in West Germany. The German respondents hold that the current NATO policy of relying on both nuclear and conventional arms is sound and rational. They write with a sense of urgency about keeping the peace "because in case of war nuclear weapons could first be used" on German territory.

The West Germans affirm the current doctrine of "flexible response," which insists that NATO have the capability "to react effectively at every level of aggression" and "the flexibility to choose" either nuclear or conventional means or both. A no-first-use pledge would rob NATO of its present deterrent strength. Such a pledge would invite Moscow to launch a large-scale conventional attack against Western Europe, confident "that its own land would remain a sanctuary as long as it did not itself resort to nuclear weapons."

Further, the German writers insist that the conventional build-up by NATO countries necessary to compensate for the neutralization of Western nuclear arms would be prohibitively costly in both financial and political terms. The Soviet Union would immediately increase its already massive conventional superiority over NATO forces in Europe, and a destabilizing arms race would ensue. Another great Soviet advantage is geographical: the Soviet Union borders on Western Europe, while the United States is three thousand miles away.

The authors endorse the NATO double-track decision of an arms build-up combined with arms control negotiations and the zero-option proposal of President Reagan for eliminating both NATO and Warsaw Pact medium-range missiles (see selections 27, 28, and 29).

Karl Kaiser is director of the Research Institute of the German Society for Foreign Affairs, in Bonn. **Georg Leber,** a member of the Social Democratic party, is vice-president of the West German Bundestag; he was defense minister of the Federal Republic 1972-78. **Alois Mertes** is a Christian Democratic member of the Bundestag and serves on its Foreign Affairs Committee. He is his party's foreign policy spokesman. General **Franz-Josef Schulze** (ret.) was commander-in-chief of Allied forces in Central Europe from 1977 to 1979.

THE APPROPRIATE STRATEGY for the use of nuclear weapons has been the subject of discussion since the North Atlantic Alliance was founded. Open debate on these problems is part of the natural foundations of an Alliance consisting of democracies which relate to each other as sovereign partners. It is not the first time in the history of the Alliance that fears about the danger of nuclear war have caused concern and anxieties in all member countries, although these are more pronounced today than before. They must be taken seriously. The questions posed demand convincing answers, for in a democracy, policy on questions of peace and war requires constantly renewed legitimization.

When McGeorge Bundy, George F. Kennan, Robert S. McNamara, and Gerard Smith submit a proposal to renounce the first use of nuclear weapons in Europe, the mere fact that it comes from respected American personalities with long years of experience in questions of security policy and the Alliance gives it particular weight. Their reflections must be taken particularly seriously in a country like the Federal Republic of Germany which has a special interest in preserving peace, because in case of war nuclear weapons could first be used on its territory.

All responsible people must face the issues of the discussion initiated by the four authors. It is necessary to think through all questions posed and not to select only those ideas which cater to widespread anxieties. What matters most is to concentrate not only on the prevention of nuclear war, but on how to prevent *any* war, conventional war as well. The decisive criterion in evaluating this proposal—like any new proposal—must be: Will it contribute to preserving, into the future, the peace and freedom of the last three decades?

Unfortunately, the current discussion on both sides of the Atlantic about the four authors' proposal has been rendered more diffi-

Reprinted by permission from the Summer 1982 issue of *Foreign Affairs* (© 1982 by the Council on Foreign Relations, Incorporated).

cult by a confusion between the option of the "first use" of nuclear weapons and the capability for a "first strike" with nuclear weapons. The authors themselves have unintentionally contributed to this confusion by using both terms. "First use" refers to the first use of a nuclear weapon regardless of its yield and place; even blowing up a bridge with a nuclear weapon in one's own territory would represent a first use. "First strike" refers to a preemptive, disarming nuclear strike aimed at eliminating as completely as possible the entire strategic potential of the adversary. A first strike by the Alliance is not a relevant issue; such a strike must remain unthinkable in the future as it is now and has been in the past. The matter for debate should be exclusively the defensive first use of nuclear weapons by the Western Alliance.

The Rationale of NATO Strategy

The current NATO strategy of flexible response is intended to discourage an adversary from using or threatening the use of military force by confronting him with a full spectrum of deterrence and hence with an incalculable risk. The strategy also aims at improving the tools of crisis management as a means of preventing conflict. The deterrent effect of the doctrine rests on three pillars:

—the political determination of all Alliance members to resist jointly any form of aggression or blackmail;

—the capability of the Alliance to react effectively at every level of aggression; and

—the flexibility to choose between different possible reactions—conventional or nuclear.

The primary goal of this strategy is the prevention of war. To this end it harnesses the revolutionary, new, and inescapable phenomenon of the nuclear age for its own purposes. Our era has brought humanity not only the curse of the unprecedented destructive power of nuclear weapons but also its twin, the dread of unleashing that power, grounded in the fear of self-destruction. Wherever nuclear weapons are present, war loses its earlier function as a continuation of politics by other means. Even more, the destructive power of these weapons has forced political leaders, especially those of nuclear weapons states, to weigh risks to a degree unknown in history.

The longest period of peace in European history is inconceivable without the war-preventing effect of nuclear weapons. During the same time span more than a hundred wars have taken place in Asia, Africa, and Latin America, where the numbers of dead, wounded, and refugees run into the millions.

The continuous increase in the number of nuclear weapons—now comprising many thousands of warheads with ever more refined delivery systems—instills in many people, for understandable reasons, anxieties about the consequences of a war with a destructive power that exceeds the human imagination. But the only new factor here is that more people realize these consequences than in the past. Many political and military leaders were already aware of them when these weapons were developed and the first test results were presented. The fear of the consequences of such a war has to this day, fortunately, led to a policy which has made an essential contribution to preventing war in Europe—but which at the same time has regrettably stimulated the build-up of arsenals, since neither side wanted to lapse into a position of inferiority.

The strategy of flexible response attempts to counter any attack by the adversary—no matter what level—in such a way that the aggressor can have no hope of advantage or success by triggering a military conflict, be it conventional or nuclear. The tight and indissoluble coupling of conventional forces and nuclear weapons on the European continent with the strategic potential of the United States confronts the Soviet Union with the incalculable risk that any military conflict between the two alliances could escalate to a nuclear war. The primary function of nuclear weapons is deterrence in order to prevent aggression and blackmail.

The coupling of conventional and nuclear weapons has rendered war between East and West unwageable and unwinnable up to now. It is the inescapable paradox of this strategy of war prevention that the will to conduct nuclear war must be demonstrated in order to prevent war at all. Yet the ensuing indispensable presence of nuclear weapons and the constantly recalled visions of their possible destructive effect, should they ever be used in a war, make many people anxious.

The case is similar with regard to the limitation of nuclear war: the strategy of massive retaliation was revised because, given the growing potential of destruction, the threat of responding even to low levels of aggression with a massive use of nuclear weapons became increasingly incredible. A threat once rendered incredible would no longer have been able to prevent war in Europe. Thus, in the mid-1960s the Europeans supported the introduction of flexible response, which made the restricted use of nuclear weapons— but also the limitation of any such use—an indispensable part of deterrence aimed at preventing even "small" wars in Europe. Critics of nuclear deterrence today misinterpret this shift in strategy, drawing from it a suspicion of conspiracy between the superpowers to wage a limited nuclear war on European territory and at the expense of the Europeans.

A renunciation of the first use of nuclear weapons would certainly rob the present strategy of war prevention—which is supported by the government and the opposition in the Federal Republic of Germany, as well as by a great majority of the population—of a decisive characteristic. One cannot help concluding that the Soviet Union would thereby be put in a position where it could, once again, calculate its risk and thus be able to wage war in Europe. It would no longer have to fear that nuclear weapons would inflict unacceptable damage to its own territory. We therefore fear that a credible renunciation of the first use of nuclear weapons would, once again, make war more probable.

A decisive weakness of the proposal by the four authors lies in their assertion that a no-first-use policy would render wars less likely, without producing sufficient evidence. Even though the restoration of the conventional balance which they call for (and which will be examined below) increases the conventional risk for the Soviet assault formations, such a policy would liberate the Soviet Union from the decisive nuclear risk—and thereby from the constraint that has kept the Soviet Union, up to now, from using military force, even for limited purposes, against Western Europe. The liberation from nuclear risk would, of course, benefit the

United States to the same degree. It must be questioned therefore, whether renunciation of first use represents a contribution to the "internal health of the Western alliance itself" or whether, instead, a no-first-use policy increases insecurity and fear of ever more probable war.

The argumentation of the four American authors is considerably weakened by their tendency to think in worst-case scenarios. They assume, almost fatalistically, a total irrationality of state behavior and the impossibility of controlling a supposedly irreversible escalation. We share the authors' opinion that the kind of Soviet adventurism that would undertake a nuclear first strike against the United States can be excluded as a serious possibility. We are also familiar with the recent studies which assert that a limited nuclear war probably becomes more and more difficult to control with increasing escalation. Here we cannot disagree. However, one must at the same time ask under what circumstances a first use of Western nuclear weapons in Europe—should it happen at all— would be probable. This is only thinkable in a situation where a large-scale conventional attack by the Warsaw Pact could no longer be countered by conventional means alone, thus forcing NATO to a limited use of nuclear weapons: small weapons in small quantities, perhaps, even, only a warning shot. All indications suggest that both sides would be extremely cautious, in order to avoid precisely the dreaded, possibly uncontrollable, escalation which some studies rightfully present as a danger, and which the advocates of a no-first-use policy present as a certainty.

The Alliance Requires Mutual Commitment

The Western alliance is an alliance of equals. Its cohesion is therefore based on the greatest possible realization of the principles of equal risks, equal burdens, and equal security. The present NATO strategy reflects this principle. It guarantees that the American military potential with all its components, conventional and nuclear, is included in the defense of Europe. Not only the inhabitants of the Federal Republic of Germany but also American citizens help bear the risks, the conventional as well as the nuclear.

The indivisibility of the security of the Alliance as a whole and of its territory creates the credibility of deterrence.

The conclusions that can be drawn from the four authors' recommendations with regard to the commitment of the United States to the defense of Europe are profoundly disturbing. To be sure, they assert that no-first-use does not represent an abandonment of the American protective guarantee for Western Europe, but "only its redefinition." Indeed, that would be the case, but in the form of a withdrawal from present commitments of the United States.

The opinion of the four American authors that "the one clearly definable firebreak against the worldwide disaster of general nuclear war is the one that stands between all other kinds of conflict and any use whatsoever of nuclear weapons" amounts to no less than limiting the existing nuclear guarantee of protection by the United States for their non-nuclear Alliance partners to the case of prior use of nuclear weapons by the Soviet Union. Even in the case of a large-scale conventional attack against the entire European NATO territory, the Soviet Union could be certain that its own land would remain a sanctuary as long as it did not itself resort to nuclear weapons. This would apply even more to surprise operations aimed at the quick occupation of parts of Western Europe which are hardly defensible by conventional means.

In such a case, those attacked would have to bear the destruction and devastation of war alone. It is only too understandable that for years the Soviet Union has, therefore, pressed for a joint American-Soviet renunciation of first use of nuclear weapons, on occasion in the guise of global proposals. If the ideas of the authors were to be followed, conventional conflicts in Europe would no longer involve any existential risk for the territory of the Soviet Union and—despite the increased American participation in the conventional defense of Europe suggested by the authors—would be without such risk for the territory of the United States as well.

The authors' suggestion that "even the most responsible choice of even the most limited nuclear actions to prevent even the most imminent conventional disaster should be left out of authorized policy" makes completely clear that a withdrawal of the United States from its previous guarantee is at stake. They thus advise

Western Europe to capitulate should defeat threaten; for example, if the Federal Republic were in danger of being overrun conventionally. The American nuclear guarantee would be withdrawn.

The authors assert that the implementation of their astonishing proposal would not be taken in Europe, and especially in the Federal Republic, "as evidence of a reduced American interest in the Alliance and in effective overall deterrence," but that, on the contrary, it would be the best means "for keeping the Alliance united and effective." On this point we beg to differ: the proposed no-first-use policy would destroy the confidence of Europeans and especially of Germans in the European-American Alliance as a community of risk, and would endanger the strategic unity of the Alliance and the security of Western Europe.

Given a renunciation of nuclear first use, the risks of a potential aggressor doubtlessly become more calculable. Moreover, the significance of Soviet conventional superiority would thereby increase dramatically. Conventional war in Europe would once again become possible. It could again become a continuation of politics by other means. Moreover, NATO would face a fundamentally different conventional threat. The elimination of the nuclear risk would free the Warsaw Pact from the necessity to disperse attack forces. As a result, NATO would have to produce significantly higher numbers of combat forces than today.

Obstacles to a Conventional Balance

The assertion of the four American authors that there is a tendency to overestimate the conventional strength of the Soviet Union does not correspond to the most recent East-West force comparison by NATO [see page xii]. They do admit, however, that a no-first-use policy requires stronger conventional forces; in their opinion the Alliance is capable of accomplishing such a build-up within realistic budgets. We believe the authors considerably underestimate the political and financial difficulties which stand in the way of establishing a conventional balance through increased armament by the West. The case would be different if, through negotiations, a conventional balance could be reached by reductions in Warsaw Pact forces. The authors do not explore this possibility, but the long years of as yet unsuccessful negotiations for mutual and balanced force reductions (MBFR) demonstrate the obstacles on this path.

The establishment of balance through the build-up of Western conventional forces would likewise be extremely difficult. The costs would be of a magnitude that would dramatically exceed the framework of current defense budgets. Suggestions by the authors about possible savings in the nuclear area in case of no-first-use are of little benefit for the non-nuclear-weapons states of Europe. (Such savings, incidentally, imply a significant reduction of the Western nuclear arsenal.) In our judgment, the United States and Great Britain would have to introduce the draft, and the European countries would have to extend their period of military service. Because of the necessity for a significantly higher number of military forces, the Federal Republic of Germany would have to accept on its territory large contingents of additional troops, those of the Allies and its own: the Federal Republic would be transformed into a large military camp for an indefinite period. Do the four American authors seriously believe that the preconditions for the build-up required by their proposal exist in Western Europe—and the United States?

Even if an approximate conventional balance could be achieved in Europe, two disadvantages to the detriment of Western Europe would remain: first, the Soviet Union has a geographic advantage—it can always quickly change the balance of forces from the relative proximity of its territory; second, there would always be the possibility, not even excluded by the American authors, that, despite no-first-use, conventional war could in an advanced phase degenerate into nuclear war.

Moreover, in commenting skeptically about the idea of a nuclear-free zone, the authors themselves point out that the Soviet Union can move nuclear weapons relatively quickly from deep within its territory into such a zone. If a no-first-use policy is linked with a complete or at least substantial withdrawal of tactical nuclear weapons—and that is apparently meant by the authors—it would, moreover, be easier for the Soviet Union to reach Central Europe with nuclear weapons from its own territory than for the United States.

For Germans and other Europeans whose memory of the catastrophe of conventional war is still alive and on whose densely populated territory both pacts would confront each other with the destructive power of modern armies, the thought of an ever more probable conventional war is terrifying.

To Germans and other Europeans, an ever more probable conventional war is, therefore, no alternative to war prevention through the current strategy, including the option of a first use of nuclear weapons. While the four authors link their proposal with the laudable intention of reducing European anxieties about nuclear war, its implementation could result in anxieties about a more probable conventional war soon replacing anxieties about the much less probable nuclear war. The anti-nuclear protest movement in Europe suspects the United States and the Soviet Union of intending to wage a limited nuclear war on the territory, and at the expense, of the Europeans. Were the movement to apply the logic of its argument to the case of no-first-use, it would naturally arrive at a new suspicion: that a conventional war could now also be waged on European territory and at European expense—particularly since a nuclear risk for the superpowers would no longer exist. All that would then be necessary would be to paint a vivid picture of the terrors of conventional war—once again thinkable—and the insecurity of the Europeans would receive new and dangerous reinforcement.

The Exposed German Position

We are grateful for the manner in which the four American authors of a no-first-use proposal have evaluated the particularly exposed position of the Federal Republic of Germany and the special difficulties which ensue for its security policy. It is, however, striking that they do not deal at all with a problem which does not, to be sure, pose itself for a world power like the United States, but which the Federal Republic of Germany and all European Alliance

partners have to keep in mind: the problem of protecting themselves from political pressure and preserving their free society.

The protection of a free society based on the rule of law is just as
important a part of policy of preserving peace as the prevention of
war. War can always be avoided at the price of submission. It is
naturally more obvious to Europeans (and in particular to Germans in their precarious position within a divided country) than to
the population of the American superpower that an actual military
superiority of the Soviet Union, or a feeling of inferiority in Western Europe, can be exploited to put political pressure on Western
Europe.

The feeling of vulnerability to political blackmail, as a result of
the constant demonstration of superior military might, would be
bound to grow considerably if the nuclear protector of the Atlantic
Alliance were to declare—as suggested by the four authors—that
it would not use nuclear weapons in case of a conventional attack
against Europe. This applies in particular to those exposed areas
which, even with considerable improvements of conventional
forces, can be conventionally defended only with great difficulty,
or not at all: these include, for example, north Norway, Thrace,
and, in particular, West Berlin. The protection of these areas lies
solely in the incalculability of the American reaction.

The advice of the authors to renounce the use of nuclear
weapons even in the face of pending conventional defeat of Western Europe is tantamount to suggesting that "rather Red than
dead" would be the only remaining option for those Europeans
then still alive. Were such advice to become policy, it would destroy
the psychological basis necessary for the will to self-defense. Such
counsel would strengthen tendencies in Europe to seek gradual,
voluntary, and timely salvation in preventive "good conduct" and
growing subservience vis-à-vis the Soviet Union for fear of war and
Soviet superiority. The result would be to restrict the very freedom
that the Alliance was founded to protect.

The four American authors advance a number of skeptical arguments about the NATO two-track decision of December 1979
which amount to a rejection of this decision. They attack one
alleged motive for the double-track decision, the desire for balance

below the intercontinental level of nuclear weapons. Although the notion of balance did occasionally appear in public discussion by politicians who advanced it to legitimize the NATO decision in view of the growing Soviet medium-range nuclear potential, balance was not a *leitmotiv* and did not play an essential role in shaping the decision itself. Were that the case, the potential of the Western nuclear weapons envisaged (should negotiations fail) would have had to be significantly larger than the planned 572 systems, which—together with the already existing Western weapons—amount to only a fraction of comparable Soviet systems. From the very beginning, the double-track decision was essentially conceived to couple the intercontinental with the Europe-related nuclear weapons force.

In Support of the Two-Track Decision

We share the concern which the four authors express about the potentially negative impact which the controversies on the NATO double-track decision could have on the Alliance. However, unlike them, we do not conclude that NATO should forgo the double-track decision. Our conclusion is based on three arguments in particular:

First, the Soviet Union must recognize that it would also be to its own advantage to abandon its absolute notion of security—for such a notion condemns any attempt at stabilizing the East-West relationship to failure. The Soviet decision to develop, produce, and deploy the SS-20 missile in Eastern Europe was made during the first half of the 1970s, i.e., during the period in which the West actively pursued genuine détente. It must have been clear to every Soviet planner that, given the quality of this weapons system, located below the strategic level (which was moving toward parity and accordingly codified in SALT), its expansion would dislocate the nuclear deterrence system by regionalizing the threat.

Messages from Western and German sources directed with great urgency at the Soviet Union during the 1970s—among them a meeting between Federal Chancellor Helmut Schmidt and General Secretary Leonid Brezhnev in May 1978—were simply ignored. The build-up of this rocket arsenal continued relentlessly and still does. In addition, new modern systems of shorter and medium reach were developed; they are now in production and deployment. All of these add a new quantitative and qualitative dimension to Soviet armament.

These developments raise the depressing question of whether and how the dynamics of Soviet armament policy can be influenced at all. In any case, in the interests of security and peace, such attempts must not be abandoned. Only an announcement and demonstration of the capacity to implement a Western medium-range armament program (572 Pershing II and cruise missiles) which would result in a loss of military and political options for the Soviets could, if at all, induce the Soviet leadership to halt and reduce its armament.

Second, where would such a development end if, by renouncing the implementation of the double-track decision, the Alliance were to let the Soviet medium- and short-range nuclear potential grow to thousands of systems without an adequate counterweight on the Western side and with continued strategic parity?

Two consequences would emerge: in the first place, the American nuclear guarantee for Europe would lose its credibility. The view, also shared by the four authors, that the Soviet medium-range potential can be dealt with by American systems assigned to NATO (which are, by the way, counted in SALT and not well usable for tactical functions) lacks conclusiveness. As such a striking Soviet superiority increasingly develops, the United States loses the capability for escalation and thereby its credibility. This has a destabilizing effect.

In the second place, we are concerned by the possibility that with an acceptance of further growth of Soviet nuclear superiority below the intercontinental level, a potential for threat emerges which can be used for political pressures. In this case, the well-meant advice that only those can be blackmailed who let themselves be is of little use, since these weapons are assumed to be unusable because of the risk involved. In 1956 Khrushchev threatened Paris and London with nuclear weapons. At that time his threats had little impact under conditions of American strategic superiority. Imagine what a repetition of such threats would be like under conditions of striking Soviet superiority in the field of medium-range weapons and of the anxieties of the West European public caused by the nuclear debate. Under these circumstances politicians in the Western democracies would be put under a degree of pressure unimaginable in the 1950s.

Third, the long-term impact of a failure of the double-track decision is a cause of concern to us. The anti-nuclear protest, in our opinion, will not disappear but will in all probability remain a permanent characteristic of the political situation in Western Europe for years. This protest and the legitimate concerns which it expresses must be taken very seriously, but at the same time it should not be overlooked that it represents a minority—which, however, enjoys powerful support from the media on both sides of the Atlantic. Security policy, like any other policy in democracies, is determined by majorities and must be accepted by minorities. If, in the case of the double-track decision, the existing clear majority should fail to prevail in the face of a minority in fundamental opposition to it—and one likely to persist in the future—much more would be at stake than the decision in question. This has been recognized by parts of the protest movement—and in Moscow as well. The capability of democratic majorities to define and implement security policy in the future is also at stake in the double-track decision.

Renouncing One Form or All Forms of Force?

Special emphasis on the renunciation of *one* form of force—the first use of nuclear weapons—decreases the importance of the general prohibition against the use of force laid down in Article 2 of the U.N. Charter, resulting for all practical purposes in a diminution of the prohibition against the use of conventional force. The Federal Republic of Germany has always adhered to the principle of the general renunciation of the use of force. It reconfirmed this commitment when entering NATO, as well as in the Eastern Treaties of the early 1970s and the Final Act of Helsinki in 1975. The Federal Republic shares with other Alliance partners the view that it is legally questionable and politically harmful to separate the question of specific arms from the general renunciation of the use of force.

Government and opposition within the Federal Republic are in complete agreement on this issue. Indeed the question must be posed whether, with a prohibition of the first use of nuclear weapons, the first use of other weapons becomes less prohibited and whether a country threatened by a conventionally highly armed neighbor will then be less protected by the prohibition of the use of force.

To an essential degree the anti-nuclear protest in Europe derives from the rejection of nuclear arms procurement up to barely imaginable potentials of destruction, from the waste of resources which it engenders in a world of poverty, and from the possibility of war under nuclear conditions. We consider these concerns legitimate, although we do not share essential conclusions of the movement. In view of the burdens of defense policy in the nuclear age which the citizens in our democracies have to bear, it is the constant duty of government and opposition to exploit all available possibilities to decrease tensions and potentials for destruction by means of cooperation, confidence-building measures, arms control, and disarmament.

Unlike the four American authors, we do not consider a renunciation of the option of a first use as the answer to the existing concerns and anxieties over nuclear weapons. Instead, we see the answer in a creative and realistic policy of arms control and disarmament. We consider the NATO double-track decision of December 1979, combining arms control negotiations and the announcement of armaments in case of failure, as an innovative step. We welcome the beginning of negotiations on medium-range weapons in Geneva and the "zero option" proposed by President Reagan. The reduction of excessive Soviet armament is the main goal of this proposal; in a way comprehensible to everybody, it now places on the Soviet Union the responsibility for potential armament measures of the West. We welcome, furthermore, the readiness announced by both world powers to open negotiations on strategic weapons, as well as the proposals on START [Strategic

Arms Reductions Talks] presented by President Reagan at Eureka on May 9. The NATO ministerial meeting of May 1981 and the declaration of the NATO summit in Bonn of June 1982 unequivocally express the continuity of the basic philosophy of the Alliance, which seeks security only through a combination of adequate defense capacity and a policy of cooperation and negotiations to eliminate the causes of tensions.

The four American authors hope that a policy of no-first-use could help to clear the way towards a serious reduction of nuclear weapons on both sides. Their further comments on this topic, however, suggest that they themselves do not entertain exaggerated hopes. Indeed, the experience of recent years in the field of tactical nuclear weapons gives little cause for hope that the Soviet side is ready for genuine reductions. Moreover, it is questionable whether the Soviets are ready to renounce their conventional superiority built up at great sacrifice, stubbornly defended during decades, and energetically expanded in recent years, at the very moment when such a superiority would be given an increased and decisive importance by a NATO renunciation of first use of nuclear weapons.

We share many of the concerns about the risks of nuclear war. They lead us to conclude that an energetic attempt to reduce the *dependence on an early first use* of nuclear weapons must be undertaken. To be sure, the authors also mention a "no-early-first-use" policy as a possible alternative, but in the last analysis they discard it as a mere variation of nuclear options and therefore call for a clear decision in favor of a renunciation of "any first use of nuclear weapons."

A reduction of dependence on an early use of nuclear weapons should, in the first place, be attempted through mutual, balanced, and verifiable reductions of conventional forces by means of East-West negotiations which result in an adequate conventional balance. We have pointed out how difficult it would be to restore such a balance by the build-up of Western conventional armament. In our opinion the essential precondition posed by the authors for their suggested renunciation of first use can, therefore, not be fulfilled.

In sum, we consider efforts to raise the nuclear threshold by a strengthening of conventional options to be urgently necessary. The reduction of the dependence on first use, in particular on early first use, of nuclear weapons, should be a question of high political priority in our countries.

The Western Alliance has committed itself to a renunciation from the very beginning: the renunciation of the first use of *any* force. The entire military planning, structure, and deployment of forces are geared exclusively toward defense. The presence of nuclear weapons has contributed essentially to the success of the Alliance in preventing war and preserving freedom for three decades. We are convinced that a reduction of the dependence on an early use of nuclear weapons would serve this purpose. Under the circumstances of the foreseeable future, however, a renunciation of the option of first use would be contrary to the security interests of Europe and the entire Alliance.

3. *Defending Europe Without the Bomb*

By THE EDITORS OF 'THE ECONOMIST'

Focus

This editorial in the respected London *Economist* is based on an analysis of the relative military strengths of NATO and Warsaw Pact forces in 1982, which are graphically portrayed in the chart on page xii. NATO must come to grips with the vast superiority of the Warsaw Pact in tanks, anti-tank weapons, artillery, and other vehicles, to say nothing of manpower, if it is to deter effectively a Soviet attack against Western Europe.

The editors conclude that "if the Russians attacked Western Europe they would probably win the war within a couple of weeks or so unless the defending NATO armies fired their battlefield nuclear weapons." They believe that NATO must strengthen its conventional forces and that this can be done by a 1.5 per cent increase over 1982 expenditures. On this point, the *Economist* editors are in general agreement with the four Americans in selection 1. But in their larger analysis of the threat, they are closer to the West German statement (selection 2). They oppose both the nuclear freeze proposal (see selections 5 and 8) and a no-first-use declaration. The editorial points out that the conventional upgrading needed for nuclear reductions "would cost more money . . . but by no means an unbearable amount."

The editors assert that in preparing the editorial and the article it accompanied, they relied on information from "generals, admirals, defense ministry officials, and defense industry specialists on both sides of the Atlantic (and on both sides of the Iron Curtain)."

I T IS MORE THAN sixty-eight years since the start of the First World
War, which killed 15 million people. Another doomed generation later, British soldiers were digging their heels in at a place
called Alamein, and German soldiers were panzering up to a place
called Stalingrad; though few of them guessed it, the turning-point
was approaching of the Second World War, which killed 51 million
people. Bear these non-nuclear things in mind as you read about
how it might be possible to defend Western Europe without nuclear weapons.

Of all the away-with-the-thing arguments produced in the past
year's new wave of ban-the-bomb anxieties, only one seems to
stand up to examination. This is the idea that NATO really ought to
be able to block a Soviet attack into the heartland of non-Communist Europe with men and tanks alone, without more or less assuming that it will have to pull the nuclear trigger in the process. By
comparison, the "peace" movement's other suggestions all ring
horribly hollow.

A worldwide freeze on nuclear weapons, popular among left-
wing American Democrats, is the undefinable in pursuit of the
inequitable. It would freeze Russia's current nuclear lead, while
requiring the counting of uncountable things like bomb-making
nuclear explosive material. The European unilateralist notion that
a nuclear Soviet Union would beam peaceably upon a wholly
denuclearized Western Europe, or even be embarrassed into taking its own nuclear clothes off, is merely the stuff that dreams are
made of. Another dream, in which a given country thinks it can
declare itself exempt from nuclear attack by going non-nuclear,
has already been disproved by history. Japan was non-nuclear, but
it was not exempt from Hiroshima and Nagasaki. And the hope of
abolishing every nuclear weapon from the face of the globe is, in

Reprinted by permission from the July 31, 1982, issue of *The Economist* (© 1982
by The Economist Newspaper Limited, London).

straight logic, a non-starter. Only a world government could enforce total abolition, and a world government would need nuclear weapons to do it.

Can Europe Be Conventionally Defended?

Instead of clutching at such straws, consider the idea that NATO might at least be able to protect Western Europe without using nuclear firepower. This has real substance.

At the moment, it is reckoned that if the Russians attacked Western Europe they would probably win the war within a couple of weeks or so unless the defending NATO armies fired their battlefield nuclear weapons (which would probably be the start of an all-out nuclear bust-up). The Russians would probably win an ordinary war because they have bigger and better non-nuclear forces in central Europe. This newspaper has been trying to work out how many extra men and how much extra equipment NATO would need to put this right, so that it could hold the line without the implied threat to fire those battlefield nuclear weapons. To achieve, in short, non-nuclear deterrence in Europe.

They are surprisingly cheerful. The gap between today's unsolid NATO defense system and a more solid one is not huge. For an addition of about 1.5 per cent a year in what the NATO countries spend on defense—only half as much again as the increase they promised in 1978—we reckon that they could strengthen their armed forces enough to have a good chance of fighting off a Russian attack for about a month. That alone would not be sufficient, since the Russians could decide to fight for more than a month. Some further preparation would be needed to cover the period between the end of that first month and the time when NATO's ordinary mobilization schemes would anyway be starting to bring in a flow of reinforcements. That would cost more money, and a lot of irksome planning. But by no means an unbearable amount.

For anyone who wants to reduce the West's present dependence on nuclear arms, this modest rearmament for the sake of practicable denuclearization should now become the centerpiece of the defense debate. The extra money will not be easy to find in a Western world where economies are moving like tortoises, if they are moving at all. It will be particularly hard to come by in countries where there are so many people without work that it is an agony to say no to the social security budget but yes to defense. The irony is that it is the anti-nuclear movement which, on its own principles, should most want to say yes. The anti-nuclear people differ from those of us who believe that a nuclear armory, properly maintained, will protect the West from attack and preserve the peace. They argue that nuclear weapons will lead to nuclear war. They should therefore be willing to support this proposal for a little more non-nuclear rearmament, once they bring themselves to realize what it would achieve.

What it would not achieve, let it be clear, is the removal of all nuclear weapons from Europe. The Russians would presumably keep theirs. So NATO would have to hold on to some of its own, to make it plain that the Russians would not have a European nuclear monopoly which they could use at will. Otherwise NATO's armies, however brilliant their non-nuclear accoutrements, would be like cavalry sent into the teeth of the machine guns.

The Implausibility of No-First-Use

Nor is there much point, in our view, in a NATO declaration promising "no first use" of nuclear weapons. These things sound marvelous when they are first said, but they are, after all, only declarations—uncheckable, unenforceable, and, when a healthy realism reasserts itself, unbelievable. Not many people believe that President Brezhnev's recent "no first use" declaration would stop his ordering the use of Soviet nuclear weapons if he thought they could save his country from an invading army. No healthy realist should long believe a Western declaration to the same effect if the issue were the saving of Western Europe. Indeed, to the extent that the Russians gave it any credence, such a Western declaration could actually make war more likely. When Russia weighs the arguments for and against risking an invasion of Western Europe, every ounce on the side of caution helps. The thought that NATO has not made even an implausible "no first use" promise is worth quite a few ounces.

For all that, the non-nuclear strengthening we propose for NATO would make a big difference to Europe's nuclear heartache. It would make it possible for the Western alliance to plan a battle for the defense of Hamburg and Frankfurt—and behind them Paris, Rome, and London—without assuming the probable use of nuclear weapons. That in turn would make it possible to remove some, if not all, of the battlefield nuclear missiles and artillery which that assumption makes necessary. It might even make it possible to reduce the number of cruise and Pershing II medium-range missiles which NATO wants to deploy as a link between the battlefield nuclear arms and the intercontinental monsters based in the United States. And if this strengthening of NATO made the Russians more reluctant to risk any sort of attack, it would thereby make war less likely. That seems to be worth an extra 1.5 per cent on the insurance premium.

There is one large, and obvious, qualification. If NATO's calculations turn out to be wrong—if the stronger NATO forces are still not strong enough to deter a Russian attack or to block it if it comes—then the defenders will be forced back on the terrible choice of either using their nuclear weapons after all (though these will now be weaker than they would otherwise have been) or fighting a non-nuclear war through to the bloody finish. ... Let nobody think that the alternative to nuclear preparedness is a return to the civilities of medieval chivalry—let alone a settling down to assured peace.

Nevertheless, the 1.5 per cent option seems to be the most promising way of inching back from the nuclear brink. The bomb, like the flying machine and the internal-combustion engine, was an invention of man's will to master nature. It will not be disinvented. The only hope is to bring its worst dangers under control, and that involves man's will to master himself. The first step could be a Western will to spend a little more money on non-nuclear arms on the plain of central Europe.

4. Western Europe Needs a Nuclear Option

By EDWARD N. LUTTWAK

Focus Emphasizing that the Warsaw Pact forces are designed for offense and the NATO forces solely for defense, Edward Luttwak insists that NATO needs a nuclear option to deter a Soviet attack and, if necessary, to counter one. In this he concurs with the four German leaders (selection 2) and disagrees with the editors of the *Economist* (selection 3).

Luttwak notes the superiority of Warsaw Pact forces over NATO forces in Europe: while NATO has a slight edge in active-duty troops, the Warsaw Pact can draw upon a huge and ready reservoir of Soviet manpower. In major land and air weapons the Soviet Union has a great advantage over NATO: in tanks 2.65 to 1, artillery 2.05 to 1, missile launchers 3.45 to 1, bombers 4.5 to 1, fighters 7.67 to 1, interceptors 2.61 to 1, and so on.

Since "the Soviet army has a valid method of offensive war, while NATO for its part has no valid method of defense," Luttwak concludes: "In the absence of an offensive capacity by NATO and a lively willingness to preempt invasion," the West can protect itself only by nuclear weapons, or, "more precisely, by the architecture of nuclear deterrence which is now in place."

Luttwak takes exception to the view that any use of nuclear arms would automatically escalate into general nuclear war. On the contrary, he says, for

psychological reasons, "by far the most likely outcome is that a war would end very soon if any
nuclear weapons, however small, were actually detonated by any side on any target."

Edward N. Luttwak is a senior fellow at the
Georgetown University Center for Strategic and
International Studies and a leading strategic affairs
consultant. Among his books are *Coup d'Etat* and
The Israeli Army.

Now that the United States is belatedly acting to restore a tolerable balance in forces nuclear as well as conventional, a vast chorus of protest has been heard from those who hold that deterrence is a policy not merely dangerous but irrational, and who therefore demand an immediate "freeze." Others have made a narrower protest, against the reliance of the United States and its allies on nuclear deterrence to dissuade a Soviet invasion that might be accomplished by the great non-nuclear forces of the Soviet army. And then there has been the broadest of claims, in which pastors and priests, rabbis and bishops, have been most prominent: that nuclear deterrence, and indeed nuclear weapons as such, are in themselves immoral.

Along with the arguments and the claims there has been a great outpouring of horrific imagery of Hiroshima and its victims, of mushroom clouds and radiation burns—imagery abundantly relayed in the complaisant press and in the visual media. The purpose has been to frighten those whom the arguments have not persuaded, so that the electorate which deliberately rejected Carter's strategy of weakness might now be terrorized into repudiating Reagan's strategy of strength.

Yet instead of reaffirming its strategy, the Reagan administration has for the most part responded to the arguments and the claims, to the words and the manipulative imagery, by appeasing the protesters, the churchmen, and the media. From those who once could explain quite lucidly the fundamental and unchanging reasons for the inevitable failure of arms control, we now hear much talk about the virtues of that very process. From those who started off resolutely determined to explain strategic realities, we now hear only great declarations of their love for peace, their revulsion against war, and their sincere dislike of nuclear weapons.

Excerpted by permission from the May 1982 issue of *Commentary* (all rights reserved).

Outside the Administration, too, all manner of people once very attentive to the delicate texture of strategy have now come forward to mollify protest by offering schemes and plans designed to reduce the role of nuclear weapons in our defense, sometimes offering a non-nuclear substitute, and sometimes not.

And yet every one of the claims which sustain the protests large and small is false; each of the arguments, both strategic and moral, can be utterly refuted.

The "front" that the North Atlantic Treaty Organization sustains against the Soviet Union and its client-states divides not nations but political systems. On the one side there is the system of production, of individual welfare and social amelioration, while on the other side there is a system that proclaims those same goals very loudly, even while subordinating them to the preservation of totalitarian control and the accumulation of superior military power.

If nuclear weapons were now disinvented, if all the hopes of the nuclear disarmers were fully realized, the Soviet Union would automatically emerge as the dominant power on the continent, fully capable of invading and conquering Western Europe and beyond if its political domination were resisted.

Comparing Conventional Power

But why should that be so in a non-nuclear world? After all, our side has all the men and all the means that would be needed to outmatch the conventional forces of the other side. Already now, by the storekeeper's method of making up an inventory, the forces of NATO can appear as strong as or even stronger than those of the Soviet Union and its not-necessarily-reliable client-states. Compare, for example, total manpower in uniform, on active duty: 4.9 million for NATO and the United States versus 4.8 million for the Soviet Union and its client-states (and remember that out of that total the Soviet Union must provide the large forces deployed against the Chinese). Compare total manpower in ground forces: 2.7 million for us versus 2.6 million for them (with the same Chinese qualification, to make us feel even better). Compare total ground forces in Europe itself: 2.1 million on our side and only 1.7 million on the other (and one must make allowance for Polish, Hungarian, and other client-state troops that prudent Soviet military planners would not want to rely upon except to add sheer mass to a successful offensive). In naval forces, the U.S.-NATO advantage is large in almost every category, even if ships are counted by the prow, as in Homer, and not by tonnage (in which Western superiority is still greater).

If one delights in these comparisons, one can come up with more numbers that are comforting. But there are also some other numbers that are less reassuring. Tanks: 17,053 for NATO in Europe (U.S. included) versus a total of 45,500 on the other side, including 32,200 in reliable Soviet hands (Hitler had only some 3,000 in 1941 for "Barbarossa," the German invasion of Russia); artillery pieces: 9,502 versus 19,446; surface-to-surface missile launchers: 355 versus 1,224 for the Soviet camp (all the nuclear warheads are in Soviet hands exclusively); antitank guns (a rather antique category by conventional wisdom): 964 versus 3,614.

As for combat aircraft in Europe, the numbers go the same way: 2,293 fighter-bombers for NATO-Europe versus 3,255 in Soviet and Warsaw Pact air forces (but predominantly Soviet); fighters: only 204 on the NATO side (the U.S. Air Force believes in heavier multipurpose aircraft) versus 1,565 on the other side; interceptors (another depreciated category): 572 on the part of NATO versus 1,490 in Pact air forces.

Each set of numbers means little in itself. But ignoring all the details, there is one very striking fact that emerges—a fact that begins to tell us the real story about the "military balance" on which there is so much controversy now that McGeorge Bundy, George F. Kennan, Robert S. McNamara, and Gerard Smith have jointly proposed [see selection 1] that NATO should renounce the "first use" of nuclear weapons to deter a nuclear invasion. That fact, indeed very remarkable, is that the rich are seemingly armed as poor men are armed, with rifles, while the poor are armed as rich men are armed, with heavy weapons. Recalling that comparison of "total ground forces in Europe" in which NATO is shown with 2.1 million troops on active duty versus a mere 1.7 million for the

Warsaw Pact—a ratio of 1.27:1 in favor of our side—we now discover that the ratios for the major weapons which modern ground forces need go the other way, in favor of the Soviet side: 2.65:1 for tanks; 2.05:1 for artillery; 3.45:1 for missile launchers; and so on.

More remarkable still, the poorer and less advanced have more combat aircraft, by ratios of 4.5:1 (bombers), 1.4:1 (fighter-bombers), 7.67:1 (fighters), 2.61:1 (interceptors), and so on. Never mind that on each side one should sort out old aircraft in each category, and never mind also that Soviet aircraft are judged inferior to their U.S. counterparts (though to take Israeli-Syrian combat outcomes as an index is totally misleading, since Soviet aircraft would do very nicely in Israeli hands, just as they performed quite well against our own fighter-bombers in Vietnam, and also in Indian hands against the Pakistanis). In spite of all qualifications large and small, the fact stands, and it is a great fact: the poor are far more abundantly armed, even in air power, which is the quintessential arm of the rich.

How can this be? What does this mean? How and why have the rich come to be poorly armed as compared with the Soviet Union (whose gross national product is now 60 per cent of the American and a mere 25 per cent of the U.S.-NATO total)? There is, of course, a very simple answer revealed by the statistics themselves. That famous number, the count of NATO ground forces in Europe in the amount of 2.1 million (as compared to 1.7 million for the Pact), is actually made up of 980,000 men in the armies of Western Europe and another 922,000 men in the Greek, Italian, and Turkish armies which mainly consist of lightly armed infantry disqualified by location, training, and equipment from fighting seriously against Soviet-style armored divisions.

But that too is no more than a circumstantial fact: it is not the ineluctable consequence of unalterable limits. NATO *could* have forces much larger *and* better equipped *and* in the right places, for it has a much larger population than the Pact, and also a far greater production. Why then do our richer allies in Western Europe fail to remedy the imbalance? Is it greed that dissuades them from spending enough, or is it perhaps defeatism? Both are in evidence in some degree. But the decisive reason is strategic: those in Europe who understand such matters know that an increased effort would not improve the balance unless it were truly huge, because there are two fundamental military factors at work which make NATO weak and the Soviet Union strong—and these are of such powerful effect in combination that they would nullify the benefits of any marginal increase in defense spending, just as they already out-weigh every one of the disadvantages that afflict the Soviet Union, including the unreliability of some of its East European subjects, the hostility of China, and the technical inferiority of some Soviet weapons. Much more than the numbers, it is these two factors that truly determine the present military imbalance in non-nuclear strength.

NATO Is For Defense

The first of the two fundamental military factors is, quite simply, that NATO is a defensive alliance—defensive not just in declared intent, as all self-respecting alliances will claim to be, but rather in actual military orientation. Specifically, the forces of NATO on the "central front"—the 600-kilometer line running from the Baltic Sea to the Austrian border—are incapable of offensive operations on a large scale. There are no plans for a NATO offensive against East Germany; there has never been suitable training, or any army-sized exercises for offensive action. In spite of the abundant claims to the contrary in Soviet propaganda at its most implausible, Soviet military planners must know that NATO could not launch an offensive against their front. The notion that Belgian, Dutch, British, German, and U.S. forces would suddenly march across the border to invade is quite simply fantastic.

This means that the Soviet high command can concentrate its own forces for offensive action without having to allocate signifi-cant strength for defense. To be sure, many Soviet divisions are either deployed on or assigned to the very long Chinese border. But there too the Soviet Union need not disperse its forces to provide a territorial defense, since the Chinese, for all their mil-lions of troops and tens of millions of rifle-armed militiamen, have no real capacity to mount significant offensive operations. At the very most, at a time of great opportunity such as a Soviet attack upon the West might present, the Chinese could mount a very limited and very shallow move against some segment of the Trans-Siberian railway where it runs near their territory.

The Soviet army, which was greatly diminished in size during the 1950s but which has grown again during the last two decades, can now mobilize so many divisions that it can cover the Chinese border very adequately; provide more divisions to maintain a threat against Iran, Eastern Turkey, and Pakistan; keep the forces now in place in Afghanistan; and still send more divisions against the "central front" than NATO could cope with.

Not counting at all the divisions of the East European client-states (even though some at least could in fact be used), the arithmetic runs as follows: if 10 more Soviet divisions are added to the Chinese "front" (in addition to the 46 stationed there already); and if a further 18 divisions are kept in reserve to deal with all the contingencies that a prudent and well-provided military leadership can imagine; and if there is no reduction in the generous allowance of 26 divisions now deployed on the Soviet Union's "southern front" (opposite the underequipped Turks, the chaotic Persians, and in Afghanistan); then, finally, the Soviet Union, upon mobilization, could launch 80 divisions against NATO in Central Europe—that is, against the West German border. And since NATO is a defensive-only alliance, the Soviet army could concentrate its forces in powerful offensive thrusts aimed at narrow segments of that front.

By another estimate, produced by the International Institute for Strategic Studies, the Soviet army could send a total of 118 divisions against NATO, the greater number being obtained by assuming that no central reserve is maintained at all (the Soviet Union does after all keep 500,000 KGB and MVD troops, which are heavily armed) and that no reinforcement would be made to the Chinese "front."

As against this, NATO can claim a total of 116 divisions, only two fewer than the higher estimate of the Soviet divisions that could be sent against it—and actually 36 divisions more than the Soviet total estimated more conservatively.

But that is truly a hollow number, since NATO's 116 divisions include more than 16 American National Guard divisions that would have to be mobilized, remanned, re-equipped (with what?), trained for weeks or months, and then transported to Europe by way of ports and airfields benevolently left intact by Soviet forces. The 116 divisions include more than 29 Italian, Greek, and Turkish divisions that are stationed far from Central Europe and are neither trained nor equipped to fight on that front. And they include 9 other divisions of foot infantry of various kinds. Once all these make-weights are removed from the count, we discover that against 80 Soviet divisions, NATO might field no more than 58 divisions of its own, including more than 12 French divisions whose participation in a fight is uncertain but whose scant armament for such combat is, unfortunately, not in doubt.

In fact, we might estimate even more truly by measuring NATO forces in terms of *Soviet* division-equivalents, whereupon we obtain 35 divisions upon full mobilization and with the transfer of all earmarked U.S. forces. The numerical imbalance thus finally emerges as a sharp one indeed: 80 Soviet divisions versus 35 for NATO. And then the defense/offense asymmetry intervenes to make the true combat imbalance even greater, since the Soviet divisions can be concentrated during an offensive against a few narrow segments of the front while NATO's divisions must defend all along a 600-kilometer border.

A Soviet Armored Blitzkrieg

Under any circumstances, the numerical imbalance in real capabilities would make things very difficult for NATO. But it would not be decisive were it not for the second great factor that makes NATO weak, which arises from the very nature of armored warfare. Nowadays, there is only one army in the world that has actual hands-on expertise in the reality of armored warfare, in the combined use of large numbers of tanks, troop carriers, and self-propelled artillery to stage offensives of deep penetration, whereby enemy forces are not merely destroyed piecemeal by fire-fights but are defeated by being cut off and forced into surrender—and that, of course, is the Israeli army. But if there is one army in the world that seriously strives to overcome its lack of recent and relevant combat experience, it is the Soviet army. It is the only one which stages vast army-sized exercises to educate its officers and men in the broad art and the detailed craft of armored warfare.

The Soviet army would not be lined up unit by unit along the 600 kilometers of the German frontier, there to fight it out in head-on combat with the forces of NATO similarly arrayed (hence the worthlessness of inventory comparisons which imply such front-to-front combat). Instead, its 80 divisions would be formed into deep columns and multiple echelons poised to advance by swift penetrations of narrow segments of the front. Having learned the art of armored warfare in the hard school of war itself, at the hands of the best masters, and having made the method at once simpler and much more powerful by employing the sheer mass of great numbers to relieve the need for fancy German-style maneuvers, the Soviet army would not employ its forces to launch a set-piece offensive on a preplanned line of advance (which would be detectable and vulnerable), but would instead seek to advance opportunistically, just as water flows down a slope, its rivulets seeking the faster paths. Initially, the advance regiments would probe for gaps and weak sectors through which a swift passage might be achieved. Any Soviet forces that could make no progress would be left in place, to keep up the threat and prevent the NATO commands from switching their forces to strengthen the front elsewhere. But Soviet reinforcements would only be sent where successful advances were being achieved in order to add to the momentum. First more regiments, then divisions, then entire "armies" would thus be channeled forward to keep up the pressure and push deep into the rear of the NATO front.

By feeding reinforcement echelons into avenues of penetration successfully opened, the Soviet high command could obtain the full effect of the classic *Blitzkrieg* even without having to rely on the skill and initiative of regimental officers, as the Germans once did. Instead of a fluid penetrating maneuver obtained by free improvisation, theirs would be an advance just as fast, achieved by mass and momentum directed from above.

Soon enough, advancing Soviet columns would begin to disrupt the entire defensive structure of NATO, by cutting across roads on which Western reinforcements and resupply depend by overrunning artillery batteries, command centers, supply depots, and finally airfields—until the very ports of entry on the Atlantic shore would be reached. With NATO's front cut in several places, with Soviet forces already in their deep rear, the choices open to NATO formations in such non-nuclear combat would be either to stand and fight for honor's sake even without true military purpose, or else to retreat—thus opening further gaps in the front. In any case, the relentless advance would soon enough impose a broader choice at a much higher level of decision, for the Germans first and the others not much later: capitulation or military destruction.

Thus in the absence of nuclear weapons, it is not the numerical imbalance in itself that would bring the dismal results, but rather the fact that the Soviet army has a valid method of offensive war, while NATO for its part has no valid method of defense. For obviously the envisaged attempts to block Soviet advances by switching defensive forces back and forth along the line (right in front of Soviet forces which would have every opportunity to disrupt such lateral movement by fire and by their own thrusts) must fail. Indeed, it can be said that even if NATO had a perfect numerical equality, it would still find it impossible to match Soviet concentrations with its own, in order to block their advance right at the front line itself. The reason for this inherent defect is not any lack of military expertise on the part of NATO commanders and planners (although their unfamiliarity with modern armored warfare does show when some pronounce on the military balance by the bookkeeper's method). The defect rather is caused by the combination of NATO's defensive-only orientation and the character of large-scale armored warfare.

A Nuclear Option Is Vital

In the face of an offensive threat by an armored-mobile army (unless the defenders are *vastly* superior in sheer strength), one of two conditions must obtain to make a successful defense possible:

either the defenders must be ready and willing to attack first, in order to disrupt an offensive preemptively; or else the defense must have considerable geographic space in which to maneuver and fight in a defense-in-depth strategy. If NATO had the political will, the training, and the organization to strike first in the face of massing Soviet forces, the latter could not safely form up in deep columns for the attack and would instead have to dilute their strength to form a defensive array of their own.

This option is purely theoretical in NATO's case. It is impossible to imagine that so many diverse governments would agree to let their national forces engage in a preemptive attack to anticipate a Soviet invasion before the outbreak of war. More likely, in the face of a Soviet mobilization and a build-up of divisions opposite NATO, there would be demands for negotiations to settle the crisis by what would no doubt be called "political means," i.e., eager concessions.

As compared with a wholly unrealistic strategy of preemptive attack, the second opinion, a defense-in-depth, may seem a feasible alternative; and it would offer the possibility of a very powerful defense indeed for NATO. Under such a strategy, Soviet invasion columns would *not* be intercepted by NATO's main defensive forces right in the border zone. Instead, advancing Soviet forces would encounter only a mere border guard along the frontier itself, thereafter being harassed, delayed, and clearly revealed by light and elusive forces as they continued to advance, being steadily weakened by the loss of momentum imposed by time, distance, breakdowns, mined barriers, multiple obstacles at river crossing points, canals, and towns—and also by successive battles with strongholds along the way. Then too, NATO air forces operating quite freely over their own territory, where Soviet air defenses would be very weak, could attack advancing Soviet forces heavily and frequently. Only then would the major combat on the ground finally take place, with fresh NATO divisions maneuvering to strike at the stretched-out and by then ill-supplied Soviet columns (air strikes would do much more damage to supply vehicles than to the Soviet armored forces themselves).

In such a setting, with a thin line of NATO covering forces on the border itself, with multiple barriers and strongholds in depth, and with the main line of resistance 100 or 200 kilometers to the rear, NATO could indeed have a very solid non-nuclear defense, and one which could moreover deter non-nuclear invasion all by itself—since any competent Soviet planner would have to estimate that defeat would be the most likely outcome. And that, of course, would be a defeat which would deprive the Soviet army of one-half of its divisions, and thus the Soviet empire of much of its gendarmerie as well as all of its prestige, no doubt triggering unrest at home and perhaps outright insurrection in the client-states.

But to imagine such a defense in depth for the NATO central front in Germany is not to consider a live option. It is, rather, to indulge in sheer fantasy—and malevolent fantasy at that. For that zone of deep combat happens to correspond to the territory where tens of millions of Germans live. Quite rightly, what the Germans demand is not merely an eventual ability to defeat an aggression at some ultimate point in time and in space, but rather an actual provision of security for themselves, their families, their homes, and their towns. The British, French, or Americans might obtain satisfaction from the defeat of an invading Soviet army in the depth of West German territory, but such a victory would be of little worth to the Germans themselves. What the European system of peaceful construction needs is a preclusive method of protection, not ultimate victory after much destruction and millions of deaths.

In the absence of an offensive capacity by NATO and a lively willingness to preempt invasion, such protection can only be assured by nuclear weapons—or more precisely, by the architecture of nuclear deterrence which is now in place. If the Soviet Union does attack, its offensive would be met in the first instance by a non-nuclear defense of the forward areas close to the border. If NATO could not hold the front by non-nuclear combat, it would warn the Soviet Union that (small-yield) nuclear weapons would be used to strike at the invading Soviet forces. And then it would strike with such weapons if the warning went unheeded.

At that point the Soviet Union would realize that the alliance was standing up to the test, that it did have the will to defend itself in its moment of truth. One Soviet reaction might be to call off the war—a quite likely response if the invasion has been launched out of some hope of gain, but much less likely if it were the desperate last act of a crumbling empire.

Another Soviet reaction might be to respond to the threat by a wider threat against the cities of Europe, or else—and more likely—to reply in kind. With its own forces weakened by nuclear attack, it might employ nuclear weapons to make its invasion easier, by blasting gaps through the NATO defenses. Or else, the Soviet Union might want to avoid the intermediate steps, and try to impose a capitulation by threatening to attack European cities if any more battlefield nuclear weapons were used.

An Answer in Kind

Such a verbal threat might in turn be averted by being answered in kind, in the first instance perhaps by the British and the French—assuming that their cities had also come under the threat. But a better response to such a Soviet threat would be possible if by then NATO had acquired its own theater nuclear forces which, like the Soviet forces that already exist in considerable numbers, would be suitable to threaten not merely cities indiscriminately, but rather such specific targets as political and military command centers, airfields, nuclear storage sites, and even large concentrations of ground forces—that threat being all the more credible for being less catastrophic.

Much more complex exchanges and many more variations can be envisaged. But by far the most likely outcome is that a war would end very soon if any nuclear weapons, however small, were actually to be detonated by any side on any target. The shock effect upon leaders on both sides—but especially on the Soviet leaders who had started the war—and also the devastating psychological impact upon the forces in the field, would most likely arrest the conflict there and then. It is fully to be expected that military units whose men would see the flash, hear the detonation, feel the blast, or merely hear of such things, would swiftly disintegrate, except perhaps for a handful of units particularly elite, and also remote from the immediate scene. The entire "software" of discipline, of morale, of unit cohesion and *esprit de corps* and all the practices and habits that sustain the authority of sergeants, officers, and political commissars, are simply not built to withstand such terror as nuclear weapons would cause—even if at the end of the day it were to be discovered that the dead on all sides were surprisingly few.

The time has come to deal forthrightly with the anti-nuclear agitation. To do as the Reagan administration has done, to concede and appease, is highly dangerous. Because if the false argument is admitted, sound strategy is thereby delegitimized and then in due course policies of weakness will inevitably follow through congressional decision and public pressure.

If, for example, the Bundy-Kennan-McNamara-Smith proposal is accepted on the argument that it is good public relations to do so, and that only a verbal change would be involved, it will soon be discovered that once NATO's "first-use" policy is renounced it will be impossible to obtain approval for the upkeep of battlefield nuclear weapons. Why, it will be said, should we keep those nuclear-capable guns so near the border if we no longer seek to deter a non-nuclear invasion by nuclear deterrence? Thus the nuclear shells of the artillery will be withdrawn—they being the smallest of our nuclear weapons, and yet very likely the most powerful for deterrence because of their immediacy and the circumscribed effect that makes use credible.

Similarly, if the principle of arms control negotiations for this or that class of weapons is once accepted, actually for purposes of public relations but ostensibly for the sake of peace and survival, how will the demand for more concessions be resisted? After all, it will be said, what petty diplomatic concern, what minor strategic advantage, is more important than peace and survival? Not to stand and assert the truth in the war of ideas means to suffer delegitimization now, and then eventual defeat in the practical realms of policy and strategy.

5. *A Global Freeze on Nuclear Weapons*

By EDWARD M. KENNEDY

Focus Early in 1982, Democratic Senator Edward M. Kennedy co-sponsored with Republican Senator Mark O. Hatfield a resolution calling for a global and verifiable freeze on nuclear arms instead of simply a freeze confined to Europe as proposed by Soviet President Leonid I. Brezhnev (see selection 30). By March 1982 the resolution had garnered the signatures of 165 members of the U.S. Senate and House (where it was introduced by Representative Edward Markey of Massachusetts), but by late fall neither chamber had passed it.

In this brief statement, Senator Kennedy insists that a general freeze "would not consign the United States to a position of global inferiority with the Soviet Union" because "perhaps for the first time in the atomic age" there is an overall nuclear balance. "Instead of worrying about a theoretical and exaggerated 'window of vulnerability,'" says Kennedy, "we should focus on this window of opportunity for arms control." The freeze must be seen as a first and necessary step to arms control and reductions. In this, the senator supports the general approach of other freeze proponents (see selection 8).

Kennedy accuses the Reagan administration of paying lip-service to arms reductions: "Our government has a weapons policy, a massive and expensive build-up, but no effective peace policy." (The Reagan administration's views are found in

63

64

selections 27-29.) He believes that Soviet "misdeeds in other areas" should not impede us from seeking a global freeze, which may help "to postpone the moment of humanity's final conflict." This reference to the "final conflict" suggests that Senator Kennedy may be influenced by the apocalyptic premise advanced by Jonathan Schell (see selection 15) and others.

Edward M. Kennedy is the senior U.S. senator from Massachusetts.

THE ISSUE OF ARMS CONTROL—perhaps the most critical issue of our time, or of all time—has now reached the point of stalemate. Soviet President Leonid I. Brezhnev is offering a self-serving and unacceptable proposal to freeze nuclear weapons in Europe alone. The Reagan administration properly rejects that, but refuses to respond with any comprehensive counteroffer. At the talks on intermediate weapons in Europe, the Administration has put forward a plan as unacceptable to the Soviets as theirs is to us; as a result, the talks are stalled. The Reagan Strategic Arms Reduction Talks (START) on strategic weapons have not begun, and no date for the discussion has been set.

Both sides are engaging in a dialogue of the deaf, making propaganda instead of talking peace. In the meantime, a grass-roots movement across the country, reaching from a ballot initiative in California to town meetings in New England, has called for a third alternative that can break the deadlock. That alternative, a global freeze on the nuclear arsenals of both sides, has been incorporated into a congressional resolution, which already has the support of 165 members of the Senate and the House. The resolution calls both for a global freeze and for the negotiation of reductions in American and Soviet weaponry.

The Administration and a number of other critics have reacted intensely and often inaccurately to the congressional proposal, which I am co-sponsoring with Republican Senator Mark O. Hatfield of Oregon. It is important to make clear what the resolution does—and does not—mean.

First, we are not suggesting a continental freeze in Europe alone. That is the Brezhnev proposal—and we categorically reject it. We favor a comprehensive freeze. Administration officials have sought to blur the difference—and then have cited a range of conflicting statistics to attack our resolution. Secretary of State Alexander M.

Reprinted by permission of Senator Edward M. Kennedy from the March 21, 1982, issue of the *Los Angeles Times* (© 1982 by Edward M. Kennedy).

Haig, Jr., first said it would leave the United States with a 6 to 1 inferiority in Europe; later, the President said it might be 3 to 1. It is baffling that on this basic question, the Administration cannot even keep its numbers straight. In fact, the Soviets have 2,004 available warheads in Europe, and we have 1,168. This does not count other American nuclear forces outside of Europe and at sea, which could be used to defend the NATO nations. Is the Administration suggesting that it would not call on those forces in the event of a crisis? Any such suggestion would represent a fundamental and destabilizing change in American policy.

Second, the global freeze proposed in the congressional resolution would not consign the United States to a position of global inferiority with the Soviet Union. The Administration asserts that it would, but advances no proof. Presidential Counselor Edwin Meese III has likened the U.S.-Soviet nuclear balance to a football game where one side is ahead 50-0. But the analogy, which is wrong even as it applied to Europe, is very far from the worldwide reality. The more relevant numbers are the count of strategic nuclear warheads: this country has 9,400 and the Soviets have 7,500. They are ahead in some areas, such as throw-weight; we are ahead in others, such as sea-based missiles. There is, perhaps for the first time in the atomic age, an overall nuclear balance.

Instead of worrying about a theoretical and exaggerated "window of vulnerability," we should focus on this window of opportunity for arms control. But the opportunity could shatter with a further escalation in weaponry, including a new round of the MX missile and the B-1 bomber on our side, and new generations of missiles already on the Soviet drawing board. Thus a freeze makes not only common sense, but strategic sense. For example, a freeze can ensure that nuclear reductions negotiated in the future will not be made meaningless by the development and deployment of new and destabilizing weapons. Together, a freeze and reductions will move the United States and the Soviet Union to run the arms race in reverse. By combining these two policies, the freeze resolution goes beyond a codification of the existing nuclear balance, and could move us quickly toward more stable deterrence and a safer world.

Third, despite administration rhetoric claiming that our proposal does not go far enough, the wording of the resolution plainly and explicitly calls for "mutual and major reductions" in existing nuclear stockpiles. Perhaps the President has not read the resolution itself. His administration pays lip-service to reductions, but its arms control policy is now going absolutely nowhere. Our government has a weapons policy, a massive and expensive build-up, but no effective peace policy. Today the two superpowers have in their possession the equivalent of one million Hiroshima bombs— nearly four tons of TNT for every man, woman, and child currently living on this planet. A freeze would be a first, far-reaching step in the thousand-mile journey to reductions. Instead of piling overkill on overkill, why not start with a freeze?

Fourth, our proposal is not based on trust for the Soviet Union or tolerance of Soviet misdeeds in other areas. We do not accept the concept of reverse linkage—that we must accept Soviet repression in Poland and elsewhere in order to coax them into arms control. We should not enter upon a nuclear freeze or reductions because we like the Soviets or they like us, but because both of us prefer existence to extinction. Every measure we would take depends on strict verification. And our resolution does not call for unilateral action but for mutual agreement. It will not weaken but strengthen our defenses. Some of the resources that are freed can be reallocated to our conventional military forces, which is where we do need to do more.

Finally, some critics have suggested that our resolution involves a dangerous excess of democracy—that it invites the public into a debate where only experts dare to tread. We do not share the notion that a professional elite deserves a monopoly on what could become the ultimate issue of personal survival for hundreds of millions of people. While the negotiators have been debating the nuclear version of the question of how many angels can dance on the head of pin—which is, precisely how high can each side make the rubble bounce?—concerned citizens have developed and lobbied for a sane alternative. We regard it as a strength of our system that free men and women can stand up and speak out. They have offered a proposal in the American free marketplace of ideas; and every citizen of the world, including the people of the Soviet Union, who do not have the right to speak, will be in their debt if this initiative helps to postpone the moment of humanity's final conflict.

In reality, the nuclear-freeze resolution commands support not only in Congress and among religious and business leaders, but among many past officials of the Defense and State departments. They have seen the nuclear danger up close, and they know that a freeze followed by reductions may be our last great chance to avert the last great war. They know that we are rapidly nearing the point of no return in the nuclear arms race. Soon both sides will fear that the other has a first-strike capability that could destroy its deterrent. Once this point is passed, arms control may become little more than rule-making for the rearrangement of the deck chairs on the Titanic. People in communities across America have seen the looming iceberg, and they hope the captain will see it too. We cannot afford to live in a world of hair-trigger nuclear missiles, where human beings will have only minutes to decide whether to fire them, and where human error could launch an accidental nuclear exchange. This is not a way of life at all; it is a way to nuclear death.

In the second year of the Reagan administration, apprehension about the nuclear danger has stirred our own nation and strained relations with our NATO allies. Both the Administration and the Soviet leadership deliver speeches about nuclear disarmament, while each relentlessly pursues the phantom of nuclear advantage. In the words of my colleague, Senator Hatfield, "The result is upward arms management rather than downward arms control." There is broad agreement that the latest Soviet proposal for a limited freeze in Europe is unequal and unacceptable. But there is also an urgent need to challenge the Soviets to go further, to freeze more, to take a bigger step back from the brink. With the world trapped between the seemingly irreconcilable positions of the Administration and the Kremlin, only the emerging initiative for a nuclear freeze and reductions can break the deadlock that consistently defeats the chance for a stable peace.

6. In Defense of Deterrence

By CHARLES KRAUTHAMMER

Focus
In April 1982 the *New Republic* acknowledged the strength of the pro-freeze movement in the United States with a lead article in which Charles Krauthammer, a senior editor, declares that fear is "the animating force" behind the freeze campaign. The crusaders enlist new adherents by scare tactics, he says, showing "graphic stills of Hiroshima victims and the maps with concentric circles radiating from ground zero in everyone's hometown"—as though people needed to be convinced that a nuclear war would be horrible.

Krauthammer stoutly rejects the no-first-use pledge by the United States and the nuclear freeze approach as dangerous and ineffective. He also addresses the "overkill" argument: "In their zeal to curb overkill, freeze advocates ignore the requirements of deterrence and, in particular, the requirement for survivability of the deterrent." Quoting Winston Churchill, he says a "balance of terror" is better than an imbalance of terror: "Safety will be the sturdy child of terror, and survival the twin brother of annihilation."

Working to reduce the chances of nuclear war, says Krauthammer, is not a romantic task or "an exercise in psychotherapy" but "mundane work in pursuit of mundane objectives: a modest program of nuclear modernization, SALT II, and a bigger conventional defense."

Charles Krauthammer is a senior editor of the *New Republic*. A section on Jonathan Schell is omitted from the essay because Schell is discussed elsewhere in this volume.

S AFETY WILL BE the sturdy child of terror, and survival the twin brother of annihilation." That was Winston Churchill's description of what he called "the balance of terror." Each superpower has the ability to incinerate the defenseless population of the other many times over; each refrains from attacking because it fears retaliation in kind; each knows that aggression is tantamount to suicide. That is deterrence. Sometimes deterrence is called MAD, mutual assured destruction. By whatever name, deterrence has prevented the outbreak of nuclear war, indeed any war, between the United States and the Soviet Union for a generation.

Living in a world of deterrence is very uncomfortable. Every American and Soviet city dweller knows that he is targeted for destruction by nuclear weapons five thousand miles away. But the physical danger is only part of the problem. The world of deterrence is a world of paradoxes. Weapons are built in order never to be used. Weapons purely for defense of helpless populations, like the antiballistic missile systems, become the greatest threat to peace. Weapons aimed at people lessen the risk of war; weapons aimed at weapons, increase it.

The strains of living in such a world are enormous. A vast anti-nuclear movement is now rising in the United States, animated principally by weariness and revulsion with this arrangement. Why now? Ronald Reagan is much of the answer. He helped defeat the SALT II treaty before his election, and has been reluctant to engage the Soviets in strategic arms talks since. For the first time in more than a decade, the United States and the Soviet Union are not engaged in negotiations to control strategic nuclear weapons. Worse, Mr. Reagan and some of his advisers have spoken in frighteningly offhand ways about "limited nuclear war" and nuclear warning shots. The Carter administration's mobile MX

Reprinted with adaptations by permission of *The New Republic* (© 1982 by The New Republic, Incorporated).

plan played a part, too. It appeared such an enormously cumbersome and expensive contrivance that people began to wonder if the experts had not lost touch with reality. So millions of Americans have decided it is time for them to take the problem into their own hands, and an anti-nuclear grass-roots crusade has emerged.

Like all crusades, it has its bible: Jonathan Schell's *The Fate of the Earth* [see selection 15]; and it has its banner: "the freeze." It has also acquired an auxiliary brigade: four members of the American foreign policy establishment who opened a wholly new front by calling for a U.S. renunciation of any first use of nuclear weapons [see selection 1]. The bible, the banner, and the brigade approach the nuclear dilemma from different directions, but they all challenge the established doctrines of deterrence. The brigade wants to limit deterrence; the freeze proponents want to ignore it; and Jonathan Schell wants to abolish it. Each deserves the closest scrutiny. . . .

The Sword of Damocles

Fear is the animating force behind a new mass movement—the freeze campaign. The movement demands a mutual halt in the development, production, and deployment of all nuclear weapons, "because," as the campaign slogan puts it, "no one wants a nuclear war." Like Schell, freeze proponents are deeply concerned, and rightly so, about the prospect of living in a world in which we have the capacity to blow ourselves to bits at any moment. The freeze crusade has enlisted hundreds of thousands of Americans by showing what happens if the Sword of Damocles ever drops. Thus the graphic stills of Hiroshima victims and the maps with concentric circles radiating from ground zero in everyone's hometown. Schell recognizes that removing this sword requires renunciation not just of overkill but of minimal deterrence, of the simple capacity to destroy the other side *once*. But very few freeze proponents advocate reducing levels below "sufficiency," because they recognize that in a pre-messianic world this would destabilize the nuclear balance and increase the chances of war. Under a freeze—indeed, under even the most radical of arms proposals, such as former

Ambassador George Kennan's proposal to cut nuclear levels in half—the superpowers would still retain the capacity for the total destruction of the other society. Insofar as people support the freeze because they can't stand the thought of being a target for Soviet missiles, they have joined the wrong movement. The freeze offers no solution to that problem. They should be with Jonathan Schell's total disarmament movement, working on the "awesome, urgent task" of remaking human nature.

Some might argue that there is another way, short of universal brotherhood, to remove the Sword of Damocles. That is unilateral disarmament. But quite apart from the fact that such a move would mean the surrender of our values, it would do little to secure our survival. The historical record does not support the proposition that helplessness is a guarantee of safety. There has been one nuclear war on record; in it a non-nuclear Japan lost Hiroshima and Nagasaki. So far there has been only one biological war, the one going on today in Laos and Cambodia. These weapons, now used against helpless tribesmen, were never used against American troops fighting the same Vietnamese forces in the same place. The Hmong, unlike the Americans, lack the capacity to retaliate in kind.

The freeze is not unilateralist, nor do many of its advocates reject deterrence. They say they reject overkill. "Enough is enough," they say. "Why waste billions on useless weapons if all they will do, as Churchill said, is to make the rubble bounce?" (It is sometimes also argued, somewhat anomalously, that having useless, rubble-bouncing weapons is at the same time dangerous.)

The problem is that in their zeal to curb overkill, freeze advocates ignore the requirements of deterrence and, in particular, the requirement for survivability of the deterrent. Our weapons must be able to withstand a first strike and penetrate Soviet defenses in a retaliatory strike (and vice versa). If either side finds the survivability of its weapons systems declining, the world becomes less safe. In an international crisis, each side, particularly the more vulnerable side, has incentive to strike first: the invulnerable side to use its advantage, the vulnerable side to strike before it is too late.

What would happen under a freeze? The U.S. retaliatory capacity depends on the three legs of its strategic triad: the land-based ICBMs, the bomber force, and submarines. Because of the increasing accuracy, power, and numbers of Soviet missiles, the U.S. land-based missile force will soon become vulnerable to a first strike. (It is precisely to eliminate that vulnerability that President Carter proposed hiding the MX in multiple shelters, a scheme now abandoned.) That leaves the bomber and submarine forces. The bomber force consists of aging B-52s that are increasingly vulnerable to attack while still on the ground, and to being shot down while trying to penetrate Soviet air space. Hence President Carter's decision to deploy air-launched cruise missiles, which would be better able to penetrate Soviet defenses and would allow the B-52s to remain outside Soviet air space. The freeze proposal would prevent deployment of these missiles. It would also prevent production and development of a new bomber, either the B-1 or the Stealth, which would be better able to elude destruction on the ground and Soviet defenses in the air. Note that the B-1 or the Stealth would not be any more destructive than the B-52. They would not make the rubble bounce any higher. They would simply be more likely to get to the target, and therefore present the Soviets with a very good reason never to launch a first strike.

That leaves the submarine force, which the United States is now in the process of modernizing to make more survivable. The new Tridents are quieter than existing subs, and because they have longer-range missiles they can hide in larger areas of the ocean. The freeze would stop their deployment.

The freeze, a proposal devised for its simplicity, does not deal very well with paradox. It is one of the paradoxes of deterrence that defensive weapons (the ABM, for example) can be more destabilizing and therefore more dangerous to peace than offensive weapons. The freeze fixates on nuclear weapons because they appear more terrible than others. And indeed they are. But they are not necessarily more destabilizing. As former Under Secretary of the Navy James Woolsey points out, the freeze does nothing to prevent non-nuclear anti-submarine and anti-aircraft advances, which weaken deterrence. But it does prevent the modernization of nuclear systems designed for survivability, which enhances deterrence.

What exactly does it mean to say that if survivability declines, war becomes more likely? One quick fix for a vulnerable deterrent is to adopt a policy of launch-on-warning: as soon as we detect enemy missiles leaving their silos, we launch our missiles before they can be destroyed. (Some officials unsuccessfully urged President Carter to adopt launch-on-warning as an alternative to building the mobile MX.) But this creates a hair-trigger situation, where the time for the world's most important decision is not a matter of minutes but of seconds, too short to check out a faulty radar reading or a misinterpretation of data. That's the price of ignoring deterrence.

This analysis looks simply at what would happen if the freeze were already a reality. But however fervently American citizens may wish it, they cannot vote a "mutual verifiable freeze" into existence. Unfortunately, that must be negotiated with the Soviets. And bad as a freeze would be as an end point, it would be worse as a U.S. negotiating position—which is exactly what it would be if, say, the Kennedy-Hatfield amendment were adopted. First, it is certain to delay other arms control initiatives. The freeze appeals to American voters because of its simplicity, but a mutual freeze would involve complex negotiations with the Soviets. What exactly would be frozen? At what stage? How would it be verified? The production, stockpiling, and qualitative upgrading of nuclear weapons cannot be detected by satellite, and the Russians have always refused on-site inspection. That problem alone turns the freeze into either a non-starter or a source of interminable negotiation.

The SALT Path to Arms Control

Ironically, there does exist an arms control proposal which, though very complicated, poorly understood by the American people, and unsuited for two-hour ratification by town meetings, is very well understood by the Soviets: SALT II. They have already signed it. If the aim of the freeze movements is a quick, simple, bold move in arms control that would allow us to proceed to real reductions, then the answer is not a freeze but SALT II. Representative Les Aspin has already pointed out with dismay the American penchant for reinventing the arms control wheel every four years.

In 1977 President Carter rejected the Vladivostok Accords negotiated by President Ford and proposed drastic reductions instead. The Soviets rejected his proposal out of hand. It took more than two years to renegotiate SALT II on the original lines of Vladivostok. President Reagan in turn rejected SALT II and called for as yet unspecified START talks. The freeze proponents are doing precisely the same thing. It simply makes no sense to propose a freeze that would require years of negotiations when SALT II is at hand, has already been approved by the Soviets, and could be adjusted in small details and ratified quickly. Of course, SALT is not as catchy a slogan as the freeze. But it is certainly a better, quicker, and more serious path to arms control.

Another aim of the freeze campaign is to move to real reductions. But to arm a U.S. negotiating team with a freeze offer is to ensure that it will have no leverage with which to bargain the Soviets into reductions. We will have unilaterally announced our willingness to forgo all our modernization programs, like the Trident, the cruise missile, and the Stealth bomber. The theory is that this gesture will elicit from the Soviets a more conciliatory negotiating position. The theory is in conflict with history. The Soviets do not have a good record of responding to unilateral gestures. At the Glassboro Summit in 1967, President Johnson tried to interest Premier Kosygin in ABM negotiations. Kosygin demurred. A year later, the Senate defeated an amendment to deny funds for an American ABM system. Three days later Soviet Foreign Minister Andrei Gromyko announced the Soviets' willingess to negotiate arms control. Eventually they agreed to an almost total ban on ABMs. We are using the same strategy today in Geneva, offering systems that we propose to build as bargaining chips. We offer to forgo deployment of the Pershing II and ground-launched cruise missiles in Europe if the Soviets dismantle their SS-20s. Under a freeze, our position in Geneva would collapse and the SS-20s would remain in place. (Brezhnev calls *that* arrangement a freeze.) In strategic arms talks, any attempts on our part to, say, bargain away one of our new systems against the Soviets' destabilizing silo-killing ICBMs would fail.

The freeze is not a plan; it is a sentiment. (Montana's proposed freeze resolution, for example, opposes "the production, development, and deployment of nuclear weapons by any nation." It will unfortunately not be binding on President Zia of Pakistan.) The freeze reflects the deeply felt and wholly laudable wish of millions of Americans that something be done to control nuclear weapons. But when taken seriously as a plan, the freeze continually fails on its own terms. It seeks safety, but would jeopardize deterrence; it seeks quick action, but would delay arms control; it seeks real reductions, but removes any leverage we might have to bring them about.

Finally, it mistakes the most likely cause of an outbreak of nuclear war. In its fixation on numbers, the freeze assumes that somehow high weapons levels *in themselves* make war more likely. True, an uncontrolled arms race breeds suspicion between the superpowers and can increase the risk of war; but arms control measures (like SALT I or II) can allow higher levels, and still decrease the risk by building confidence on both sides and letting each know precisely what the other is doing. If nuclear war ever comes, it most likely will be not because the weapons fire themselves, but because some national leader, in order to preserve some national interest, orders them fired. When did we come closest to nuclear war in the last thirty-six years? In October 1962, when President Kennedy decided to threaten Khrushchev with war unless he obeyed our ultimatum on the Cuban missiles. In 1962 the level of nuclear arms was much lower than it is today. And when was the chance of nuclear war smallest? Probably at the height of détente, during the Apollo-Soyuz love fest, when U.S.-Soviet relations were good, even though each side had the capacity for multiple overkill.

The absolute level of nuclear weapons is only one factor, and a relatively small one at that, in determining the likelihood of nuclear war breaking out. (It is certainly less important than the balance of vulnerabilities on each side, i.e., the stability of deterrence.) The most likely source of nuclear war is from a regional conflict between the superpowers, where one or the other has important interests but finds itself at a conventional disadvantage. That is the American situation today in Europe and in the Persian Gulf. To prevent the Soviets from taking advantage of their superiority in conventional arms, the United States has reserved the option of using nuclear weapons to respond to a non-nuclear Soviet attack. This policy of extending nuclear deterrence to conventional conflicts has kept the peace. But it is dangerous. It blurs the line between conventional and nuclear war, and by threatening "limited" nuclear war it opens the door to a nuclear holocaust, since no one knows whether a limited nuclear war can be kept limited. The most effective way to eliminate that danger, and thus eliminate the greatest existing risk of nuclear war, is to make this kind of extended deterrence unnecessary: to right the conventional balance by radically bolstering Allied forces, particularly on the West European frontier. NATO could then deter a conventional attack without having to threaten to wage nuclear war.

The High Cost of Conventional Defense

The freeze crusade, which springs from deeply felt anti-war and anti-armament sentiments, is not comfortable with the thought that preventing nuclear war may require a radically enlarged conventional defense. Furthermore, one of the major appeals of the anti-nuclear movement is the promise to halt the economic drain caused by "useless" nuclear weapons and to redirect resources to human needs. But a shift away from strategic to conventional weapons would be very expensive. Our reliance on nuclear weapons—and the current conventional balance in Europe—results in large part from a desire to *reduce* defense spending. In the 1950s we decided to buy defense in Europe on the cheap. Rather than match the vast armies and tank forces of the Warsaw Pact, we decided to go nuclear, because, as John Foster Dulles put it, it offered "more bang for the buck."

But the European defense balance has become more unstable since Dulles's day. In the 1950s the United States threatened "massive retaliation." If the Soviets crossed into Western Europe, we would attack the Russian homeland with a strategic nuclear strike. When the Russians acquired the same capacity against the United States, that threat lost its credibility. The Kennedy administration adopted a new policy of "flexible response," a euphemism for a limited nuclear war. Under the new doctrine, the United

States reserved the right to use theater nuclear weapons on the battlefield to thwart a conventional Soviet attack. That has been our policy ever since. (Ronald Reagan did not invent it, although he has the habit of throwing it around more casually and publicly than other presidents.) This doctrine has troubled many Americans, but as long as the United States was not prepared to challenge the Soviet conventional superiority in Europe, nor prepared to abandon its European allies, there seemed no other choice.

Enter the auxiliary brigade of the anti-nuclear movement: four former high administration officials, two of whom, under President Kennedy, gave us "limited nuclear war" (Robert McNamara and McGeorge Bundy); one of whom gave us "containment" (George Kennan); and one of whom gave us SALT (Gerard Smith). In the spring of 1982 they opened an entirely new front in the crusade. They called for the adoption of a "no-first-use" policy on nuclear weapons. It was a renunciation of "flexible response" and of "extended deterrence." (They would retain extended deterrence in one restricted sense: as a retaliation for a Soviet *nuclear* attack on Western Europe, an unlikely possibility since the Soviets are prepared to renounce first use, and since with their conventional advantage they have no reason to attack with nuclear weapons.)

No-First-Use: A Greater Nuclear Threat

The problem with folding our nuclear umbrella, as the four wise men themselves acknowledged, is that, unaccompanied by conventional rearmament, it means the end of the Western alliance and the abandonment in particular of West Germany to Soviet intimidation and blackmail. The other problem with a no-first-use policy is that it might paradoxically increase the chances of nuclear war. Today a war between the United States and the Soviets is deterred at its origin: since even the slightest conventional conflict between them carries the threat of escalating into a nuclear one, neither happens. The no-first-use policy moves the "firebreak" from the line dividing war from peace to the line dividing conventional war from nuclear war. It trades the increased chance of conventional war (because now less dangerous and more "thinkable") for a decreased chance of such a war becoming nuclear. But no one can guarantee that *in extremis,* faced with a massive Soviet invasion of Western Europe, the United States would stick to its no-first-use pledge. Thus, by making a European war thinkable, this policy could, whatever its intentions, lead to a nuclear war.

Unless, that is, we have the conventional forces to preserve the original firebreak between war and peace. Thus, to prevent both political and (possibly) nuclear calamity, a no-first-use pledge must be accompanied, indeed preceded, by a serious conventional build-up of Western forces on the European frontier. The problem with McNamara *et al.* is that although they acknowledge this need, they treat it very casually—certainly with nothing like the urgency with which they call for abandoning extended deterrence. They speak only vaguely of the need for "review" and "study" of conventional military needs, of whether the political will exists in the West for such a build-up, and of "whether we Americans have a durable and effective answer to our military manpower needs in the present all-volunteer active and reserve forces" (they cannot quite bring themselves to say the word "draft"). Their eagerness to be the first off the blocks with a no-first-use policy is obvious. Their reluctance to urge on their anti-nuclear allies the only responsible and safe (and costly) means of achieving it is lamentable. The result of their highly publicized, grossly unbalanced proposal is predictable: another support in the complex and high vulnerable structure in deterrence has been weakened. The world will be no safer for it.

Despite the pandering of the freeze-riding politicians and the posturing of the four wise men—and the good intentions of millions of concerned Americans caught up in the anti-nuclear maelstrom—there is no need to reinvent nuclear policy. There *is* a need for arms control: SALT II is the best transition to real reductions. There *is* a need to avoid limited nuclear war: rebuilding our conventional strength and perhaps reintroducing the draft would reduce the risk. These proposals are neither new nor exciting. Unlike Schell's crusade, they don't promise to restore "the wholeness and meaning of life." They don't suggest that "the passion and will that we need to save ourselves would flood into our lives. Then the walls of indifference, inertia, and coldness that now isolate each

of us from others, and all of us from the past and future generations, would melt, like snow in the spring." They don't promise to
set right "our disordered instinctual life." That is because working
to reduce the chances of nuclear war is not an exercise in
psychotherapy. It is not a romance. It is mundane work in pursuit
of mundane objectives: a modest program of nuclear modernization, SALT II, and a bigger conventional defense. These measures
will not cure anomie but will help to maintain deterrence, that
difficult abstraction on which our values and our safety depend.

7. 'No First Use' Requires a Conventional Build-up

By IRVING KRISTOL

Focus A self-confessed "hawk" on foreign policy predictably sees in the massive Soviet military build-up a grave danger to the United States and its allies. Yet Irving Kristol since Hiroshima has favored a U.S. policy of no first use of nuclear weapons. He stresses the moral issue: "A just war loses its moral legitimacy if it is unjustly conducted—i.e., if the destruction of life and property is markedly and obviously disproportionate ... to the war aims. ... Nuclear weapons are so indiscriminately destructive ... that their use is morally justified only in the most extreme conditions."

He argues that overdependence on nuclear arms, in part because they are cheaper than conventional forces, "will gradually but surely produce a weakening in the military ethos and, indeed, a decline in patriotic spirit. We have seen this happening in the Western world, and the proper term for it is decadence."

Kristol calls instead for a substantial build-up in conventional arms by the United States and its NATO allies. It would be a heavy burden, he says, but "if we and they are unwilling to shoulder that burden, then we are simply unworthy of the liberties we seek to preserve." Kristol's views on conventional arms are in general agreement with those

84

of the *Economist* editorial (selection 3) and at variance with those of Edward Luttwak (selection 4) and Charles Krauthammer (selection 6).

Irving Kristol is a political philosopher, editor, and writer. He is a co-editor of *The Public Interest* and the author of *On the Democratic Idea in America* and *Two Cheers for Capitalism*, among other works.

FOR MORE THAN THIRTY-FIVE YEARS, ever since the explosions at Hiroshima and Nagasaki, I have favored a doctrine of non-first-use of nuclear weapons by the United States. Since I am generally—and correctly—regarded as a "hawk" on foreign policy, this view has puzzled and irritated many of my political associates. They have tended to regard it as an inexplicable aberration. Today, with the rise of a powerful, popular anti-nuclear movement, they may wish to reconsider the issue.

The arguments in favor of non-first-use are, as they always have been, threefold: moral, psychological, and strategic.

The moral issue is clear enough. A just war loses its moral legitimacy if it is unjustly conducted—i.e., if the destruction of life and property is markedly and obviously disproportionate either to the occasion of the conflict or the war aims that are being pursued. Nuclear weapons are so indiscriminately destructive, and on such a relatively large scale, that their use is morally justified only in the most extreme conditions.

In fact, ever since the end of World War II our Pentagon and State Department have always had an intuitive, common-sense perception of this truth, though pretending it does not exist. For instance, can anyone imagine a circumstance in which the United States will use nuclear weapons against a non-nuclear power? We did not use them in Vietnam and, had we gone to war with Iran over the hostages, we would not have used them there either. Nor is it conceivable that we should use them against Cuba or Nicaragua. The foreseeable revulsion of public opinion, both at home and abroad, excludes any such possibility.

So why doesn't the Pentagon at least openly say that we will not use nuclear weapons against non-nuclear nations? Why does it bridle at any such suggestion? Why does it persist in the pretense

Reprinted by permission from the March 12, 1982, issue of the *Wall Street Journal*.

that nuclear weapons differ only quantitatively, not qualitatively, from more conventional weapons?

The answer from military officials is that it is to our advantage to keep those nations uncertain with regard to our possible use of nuclear weapons—the assumption being that, in such a state, they will behave more circumspectly toward us. But is there the slightest shred of evidence that Iran or Cuba has been in any way intimidated by our nuclear arsenal? Is there even any hint of uncertainty in their actions? They *know* we are not going to use nuclear weapons against them. The Pentagon, deep down, knows it too. The only ones who are intimidated by our present posture are the American people and our allied populations, who keep fearfully wondering whether the Pentagon, in a moment of pique or panic, might actually do the unthinkable.

The psychological argument in favor of a doctrine of non-first-use points to the corrupting effects of the illusion of military security that nuclear weapons create. Neither the United States nor our NATO allies have been willing to make the necessary sacrifices, in money and manpower, so that we can effectively cope with the inevitable crises in a decaying world order. The United States does not even have the conventional strength to confront Cuba in a convincing way. As for our European allies, they have become utterly insular—citizens of a "little Europe."

This situation has come about not only because nuclear weapons are seemingly so powerful as to provide an invincible "deterrent," but because they are so much cheaper than conventional armies, navies, and armaments. As a consequence, politicians in the free world inevitably gravitate toward a policy of steadily diminishing *usable* military strength while investing in nuclear arms to protect "national security," defined in the most limited and parochial way. Any such policy will gradually but surely produce a weakening in the military ethos and, indeed, a decline in patriotic spirit. We have seen this happening in the Western world, and the proper term for it is decadence.

The strategic argument in favor of a doctrine of non-first-use derives from the parity of nuclear power that now exists as between the United States and the Soviet Union. That such a parity would one day exist was predicted. But the implications of parity are only beginning to dawn upon us. Those implications now threaten an imminent collapse of the NATO alliance and are also visible in the growing popularity of an anti-nuclear campaign in Western Europe and the United States.

A Hole in the Nuclear Umbrella

In the years shortly after World War II, when Western Europe was disarmed, when we were "bringing the boys home" while the Soviet military remained near full strength—at that time the idea of an American nuclear response to Soviet aggression in Western Europe may have made temporary strategic sense. It really did provide the nations of Western Europe with an "umbrella" under which they could rebuild their economies and reconstruct their military establishments.

Shortly thereafter, when the Soviet Union developed its first atomic bombs, the "umbrella" was perceived to have a hole in it. The United States, for obvious reasons, became a lot less enthusiastic about the prospect of an automatic, immediate nuclear response to Soviet aggression. And so NATO was invented.

From the outset, the military philosophy behind NATO was ambiguous. The United States saw NATO as eventually becoming a military force powerful enough to repel a Soviet onslaught—all at the conventional level, of course. To that end we stationed some 350,000 U.S. soldiers in Europe. The Europeans saw NATO's eventual capability as being sufficient merely to "check" and slow down any Soviet movement across NATO's borders, providing time for the Soviets to contemplate the inevitable consequence of continued action. That consequence was an American nuclear attack on the Soviet Union. Those American troops in Europe were a "tripwire"—hostages, really—to make this consequence both credible and inevitable.

Note how attractive this situation was at the time, from the European point of view. Should a full-scale war actually take place, the Soviet Union would be annihilated, the United States would suffer a fair degree of devastation from Soviet nuclear retaliation, while Western Europe would experience only minimal or moderate damage.

Alas, this agreeable prospect was not to endure. By the 1960s, it became clear that the nations of Western Europe preferred to expand their welfare states rather than their military establishments, even while the Soviets were closing their "missile gap." The "umbrella" was looking a bit porous. So tactical nuclear weapons were inserted into the NATO arsenal. This did not alarm the Europeans too much, since it was assumed their use on European soil would be limited and short-lived. They would "signal" the Soviets that an act of aggression had passed the nuclear threshold. If the Soviets then persisted, an American-Soviet nuclear exchange would occur—over the heads of Europeans, as it were.

The 1970s witnessed the emergence of U.S.-U.S.S.R parity at the nuclear level, and of Soviet superiority vis-à-vis Western Europe at all levels. The Soviets now had at least as many tactical nuclear weapons as NATO. They had, moreover, a new arsenal of intermediate-range missiles, pointing to all major European cities. At that point we and our European allies, reacting like automatons, decided that NATO too needed such intermediate-range missiles on European soil. And that is when the current crisis broke out and the anti-nuclear movement assumed mass proportions.

The Umbrella Is Now Imaginary

Behind this crisis in NATO is the recognition of two facts. First, the American "umbrella" is now purely imaginary. It is always possible that, if the Soviets overrun Western Europe, an American President will press the button that will bring about the mutual, assured destruction of both the United States and the Soviet Union. It is possible—but how likely? What would be the sense of such an action? The people of Western Europe have perceived that any such reaction by any U.S. president is very, very unlikely—would, indeed, be stupid. Their governments continue to say otherwise, but they are speaking into the wind, with hollow voices.

The second fact is that any Soviet aggression against Western Europe will now mean that Western Europe becomes a nuclear battlefield, as NATO's "unbroken spectrum" of weaponry, from conventional to nuclear, unfolds. In short, NATO has now maneuvered itself into a position where Western Europe is doomed to near-annihilation if it resists—however successfully or unsuccessfully, whatever that means—a Russian attack! Is it any wonder that a spirit of defeatism is beginning to pervade the political atmosphere in Europe? And, of course, various left-wing groups are only too eager to turn this spirit into an active policy of appeasement—which they are doing, with much success.

The root cause of this disaster in foreign policy has been our failure, and the failure of our European allies, to insist on a clear line of demarcation between the use of conventional weapons and nuclear weapons. Such an insistence would be possible *only* if we were fully prepared to be a match for the Soviets at the conventional level, just as they have shown themselves prepared to make the sacrifices necessary to match us at the nuclear level. With such matching strength, it might be possible to negotiate a reduction in nuclear armaments. But without it, there is a mismatch that can result only in a tilt of world power toward the Soviets.

A doctrine of non-first-use would reassure the American people and the world that we are doing our best to avoid a nuclear holocaust, large or small. It would also place upon the Americans and their allies the burden of large, expensive, conventional military establishments, so that we can meet our responsibilities without always and immediately raising the specter of nuclear disaster.

If we and they are unwilling to shoulder that burden, then we are simply unworthy of the liberties we seek to preserve. A nation or an alliance that prefers mass annihilation to higher taxes or a diminution of social services will, when the crunch comes, surely decide that appeasement is preferable to both.

PART TWO

The Peace Movement

8. Revive the Ban-the-Bomb Movement

By SIDNEY LENS

Focus Long a participant in the American anti-war movement, Sidney Lens views the current nuclear freeze crusade "as only the first step toward our *real* goal"—"the abolition of all nuclear weapons on this planet."

Only recently, says Lens, has the Left, after its long preoccupation with Vietnam, shifted its attention once again "to the fundamental threat of the arms race." Now the old peace forces such as *The Progressive*, the War Resisters League, the Fellowship of Reconciliation, and Pax Christi are joined by a far broader-based coalition, and the freeze campaign "has reached into such unlikely precincts as Loudoun County, Virginia, where the county supervisors unanimously approved a freeze resolution."

Applauding the American "peace demonstrations" as the will of the people to stop the "nuclear arms race," Lens asserts that on this issue "the government of the United States no longer represents the American people." He concludes that "the aim of the U.S. government—not only of the Reagan administration, but of its predecessors for three decades—is to subject the *Soviets* to Finlandization by arraying against them so formidable a nuclear threat that they will have no choice but to bow to Washington's will." One tactic used by the

94

Reagan administration in its "attempt to Finlandize the Soviet Union," he says, is to impose "McCarthyite restraints at home, so that no effective opposition will rise against the government policies."

Sidney Lens is a senior editor of *The Progressive*. He has been active in the peace, war resistance, and anti-nuclear movements and is the author of *The Day Before Doomsday* and *The Bomb*.

W HEN *The Progressive* devoted most of its February 1976 issue
to my article "The Doomsday Strategy," Editor Erwin Knoll
told me that while he was in full agreement with my analysis, he
couldn't subscribe to my conclusion that a nuclear holocaust was
virtually unavoidable. "I just can't believe we are headed toward
extinction," Knoll said. He offered no argument or explanation; he
simply felt we would manage, somehow, to head off the holocaust.

At that time, the nuclear arms race had virtually been
forgotten—even by the peace movement. For years we had been
focusing on Vietnam. Anti-war activists were wholly unfamiliar
with the arcane jargon of nuclear strategy—"counterforce,"
"damage limitation," "mutual assured destruction," and the
like—and incapable of mounting a factual challenge to the Pentagon's claims.

Our intent was to shift the Left's attention back to the fundamental threat of the arms race—and to some extent we succeeded.
One consequence, after "The Doomsday Strategy" appeared, was
the formation of a new national peace coalition, the Mobilization
for Survival. But we saw little likelihood then that thousands—
even millions—of Americans would be enlisted in a massive and
vocal crusade against nuclear weaponry.

That was six years ago. Four years later, in 1980, the peace
movement had grown, to be sure, but it was still by no means a
force to be reckoned with. It was, in fact, deeply divided over
ratification of the SALT II agreement that had been initialed by
Jimmy Carter and Leonid Brezhnev in June 1979.

The Progressive, along with the War Resisters League, the Fellowship of Reconciliation, Jonah House, Pax Christi, and a few
other organizations, opposed the treaty on grounds that it would

Reprinted with adaptations by permission from the May and August 1982 issues
of *The Progressive* (409 East Main Street, Madison, Wisconsin 53703; © 1982 by
The Progressive, Incorporated).

perpetuate rather than curb the arms race, permitting the addition
of some 4,000 warheads to each side's nuclear stockpile. But that
was a minority position within the peace movement, and an unpopular one: the majority worked for approval of SALT II, though
with misgivings, because it feared that the weapons build-up without the treaty might be even greater than what the treaty allowed.

At that point, Senator Mark Hatfield, Oregon Republican, introduced a significant new element—a proposed amendment to
SALT II that would add a "freeze" provision barring research,
testing, development, manufacture, and deployment of new nuclear weapons and delivery systems. It was a compromise to which
the "left-wing" critics of SALT II—like *The Progressive*—could
and did subscribe. Unfortunately, the Right wanted no part of it,
and most of the peace movement, after expressing initial support
for the Hatfield Amendment, dropped it in fear that it would
jeopardize the chances of ratifying SALT II. As it turned out,
SALT II was a dead letter either way.

But look at what has happened since! Suddenly a revived freeze
campaign, organized on the initiative of Terry Provance of the
American Friends Service Committee and Randall Forsberg of the
Boston Study Group, has swept the country. Here are a few of its
manifestations:

• Initiatives for a freeze have been approved in 159 Vermont
town meetings, at 28 town meetings in New Hampshire, at least a
half dozen in Massachusetts, and a scattering in several other
states.

• State legislative bodies in Massachusetts, Oregon, Connecticut, New York, Wisconsin, Vermont, Minnesota, and Kansas
have approved resolutions endorsing the freeze, and action is
pending in others.

• Well over one million Americans—some 500,000 in California alone—have signed petitions calling on the United States and
the Soviet Union to adopt "an immediate and mutual freeze of all
further testing, production, and deployment of nuclear weapons
and missiles and new aircraft designed primarily to deliver nuclear
weapons [as] an essential verifiable first step toward lessening the
risk of nuclear war and reducing the nuclear arsenal."

- The freeze campaign has reached into such unlikely precincts as rural Loudoun County, Virginia, where the county supervisors unanimously approved a freeze resolution. And in Kalamazoo, Michigan, 300 residents raised $10,000 to buy a message on seventeen billboards in the Washington, D.C., area: "Hear Us ... Nuclear War Hurts Too Much."

With that sort of momentum building, about 150 members of the U.S. House of Representatives and two dozen senators have signed on as co-sponsors of a resolution urging the two superpowers to "decide when and how to achieve a mutual and verifiable freeze" on testing, production, and further deployment of nuclear weapons and delivery systems, and later to seek "mutual and verifiable" reductions in thermonuclear stockpiles.

In addition to its congressional sponsors, the freeze resolution has drawn support from such prominent figures as former Vice President Walter Mondale and former ambassador to Moscow George F. Kennan. Perhaps even more indicative of its growing impact, however, is the increasingly shrill opposition. President Reagan, departing from the prepared text of a speech to the Tennessee legislature in mid-March [1982] warned that the freeze "legitimates a position of great advantage for the Soviet Union" and "would leave us and our allies on very thin ice." Secretary of State Alexander Haig and Pentagon officials have also scorned the freeze idea, and in a March 22 editorial headed "Peddling Nuclear Fear" the *Wall Street Journal* dismissed the freeze campaign as "hysteria" and "apocalyptic ban-the-bomb mentality."

What brought the peace movement to a point where it merited such denunciations? How did the movement suddenly become the subject of a *Time* magazine cover, of television specials, of attention in the daily press? One significant factor, certainly, was the eruption of anti-nuclear demonstrations in Western Europe, triggered by U.S. plans to install new missiles aimed at the Soviet Union. Another factor was some reckless, almost casual talk by Reagan administration officials—including the President himself—about the possibility of "winning" a "limited" nuclear war. Increasingly vocal opposition to the arms race by church leaders in Europe and in the United States—and especially by the

U.S. Catholic bishops—has made it difficult to put a "pro-Communist" label on the peace movement.

Economic considerations also figure significantly in the sudden surge of anti-war sentiment. Millions of Americans, buffeted by unemployment, high interest rates, inflation, and drastic cutbacks in social services, have rediscovered the ancient truth that a nation can't have both guns and butter. They realize that both the United States and the Soviet Union have acquired massive overkill capacity far in excess of any "national security" rationale, and that to add still more to the stockpiles of weapons is not only terribly wasteful but terribly dangerous.

There is, in fact, a real possibility that the organized peace movement—and especially the freeze campaign—will lag behind its natural and potential constituency among the American people. Before we cheer too loud and long for what has been achieved in recent months, we should take note of some serious problems inherent in the freeze—problems that stem from an excess of caution among its organizers.

The petition being circulated in most parts of the country falls notably short, for example, even of matching the language of the congressional resolution, itself quite a timid document. The congressional sponsors call for negotiations after a nuclear freeze has been instituted, to bring about a *reduction* in atomic arsenals on both sides. The petition, on the other hand, merely asserts that the freeze "is an essential verifiable first step towards . . . reducing the nuclear arsenal," but suggests no further steps, bilateral or unilateral, to bring about such reduction.

A freeze alone would simply obligate the United States and the Soviet Union to stop producing or deploying new warheads or delivery systems. That would leave in place some 30,000 U.S. warheads and some 20,000 Soviet warheads, equal in aggregate power to more than a million bombs like the one that devastated Hiroshima in 1945. The *initial* demand of the freeze campaign is, therefore, an exceedingly modest one—and one that would barely diminish the risk of a nuclear holocaust.

The word *verifiable* in the freeze proposal poses another problem. Verification has served for three decades as a pretext for blocking disarmament proposals. The 1946 Baruch Plan stipulated that before there could be any disarmament, the Soviets would have to admit United Nations verification teams to map Soviet territory and inspect military installations. In 1955, when the Soviets accepted in principle an American-British-French disarmament plan that would have eliminated nuclear weapons and substantially reduced conventional forces, President Eisenhower withdrew the plan and substitued an unacceptable verification system. It was the question of verification that turned the first SALT agreement for a disarmament plan into a mere "arms control" measure, though the current capability of satellite surveillance makes the notion of verification obsolete.

Arms Control Is Not Enough

The freeze campaign itself could easily be co-opted and converted into an "arms control" effect. The danger is that in its eagerness to enlist mass support—and congressional sponsors—the movement will dilute its demands to the point where they are rendered meaningless. After all, most of the senators and representatives who have endorsed the freeze vote regularly and without protest for increased military budgets. They may now favor a standstill in the arms race, or even a reduction of each superpower's nuclear stockpile—but they would still insist on the "sufficiency" of what former Defense Secretary Robert S. McNamara called "mutually assured destruction."

That isn't a good enough goal for those of us who care about the survival of the human species. We cannot be content with a freeze that leaves our future mortgaged to the nuclear monster. Our goal should be the one stated in the International Peace Petition, which calls on the two superpowers not only to institute a freeze but to "progressively, but quickly, destroy present stockpiles."

We should regard the freeze as only the first step toward our *real* goal—and we have a moral obligation not to disguise or conceal that goal. It is the abolition of all nuclear weapons on this planet. That goal may seem remote—and even impossible of achievement—today. But who would have thought, six years ago, that so many Americans would be enlisted in a campaign for a nuclear freeze?

In an astonishingly short time a remarkably large number of Americans have recognized the danger of the nuclear arms race and embraced the idea that it must stop. On this issue, it now seems clear, the government of the United States no longer represents the American people.

Every recent public opinion poll has affirmed that a substantial majority wants the arms race ended. Advocates of disarmament, dismissed not long ago as kooks and political pariahs, enjoy new respectability. Protests against nuclear weaponry are part of the mainstream coverage on the evening newscasts right alongside Henry Kissinger's speeches to the Foreign Policy Association. Ann Landers, whose syndicated advice is dispensed to some 70 million readers, devotes a full column to a plea for a nuclear freeze. Big-city mayors assemble in Minneapolis and call for less military spending and more money for human needs. The media are suddenly full of features on the damage done to the psyche of young children by the fear of nuclear holocaust.

From the big stage in New York's Central Park, the massive crowd that assembled on June 12 [1982] seemed endless. It was estimated to number more than 700,000, perhaps a million, and it was the largest turnout ever for a political demonstration in this country. Some of the marchers who had come from hundreds or thousands of miles away were never able to get within sight or earshot of the stage.

That may have been just as well. There were sixty or eighty speeches—I lost count—and few of them stayed within the three-minute limit. Though there were notable exceptions (including Helen Caldicott and Randall Forsberg), most speakers were neither especially inspiring nor even informative. There was none of the chanting and cheering, little of the spark that marked the great anti-war rallies of the late 1960s and early 1970s.

But the factional squabbles that typically characterized some of the planning for the rally were overcome. The Reagan administration's petty denial of entry visas to hundreds of Japanese peace activists helped kindle a militant spirit. The commitment at the great peace demonstration was visible and deep, and it encompassed Americans of all ages, classes, races, and interest groups.

Earlier, outside the United Nations, Monsignor Bruce Kent, the leader of the British Campaign for Nuclear Disarmament, reported that his movement's London demonstration on June 10 had been the largest ever. In Bonn, too, record crowds had turned out. Throughout the Western world, the message in June (and before and after) was simple and direct: End the nuclear arms race and end it *now*. That was also the message of the 1,600 nonviolent protesters arrested while committing civil disobedience in front of the U.N. missions of the five nations known to possess thermonuclear weapons, and of the similar number arrested a week later at the Lawrence Livermore Laboratories of the University of California, while demonstrating against weapons work.

The Administration: Standing Firm

The Reagan administration has, of course, not been moved. It persists in its plan for a five-year, $1.6 trillion military build-up, allocating almost $200 billion to weapons that will pose critical new threats to human survival on this planet—the MX, cruise, and Pershing missiles; the Trident submarine and missile; the B-1 and Stealth bombers, and the Mark 12-A reentry vehicle.

In Europe, attempting to soften the hawkish image that has generated a new surge of anti-American sentiment, President Reagan stated over and over that he understood and sympathized with the concerns of the disarmament demonstrators. But he asserted that his peculiar process of arms-reduction-by-arms-build-up was the only way; that the United States must first "catch up" with the Soviet Union before it can begin to contemplate a freeze or cutback.

Administration officials have mounted an energetic counter-offensive against the reborn peace movement. Defense Secretary Caspar Weinberger and others now concede—in a departure from some of the most alarming statements issued during Reagan's first year in office—that "we don't believe a nuclear war can be won." But they insist against all logic that they require more nuclear weapons so they can fight an *unwinnable* war, if necessary. They don't explain how more weapons will provide more security, in light of the certain destruction that awaits all participants in any direct nuclear confrontation.

Most of the Reagan policy planners have shown themselves to be quite adept at personal finance. Not one of them, we can assume, would invest a single dollar in a business that had been demonstrated to be a sure loser. But they are clearly willing to invest trillions of dollars—and billions of lives—in an arms race that is a sure loser. And they are waiting, hoping to outlast the wave of public concern, expecting the movement to succumb to demoralization and disintegration, certain that they will be able to perpetuate the endless cycle of escalation.

Why? Surely not to trigger an actual nuclear war between the United States and the Soviet Union, with all the horror and devastation that would entail. U.S. strategic planners are not suicidal psychopaths, after all. But they do have an objective they call *victory,* and what they mean by that is the power to organize the world to suit the interests of corporate America and to rule it without interference from the Soviet Union or from "Soviet-inspired" Third World regimes. They want what Sir Solly Zuckerman, the British Nobel laureate, has described as the best kind of victory—one in which the enemy surrenders to superior force without a shot being fired.

The aim is to *Finlandize* the Soviet Union. In the lexicon of the American Right, Finlandization is the process by which the Soviets intimidate a weak nation—Finland—while leaving it with a modest measure of autonomy. But the aim of the U.S. government— not only of the Reagan administration, but of its predecessors for three decades—is to subject the *Soviets* to Finlandization by arraying against them so formidable a nuclear threat that they will have no choice but to bow to Washington's will.

The Reagan administration's attempts to Finlandize the Soviet Union rests on a three-part strategy:

• A military build-up that far exceeds any effort mounted in the past, moving in less than a decade toward an increase of 400 to 500 per cent in annual spending.

• A tighter and tighter squeeze on the Soviet economy.

• An imposition of McCarthyite restraints at home, so that no effective opposition will rise against the government policies.

The military expansion focuses on new weapons against which the Soviets have not yet developed any effective defense. By the end of this decade, the Reagan administration hopes, the Russians will be at such great technological disadvantage that they will have to yield.

The hundred or so Pershing missiles in West Germany will be able to strike the Soviet Union within four to six minutes of launch. The thousands of cruise missiles soon to come off the assembly lines will be launchable from B-1 and Stealth bombers, and will travel to their targets at low levels invisible to radar. The Trident submarine will be able to direct its warheads at Moscow from a distance of 4,000 miles. The space shuttle will place satellites in the sky capable of immobilizing Soviet command and navigation.

To complete its encirclement of the Soviet Union, the United States plans to consolidate its alliance with the People's Republic of China, which has already tested a 7,500-mile-range missile and a four-megaton hydrogen bomb.

In these circumstances, Washington hopes, the Finlandization of the Soviet Union will be achieved. But even if it isn't, the cost to the Russians of attempting to keep up with arms escalation will put severe strains on the Soviet economy and severe hardships on the people of the Soviet bloc, leading to what George F. Kennan, author of the "containment" policy of 1947, has called "the breakup and gradual mellowing of Soviet power."

The economic squeeze on the Soviets is being tightened directly, too—by raising the cost of Western bank credits, for example, and denying export licenses for such high-tech goods as the gas turbine blades needed for the Russians' 3,700-mile natural gas pipeline to Western Europe. The Administration has reason to fear that if France, West Germany, and other Western nations were to become dependent on the Soviet Union for much of their natural gas, they would not continue to steer a hard anti-Soviet course.

But economic measures that injure U.S. allies are likely to encounter political resistance abroad, just as the Administration's foreign and domestic policies are meeting with more and more resistance at home. That is why the first steps toward repression have already been taken—in restoring the CIA's franchise to engage in domestic spying, for instance, and in curbing the right of

Americans to travel in Cuba. After years of disuse, the old, discredited McCarren Act of 1952 was dusted off by the Administration to bar several hundred Japanese visitors from attending the U.N. Special Session on Disarmament.

The massive popular mobilization against nuclear arms that turned out so forcefully in June can prevent this comprehensive Reagan program from being put into effect. But the Administration assumes that the movement will be in no position to do so—that it will fade away without attaining any of its goals.

Our answer must be to escalate the opposition to nuclear weaponry and give it a strong moral base. During the Vietnam war, the peace movement shifted from a demand for "negotiations" to a demand for "withdrawal," and from tactics of peaceable assembly to tactics of confrontation and civil disobedience. Similarly, we will soon face the challenge of moving from the goal of a nuclear "freeze" to the demand for total abolition of all nuclear weapons.

It is time to revive the slogan "Ban the Bomb," and to devise a strategy of resistance to a government that would march us down the road to nuclear extinction. In this age of peril, business as usual is a luxury we can no longer afford.

9. *Ban Whose Bomb?*

By WILLIAM E. GRIFFITH

Focus In this brief essay, a professor of international politics at MIT criticizes the "new American peace movement." He calls it the "kid brother of the West European anti-nuclear movement, which was reactivated in 1977 after the Russians began deploying, and aiming at Western Europe, many of their 3,000-mile-range SS-20 missiles. When the United States later proposed installing countervailing missiles, many Europeans feared nuclear war."

The fear of nuclear war on both sides of the Atlantic is genuine and should be respected, but the author objects to "the simplistic proposal that U.S. and Soviet arsenals be frozen at present levels or, even more naïve, that America undertake one-sided cutbacks."

Professor Griffith asserts that Moscow has been actively manipulating peace sentiments in the West. The "small minority of Communists in the peace movement do not control it," he says. "However, the Soviets have fed funds and propaganda to some European groups, and the World Peace Council, a Soviet-front organization, has allied itself with the movement." (The Soviet connections with the peace movement are elaborated in selections 10, 11, and 12.)

Griffith is particularly critical of Brezhnev's call for an immediate nuclear freeze in Europe (selection 30), which "would pose a dangerous disadvantage to NATO and the West since the Soviets are so far ahead with their SS-20s." If we accepted this proposal, says Griffith, we would need on-site inspection to verify Soviet compliance—something Moscow has never permitted. Further, Brezhnev's proposal "would leave the Russians free to deploy, in the Asian part of the Soviet Union, still more SS-20s, targeted on Europe."

William E. Griffith is Ford Professor of Political Science at the Massachusetts Institute of Technology, and an adjunct professor of diplomatic history at the Fletcher School of Law and Diplomacy, Tufts University.

L ESS THAN A DECADE after the tumultuous protests against the Vietnam war, another peace movement is burgeoning in this country and in Western Europe. Last fall [1981], massive rallies in Bonn and London drew some 400,000 people, and on November 11, Veterans Day, more than 100,000 American students turned out for anti-nuclear "teach-ins" at 150 colleges and universities.

Concern over nuclear weapons is not, of course, confined to this peace movement. And there is nothing wrong with airing such worries in public discussion. My objection is to the simplistic proposal that U.S. and Soviet arsenals be frozen at present levels or, even more naïve, that America undertake one-sided cutbacks.

The new American peace movement is the kid brother of the West European anti-nuclear movement, which was reactivated in 1977 after the Russians began deploying, and aiming at Western Europe, many of their new, 3,000-mile-range SS-20 nuclear missiles. When the United States later proposed installing countervailing missiles, many Europeans feared nuclear war. The Senate's rejection of the Strategic Arms Limitation Talks (SALT II) agreement, President Reagan's denunciation of détente, and incautious American talk of limited nuclear war in Europe fed these fears and gave impetus to the current peace movement.

Moscow always sought to split or weaken the NATO alliance and has been quick to manipulate the situation. The small minority of Communists in the peace movement do not control it. However, the Soviets have fed funds and propaganda materials to some European groups, and the World Peace Council, a Soviet-front organization, has allied itself to the movement.

A major theme on both sides of the Atlantic is that if we begin cutting back on nuclear weapon production, Moscow will do the

Reprinted with adaptations by permission from the June 1982 issue of *Reader's Digest* (© 1982 by The Reader's Digest Association, Incorporated).

same. But something similar to this has already been tried—and most emphatically did not work.

Back in the 1960s, when our intercontinental ballistic missiles vastly overshadowed the Russians', the Johnson administration imposed a unilateral freeze on ICBM production, halting the number at 1,054. We tried to persuade the Soviets to do the same, but Russia continued missile production. Today, with nearly 1,400, it has passed us.

The West's Military Disadvantage

Many nuclear critics maintain that U.S. military power is as much of a threat to world peace as is the Soviet Union's. But the United States is already running second in important aspects of military preparedness, while the Soviet Union has been carrying out the most massive military build-up, nuclear weapons included, in the history of mankind. While we devote 5.9 per cent of our gross national product to military spending, the Russians spend an estimated 12 to 14 per cent of theirs. The Soviet Union now has a first-rate navy and enough long-range airpower to transport troops any place on earth.

The Red Army is so superior to NATO in conventional weaponry that it could probably conquer Western Europe in a few weeks. Only the U.S.S.R.'s fear that we would use tactical nuclear weapons against Soviet tanks has prevented this. A nuclear NATO thus has been the real guarantor of peace.

But today the additional SS-20s upset this balance and give the Russians a significant advantage within the European theater. These missiles can hit targets throughout Western Europe. The Russians already have 300 SS-20s in place at this writing. Each SS-20 has three warheads that can be targeted independently, thus providing an annihilating force of 900 large nuclear bombs.

The Soviets have had SS-4 and SS-5 nuclear missiles targeted at Western Europe for years. But the SS-20s are far more threatening. Moreover, unlike older missiles, they can be moved from one location to another on tracked vehicles, and are more difficult to detect. NATO's Pershing I missiles have a range of only 450 miles, far short of Soviet frontiers.

Largely at the urging of NATO members, the United States prepared to deploy 108 Pershing II and 464 ground-launch cruise missiles. Their ranges, up to 1,800 miles, were enough to cover the western portion of the Soviet Union and thus serve notice that Moscow could not bend Europe to its will by a display of brute force.

Then, last November [1981], in the face of nuclear war fears, President Reagan offered to cancel plans to deploy these missiles if the Russians would dismantle their SS-4, SS-5, and SS-20 missiles. The Kremlin rejected the offer, and subsequent arms negotiations in Geneva, Switzerland, made little progress.

In March [1982] Soviet President Leonid Brezhnev offered to suspend further deployment of SS-20s in European Russia and called on NATO to cancel plans to deploy U.S. missiles in Europe. Reagan responded by endorsing a bipartisan Senate resolution that seeks either to erase the Soviet lead or to reach an agreement with Moscow for substantial reduction.

The Danger of an Immediate Freeze

Brezhnev's insistence on an immediate freeze would pose a dangerous disadvantage to NATO and the West, since the Soviets are so far ahead with their SS-20s. And the only way we could ascertain whether Moscow was living up to the agreement would be with on-the-ground inspections within the Soviet Union— which has always forbidden them. Brezhnev's proposal also would leave the Russians free to deploy, in the Asian part of the Soviet Union, still more SS-20s, targeted on Europe.

Assuming the Russians persist in their refusal to dismantle their SS-20s, then some Pershing IIs and cruise missiles can be in place by next year [1983]. Clearly, this would be a defensive response to a hostile move by the Soviets; yet U.S. and European demonstrators accuse the United States of provoking nuclear war. Their outrage is one-sided; few condemned the Soviet Union for deploying their SS-20s.

The United States has no choice but to maintain rough nuclear parity with the Soviets in Europe. The Europeans are our most important allies and trading partners. If we allow the nuclear balance to tip strongly in Moscow's favor, Western Europe will inevitably be brought under predominant Soviet influence. Europe's trade and technology would shift to the U.S.S.R.; Japan, China, and the oil-producing countries would similarly come to terms with Moscow. The United States would be reduced to an isolated, second-rate power.

The same might occur if we were to overreact to the peace movement. Some Americans, disappointed with our allies, seek a cutback on U.S. troops in Europe. But a U.S. withdrawal is exactly what Moscow has been trying to achieve since World War II.

It is important, therefore, that we keep our perspective on—and do not get taken in by—the peace movement. Instant television reporting can create a political illusion by making well-organized groups appear far more numerous and influential than they actually are. In fact, an ABC/*Washington Post* poll found that 54 per cent of American respondents felt the Reagan administration's increased defense spending was at or below the right level. And more than 60 per cent of those interviewed by German pollsters favor retention of American nuclear weapons and American troops on German soil.

I strongly favor arms control negotiations with the Russians. They will not accept deep cuts, but they did accept ceilings on intercontinental-nuclear-weapon systems in the SALT negotiations. In time they may also accept ceilings on SS-20s and equivalent Western missiles. Meanwhile, we should stand firm in our resolve to build up our military power. We must negotiate from strength, not from a weakness brought about by unilateral cutbacks. Only then can we re-establish European nuclear equality and thus keep our NATO alliance firm.

10. The KGB's Magical War for 'Peace'

By JOHN BARRON

Focus Since the early 1950s, the Soviet Union has been active in promoting peace and disarmament movements in the United States and Western Europe. Its efforts to disarm NATO have been orchestrated largely by the KGB, the Soviet Committee for State Security, known as the "Sword and Shield of the Communist Party." In this essay a distinguished researcher-journalist, John Barron, documents the recent Soviet peace campaign, relying heavily on well-informed defectors from the KGB.

Barron says the KGB's "Active Measures" to disarm the United States and divide it from its European allies include "overt and covert propaganda, manipulation of international front organizations, forgeries, fabrications and deceptions, acts of sabotage or terrorism committed for psychological effect, and the use of agents of influence." In sum, the KGB seeks to demoralize the West by "inverting reality." As a leading defector put it: "The KGB plans and coordinates campaigns to persuade the public that whatever America does endangers peace and that whatever the Soviet Union proposes furthers peace."

Barron details the role of KGB operatives in persuading articulate groups in the West to oppose U.S. deployment of the so-called neutron bomb, designed to deter a Soviet attack on Europe at less human cost than the present tactical weapons

111

there. The deployment was canceled. Emboldened by this success, the KGB turned its attention to opposing the deployment of Pershing II missiles in Western Europe. The Pershing II missile is designed to deter the 315 Soviet SS-20 missiles, which in fifteen minutes "could obliterate 945 European targets—including every sizable city from Oslo to Lisbon, from Glasgow to Istanbul."

On March 20, 1981, "less than one month after Brezhnev called for a nuclear freeze," reports Barron, the first national strategy conference of the American Nuclear Freeze Campaign convened for three days at Georgetown University in Washington. Two KGB operatives played a significant role in the meeting. Also on March 20, a new organization called International Physicians for the Prevention of Nuclear War held its first conference, in Virginia; the Soviet delegation was headed not by a doctor but by Georgi Arbatov, "one of the masterminds of the Active Measures campaign." KGB operatives have "made numerous visits to Riverside Church" (New York), whose senior minister, William Sloane Coffin, is active in the freeze campaign, and they have shown up at pro-freeze meetings across the country.

John Barron is the author of: *KGB: The Secret Work of Soviet Secret Agents* and, with Anthony Paul, *Murder of a Gentle Land* (Cambodia). This essay is excerpted from his new book on the KGB, to be published early in 1983.

IN THE OLD LUBYANKA PRISON on Dzerzhinsky Square in Moscow, the screams of the tortured and the pleas of the doomed are heard no more. Drunken executioners no longer ram pistols into backs of heads and blow out the faces of "enemies of the people." No longer must cleaning crews come every few hours to wash blood from the stone walls, swab gore off the oak floors, and cart away former comrades' remains.

Today the Communist party torturers and executioners perform their duties elsewhere, and Lubyanka, whose name still kindles fear in Russians, has undergone a reincarnation. Unknown to the general public, its cells, torture chambers, and execution cellars have been remodeled into offices and made part of the "Center"—the headquarters of the Committee for State Security, or KGB.

Sitting in a mahogany-paneled office on the third floor of Lubyanka is the new KGB chairman, Vitaly Fedorchuk. He must still concern himself, first of all, with the continuing subjugation of the Soviet people on behalf of the Party. He and his deputies must still supervise some 5,000 KGB officers abroad who daily endeavor to steal the scientific, military, and state secrets of other nations. But today, as never before, the KGB leadership is preoccupied with prosecution of what the Russians call Active Measures.

As a result of a disastrous KGB loss, the West has gained encyclopedic, inside knowledge of how the Soviet Union conceives and conducts Active Measures. In late 1979 Major Stanislav Aleksandrovich Levchenko escaped from Japan to the United States, and he turned out to be one of the most important officers ever to flee the KGB. Levchenko had worked at the Center as well as in front organizations in Moscow. At the time of his escape he was

Reprinted by permission from the October 1982 issue of the *Reader's Digest* (© 1982 by The Reader's Digest Association).

Active Measures Officer at the KGB's Tokyo Residency. From his unique background, he disclosed strategy, tactics, and myriad examples of Active Measures, while unmasking Soviet fronts and key KGB operatives.

"Few people who understand the reality of the Soviet Union will knowingly support it or its policies," Levchenko states. "So by Active Measures, the KGB distorts or inverts reality. The trick is to make people support Soviet policy unwittingly by convincing them they are supporting something else. Almost everybody wants peace and fears war. Therefore, by every conceivable means, the KGB plans and coordinates campaigns to persuade the public that whatever America does endangers peace and that whatever the Soviet Union proposes furthers peace. To be for America is to be for war; to be for the Soviets is to be for peace. That's the art of Active Measures, a sort of made-in-Moscow black magic. It is tragic to see how well it works."

Today, the KGB is concentrating on one of the largest Active Measures campaigns mounted since World War II. Its objective is to secure military superiority for the Soviet Union by persuading the United States to abandon new weapons systems that both American political parties and numerous strategists judge essential to Western military security. The name of the campaign is "nuclear freeze."

This worldwide campaign thus far has been remarkably successful, for the KGB has induced millions upon millions of honorable, patriotic, and sensible people who detest Communist tyranny to make common cause with the Soviet Union. Most of these millions earnestly believe they are doing what they must to spare mankind the calamity of nuclear war. In appealing to their admirable motivations, the Soviet Active Measures apparatus follows a strategy not unlike that of cigarette advertisers. Tobacco companies do not ask people to consider thoughtfully the fundamental issue of whether the pleasures of cigarette addiction offset indisputable perils to health. Rather, by simple slogans and alluring illustrations, they evade the issue. Similarly, Active Measures, by holding out the allure of peace through simple slogans and simplistic proposals, try to evade the fundamental and extremely complex issue of arms limitation. And, as Levchenko suggests, they try to persuade everybody that the way to peace lies down the path the Russians are pointing to.

KGB Forgeries and Fronts

In the Soviet lexicon, Active Measures include both overt and covert propaganda, manipulation of international front organizations, forgeries, fabrications and deceptions, acts of sabotage or terrorism committed for psychological effect, and the use of Agents of Influence.*

The KGB has concocted more than 150 forgeries of official U.S. documents and correspondence portraying American leaders as treacherous and the United States as an unreliable, war-mongering nation. One of the most damaging was a fabrication titled *U.S. Army Field Manual FM30-31B* and classified, by the KGB, top secret. Field manuals *FM30-31* and *FM30-31A* did exist; *FM30-31B* was entirely a Soviet creation. Over the forged signature of General William Westmoreland, the manual detailed procedures to be followed by U.S. military personnel in friendly foreign countries. These fictitious instructions told U.S. military forces or advisers how to interfere in internal political affairs and, in certain circumstances, how to incite ultra-leftist groups to violence so as to provoke the host government into militant anti-Communist actions.

The KGB forgery proved invaluable after terrorists from the radical leftist Red Brigades murdered Aldo Moro, president of the Italian Christian Democratic party, in March 1978. Although Moro's murder constituted a grievous loss to the United States, Radio Moscow began broadcasting charges that he had been assassinated by the CIA. Initially, few people paid any attention to the totally undocumented allegation. Then, according to congressional

---

*The classic Soviet espionage agent steals secrets. An Agent of Influence strives to affect the public opinion and policies of other nations in the interests of the Soviet Union. His or her advocacy may be open or concealed, direct or subtle. Always, though, the Agent of Influence pretends that he or she is acting out of personal conviction rather than under Soviet guidance.

testimony, Cuban intelligence officer Luis Gonzalez Verdecia offered a Spanish newspaper the forged Army manual along with an analysis by Fernando Gonzalez, a Spanish Communist who dealt with the KGB. In his article Gonzalez cited the manual to support claims that the United States was involved with various Western European terrorist groups, including the Red Brigades.

The leftist Spanish magazine *El Triunfo* published both Gonzalez's article and parts of the forgery on September 23, 1978. Immediately, Italian and other European newspapers replayed the Spanish story. Soviet propagandists now set up a new hue and cry, citing the articles in the non-Communist European press as "evidence" that the CIA had assassinated Moro and that the United States was the actual sponsor of left-wing terrorists all around the world.

Soon, the press in twenty countries published the allegations against the CIA along with the forged manual or excerpts from it. In the minds of millions, the KGB had succeeded in inverting reality.

In all nations the KGB attempts to recruit agents—within the political system, press, religion, labor, the academic world—who can help shape public attitudes and policies to Soviet interests. Pierre-Charles Pathé, a French journalist, was an archetypical Agent of Influence until his arrest in 1979. KGB officers, working in Paris under diplomatic cover, regularly supplied him with data that he transformed into articles or passed along to other journalists as his own research and thought. For nearly twenty years Pathé initiated more than 100 articles on Latin America, China, NATO, the CIA and other topics, all in tune with KGB goals. With KGB funds, he published a newsletter read by leaders in government and industry. A French court judged Pathé's actions so potentially damaging to France's military, political, and essential economic interests that it sentenced him to five years' imprisonment.

The Soviets also discreetly encourage terrorism as a form of Active Measures. At a school where KGB personnel formerly trained, near the village of Balashikha, east of Moscow, officers of Department V, responsible for sabotage and assassination, bring in contingents of 100 or so young people each year from the Middle East, Africa, and Latin America to be taught terrorism. The majority of trainees return to their homelands without specific missions, the KGB calculating that the Soviet Union benefits from any mayhem committed in the Third World. But a few are recruited to be KGB agents within the terrorist movements back home. And the best and most ideologically reliable are recruited to serve the KGB independently.

Beyond these types of Active Measures for which it is exclusively responsible, the KGB assists the International Department of the Central Committee in maintaining an interlocking web of front organizations. While all are controlled from Moscow, they are not popularly perceived as subversive. The most important fronts in the current "peace" campaign are the World Peace Council (WPC) and the Institute for the U.S.A. and Canada.

Soviet Control of the World Peace Council

The World Peace Council emerged in Paris in 1950 to foment "Ban the Bomb" propaganda at a time when the Soviets had not succeeded in arming themselves with nuclear weapons. Expelled from France for subversion in 1951, the WPC took refuge in Prague until 1954, when it moved to Vienna. The Austrians also evicted the group because of subversive activities in 1957, but the WPC retained a European outpost in Vienna through a branch titled the International Institute for Peace. In 1968 the WPC established headquarters in Helsinki to orchestrate the global propaganda campaign to compel withdrawal of American forces from Vietnam.

The president of the council is Indian Communist Romesh Chandra, who long has been a controlled and witting Soviet agent. Intelligent, vain, and arrogant, Chandra is almost embarrassing in his slavish adherence to Soviet dictates and his paeans to all things Soviet. "The Soviet Union invariably supports the peace movement," Chandra said a few years ago. "The World Peace Council in its turn positively reacts to all Soviet initiatives in international affairs."

Nevertheless, the Russians supervise Chandra closely by assigning both International Department and KGB representatives to the permanent secretariat of the WPC in Helsinki. The public record amply demonstrates the totality of Soviet control. In its thirty-two years of existence, the WPC has not deviated from the Kremlin's line of the moment. It did not raise its voice against Soviet suppression of Polish and East German workers in 1953, Soviet slaughter of Hungarians in 1956, Soviet abrogation of the nuclear-test moratorium in 1961, the clandestine emplacement of nuclear missiles in Cuba in 1962, the invasion of Czechoslovakia in 1968, the projection of Soviet military power in Angola, Ethiopia, and Yemen. The WPC has failed to criticize a single Soviet armament program; only those of the West. And it endorsed the Soviet invasion of Afghanistan.

WPC finances further reflect Soviet control. Huge sums are necessary to maintain the offices and staff in Helsinki, Vienna, and, since 1977, Geneva; to pay for continual global travel by WPC officials; to publish and distribute around the world monthly periodicals in English, French, German, and Spanish; to finance international assemblies for which hundreds of delegates are provided transportation, food, and lodging. Yet the World Peace Council has no visible means of support. Virtually all its money comes clandestinely from the Soviet Union.

Even so, many people, including diplomats, politicians, scientists, and journalists, choose not to see the WPC for what it is. The United Nations officially recognizes the WPC as a "nongovernmental organization" and joins it in discussions of issues such as disarmament and colonialism. The national peace committees with which the WPC maintains both open and secret ties in more than 100 nations rarely are stigmatized in the press as puppets of the Politburo.

Given the façade of an earnest institution that unites sincere men and women from all parts of the world in the quest for peace, given the expertise of KGB and International Department specialists in Active Measures and propaganda, given virtually limitless funds, the World Peace Council frequently rallies millions of non-Communists to Communist causes.

Another front, the Institute for the U.S.A. and Canada, affords disguised Soviet operatives entrée into much higher levels of American society than does the WPC. Its director, Georgi Arbatov, an intimate of former KGB chairman Yuri Andropov, has in recent years been a regular commuter to the United States, where he hobnobs with prominent politicians and preaches the gospel of disarmament on national television.

Fully a third of the Institute's staff are regular officers of the KGB; one of its deputy directors is Radomir Georgovich Bogdanov, a senior KGB colonel, who has been subverting foreigners for a quarter century. He labored more than a decade to recruit English-speaking leaders in India and did so well that the KGB promoted him to Resident in New Delhi. As such, he helped develop Romesh Chandra into an Agent of Influence in the 1960s and has worked with him intermittently ever since.

In the mid-1970s the KGB assigned Bogdanov to the Institute and to American targets. His pose as a scholar and disarmament specialist questing for peace and understanding earns him access to U.S. politicians and academicians who genuinely do desire peace and understanding. Bogdanov has turned up at disarmament conferences—in Washington, New York, and Europe—peddling the Soviet line and hunting for Americans who can be seduced into following it.

Soviet Subsidy of Foreign Communist Parties

The KGB also assists the International Department in sustaining foreign Communist parties. Many of the parties survive only through secret Soviet subsidies, often delivered by the KGB. The Russians, for example, long have smuggled between $1 million and $2 million annually to the U.S. Communist party.

The U.S.S.R. spends millions on the foreign parties because, even if bedraggled and numerically small, they still contribute significantly to Active Measures. Their members can be counted upon to circulate pamphlets and promulgate Soviet themes that subsequently creep into respectable discourse. Members elected to democratic parliaments can insert these themes into the reportage of the non-Communist press by echoing them in official debates. The parties constitute a ready reservoir of disciplined demonstrators who can take to the streets simultaneously in cities throughout the world to foster an illusion of spontaneous concern. They provide the indefatigable cadre of planners, organizers, and agitators who help stage mass demonstrations that attract non-Communists.

The vast Soviet Active Measures apparatus—the overt propaganda organs, foreign Communist parties, international fronts, KGB Residencies around the world, the factories of forgery and disinformation, the Agents of Influence—is well coordinated and disciplined and can respond to commands rapidly and flexibly. When the KGB or International Department senses opportunity, a detailed operational plan is submitted to the Politburo. Once the Politburo approves, everybody from Brezhnev on down pitches in. The basic themes and subthemes of the campaign then are massively and thunderously propagated, like some primitive chant, to drown out reasoned debate or dissent.

Neutron Bomb, Soviet Bombast

The Soviets' current peace campaign began five years ago in reaction to the enhanced-radiation warhead (ERW), which soon was mislabeled the neutron bomb. The ERW was born of the most realistic considerations. By 1976 the Soviet Union and its satellites had deployed some 20,000 battle tanks against West Germany.

NATO, with only some 7,000 tanks and numerically inferior ground forces, could be sure of repelling an onslaught by Soviet armor only through the use of tactical nuclear weapons. However, the smallest of the nuclear weapons then stored in Europe had a destructive force roughly equivalent to that of the bomb dropped on Hiroshima. The blast and heat from such a weapon would wipe out not only Soviet invaders but everybody and everything within a four-mile radius of the detonation point. Radiation would kill men, women, and children within an even wider area.

Through their hydra-headed propaganda apparatus, the Russians were able to say, and in effect continue to say, to the West

Germans: If there is war, that is, if we attack you, the Americans will lay waste to your country and people. Since defense is impossible without annihilation, you should quit NATO, cease being pawns of the Americans, and come to peaceful and profitable terms with us.

The Russians' most imminent objective in arraying armor on West German borders in such profligate numbers was to reinforce this argument; not to attack, but to intimidate and fragment by threat.

The United States developed the ERW solely to neutralize this threat. Fired from a howitzer or short-range missile, the ERW obliterates everything within a radius of about 120 yards, inflicting no physical damage beyond. It releases neutrons, which flash through the thickest armor with the ease of light passing through a window. The neutrons instantly kill tank crews, soldiers, and anybody else in a radius of 500 yards, and cause death within hours or days to all inside a radius of one mile. The radiation effects dissipate quickly, though, and the area affected may safely be entered only hours later.

After technological breakthroughs in the mid-1970s made production of an ERW feasible, military strategists advanced the following arguments: The ERW would render the 20,000 Communist tanks menacing NATO by and large useless, militarily and politically. The ERW could wipe out the crews of entire Communist armored divisions, while causing minimal civilian casualties and physical devastation. In other words, NATO could defend Western Europe without destroying much of the area and its population.

Accordingly, President Gerald Ford in April 1976 approved the enhanced-radiation warhead. But in June 1977 President Jimmy Carter announced that he would delay a final decision until November.

Now the Russians had time and opportunity to initiate a worldwide campaign to pressure President Carter to do as they wished. In little more than a month, the Politburo, the International Department of the Central Committee, the KGB, their worldwide web of agents and front groups, and the Soviet press were ready. They began July 9, 1977, with a cry from TASS aimed at Carter himself: "How can one pose as a champion of human rights and at the same time brandish the neutron bomb, which threatens the lives of millions of people?" The Kremlin then warned the world that the neutron bomb can "only bring the world closer to nuclear holocaust."

Throughout July the Soviet press and radio, in an ever-rising chorus, sounded variations of this refrain: The ghastly new American weapon, the neutron bomb, threatens mankind with nuclear extinction. To be for the neutron bomb is to be for war. To oppose the neutron bomb is to be for peace.

Faithfully, the state-controlled media of Eastern Europe and the newspapers of Communist parties in Western Europe echoed the bombast emanating from Moscow.

Soviet-Sponsored Peace Demonstrations

Initially, the Active Measures against the ERW were mostly overt, and the propaganda was traceable to Communist sources. But in August the campaign advanced into semi-covert and clandestine phases. The World Peace Council proclaimed August 6-13, 1977, a Week of Action, and its front groups, abetted by the KGB and local Communist parties, promoted public demonstrations whose Soviet sponsorship was less perceptible. That week crowds, pleading in the name of humanity against the "killer neutron bomb," demonstrated before U.S. consulates or embassies in Bonn, Stuttgart, Frankfurt, and Istanbul. Though subtly directed by Soviet agents, the demonstrators—in Germany and the Netherlands at least—were mostly non-Communists attracted by intensive advertising, and motivated by a variety of impulses: anti-Americanism, pacifism, abhorrence of all nuclear weapons, and a sincere longing for peace.

Elsewhere, in lands where the ERW never would be used, KGB Residencies did their job by planting disinformation in the local press. One prestigious Latin American newspaper published an anti-neutron-bomb article attributed to the International Institute for Peace in Vienna, which was not identified as the Soviet front that it is. A small Communist claque in Lima dispatched a formal protest to the United Nations. A spate of Soviet-inspired articles appeared in India, Pakistan, Mauritius, Ghana, Ethiopia, and Libya.

Concurrently, within its own empire, the Soviet Union beat the propaganda drums in a new crescendo. From East Berlin, Reuters on August 8 reported: "Twenty-eight European and North American Communist parties today joined in an unusual display of public unity to call on the United States to ban production of the neutron bomb." A sturdy worker in Moscow recalled the suffering of World War II; by coincidence, another man 1,500 miles away in Uzbekistan spoke almost exactly the same words.

In October, Secretary of Defense Harold Brown announced President Carter would approve production of the ERW only if NATO allies agreed in advance to its deployment on their territories. Western European leaders recognized the ERW as a much safer, more credible deterrent than the nuclear warheads already on their soil, and privately wanted it added to NATO defenses. But by temporizing and publicly shifting the burden of decision to them, Carter exposed Allied leaders as well as himself to intensified pressures.

Accurately assessing Carter as a devoted Baptist, the Russians played upon his deep religious faith. In a dispatch quoted by the American press, TASS reported: "Soviet Baptist leaders today condemned production of the neutron bomb as 'contrary to the teachings of Christ' and urged fellow Baptists in the United States to raise their voices in defense of peace." As President and Mrs. Carter worshiped at the First Baptist Church in Washington on Sunday, October 16, 1977, six outsiders disrupted the service with shouts against the neutron bomb. And on two more occasions, protesters harassed the Carters at church.

In January 1978 Brezhnev sent letters to the heads of all Western governments asserting that the neutron bomb would "pose a grave threat to détente." Western members of parliament received similar letters from members of the Supreme Soviet and Soviet trade-union leaders.

Emboldened by the initial furor the Active Measures campaign had incited, the KGB and International Department moved on the U.S. Congress. American Communists, joined by non-

Communists, formed a National Committee to welcome Romesh Chandra and the World Peace Council presidential bureau to a "Dialogue for Disarmament and Détente" held in Washington from January 25 to 28. United States Representative John Conyers, Jr., heartily greeted the group. "You have joined us to give us courage and inspiration in our fight for disarmament and against the neutron bomb," he said.

The KGB provided the star of this show at the Capitol. Reporting the proceedings, which included a luncheon in the House of Representatives, the Communist *Daily World* said: "Every now and then one of the speakers would strike an emotional chord that was both personal and political, a human plea that sank deeply into the listeners. One such speaker was Radomir Bogdanov of the Soviet Academy of Sciences." The *Daily World* neglected to mention that Bogdanov is a KGB officer.

Having given "courage and inspiration" to U.S. congressmen, agent Chandra and Colonel Bogdanov proceeded to New York, where the WPC group had "long and fruitful discussions" with U.N. Secretary-General Kurt Waldheim.

In late February, 126 representatives of peace groups from fifty nations gathered in Geneva to denounce the neutron bomb. They attracted attention from an uncritical press that did not ask who was paying for this extravaganza allegedly sponsored by a heretofore unknown outfit calling itself the Special Nongovernmental Organizations Committee on Disarmament. The actual organizers and sponsors were the World Peace Council, its Swiss allies, and Eastern European "diplomats" accredited to the United Nations in Geneva. The presiding officer was the ubiquitous agent Chandra.

On March 19, in a rally organized primarily by the Dutch Communist party, some 40,000 demonstrators, drawn from throughout Europe at considerable expense to the rally's sponsors, marched through Amsterdam inveighing against the horrors of the neutron bomb and the nuclear holocaust it surely would precipitate. The protest, part of the International Forum Against the Neutron Bomb, doubtless constituted evidence to many that the neutron bomb must be very bad indeed.

Despite the illusion of a worldwide tide of sentiment welling up against the ERW, President Carter's three principal foreign-policy advisers—Secretary of State Cyrus Vance, Secretary of Defense Harold Brown, and National Security Adviser Zbigniew Brzezinski—all urged production. So did the Washington *Post* and the New York *Times*. Declared the *Times*: "Ever since the Carter administration asked Congress last summer for funds to produce enhanced-radiation nuclear warheads, critics ranging from Soviet propagandists to Western cartoonists have had a field day attacking the so-called 'neutron bomb.' The archetypical capitalist weapon, Moscow has called it, a destroyer of people but not property. Grim forecasts of lingering radiation deaths have filled newspaper columns worldwide. Rarely have the relevant questions been asked: Is the neutron weapon really more terrible than other nuclear weapons? And more important, would its deployment make nuclear war more likely?

"The answer to both these questions is almost certainly 'No.'. . . Neutron weapons in Western hands would significantly complicate Soviet tactical planning: If its tanks were to attack in mass, they would be highly vulnerable. If they were to disperse, they would be easier targets for conventional precision-guided anti-tank weapons. . . ."

Canceling the 'Neutron Bomb'

Such logic was unavailing. On April 7, 1978, President Carter announced the ERW's cancellation. The Communists gloated. "The political campaign against the neutron bomb was one of the most significant and successful since World War II," boasted Janos Berecz, chief of the Hungarian Communist party's International Department. And Leonid Brezhnev himself decorated Soviet Ambassador Aleksandr Yosipovich Romanov for his services in inciting the Dutch demonstrations.

In unilaterally abandoning plans to produce the enhanced-radiation warhead, the United States secured no reciprocal or compensatory concessions from the Soviet Union. Abandonment gained no good will from those people endemically hostile to the plan or those convinced that it had pushed the world to the precipice of nuclear war by developing a ghastly new weapon.

By arming NATO with the enhanced-radiation warhead, the United States had intended to demonstrate to friends that it possessed the will and capacity to participate effectively in their defense. By vacillating, then capitulating before the pressures of Soviet Active Measures, the United States showed itself to be irresolute and, in the eyes of many friends, witless.

The retreat especially frightened Europeans threatened by the Soviets' newest weapon of mass destruction, the SS-20 missile. The SS-20 is an accurate, mobile weapon that can be concealed from detection by space satellites and reconnaissance aircraft. In 1977 the Russians had begun deploying the first of 315 of these missiles, each with three nuclear warheads that can be directed at separate targets. Thus the Soviet Union now had an intimidating new force, which within fifteen minutes from launch could obliterate 945 European targets—including every sizable city from Oslo to Lisbon, from Glasgow to Istanbul.

At the insistence of the Western Europeans and particularly West German Chancellor Schmidt, the Carter administration finally agreed to emplace, under joint U.S.-NATO control, 572 Pershing II and cruise missiles as a counterpoise to the SS-20s. Unlike the old missiles they would replace, the intermediate-range Pershing II and cruise missiles could reach Moscow and other cities in the western Soviet Union. Both are mobile, can be hidden, and could probably survive a surprise attack. Unlike the SS-20, the new American missiles would be armed only with a single warhead.

NATO strategists reasoned that the 572 warheads would suffice to void the threat of the SS-20 by convincing the Russians that attack upon Western Europe automatically would bring a catastrophic counterattack. The balance of nuclear terror, which has kept peace in Europe for more than three decades, would be restored; neither side could credibly threaten the other with nuclear assault. NATO ministers in December 1979 overwhelmingly approved deployment of the modern missiles, and the United States promised to put them in place by late 1983.

Throughout the 1980 presidential campaign, candidate Ronald

Reagan declared that, if elected, he would restore American military power to the degree necessary to deter Soviet intimidation or attack. A few days after Reagan won, the Soviet Union instigated the great new Active Measures campaign to prevent NATO from countering the SS-20s and to reverse the American election results by nullifying the rearmament program implicitly mandated by the voters. After the success of the anti-neutron-bomb campaign, their expectations were high.

Why Brezhnev Wants a Freeze

On February 23, 1981, Leonid Brezhnev, addressing the Twenty-Sixth Communist Party Congress, issued an official call for a nuclear freeze—an immediate cessation of development of any new weapons system.

Such a moratorium would achieve the fundamental Soviet objective of aborting American production and deployment of the enhanced-radiation warhead (re-initiated by Reagan), the mobile MX, Pershing II, and cruise missiles, and a new manned bomber, the B-1. It would leave Western Europe vulnerable to the relentlessly expanding Communist forces—now including an astonishing 42,500 tanks and 315 deadly SS-20 missiles. It would leave the United States with a fleet of old, obsolete strategic bombers unlikely to penetrate Soviet air defenses and with an aging force of fixed land-based missiles vulnerable to a first strike by gigantic new Soviet missiles.

Instantly the KGB, the International Department, and the immense Active Measures apparatus heeded Brezhnev's call. With the World Peace Council, its foreign affiliates, and local Communist parties again the principal organizers, a new series of mass demonstrations occurred in Europe. An estimated 250,000 people marched in Bonn, protesting against any new missiles or nuclear weapons. Soviet fronts helped assemble a throng estimated at 350,000 in Amsterdam, a reported 400,000 in Madrid, and 200,000 in Athens.

The KGB all along played its traditional part. Dutch authorities in April 1981 expelled KGB officer Vadim Leonov, who, in the guise of a TASS correspondent, associated closely with leaders of the Dutch peace movement. Leonov made a number of professional mistakes, including a drunken boast to a Dutch counterintelligence source. "If Moscow decides that 50,000 demonstrators must take to the streets in the Netherlands, then they take to the streets. Do you know how you can get 50,000 demonstrators at a certain place within a week? A message through my channels is sufficient," Leonov bragged. In November Norway expelled KGB officer Stanislav Chebotek for offering bribes to those Norwegians who would write letters to newspapers denouncing NATO and the proposed missiles for Europe.

In January 1982 Portugal ousted two KGB officers, Yuri Babaints and Mikhail Morozov, for attempting to incite riots against NATO. That same month the Portuguese also denied visas to Soviet Peace Committee representatives who wanted to join a Communist-sponsored demonstration against NATO and the missiles on grounds that they were Soviet subversives. The Portuguese Socialist party boycotted the Lisbon march, deriding it as a "reflection of the diplomatic and military logic of the Soviet bloc."

However, the march of about 50,000 people proceeded—with U.S. Congressman Gus Savage as one of its leaders. In a newsletter to constituents, Savage boasted of his participation in activities of the World Peace Council, which he described as "the largest nongovernmental peace organization in the world."

All the while the KGB was manufacturing a spate of forged documents intended to buttress the theme that American rather than Soviet nuclear weapons most imperil Western Europe. It succeeded in circulating in Great Britain, the Netherlands, Norway, Belgium, Malta, Greece, and France a pamphlet entitled "Top Secret Documents . . . on U.S. Forces Headquarters in Europe . . . Holocaust Again for Europe." The contents consisted of alterations and fabrications based upon authentic military-contingency plans stolen by a KGB agent, Sergeant Robert Lee Johnson, from the Armed Forces Courier Center vault at Orly Field in 1962. The fabrications purported to show that the United States planned to blow up much of Europe with nuclear weapons to save itself.

Reproducing a standard, unclassified U.S. government map of Austria, the KGB labeled it top secret and marked targets on it. Both the Austrian Communist newspaper *Volksstimme* and *Komsomolskaya Pravda* in Moscow published stories alleging that the map proved the United States planned to destroy Austrian cities and installations with nuclear bombs.

In Denmark, writer Arne Herløv Petersen, a KGB agent since 1970, helped organize a propaganda drive advocating a Nordic Nuclear Weapon Free Zone, i.e., stripping the northern flank of NATO of all nuclear defenses. As part of this effort, he composed an advertisement signed by 150 Danish artists and intellectuals and bought newspaper space with KGB money. In the summer of 1981 Petersen sponsored a peace march from Oslo to Paris, and he also published under his own name propaganda tracts written by the KGB.

Danish counterintelligence officers witnessed twenty-three clandestine meetings between Petersen and Major Vladimir Dmitriyevich Merkulov, Active Measures officer at the KGB Residency in Copenhagen. Finally, in October 1981, they arrested Petersen as a Soviet agent. Merkulov, who had been active in the Danish Cooperation Committee for Peace and Security, a Communist-dominated subsidiary of the World Peace Council, was expelled.

The U.S. Freeze Campaign

While the Soviet-inspired demonstrations against NATO and the new missiles raged across Europe, protests in America initially were scant and inconsequential. But on March 20, 1981, less than one month after Brezhnev called for a nuclear freeze, the first national strategy conference of the American Nuclear Freeze Campaign convened for three days in a meeting hall at Georgetown University in Washington. The topics of the skills-sharing workshops suggest just how farsighted and well considered the planning was. Working sessions were conducted to teach activists about: "Congressional District/Petitions Approach; Referendum/State Legislator Approach; Organizing Around Nuclear Weapon Facilities; How to Approach Middle America—

Small Group and One-to-One Techniques; Media; Reaching and
Activating National Organizations (Including Your Own); Work-
ing with the Religious Community; Working with the Medical and
Scientific Community; Working with Groups with a Human Needs
Agenda."

Virtually the entire blueprint for the nuclear-freeze campaign
that followed was drawn in comprehensive detail. Speakers
stressed that the beauty of the nuclear freeze derives from its
simplicity. It would enable all people sincerely concerned about
the danger of nuclear war to answer for themselves the question,
"What can I do?"

According to a "peace" movement newspaper, the organizers at
Georgetown comprised "between 275 and 300 predominantly
white middle-class people from thirty-three states, Great Britain,
and the Soviet Union." Records available today identify only two
of the invited Soviet guests. One was Oleg Bogdanov, an International Department specialist in Active Measures, who flew in from
Moscow. The other was Yuri S. Kapralov, who represents himself
as a counselor at the Soviet embassy in Washington. Kapralov was
not merely an observer. He mingled with disarmament proponents, urging them on in their efforts to abort new American
weapons. He was an official member of the discussion panel, and,
as one listener put it, his statements were "very impressive."

But Yuri Kapralov did not speak just for himself. Kapralov is a
KGB officer who, ever since arriving in the United States in 1978,
has dedicated himself to penetrating the peace movement. Thus,
little more than two miles from the White House, the KGB helped
organize and inaugurate the American "nuclear freeze" campaign.
While many civic and church groups of unassailable repute were to
join in advocating the "freeze," in terms of the strategy and organization of the drive, this little-noted conference at Georgetown was
a seminal meeting.

KGB officer Kapralov subsequently showed up at other American forums advocating peace and disarmament. According to press
accounts he received some of the loudest applause given speakers
by about 800 Harvard students and faculty members, and the
Boston *Globe* termed him "one of the most effective speakers."

Blaming the arms race on the United States, Kapralov said, "It's funny that when our leaders talk very clearly about their desire for peace, some of your people just discredit it as transparent propaganda. We would prefer that your leaders would talk as clearly and as forcefully for peace and arms control as ours." More applause.

When Brezhnev called for a nuclear freeze, he adjured scientists to join in warning the public of the horrors of nuclear war. On March 20, the same day the Nuclear Freeze Campaign strategy conference began at Georgetown University, a new outfit, titled International Physicians for the Prevention of Nuclear War, held its first annual conference. The Soviet delegation to the meeting in Virginia included Brezhnev's personal physician, Evgenny Chazov. But the head of the delegation was not a physician at all. He was none other than Georgi Arbatov, the International Department operative, one of the masterminds of the Active Measures campaign.

The cold war was entirely the fault of the United States, according to Arbatov. America started it by dropping an atomic bomb on Hiroshima. The Russians have always believed, declared Arbatov, that the first atomic bomb was aimed as much at them as at the Japanese. New weapons will not enhance the security of anyone, Arbatov argued. America should spend its money on the needy, the underfed, the starving; not on arms. According to the Toronto *Star*, the assembly rewarded Arbatov with "thunderous applause."

A Visit to Capitol Hill

Following the Georgetown and Virginia conferences, the U.S. Peace Council arranged for a World Peace Council delegation, with Romesh Chandra at the forefront, to tour American cities. The appearance most beneficial to them was on Capitol Hill where, in May, Representatives John Conyers, Jr., Don Edwards, Mervyn Dymally, George Crockett, Jr., Ted Weiss, and Mickey Leland invited colleagues to meet and listen to the WPC delegates. Whether or not the delegation's lobbying in behalf of Soviet interests affected any of the congressmen, the cordial welcome Chandra and his colleagues received at the Capitol lent them a useful measure of respectability as bona-fide seekers of peace.

Continuing organizational efforts orchestrated from Moscow resulted in a series of conferences at which assorted peace and allied special-interest groups planned specific actions. The strategy that emerged envisioned a rising furor of demonstrations, agitation, and propaganda against the European missiles and new U.S. weapons and in favor of the nuclear freeze proposed by Brezhnev. Various leaders repeatedly emphasized the necessity of rounding up "newly aroused individuals and constituencies" so, as one put it, "the demonstrations would not appear to be a primarily 'peace movement' event."

'Mobilization for Survival' Activities

The idea of a nuclear freeze was not new in the United States. It had been advanced two years earlier at a convention of the Mobilization for Survival (MFS), composed of three dozen or so organizations, including the U.S. Communist party, the U.S. Peace Council, and Women Strike for Peace. One energetic leader of the Mobilization for Survival is Terry Provance, a World Peace Council activist who in 1979 participated in the founding meeting of its American branch, the U.S. Peace Council. Provance earlier led the campaign against the B-1 bomber and then became coordinator of the disarmament program of the American Friends Service Committee.

When the freeze campaign revived in 1981, MFS sponsored a strategy conference attended by representatives of some forty-six peace and disarmament factions and held in Nyack, N.Y., the weekend of October 23 to 25. Provance, who had spoken at a disarmament rally in West Germany earlier in the year, discussed plans for high-profile Europeans active in the disarmament movement to come to the United States in ensuing months to stimulate the American movement. Conference participants were told that the months ahead would be "a key time to organize local public meetings and/or demonstrations," demanding a "suspension of all U.S. plans to deploy Pershing II and cruise missiles."

The action agenda adopted called for support of the nuclear freeze, solidarity with the European peace movement, "creative, dramatic actions" against large corporations, propaganda against both nuclear arms and nuclear power, and attempts to attract more followers by blaming social ills on "the military budget."

Two weeks later agent Chandra flew to New York to confer with American Communist leaders and attend a conference of the U.S. Peace Council, which attracted representatives from a mélange of peace, religious, and radical organizations. Chandra and Achim Maske of the West German peace movement both implored the Americans to redouble agitation to block the Pershing II and cruise missiles. As a pattern for their lobbying, Chandra commended recent pronouncements of Brezhnev's.

Congressman Savage spoke about how to induct blacks and other minorities into the disarmament drive. Congressman Conyers exhorted the activists to rally behind efforts to transfer funds from the defense budget to welfare programs. The executive director of the U.S. Peace Council, Michael Myerson, a longtime Communist functionary, asserted that the U.S. Peace Council had a unique responsibility to fuse the cause of disarmament with that of the Palestine Liberation Organization and guerrillas in El Salvador, Guatemala, Chile, and South Africa.

On November 15, 1981, the day the U.S. Peace Council gathering ended, Riverside Church in New York opened a conference on "The Arms Race and Us." Serving as host and hostess were the Reverend William Sloane Coffin and Cora Weiss, whom he engaged as the Riverside Church disarmament-program director.

During the Vietnam war Weiss was a leader of Women Strike for Peace. A congressional study characterized Women Strike for Peace as "a pro-Hanoi organization" which from its inception "has enjoyed the complete support of the Communist party." Even while the fighting continued, Weiss traveled to both Hanoi and Paris to consult with the North Vietnamese. Subsequently she became a director of Friendshipment, established to funnel American aid to Vietnam after the Communist victory. In 1976, she joined a coalition formed to stage anti-government demonstrations during the bicentennial celebrations. Weiss also has helped sponsor the Center for Cuban Studies, a group to which Fidel Castro personally expressed his appreciation on its tenth anniversary.

About 500 disarmament proponents from around the nation attended the conference Weiss organized. A prominent new performer on the disarmament scene, Australian-born pediatrician Helen Caldicott, did her best to instill fear and loathing. "We are on the brink of extinction," she warned. While Caldicott had no criticism of Soviet weapons, she likened the christening of a U.S. Trident submarine to christening "Auschwitz," to "a gas oven full of Jews burning up."

Caldicott, who now devotes herself fully to running another peace lobby, Physicians for Social Responsibility, did sound one positive note. She had just toured Europe, whipping up support for the freeze. "It was a wonderful feeling to be over there," she said, because "the fear was palpable but realistic." By contrast, she lamented, "the Americans seem to have no panic. Why?" Caldicott concluded by quoting an ecclesiastical appeal for unilateral American disarmament.

Surely her words heartened KGB officer Kapralov, who came up from the Washington Residency to participate in the start of the Riverside Church Disarmament Program.

Mobilization for Survival convened its climactic strategy session early last December on the campus of the University of Wisconsin in Milwaukee. Some of the MFS leaders were frank in their statements of tactics, strategy, and goals. A staff organizer from Boston, Leslie Cagan, said that current expediency necessitates a coalition that "makes it easier to call out more people to demonstrate." Construction of a coalition with "diversity of composition," she explained, requires "a common enemy as well as a common vision." As useful enemies, Cagan cited President Reagan, "our military-industrial complex, racism, and sexism."

Mel King, a Massachusetts state legislator active in both the World Peace Council and the U.S. Peace Council, demanded a more militant spirit. "We've been too damn nice," he declared. "It's time we stopped just getting mad and started getting even."

In workshops, allies of the revolutionary Weather Underground lobbied for terrorism in general, "direct action," and "armed propaganda" against installations involved in production of nuclear power and weapons. Lauded as "genuine people's leaders" were two convicts: Puerto Rican Rafael Cancel Miranda, one of the four terrorists who shot up the House of Representatives, wounding five congressmen, and American Indian Movement leader Leonard Peltier, who killed two FBI agents from ambush.

The business of the conference included the practical planning of 1982 demonstrations at air bases, missile sites, and defense plants; the formation of task forces to write letters to newspapers and importune elected officials in behalf of the nuclear freeze and against major American weapons systems. The Reverend Robert Moore, an MFS national staff member and a leader in the Nuclear Freeze Campaign, together with staff organizer Paul Mayer, stressed the advantages of bringing the campaign to a climax during the U.N. Special Session on Disarmament beginning in June.

Success in the Freeze Campaign

The World Peace Council in the December 1981 issue of *Peace Courier* happily reported that its U.S. Peace Council was progressing well in collecting signatures on petitions advocating the nuclear freeze, promoting a California referendum on the freeze, and advertising the Jobs for Peace Campaign, another plan to divert money from defense to welfare.

The World Peace Council, its parent, the International Department, the KGB, and the Politburo all had ample grounds to be pleased. Like the simple slogans of past Soviet Active Measures, nuclear freeze appealed to many Americans who honestly desired to do something about the transcendent issue of war and peace. From the East Coast to the West Coast, town councils and county boards of supervisors paused in their deliberations about zoning, sewage systems, and school budgets to pass resolutions favoring the nuclear freeze. Nearly 600,000 Californians petitioned for a referendum to record their state in favor of the freeze. Prominent religious leaders, educators, scientists, artists, entertainers, and other public figures endorsed the nuclear freeze. Helen Caldicott's Physicians for Social Responsibility toiled tirelessly to scare people by pointing to the obvious—wherever detonated, a nuclear bomb would wreak horrendous havoc.

On March 10, 1982, Senators Edward Kennedy and Mark Hatfield introduced a resolution demanding an immediate nuclear freeze, and in the House of Representatives, a parallel resolution was introduced. Even if adopted, the resolutions would be binding upon no one. But they did significantly augment the Soviet campaign to prevent the United States from producing the weapons that would ensure a balance of strategic power.

Meanwhile, on orders from the Center at Lubyanka, the KGB Residency in New York concentrated much of its manpower upon the freeze campaign. U.S. counterintelligence identified more than twenty Soviet agents endeavoring to influence elements of the peace movement, particularly leaders in religion, labor, and science.

Typical of them are KGB officers Sergei Paramonov, Vladimir Shustov, and Sergei Divilkovsky, all of whom masquerade as diplomats at the U.N. Paramonov, who participated in the inaugural meeting of the Riverside Church disarmament program, courts wives of clergymen and other women in the peace movement. A charming professional, he entices the naïve with free trips to Moscow, suggesting they can "reduce misunderstandings" between America and Russia. Shustov and Divilkovsky have made numerous visits to Riverside Church. And they have shown up at other churches and meetings of prestigious organizations concerned with peace.

The Soviets supplemented the labors of their New York and Washington residencies by sending people from the Center into the United States on temporary assignments. Even before the freeze movement materialized, a Soviet delegation including KGB officer Andrei Afanasyevich Kokoshin toured the United States, visiting Americans who were to be prominent in the campaign. Another delegation led by Nikolai Mostovets, who heads the North American section of the International Department, plotted strategy with the U.S. Peace Council.

Of the Soviets who applied for visas to attend a disarmament conference sponsored by the National Academy of Sciences in Washington in January 1982, roughly half were known intelligence officers. The State Department refused entry to most of them. Nevertheless, of those who came, almost half were co-opted KGB agents or International Department operatives. One of the Soviet "scientists" was Vitaly Zhurkin, who, back in the 1960s, when agent Chandra was being groomed in New Delhi, used to give money and orders to the Indian Communist party.

In anticipation of a massive nuclear-freeze rally on June 12, 1982, emissaries from thirteen Soviet international fronts flooded into New York City. They joined more than 700,000 Americans who paraded and spoke out for peace.

Soviet Rehearsal for Nuclear War

The following week the Soviet Union staged a terrifying rehearsal of a surprise nuclear attack on the United States and Western Europe. In a span of seven hours, they fired land- and sea-based missiles designed to kill American satellites, destroy U.S. retaliatory power, obliterate American cities, and wipe out Europe. The firings, over Soviet territory and waters, exactly duplicated wartime distances and trajectories, and produced shock among those monitoring them in Washington. Never before had there been such a realistic and comprehensive practice for starting a nuclear war.

There has been no great outcry against these ominous Soviet preparations. Neither has there been any outcry against the relentless Soviet buildup of offensive nuclear weapons.

In Europe demonstrators did not protest against the 315 new Russian missiles that can incinerate all European cities in twenty minutes. Instead, they protested against the 572 weapons that NATO *plans* to emplace to defend Western Europe. In America the demonstrators did not protest against the 1,400 intercontinental missiles aimed at America, many of which are designed to annihilate U.S. missiles in a first strike. Instead, they demonstrated against *projected* American missiles, bombers, and submarines whose deployment would more than anything else ensure that the

Soviets never will dare launch the kind of surprise attack for which they practiced last June.

While the demonstrations proceeded in Europe and the United States, seven young European tourists—a Belgian, two Spaniards, two Frenchmen, and two Italians—attempted a tiny demonstration in Moscow. On April 19, 1982, in Red Square, they unfurled a banner saying in Russian, "Bread, Life, and Disarmament." Instantly, the KGB seized them and carted them to jail before they could pass out a single leaflet in behalf of peace. On August 8, 1982, the Associated Press reported from Moscow: "A co-founder of Moscow's only independent disarmament group is being administered depressant drugs against his will in the psychiatric hospital where he is being held, his wife said today." And at Harvard, students and faculty reserved some of their loudest applause for a spokesman from the KGB, a man from the Lubyanka Center.

Once again, the KGB had succeeded in inverting reality.

11. The Counterfeit Peacemakers

By RAEL JEAN ISAAC *and* ERICH ISAAC

Focus
A wife-husband team of scholars here documents the changing character and interlocking components of the American "peace movement." Since the sixties, say the authors, traditional pacifist groups such as the Fellowship of Reconciliation and the American Friends Service Committee have moved away from their commitment to non-violence. They continue to criticize U.S. defense policies, but at the same time they often condone the "revolutionary" violence of self-styled "liberation movements" and even terrorist groups. Their argument is that to eliminate war, we must first eliminate injustice. Other more recent "peace" organizations, such as Clergy and Laity Concerned, SANE, and Women Strike for Peace, have, with fewer inhibitions, embraced revolutionary causes. They appear to be far more concerned with injustice in America than in the Soviet Union.

All Western peace movements are targets for "Soviet manipulation and penetration," say the authors. Moscow's major instrument for influence is the Soviet-controlled World Peace Council (WPC), whose first major effort was the Stockholm Peace Petition in 1950. The WPC has actively opposed many major U.S. foreign policies and supported "liberation movements" in the Third World. To reach the American audience, in 1979 the WPC created an affiliate, the United States

Peace Council, which works actively with a score of American anti-war groups. Its creation was hailed by the Communist *Daily World* as an event that "may mean the difference between life and death for humanity." The U.S. Peace Council (a tax-exempt group) has for its symbol a dove shaped into a clenched fist.

The authors summarize how the Communists work with peace groups, including church organizations, in undercutting U.S. policies. The Soviet connection is further documented by journalist John Barron in selection 10 and Soviet émigré Vladimir Bukovsky in selection 12 and is underscored by an official Soviet statement, selection 13.

Rael Jean Isaac is an author and journalist who has studied the peace movement and the political activities of American religious bodies. **Erich Isaac** is a professor of geography at the City College of New York.

B EGINNING EARLY IN 1982, what the media dubbed a "peace crusade" swept the country. It centered on something known as the nuclear freeze petition, calling for a mutual freeze by the United States and the Soviet Union on the testing, production, and deployment of nuclear weapons and their delivery systems. Nuclear freeze petitions proliferated on street corners, in front of supermarkets, in churches and synagogues. Hundreds of town meetings passed freeze resolutions, and so did a number of state legislatures. In California, a drive to put the freeze on the ballot collected the requisite 350,000 signatures in a mere two months. Polls showed Americans would vote for a freeze by a margin of three to two on local ballots. Mass demonstrations were arranged to coincide with the U.N. Special Session on Disarmament in June.

Every effort was made to galvanize the unimaginative. There were bicycle races from death, "run for your life" marathons, die-ins, lie-ins, teach-ins, and other consciousness-raising devices. A group called Physicians for Social Responsibility described to audiences the physical suffering they would experience following a nuclear explosion: the starvation, dehydration, radiation sickness, and infections. These doctors explained in vivid detail the horrible aftermath of nuclear war and their total inability as physicians to help any of the survivors. (Not that they showed any sign of wanting to improve their ability to help. Far from urging rational civil defense measures, which the Soviets have taken, a film produced by the Physicians for Social Responsibility included a statement that it is a breach of medical ethics for a physician to participate in planning for emergency medical services in the event of nuclear attack.)

While no one doubts the dreadful consequences of nuclear war and the need to avert it, this cannot explain the peace crusade. The

Excerpted with adaptations by permission from the July 1982 issue of *The American Spectator* (© 1982 by *The American Spectator*).

nuclear age has been with us since 1945. Why the sudden ferment, to the point that a front-page headline in the *Wall Street Journal* reported, "Town of Pella, Iowa, talks of little other than nuclear attack"? Where did the nuclear freeze movement come from? Where do its initiators plan to take us?

Origin of the Freeze Campaign

The nuclear freeze was initially coordinated in early 1980 by two pacifist organizations: the American Friends Service Committee (AFSC) and the Fellowship of Reconciliation. The first is wealthier and better known, but both originated at the end of World War I as religiously based organizations committed to nonviolence. The freeze quickly won the support of almost all the organizations that make up what in current jargon could be called "the peace community." These are both pacifist and non-pacifist groups devoted to reducing the prospects of war. The best established of those who signed the initial "Call to Halt the Nuclear Arms Race," as the freeze was originally titled, were Clergy and Laity Concerned and SANE (which have been the most active in procuring signatures for the freeze), Mobilization for Survival, Pax Christi (a Catholic organization), Riverside Church Disarmament Program, and Women's International League for Peace and Freedom. Once the freeze caught on, the Nuclear Freeze Weapons Campaign, consisting primarily of organizations which signed the initial "Call," decided to establish a special clearing-house in the center of the country. Using the tax exemption of one of them (the Council for a Livable World Education Fund), the clearing-house opened in St. Louis in January 1982.

Most Americans have a warm, if hazy, image of peace organizations, especially pacifist groups, whose dedication to nonviolence is seen as admirable, if impractical. A closer look, however, would produce some major surprises. The major pacifist organizations— the AFSC, the Fellowship of Reconciliation (FOR), the War Resisters League (WRL), and the Women's International League for Peace and Freedom (WILPF)—are centers of radicalism whose relation to nonviolence is highly problematic, since in practice they condone violence to achieve the goals of what the Left defines as "liberation movements." The distinction between pacifist and non-pacifist peace organizations, indeed between most peace organizations and radical left-wing political groups, has become a distinction without a difference.

Intrinsic to pacifism, of course, is the view that means and ends cannot be separated, and all the pacifist organizations continue to pay lip service to this principle. A 1980 article in the Fellowship of Reconciliation's journal states the case as eloquently as ever: "Nonviolent activists dispute the assertion that the end justifies the means: they see means and ends as one and inseparable. . . . The means invariably become embodied in the end, however noble, and skew and distort that end—often beyond recognition." The article quotes a pithy phrase: "You can't grow a rose from a cactus seed." Similar passages could readily be produced from every pacifist publication.

One dramatic example of the gap between pacifist rhetoric and reality is the attitude of these groups toward the Palestine Liberation Organization. As the world's chief terror organization, the inspiration and actual training agency for the world's proliferating terror groups, from the Baader Meinhof to the Red Brigades to a host of groups in Latin America, the PLO should be especially abhorrent to pacifists. Instead, the attitude of the pacifist organizations toward the PLO is one of warmth, even admiration. For example, in 1975 the Fellowship of Reconciliation sent a group to PLO headquarters in Lebanon. The members returned to praise the PLO officials with whom they had spoken and were particularly enthusiastic about one whom they said "spoke in near pacifist terms about guerrilla violence." (The very fact that such a phrase could be formulated says something about what has happened to American pacifism.) One member of the Fellowship group criticized Secretary of State Henry Kissinger, then engaged in his famous "shuttle diplomacy" in the Middle East, for "inviting Palestinian militants to return to terrorist tactics in the absence of any peaceful alternative for justice." If the United States did not give the PLO what it wanted, the PLO had no "alternative" except violence.

The Women's International League for Peace and Freedom seems almost obsessed with the PLO. In a recent year its journal,

Peace and Freedom, ran ten articles on the Middle East, the purport always the need to involve the PLO.

The AFSC meanwhile has done more. Its activities in Israel, ostensibly "humanitarian," provoked the Israeli government to the point where it sought to remove the AFSC's Middle East representative for pro-PLO activities. The AFSC maintains a Community Information and Legal Aid Center in East Jerusalem. While the Israeli authorities were told it would be a counselling center, it rapidly developed into a legal aid service for captured PLO terrorists. In an interview in 1979, Jean de Muralt, then its director, said: "We help the small fry. The big people have their own connections and don't need our help." In the United States the AFSC has organized lobbying efforts on behalf of the PLO and speaking tours for its propagandists.

The identification of pacifist organizations with the PLO is a particularly striking illustration of the breakdown of pacifist principles; however, instances of pacifist support for terrorist groups could be multiplied. Almost any Third World "liberation movement," provided it attacks the West, can count at the very least on full moral support from the U.S. pacifist organizations whose fundamental principle, to use the words of an AFSC brochure, is that "violence can never be right."

A Radical Conception of Pacifism

Although the breakdown of American pacifism is a phenomenon only of the last fifteen years, the tensions that led to its disintegration are much older. They stemmed from the conviction of pacifists that war would be eliminated only if the cause of war were eliminated, this cause being social injustice. With the Bolshevik Revolution, many pacifists became attracted to revolutionary Marxism and its promise to eliminate injustice once and for all. The Fellowship of Reconciliation was the most influential pacifist organization in the interwar years, and it was repeatedly battered by conflicts between those who opposed all violence and those who were convinced that class warfare was necessary to prevent international warfare. The Fellowship came down on the side of nonviolence, and in the mid-thirties, the dissidents—who at one point included the organization's executive secretary, J. B. Matthews—were forced to resign. The most famous American pacifist, A. J. Muste, briefly left the Fellowship for a fling at Communism, becoming general secretary of the Communist League of America, a section of the Trotskyite Fourth International. He returned to pacifism, and the Fellowship, in 1937.

All this ferment left its mark. While still a pacifist but undergoing the intellectual development that would make him, if only temporarily, a Communist, Muste developed a radical conception of pacifism outlined in his 1928 essay "Pacifism and Class War." Here he expanded the definition of violence, declaring that "the basic fact is that the economic, social, political order in which we live was built up largely by violence, is now being extended by violence and is maintained only by violence." He insisted that since 90 per cent of the violence in the world was perpetrated by forces of the status quo, it was somewhat "ludicrous" that public concern centered on the 10 per cent of violence used by rebels against repression. Not only did Muste minimize the importance of revolutionary violence, but he argued that it is improper even to counsel nonviolence so long as we benefit from the existing "violent" order.

After World War II, Muste's doctrines became pacifist orthodoxy. Conscientious objectors, particularly those who chose prison over the forms of alternative service offered by the government, emerged with a new conception of nonviolent tactics as the way "to shake the present order to its foundations." Although the Fellowship initially resisted, the War Resisters League (a non-religiously based pacifist group that developed out of the Fellowship in 1923) resolved in 1947 to work for "political, economic, and social revolution by nonviolent means." David Dellinger, a member of the League's executive committee, published a paper called *Direct Action* whose first issue advocated "strikes, sabotage, and seizure of public property now being held by private owners." One writer suggested that "a mass invasion of A&P supermarkets by housewives with hungry families, for the express purpose of emptying shelves, would be a good way of keeping down the profits of the masters." The editor felt called upon to object, protesting that "taking goods *surreptitiously*" would imply they rightfully belonged to store-owners, "thereby continually paying homage to capitalist ideals of property."

What happened when Muste's broadened definition of violence was accepted was that the distinction between violence and nonviolence disappeared. All governments, including democratic governments, were violent because they implicitly had the sanctions of violence behind them. There then was no way of distinguishing between the violence of the status quo and the bombs and guns of the revolutionaries who challenge it. Indeed revolutionaries were to be preferred, for they merely respond to the prior violence of the established order and seek to achieve greater justice.

Pacifists thus have so extended the meaning of violence that it no longer even refers to the use of force, implicit or explicit. According to David McReynolds, a War Resisters League staffer, nonviolence is "most deeply violated" when it is confined to the area where "the state kills people"; poor housing, racism, and sexism are equally "violent," and the violence of unemployment is as real "as napalm falling on Vietnam." An article in the Fellowship of Reconciliation's *Fellowship* claims that "where a woman is denied equal pay for equal work . . . it is an example of violence." War Resisters League President Norma Becker believes all our institutions must be overturned "because unless these institutions are eradicated," it doesn't seem likely that we "will be in a position to really practice nonviolence."

Given the breakdown of pacifism in traditional pacifist organizations, it is hardly surprising that the formally non-pacifist peace organizations that have sprung up since World War II have also come to identify with violent movements. The most important to develop prior to the Vietnam war were SANE in 1957 and Women Strike for Peace in 1961, both of which arose to protest nuclear atmospheric testing. (Physicians for Social Responsibility also dates to 1961 but became moribund until revived by pediatrician Helen Caldicott in 1979.) The Vietnam war produced a series of organizations, the most lasting of which has been Clergy and Laity Concerned about the Vietnam War (CALC). After the war was over, it dropped the last four words in its title. CALC is now simply "Concerned," chiefly about the evils of the American Empire. Several of the prominent peace organizations are coalitions: The Coalition for a New Foreign and Military Policy brings together many of the organizations active against the Vietnam war, especially the churches; the Mobilization for Survival combines anti-nuclear energy groups with disarmament and radical political groups.

Soviet Exploitation of the Movement

Insofar as they are influential, disarmament movements by their very nature serve to weaken Western defenses and inhibit the willingness of Western countries to project their forces beyond their borders. It thus goes without saying that these movements are an obvious target for Soviet manipulation and penetration. If the Soviet Union can manipulate them to focus exclusively on Western disarmament and discount the existence of external threats—or better still to serve as apologists for aggressive Soviet actions— they are even more useful to the Soviets. The point is to help the Soviet Union project an image of itself as the major force for peace in the world, its initiatives thwarted by Western militarism.

The Soviet Union has a front organization, the World Peace Council (WPC), designed to identify the Soviet Union as the world's chief force for peace among Third World countries and to manipulate Western public opinion, especially Western peace movements, on issues the Soviet Union deems vital to its interests. Created shortly after World War II, the WPC sponsored the Stockholm Peace Petition Campaign of 1950 as its first major effort. The campaign obtained almost 500 million signatures worldwide, over a million of them in the United States, where most of the signatories had no idea of the campaign's origin. In 1975 the WPC launched a second Stockholm Peace Petition, this time obtaining 700 million signatures.

While the WPC has devoted much effort to extolling the Soviet Union, promoting Soviet-backed liberation movements, and attacking the United States and its "puppets," it has in the last few years assumed an even larger role mobilizing the Western disarmament protests. It has been trying to block U.S. plans to modernize NATO's Theater Nuclear Forces with medium-range cruise and Pershing II missiles and to upgrade NATO's anti-tank capabilities with neutron bombs. In an article in *Ons Leger* in October 1981, Dutch journalist J. A. E. Vermaat analyzes the extensive role the World Peace Council and a sister Soviet front, the Christian Peace Conference, have played since 1977 in the Dutch peace movement, that major testing ground in the Soviet effort to promote Western disarmament initiatives.

Not that Soviet efforts have been confined to Holland. In November of 1981, Danish writer Arne Herløv Petersen was charged with having placed full-page ads at Soviet expense in Danish papers, urging opposition to NATO and support for Soviet peace proposals. The ads were officially sponsored by the Cooperative Committee for Peace and Security, the chief organization of the Danish peace movement, itself largely led by Communists. In Germany the West German Communist party has increasingly taken control of the peace movement, to the public discomfiture of other radical groups, such as the environmentalist Green party.

Obviously pleased by the success of the Dutch movement and its spread throughout Western Europe, Boris Ponomarev, veteran head of the Communist party's International Department, told a group of Soviet and foreign scientists in 1981 that even though the anti-war movement had reached unprecedented proportions, "the interests of preserving peace call for further development of the anti-war movement." [See also selection 13.]

The World Peace Council, of course, is the most transparent of fronts, the "peace" in its title the purest Orwellian doublethink. In 1975 the Council gave its highest award, the Frederic Joliot-Curie Gold Medal for Peace, to Yasir Arafat. That same year it gave a lesser peace award to Lolita Lebron as an "outstanding Puerto Rican freedom fighter . . . who has been in U.S. jails for the last twenty years." (Lebron was one of four Puerto Rican terrorists who opened fire on the U.S. House of Representatives from the visitors' gallery during the Truman administration.) Another former winner of the Joliot-Curie Gold Medal for Peace is Leonid Brezhnev. On its thirtieth anniversary the World Peace Council celebrated ever new "victories for peace" in "Ethiopia, Afghanistan, Iran." Presumably to help celebrate one of these Soviet "victories for peace," the WPC has scheduled its next meeting in Afghanistan.

Warm Reception for a 'Peace' Delegation

In reaching public opinion in the United States, the WPC has been aided since 1979 by the presence of an American affiliate, the United States Peace Council. The groundwork for the U.S. Peace Council was laid in 1975 when a nine-member delegation from the WPC came to this country to publicize the WPC's Second Stockholm Peace Petition.

The reaction of established U.S. peace organizations to the WPC visit was revealing. In the past, and for all their internal tensions, U.S. pacifist organizations would have been wary of Communist manipulation. "Communist-inspired 'peace campaigns' are not genuine," announced the Fellowship of Reconciliation when the first Stockholm Peace Campaign was launched, and lead "to building up the Communist party rather than pacifism or peace." This time, however, none of them decried the delegation as a fraud, and several in fact used their standing to give the delegation credibility among unsuspecting American political and religious leaders. The delegation's Washington visit, for instance, was coordinated by Edith Villastrigo, director of the Washington office of Women Strike for Peace. As a result, the WPC delegation was able to meet with twenty members of Congress (several of whom hosted a luncheon for the delegation) and was welcomed at the Methodist Church Center by leading clergymen. Thanks to preparations by various peace and church groups in the fifteen cities it visited, the delegation met with local and state officials, spoke at church meetings, campuses, even high schools (the delegation reported that following its presentation at University High School in Milwaukee many students asked if they could join the World Peace Council). Delegation members appeared on television and met with editorial boards of major daily newspapers.

Indeed, the reception accorded this delegation of the world's leading Communist front was nothing short of amazing. In New

York City, Ambassador Angier Biddle Duke, on behalf of then Mayor Abraham Beame, presented delegation members with Bicentennial Medals. In both Los Angeles and Milwaukee the delegation accepted mayoral proclamations in its honor. In Detroit the delegation won a sheriff's escort and keys to the city. It also accepted a "Spirit of Detroit Award" given to the WPC for its "substantial effort to achieve peace." In South Bend, Indiana, the delegation received keys to the city, and a luncheon in its honor was given by the Chamber of Commerce! In each community— and the delegation also visited Seattle, Cleveland, and San Francisco—the group left behind what it described as an "ongoing WPC committee." Local Peace Councils already existed in Los Angeles and Chicago. The delegation's report mentioned that the Chicago Peace Council would continue "as always to maintain contact with the WPC."

In 1978 the WPC actually held a three-day conference in Washington, sponsored by, among others, Kay Camp, president of the Women's International League for Peace and Freedom, and Edith Villastrigo of Women Strike for Peace. The conference came out for American Indian claims against the United States and for Puerto Rican independence and opposed U.S. building of "weapons of mass destruction." WPC President Romesh Chandra said the presence of the WPC group in the United States, when prior to the McGovern amendment it would have been banned from entering the country, "proves that we can win."

The seeds planted by the delegation came to fruition in 1979 with the establishment of the United States Peace Council. The Communist *Daily World* hailed its advent, saying the organization "may mean the difference between life and death for humanity." Romesh Chandra showed up for the first national conference, echoing in his speech the WPC line that liberation struggles are the peace movements of their people. In the words of this former member of the central committee of the Communist party of India:

> People ask me, "You are a peace movement. Why do you support the armed struggles in Nicaragua, Palestine, Vietnam?" And I reply, "The armed struggle in these countries *is* the peace movement. . . ."

Wherever possible, the resolutions passed by the conference packaged Soviet foreign policy objectives to appeal to segments of American society. The conference appealed to the anti-nuclear energy movement by linking the need to shut down nuclear plants with "the recognition that nuclear arms production is even more dangerous and needs to be shut down also." It appealed to distinctive American preoccupations by emphasizing the threat "the draft poses to human rights." It resolved not only to work closely with existing anti-draft registration organizations but to form a GI and Veterans Committee "to organize the thirty million American veterans and two million GIs to fight for peace."

On the whole, however, the conference simply passed resolutions conforming to major Soviet objectives: support for Third World liberation movements and U.S. disarmament. It passed a resolution, "In Solidarity with the Arab People of Palestine and Their Central Issue: Palestine," which condemned the Camp David accords as "a cornerstone of a new U.S. offensive in the Middle East." Another resolution called for withdrawal of U.S. bases from the Philippines and an end to all aid to that country. On the other hand, resolutions called for U.S. aid to Communist Vietnam, Laos, and Kampuchea. Other resolutions concentrated on cutting back U.S. defense expenditures and "forming coalitions of peace groups." Resolutions were passed opposed to all new U.S. weapons systems.

The U.S. Peace Council has established a "Peace Education Foundation," which has received tax-exempt status from the IRS. The Foundation is headed by Abe Feinglass, a World Peace Council Presidium member and secretary-treasurer of the Amalgamated Meatcutters Union. The Foundation has announced plans to explore the effects of the military budget on blacks and other minorities. At its second national conference in 1981, the U.S. Peace Council established a youth caucus, designed to reach out to junior high and high school youth with anti-draft and anti-war themes, and announced development of a curriculum guide for courses on peace in public schools.

Even the symbol at the top of U.S. Peace Council literature tells the story: It is a dove shaped into a clenched fist.

It is bad enough that established U.S. peace organizations have failed to denounce the U.S. Peace Council and its transparent effort to channel the desire for peace to serve Soviet purposes. But even worse than their silence has been that virtually all of them have become involved with the U.S. Peace Council in some way. Before its founding conference the U.S. Peace Council issued a "Call" which said:

> We who initiate this Call believe that there is a peace majority in our country. . . . We seek to help organize our peace majority in its entire spectrum because only then can our people compel peace.

Those who gave their names as sponsors of this Call in effect endorsed the U.S. Peace Council as a bona fide peace-seeking organization. Yet the sponsors included the president of the Women's International League for Peace and Freedom, the executive director of SANE, the disarmament coordinator of the American Friends Service Committee, the director of the Washington office of Women Strike for Peace (who had coordinated the 1975 WPC visit), and a leader of Clergy and Laity Concerned. For many, more than sponsorship was involved. At the founding conference the executive director of SANE, the disarmament director of the AFSC, an official of the Women's International League for Peace and Freedom, and a representative of Clergy and Laity Concerned conducted workshops. When the U.S. Peace Council took out a full-page ad in the *New York Times* in June 1979 to attack Joan Baez and others who had criticized human rights violations in Vietnam (the U.S. Peace Council ad countered that "Vietnam now enjoys human rights as it has never known in history"), it was signed not only by assorted Communists and far leftists, but by the president and vice-president of Women's International League for Peace and Freedom and by several leaders of Clergy and Laity Concerned.

Two pacifist organizations were conspicuous by their absence as sponsors of the U.S. Peace Council "Call"—the Fellowship of Reconciliation and the War Resisters League. The League did send an observer to the 1979 U.S. Peace Council conference who was sufficiently disturbed by the proceedings—she noted that

Communist party literature was "everywhere"—to prepare a critical statement which she tried to read to those assembled. The organizers, however, told her that there was "no time."

Nonetheless, the Fellowship and the War Resisters League together with the other peace organizations participated with the U.S. Peace Council in a series of strategy groups set up to plan demonstrations for the U.N. Special Session on Disarmament that was held in June 1982. Indeed the U.S. Peace Council has begun to show up regularly at meetings of the various peace organizations. Add to this the increasingly frequent references in peace-group literature to joint local projects of peace and Peace Council groups and the picture is clear: The U.S. Peace Council is fast becoming an accepted member of the "Peace Club."

The Mobilization for Survival (MFS) can serve as a model of how Communist and peace organizations have become intertwined. According to the published accounts by MFS leaders, the organization was established in 1977 after Peggy Duff, a leader in the British disarmament movement long active in the World Peace Council, told U.S. peace group representatives that the first U.N. Special Session on Disarmament (which started as a WPC project in 1975), scheduled for May 1978, was of "historic importance" and it was up to American peace groups to make sure it has maximum public impact. Labor organizer Sidney Lens, long active in the Chicago Peace Council, and sociology professor Dr. Sidney Peck, identified in a 1970 staff study prepared for the Internal Security Committee of the House of Representatives as a member of the Wisconsin State Committee of the Communist party, took the initiative in establishing the Mobilization for Survival, which then organized demonstrations in connection with the 1978 U.N. Special Session on Disarmament. According to its own no doubt generous estimate, MFS was able to produce only 25,000 demonstrators for that first disarmament session. It is a mark of the peace-movement explosion that an estimated crowd of 750,000 attended a peace rally at Central Park in New York in connection with the 1982 disarmament session. Delegations came from Europe and Japan (though several hundred of the one thousand Japanese demonstrators who flew over were denied entry visas).

The Fellowship of Reconciliation, the War Resisters League, and other pacifist organizations became part of MFS upon its founding in 1977. So did SANE and Clergy and Laity Concerned, the U.S. Communist party with three of its fronts, and in 1979 the U.S. Peace Council. The third element in MFS was anti-nuclear-energy groups. No national environmental organizations joined, but a host of local groups did, their names ranging from Mississippi Alliance for the Environment to the more colorful Appletree, Dogwood, Jackrabbit, and Crabshell alliances.

With a double constituency of anti-nuclear-energy and anti-nuclear-weapons groups, the Mobilization has worked on both fronts, using such slogans as "Zero Nuclear Weapons" and "Ban Nuclear Power." But there is little doubt that the primary interest of its leaders is in disarmament. A 1979 MFS demonstration in Washington, D.C., brought a World Peace Council delegation to address the rally, including Werner Rumpel, head of the East German Peace Council, and Nicholas Schouten, a leader of the Communist party of the Netherlands, who played a key role in organizing the anti-neutron-bomb campaign there.

Those directing MFS activities wear a variety of hats. The head of its Labor Taskforce is Gil Green, a member of the U.S. Communist party's central committee, whose major responsibility within the party has been coordinating relations with peace organizations. Head of the MFS International Task Force is Terry Provance, who also heads the AFSC's Disarmament Task Force and was one of the sponsors of the U.S. Peace Council.

Cooperation With Communists

Needless to say, what such developments as the founding and growing acceptance of the U.S. Peace Council or the unabashed fellow-traveling of the Mobilization for Survival coalition signify is that the Soviets do indeed have input into the U.S. peace movement. And whenever well-intentioned people, who are not necessarily wise people, have tried to cooperate with Communists for what they are persuaded are common goals, the results have been disastrous to the well-intentioned. So well did a socialist-pacifist like Norman Thomas learn this lesson that, shortly before America's entry into World War II, in his last-ditch effort to keep America out of the war, he cooperated with the America First movement, which he detested, but refused to cooperate with the Communists (then opposed to entering the war because the Stalin-Hitler pact was in effect). Even A. J. Muste knew better than he spoke when he encouraged pacifists to enter into coalitions with Communists during the Vietnam era. At the time of the Korean War, Muste wrote that Communists advocate coalition governments because the strictly disciplined Communist party always dominates such coalitions and before long takes them over. It is presumably a principle equally applicable to coalitions with Communists outside of government.

Does it then follow that the nuclear freeze is an example of successful Soviet manipulation? Is the specific proposal simply a target of opportunity, or is more involved? According to journalist Peter Pringle, writing in the *New Republic,* the nuclear freeze proposal had its origin in a meeting called by the American Friends Service Committee in the summer of 1979. Sidney Lens [see selection 8] writes that the freeze was "organized on the initiative" of Terry Provance and Randall Forsberg. Forsberg, formerly of the Stockholm International Peace Research Institute,* has now established her own think tank, the Institute for Defense and Disarmament Studies. Provance, as we just noted, is disarmament director of the American Friends Service Committee, head of the MFS International Task Force, and was a sponsor of the U.S. Peace Council. But he wears yet another hat. Terry Provance is one of forty official U.S. members of the World Peace Council. He was elected to this position at the WPC's 1977 meeting in Warsaw.

---

*The credibility of the Stockholm International Peace Research Institute, whose annual studies on the global balance of power constitute the bible of the disarmament forces in Western Europe, has recently suffered a number of blows. A staff member was arrested for illegally gathering intelligence in Norway and Sweden; a former researcher charged that her work on Soviet military bases was censored by the institute's Czechoslovak consultant; and Carl Bildt, a member of the Swedish Parliament's Foreign Affairs Commission from the Moderate party, charged the institute with "obsession with the details of Western weapons combined with the inability or unwillingness to see what's going on on the other side."—ED.

It is clear that the Soviets want to see the freeze movement grow. In August 1981, when the AFSC was trying to build momentum for the freeze, it staged a three-day march in New England. En route the marchers were addressed by Yuri Kapralov, a counselor at the Soviet Embassy in Washington, who said that the Soviet Union had "a very favorable view of the idea of a weapons freeze." The International Secretariat of the Christian Peace Conference, the Soviet front that targets Western churches, declared at a meeting in Moscow in January 1982 that "the principal task of the peace movement today is to support all efforts for a freeze on nuclear weapons as a first step toward disarmament." The U.S. Peace Council has thrown itself into freeze work. Its chairman, Michael Myerson, signed the initial "Call" for the freeze, and the World Peace Council's *Peace Courier* in December 1981 praised the role the U.S. Peace Council was taking in collecting signatures for it. Irving Stolberg, a U.S. Peace Council sponsor and U.S. delegate to the 1980 World Peace Council conference in Bulgaria who is also a Connecticut state legislator, coordinated the campaign that passed the freeze proposal at the state level in Connecticut.

There is small cause for wonder that the Soviet Union encourages the freeze campaign; former Secretary of State Haig, however, called it "not only bad defense and security policy . . . [but] bad arms control policy as well." The Administration's skepticism is warranted. The freeze is bad security policy because the U.S. land-based missile force is vulnerable to a Soviet first strike—and a nuclear freeze would freeze its vulnerability, ensuring the Soviet Union an enormous strategic advantage in any future negotiations. In Europe, now targeted by 300 Soviet mobile missiles (SS-20s) equipped with 900 warheads, failure to deploy the Pershing II and cruise missiles would ensure its neutralization, eventually giving the Soviet Union the kind of dominant influence it exerts over Finland. It is bad arms control policy because the Soviet Union would have no incentive to negotiate arms *reduction*—the goal of arms control policies—once its superiority was frozen. From the Soviet standpoint, the fervor over the freeze offers the opportunity to revert to earlier proposals and call them a freeze: Brezhnev has proposed that in exchange for a U.S. "freeze" in not deploying any weapons systems to counter the SS-20s, the Soviet Union will withdraw the latter beyond the Urals. Since the missiles are mobile, however, they could be returned at the Soviet Union's convenience; moreover, even from behind the Urals they could devastate any European target.

Does the Soviet Union want a freeze on nuclear weapons beyond Europe? Not if it is verifiable, i.e., with on-site inspection. (Aware of this, freeze leaders say satellite inspection will be ample.) For the Soviet Union, the ideal situation is prolonged negotiations over the content (and method of verification) of a freeze, during which the United States would be restrained by public opinion from deploying new systems or even increasing defense expenditures while the Soviet Union methodically continued to build up its arsenal.

Appealing to Common Fears

The freeze appeals to the fears everyone shares of nuclear war and presents a measure that is simple, one the man-in-the-street feels he can fully grasp. Moreover, it sounds even-handed, for it calls upon the United States and the Soviet Union to adopt a *mutual* freeze. And why should one expect the average person to think more carefully of the implications of the freeze when congressmen, with staffs hired to consider the ramifications of legislation, are jumping on the freeze bandwagon? By March 10, 1982, 129 congressmen had announced they would seek a resolution of both houses asking the President to negotiate an atomic-weapons freeze.

Why have peace organizations, both the traditional pacifist ones and the newer breed of post-World War II organizations, shown so little resistance to Soviet manipulation? Why were the organizations, under their initial leadership, so much more wary of Communism? For one thing, some of the earlier leaders had been burned by actual experience, and their subsequent vigilance sheltered a newer generation. Stalin's death was immensely important, allowing the leaders of peace organizations to delude themselves that the Communist world had been transformed. The greater sophistication of some of the post-war peace fronts also played a role. The Christian Peace Conference, for instance, which gives Soviet policies a theological aura, convinced many organiza- tions—and churches—that there are independent peace move- ments behind the Iron Curtain.

A major turning point in making cooperation with Communists acceptable was the Vietnam war. A. J. Muste's influence was again important. He eased pacifist fears of cooperating with groups that endorsed revolutionary violence by suggesting that radical pacifists were equally compromised by cooperating with those who "in practice are aligned with Western nations and are less sensitive to factors of violence, suppression, and evil in American and Western culture than in the non-Western world." Critics within the pacifist movement charged that the end result of all the coalitions of peace groups and sectarian varieties of Communists was to destroy pacifism. Albert Hassler, a Fellowship of Reconciliation staffer for thirty-two years, and executive secretary from 1960 until his re- tirement in 1974, wrote:

> The question for pacifists, I think, is whether, in their proper sympathy for the exploited and oppressed of the world, they are willing to justify the use of killing violence to rectify the situa- tion, when it is used by "liberation" movements. If they are, then pacifism itself was one of the casualties of Vietnam.

Non-pacifist peace organizations, including SANE and Women Strike for Peace, were equally affected. SANE experienced sharp divisions, with its executive director, Donald Keys, and others on the staff resigning after a number of chapters were captured by radicals. During the war years, a number of U.S. peace organiza- tions began to send delegations to participate in World Peace Council conferences which, under Soviet guidance, were designed to coordinate activities in opposition to the war.

Deliberate Communist infiltration is yet another factor that has driven the peace movements leftward. SANE and Women Strike for Peace have been Communist targets from their inception. SANE was forced to purge itself of Communists in 1960, only three years after its formation; so successful had the infiltration been that a fourth of the chapters had to be expelled from the organization. But, as we have seen, with the Vietnam war SANE was again radicalized. In 1962, Congress held hearings on Communist infiltration of Women Strike for Peace. The women achieved a publicity victory by packing the hearing room with their babies and handing flowers to each of the women called to testify. In the end, penetration continued unchecked.

Lawrence Scott, an executive of the American Friends Service Committee who initiated SANE as an attempt to reach out to non-pacifists, acknowledged the problem of Communist infiltration over twenty years ago. He believed that pacifist organizations were better protected because of their refusal to separate ends and means. Of course, with the breakdown of their commitment to that principle, pacifist groups have become equally subject to infiltration and manipulation. The process is furthest advanced in Europe. According to the annual report of the Office for the Defense of the Constitution of the West German Ministry of the Interior, Communists have leading positions in the national executive of the West German War Resisters League.

America as the 'Greatest Threat'

But by far the most important factor in facilitating the transformation of the peace organizations into channels that, for all practical purposes, serve Soviet interests has been a common view of the world all the peace groups discussed here have come to share: the vision of the United States as the greatest threat to world peace and the chief agent of militarism, imperialism, racism, and economic exploitation. In a by no means atypical article, a Women's International League for Peace and Freedom staffer writes that U.S. society is "an oligarchy composed of a very few wealthy people who have been able to spread considerable well-being among their supporters, agents, willing serfs, and the general public by plundering the ignorant and weak here and in other parts of the world." The co-chairman of Clergy and Laity Concerned, John Collins, quotes approvingly the words of another CALC official who said that corporate capitalism "needs a hungry world to enable it to operate 'efficiently.' "

There is, in other words, hardly any gap between the peace movement's perspective and that of the Soviet Union on how to create a more just global society. The World Peace Council's publications also inveigh against the evils of imperialism, militarism, sexism, racism, all of which they too define as the peculiar property of the United States and its "puppets." It is difficult to distinguish between the foreign policy the World Peace Council, under Soviet guidance, would like the United States to pursue, and the policy the peace organizations would like it to pursue. Indeed, given the identity of underlying views, is there any reason for peace organizations to resist Soviet infiltration and manipulation?

We are left, finally, with an approach to peacemaking whose essence is the double standard. After the Soviet invasion of Afghanistan, the pacifist organizations, all of which make a strong point of their belief in resistance—nonviolent resistance—to aggression, might have been expected to support U.S. responses that stopped short of violence, including the Olympic boycott and the grain embargo. In fact, they sharply opposed any U.S. efforts to counter the Soviet action. (The same thing happened after the repression of Solidarity in Poland. WILPF passed a statement that ignored events in Poland but attacked Reagan's "political and economic sanctions" and called on him "to restore ties with Poland and the Soviet Union to their previous levels.") An article in WILPF's journal by then WILPF international president Kay Camp summed up the organization's view of the invasion of Afghanistan: "While military intervention is always regrettable, the Soviet interest in having close relations with a neighboring country with which it shares a 2,000 mile border is understandable."

The peace organizations are concerned almost wholly with U.S. disarmament. David McReynolds of the War Resisters League says frankly that the only "politically realistic" approach is bold unilateral initiatives, and the League is in fact circulating a statement calling for unilateral nuclear disarmament. The Riverside Church Disarmament Program minimizes the Soviet "threat," which its publications put in quotation marks. It relies heavily on publications and speakers from the America-the-enemy think tank, the Institute for Policy Studies. This is scarcely surprising since the program is headed by Cora Weiss, daughter of Samuel Rubin, whose Samuel Rubin Foundation, directed by Cora and her husband Peter Weiss, has long served as the major funder of IPS.

We are even hearing Soviet slogans passed off as native American peace products. The Women's International League for Peace and Freedom recently announced a new program called STAR, standing for Stop the Arms Race. An innocent-enough-sounding phrase, it was the slogan of the World Peace Council's 1975 Second Stockholm Appeal campaign, repeated as a litany in its documents: To Make Détente Irreversible—Stop the Arms Race; To Defend the Peace and Build a New World—Stop the Arms Race. What the Women's International League for Peace and Freedom has been able to add is some Hollywood stars—Joanne Woodward, Marlo Thomas, Vinie Burrows, and Polly Bergen are participating in this latest World Peace Council propaganda triumph.

Disarming the United States

For all their fraudulence, the American peace organizations have grounds to hope that they may find themselves at the center of a great mass movement for disarmament in the United States. Peace organizations have been mushrooming—there are now sixty sizable ones. The older organizations are growing. The Fellowship doubled its membership last year; Physicians for Social Responsibility increased its membership sevenfold; SANE reported an 88 per cent increase; the U.S. Peace Council now boasts forty chapters around the country. Other organizations are rediscovering the bomb. The Union of Concerned Scientists, which began in 1969 as a disarmament group, turned almost all its attention in the 1970s to the then more fashionable issue of nuclear power. Now it is back with the bomb, organizing teach-ins on campuses around the country, a consciousness-raising tactic which proved effective in the Vietnam war period.

Much more important than the growth of the peace organizations themselves is the influence they are having on major institutions, especially the church. An "Abolitionist Covenant" is circulating through the churches which affirms willingness to live without nuclear weapons as a religious commitment and calls for a freeze as a first step. The Presbyterian Church, the United Church of Christ, the Disciples of Christ, the United Methodist Church, and the Episcopal Church have all voted to make "peace" their priority issue. This is being translated into such measures as the creation, by the United Church of Christ, of "Peace Advocacy" groups in every state to encourage people to "lobby for peace" in Washington. The umbrella National Council of Churches has already endorsed the freeze. The Riverside Church Disarmament Program is training Disciples of Christ ministers to become peace pastors. And the National Conference of Catholic Bishops is taking an active role, condemning any threat to use the American nuclear arsenal, even in response to Soviet prior use. In November 1981, twenty-nine Catholic bishops condemned the very possession of nuclear weapons as "immoral."

Enlisting Environmentalists

Major environmental organizations, long wary of becoming involved in defense issues, are beginning to man the peace barricades. Helen Caldicott of Physicians for Social Responsibility, who has called the nuclear arms race a case of "missile envy" stemming "from an inadequate male sexual complex on the part of world leaders," has urged the Sierra Club to come in on the ground that nuclear war would destroy mammals, birds, and the ozone layer.

The Sierra Club, whose ranks have swollen to 300,000 members in 1982, a 44 per cent increase in one year, shows every sign of indeed coming in. Its executive committee has already adopted a resolution to lend "support for worldwide disarmament," a cautious entry to be sure, but one likely to lead to what, from the standpoint of the peace movement, are better things. Environmental groups see new propaganda potentialities for their longstanding fight against nuclear power. The Environmental Policy Center now calculates the "warhead equivalent" of commercial reactors. South Carolina's anti-nuclear-energy Palmetto Alliance argues that "every time you flick a switch and it's nuclear-generated electricity, you're helping to make a bomb." The Alliance notes happily that "people really respond to that."

What explains the current runaway success of the disarmament movement? Fear of nuclear war, never far below the surface of public consciousness, has in the past been tempered by other fears and by confidence in public authorities. For the generation of World War II, the Soviet threat was real, as was belief in the need for American strength to contain it. Whatever moral reservations were held regarding nuclear bombs, the right and even necessity of their being a component of the U.S. arsenal was not generally challenged.

What is new is distrust of the U.S. government by its citizens, which in recent years has mounted to such an extent that for significant numbers the mere fact that the government states something is sufficient warrant to believe the opposite is true. Long nurtured by the extreme Left, this attitude has spilled over to segments of the media, to the universities, to the leadership of mainline churches. The resolutions passed by these churches in the last decade reflect a view of American institutions as oppressive and of America's role in the world as one of global oppressor. Such attitudes made the climate ripe for Soviet propaganda offensives conducted chiefly through the World Peace Council, which had been able to establish ties with elements of the adversary culture.

The election of Ronald Reagan was a galvanizing experience for those in the adversary culture—at the same time a shattering defeat and a proof that their worst fears were on the verge of being realized. The nuclear freeze proposal, with its evenhanded veneer, has served as a brilliant, even inspired lever by which to mobilize the public's inevitable anxieties about living in the nuclear age into a weapon to prevent achievement of the Reagan administration's keystone effort: the restoration of U.S. defense capabilities.

Only two years ago a study of peace organizations commissioned by the Institute of World Order found them discouraged and demoralized. Thanks largely to the runaway success of the freeze, they are today transformed. This is not to say that all the peace organizations are enamored of the freeze. We have already noted the objections of the War Resisters League. Roger Molander, head of Ground Zero, which in April 1982 raised consciousness by hypothesizing direct hits in several hundred cities and describing how they would look after an atomic bomb had hit them, says he does not like the freeze because it will not lead to arms reductions.

Even the most ardent proponents of the freeze see it as just the beginning. Don Ebener of the Fellowship of Reconciliation says "the freeze is only the first step toward total disarmament, and it's only to be used as a tool toward that end." Peace groups have plenty of other proposals in the works, including tax resistance, initially in the "symbolic" form of withholding the federal tax on the telephone bill. The project dearest to the heart of the peace movement is "conversion," i.e., converting military industries to civilian production. Pacifist organizations, of course, want to eliminate our war-making potential altogether. Other groups propose cutting military expenditures by 50-80 per cent, cuts they say are feasible even if no further arms agreements are reached with the Soviets.

Given the international realities, it is all too obvious where the peace movement would lead us. *Contentions,* the newsletter of the Committee for the Free World, whose executive director is writer Midge Decter, has put it succinctly:

> The people who claim to seek universal disarmament, to the extent that their efforts will succeed, will bring about only the disarmament of the democracies. A world in which the democracies have renounced the means to defend themselves against a mightily armed totalitarianism is a world in which there will be no freedom *and* no peace.

There are signs some peace organizations are aware of what lies down the road. If disarmament leads to invasion, they are calling for "transarmament," which means nonviolent resistance and non-cooperation. They assure us it will make effective occupation of this country "impossible." Indeed, an article in the War Resisters League journal suggests that it is time for the United States to start thinking about the nonviolent defense of the country.

12. The Soviet Role in the Peace Movement

By VLADIMIR BUKOVSKY

Focus — A noted Russian writer now in exile in the West here examines the fundamental motives and strategy of Soviet foreign policy—its "struggle for peace," its concept of the just war, and its multi-faceted efforts to undermine the confidence and security of the United States and its allies. According to Moscow, says Bukovsky, "the only way to save humanity from the evil of wars is to 'liberate' it from the 'chains of capitalism.'" Also, "'just wars' are those fought 'in the interests of the proletariat,'" and "the interests of the proletariat are best known to the advance-guard of the proletariat . . . by Lenin, Stalin, Khrushchev, and Brezhnev. . . ."

Bukovsky holds that the Soviet regime is brutal and aggressive, that the West is non-aggressive, and that U.S. and Western interests are threatened by Moscow's military might.

He traces the development of the Soviet peace offensive and explains how the Soviet-backed World Peace Council exploits fear and anxiety in the West, which is particularly vulnerable because of its open societies. He details Soviet manipulation of the British Campaign for Nuclear Disarmament, a group that defended the Soviet invasion of Afghanistan. He notes that a representative of the Polish junta was invited to address an international

165

peace conference in Denmark held by the World Peace Council.

Bukovsky quotes and documents many official Soviet sources that clearly indicate significant Soviet influence and control among Western peace movements; he also cites the *Program of Action 1981*, "unanimously adopted by the international community of peace lovers" and published by the World Peace Council. Comments made by a Communist official in May 1981 appear to bear out Bukovsky's conclusions (see selection 13).

Bukovsky warns the West against "a hysterical desire to survive at any price." Recent mass peace demonstrations were disastrous, he says, because participants thereby identified themselves, "willingly or unwillingly, with the rulers of Eastern countries."

Vladimir Bukovsky survived twelve years in the Soviet Gulag. He has resided in the West since 1976 and is now at King's College, Cambridge. He is the author of *To Build a Castle: My Life as a Dissenter* and other works.

*Peace will be preserved and strengthened if the people take the cause
of peace into their own hands and defend it to the end.*
                                              —JOSEPH STALIN, 1952

THE "STRUGGLE FOR PEACE" has always been a cornerstone of
Soviet foreign policy. Indeed, the Soviet Union itself rose out
of the ashes of World War I under the banner of "Peace to the
People! Power to the Soviets!" Probably from the very first, Bolshevik ideologists were aware of how powerful a weapon for them
the universal craving for peace would be—how gullible and irrational people could be whenever they were offered the slightest
temptation to believe that peace was at hand.

Once they recognized the power of "peace" as a weapon, the
Communists have never let go of it. In this respect, it must be
admitted, Soviet politics have invariably been most "peaceful."
We must at the same time bear in mind that according to Communist dogma, wars are the "inevitable consequence of the clash of
imperialist interests under capitalism," and therefore they will
continue to be inevitable as long as capitalism exists. The only way
to save humanity from the evil of wars, then, is to "liberate" it from
the "chains of capitalism." Accordingly, there is a very precise
distinction to be made between "just wars" and "unjust wars."
"Just wars" are those fought "in the interests of the proletariat." It
is perfectly simple and perfectly clear: just wars are absolutely
justifiable because they lead to the creation of a world in which
there will be no wars, forevermore. Proletarians are all brothers,
are they not? So, once the world is rid of capitalists, imperialists,
and various other class enemies, why should those who are left fight
one another?

By this same impeccable logic, the interests of the proletariat are
best known to the advance guard of the proletariat, that is, the

Reprinted with adaptations by permission from the May 1982 issue of *Commentary* (all rights reserved).

Communist party, and should be defined by Lenin, Stalin, Khrushchev, and Brezhnev, since they are in turn the advance guard of the Communist party.

As soon as we have pinned down this formula and deciphered its terminology, the course of history becomes absolutely clear. For instance, Soviet occupation of the Baltic states and Bessarabia, or the war with Finland in 1939-40, were of course perfectly just, as was the partition of Poland, achieved in cooperation with Nazi Germany in 1939. On the other hand, the Nazi attack on the Soviet Union in 1941 was blatantly unjust. By the same token, any attack by the Arabs on Israel is just, at least insofar as it is successful. If Israeli resistance to attack is successful, however, then all peace-loving peoples must protest.

It goes without saying that world public opinion must accept the distinction I have outlined above and direct every effort in the struggle for peace toward establishing it. Fortunately, there are a great many "progressive" people in the world, people for whom any direction taken by Moscow is progressive because by definition it is taken in the service of socialism. Thus, before the Molotov-Ribbentrop pact of 1939 was signed, the energies of all progressive people were mobilized against fascism, whether in Spain, Italy, or Germany. As soon as the pact was signed, the notion of what was progressive and what was not changed drastically.*

On February 2, 1940, for example, the German Communist leader Walter Ulbricht, later to become head of the East German state, was permitted by the Nazi government to publish an article in *Die Welt* in which he said: "Those who intrigue against the friendship of the German and Soviet peoples are enemies of the German people and are branded as accomplices of British imperialism."

The British *Daily Worker* adopted a similar line and greeted the new alliance as a victory for peace, as did the American *Daily Worker*. On September 19, 1939, when the war was raging in Poland, it published a declaration of the National Committee of the American Communist party proclaiming the war declared by

---

*Much of the material that follows here on the early days of World War II is taken from the book by Nikolai Tolstoy, *Stalin's Secret War* (1981), where the appropriate references can be found.

France and Britain on Nazi Germany to be an imperialist (that is, "unjust") one, which should be opposed by the workers. This appeal was immediately supported by fellow-travelers like Theodore Dreiser, and Communist trade unions set out to sabotage production in munitions factories, lest any aid reach Britain or France. Right up to the eve of the Nazi invasion of Russia, Communist propaganda did everything possible to dissuade the United States from helping the European democracies in their war against Nazi Germany. These pages in the history of the glorious "struggle for peace" by the progressive social forces are not much spoken of any more, particularly where the young might hear.

As soon as Nazi Germany turned against its great Eastern ally, the "struggle for peace" was instantly terminated. Indeed, the sudden outburst of patriotism among the "progressive social forces" was remarkable. No strikes, no condemnation of Western imperialism—as if the latter had never existed. For the remainder of World War II the Allies were to enjoy a happy time of industrial peace and a relaxation of the class struggle. The war, of course, was now a "just" one.

Oddly, the passion for peace was resurrected shortly after the war was over, while the Soviet Union was swallowing a dozen countries in Central Europe and threatening to engulf the rest of the continent. At that time, some "imperialist warmongers" were sounding the alarm over Soviet conduct and even suggesting the creation of a "very aggressive" NATO alliance. The "reactionary forces" in the world were starting a "cold war." Beyond this, the Soviet Union was lagging behind the United States in the development of nuclear weapons. For some curious reason, however, the "imperialist military-industrial complex"—all those Dr. Strangeloves—failed to drop the atom bomb on Moscow while they still enjoyed a monopoly on it. This should undoubtedly be ascribed to the success of a great movement of peace-lovers. How could it be explained otherwise, short of the reactionary suggestion that NATO generals were not in the least aggressive?

In any case, members of the older generation can still remember the marches, the rallies, and the petitions of the 1950s (particularly the famous Stockholm Appeal and the meetings of the indefatigable World Peace Council). It is hardly a secret now that the whole campaign was organized, conducted, and financed from Moscow, through the so-called Peace Fund and the Soviet-dominated World Peace Council—where a safe majority was secured by such figures as Ilya Ehrenburg and A. N. Tikhonov. This was the period when comrade Stalin presented his memorable recipe for peace that is the epigraph to this article. Stalin's formulation was enthusiastically taken up by millions, some of them Communists, some loyal fellow-travelers, a number of them muddleheaded intellectuals, or hypocrites seeking popularity, or clerics hungry for publicity—not to mention professional campaigners, incorrigible fools, youths eager to rebel against anything, and outright Soviet agents. Surprisingly, this odd mixture constitutes a fairly sizable population in any Western society, and in no time at all the new peace campaign had reached grandiose proportions. It became fashionable to join it and rather risky to decline.

A Well-Calculated Passion for Peace

The purpose of all this peace pandemonium was well calculated in the Kremlin. First, the threat of nuclear war (of which the Soviets periodically created a reminder by fomenting an international crisis) combined with the scope of the peace movement should both frighten the bourgeoisie and make it more tractable. Second, the recent Soviet subjugation of Central European countries should be accepted with more serenity by Western public opinion and quickly forgotten. Third, the movement should help to stir up anti-American sentiment among the Europeans, along with a mistrust of their own governments, thus moving the political spectrum to the Left. Fourth, it should make military expenditures and the placement of strategic nuclear weapons so unpopular, so politically embarrassing, that in the end the process of strengthening Western defenses would be considerably slowed, giving the Soviets crucial time to catch up. Fifth, since the odd mixture of fools and knaves described above is usually drawn from the most socially active element in the population, its activism should be given the right direction.

The results were to exceed all expectations. Soviet money had clearly been well spent. The perception of the Soviet Union as an ally of the West (rather than of Nazi Germany) was still fresh in people's minds, which undoubtedly contributed to the success of the "struggle for peace."

Subsequently, the death of Stalin, the shock created by the official disclosure of his crimes, the Khrushchev "thaw" in international relations, and, above all, the fact that the Soviets had caught up with the West in nuclear weapons, were to make the peace movement temporarily redundant; it ceased to exist just as suddenly as it had once appeared. Meanwhile, the inefficiency of the Soviet economy once again brought it to the point of collapse. The Soviet Union badly needed Western goods, technology, and credits. Without these, there would have to be very substantial economic reform, dangerous to continued party control over the entire economic life of the Soviet Union. At the same time, it was from the strategic point of view important for the Soviets to legitimize their territorial holdings in Eastern Europe and to secure for themselves the freedom to move further. Something new was called for. Out of the depths of the Kremlin, the doctrine of détente was born.

Though the peace movement was put in cold storage, the issue of peace was nevertheless central to this new Kremlin policy as well. The West had grown so exhausted by the constant tension of the previous decades that the temptation to relax, when offered by the Kremlin, was simply irresistible. And after a decade of a ruthless "struggle for peace," no Western government could get away with rejecting a proposal to limit the arms race—however well some of them understood that it would be senseless to try to reach an agreement with the Soviets while the essentially aggressive nature of Communist power remained in force. Probably some such recognition explains why the Western governments insisted on linking participation in the Helsinki agreements to the observance of human-rights agreements inside the Communist bloc. Their idea was to force the internal relaxation of the Soviet regime and so make it more open and less aggressive. In exchange the West provided almost everything Brezhnev demanded in his "Peace

Program" of the Twenty-fourth Party Congress in 1971. "The inviolability of the postwar frontiers in Europe"—that is, the legitimation of the Soviet territorial annexations between 1939 and 1948—as well as a substantial increase in economic, scientific, and cultural cooperation were solemnly granted by the Western countries in Helsinki in 1975. Earlier a separate treaty had perpetuated the artificial division of Germany without even a reference to the Berlin Wall.

The Western democracies had displayed such readiness to accommodate their Soviet partners that their behavior was perceived as weakness. Probably the most disgusting features of détente could be seen in Germany, where the "free flow of people and ideas" had very quickly degenerated into trading people like cattle, the right to visit one's relatives in the East becoming a kind of reward conditional on the "good behavior" of the West German government. By playing on this sensitive issue the Soviets were able to blackmail the whole country and to "modify" the policies of its government. Unfortunately, Germany is a key factor in East-West relations because in order to avoid a major split in the Western alliance the other members have to adjust their positions in accordance with Germany's. So it was that Soviet influence came to be exerted through the back door, and the West was politically paralyzed.

In addition, far from making the Soviets more dependent—as the proponents of détente had assured us—increased trade, and particularly huge Western credits, have made the West more and more dependent on the Soviet Union. The dimensions of this disaster became clear only recently, when the discussion of economic sanctions against the Polish military rulers and their Soviet masters revealed the inability of the Western countries to reduce once-established economic relations with the Eastern bloc without harming themselves even more. In fact, by now the Soviets are in a position to threaten the *West* with economic sanctions. Undoubtedly, they will take advantage of it very soon.

In the meantime, far from relaxing internally, the Soviet regime had stepped up its repressive policies, totally ignoring the weak Western protests against Soviet violations of the human-rights agreements. The weakness of these protests had in turn served only as further incitement for the Soviets to proceed in their course of repression without restraint. Clearly, the ideological war waged by the Soviets through all those earlier years had only increased in intensity during the era of détente. Nor did they try to camouflage this warfare. On the contrary, Leonid Brezhnev stated openly in his speech to the Twenty-fifth Party Congress, on February 24, 1977: " . . . it is clear as can be that détente and peaceful coexistence relate to interstate relations. Détente in no way rescinds, or can rescind, the laws of the class struggle."

Furthermore, as it transpired, instead of reducing their military expenditures and arms build-up, as the Western nations had during those years, the Soviet Union, taking advantage of Western relaxation, had significantly increased its arsenal. So much so that if in the 1960s it could be said that a certain parity between East and West had been achieved, by now the Soviets have reached a point of clear advantage over the West. We also now know that the benefits to the Soviet Union of trade with the West were invariably put to military use. For example, the Kama River truck factory built by Americans in the 1970s has recently begun manufacturing the military trucks that were observed in action during the Soviet invasion of Afghanistan.

The Final Blow to Détente

By the end of the 1970s, the West was becoming increasingly aware of these dangerous developments. The usefulness of détente, long challenged by some, was now being questioned by many. And then came the final blow—on Christmas 1979. Just at the moment when most people in the West were preoccupied with such things as Christmas cards and presents, something like 100,000 Soviet soldiers moved in to occupy neighboring Afghanistan, an officially "non-aligned" country with a population of about 17 million. The world was shocked, and the U.S.S.R. was immediately placed in isolation. Even the Communist parties of many countries condemned the Soviet action as a piece of blatant aggression. The invasion of Afghanistan, followed by the arbitrary banishment to internal exile of Nobel laureate Andrei Sakharov, followed still later by the threatening of Poland (leading, finally, to the imposition of martial law), virtually terminated the era of détente.

This termination has cost the Soviets dear. In fact, they have lost almost everything they had gradually managed to gain while the West was enjoying its bout of unilateral relaxation. Ratification of the SALT II agreement was suspended indefinitely. The Americans were awakened from their prolonged lethargy to discover with horror how weak, ineffective, and unproductive their country had become. In this new psychological atmosphere, the victory of Ronald Reagan was inevitable, promising an end to American defense cutbacks, the deployment of a new, previously shelved generation of weapons like the B-1 bomber, the cruise missile, the MX, and the neutron bomb. It seemed equally inevitable that the military budgets of all the other Western countries would be increased, while the trade, technology, and credit arrangements with the Soviets would be reduced, or at least be made more difficult to obtain.

Thus, if this trend were to continue, the Soviets would lose their position of military superiority—especially in view of the fact that their economy is so much less efficient than that of "rotten capitalism." Add to this the new wave of international hostility noticeable especially in the Muslim world (the United Nations General Assembly voted against the Soviets on Afghanistan, for the first time since the Korean War), a continuing crisis in Poland, a hopeless war in Afghanistan, and a growing unrest among the population at home caused by food shortages, and the picture grew so gloomy as to be just short of disaster. Clearly the Soviet rulers had to undertake something dramatic to avoid a total catastrophe.

I myself, to tell the truth, was not very much surprised when suddenly, within a year, a mighty peace movement came into being in Western Europe. Especially since, by some strange coincidence, this movement showed itself first of all precisely in those European countries where the old missiles were to be replaced by newer Pershings and cruise missiles. I make no claim to special prescience; it is just that after thirty-four years of life in my beloved

Communist motherland, I have some sense of its government's bag of tricks, pranks, and stunts. In fact, it was not a very difficult thing to predict, for the Soviet state is not a particularly intelligent creature. If you think of it rather as a huge, brainless, antediluvian reptile with a more or less fixed set of reflexes, you cannot go far wrong. "Well, here we are, back to the 1950s again," I thought.

What was much more amusing to observe was the ease with which presumably mature and responsible people had by the thousands fallen into the Soviet booby-trap. It is as if history were repeating itself before our eyes, offering us a chance to see how the Russian state collapsed in 1917, or how France collapsed within one month in 1940. It is also quite amusing, if one has a taste for such amusement, to be reminded of how people are practically incapable of deriving any useful knowledge from even the recent lessons of history. Once again, the universal craving for peace right now, this very moment, and at any price, has rendered people utterly illogical and irrational, and left them simply unable to think calmly. Their current arguments, if one may call them that, are so childish, senseless, selfish, that an involuntary smile comes immediately to one's lips. Even at best what one hears is a parroting of the kind of old moldy Soviet slogans and clichés that even schoolchildren in the Soviet Union would laugh at.

The Exploitation of Fear

To begin with, why is it that everyone has suddenly begun to be so apprehensive about nuclear war again? What has happened to make it more real than it was, say, two or three years ago? The entire history of East-West relations shows that the only way to force the Soviets to respect agreements is to deal from a position of strength. So are we to understand that because the Soviets might cease to be militarily superior to us, nuclear war is once again a reality? Should we, then, take this proposition to its logical conclusion and say that the only guarantee of peace is Soviet military superiority?

Meanwhile, countless TV programs have suddenly sprung up that unfold before us images of the great treasures of our civilization—paintings, sculptures, pyramids, antiquities—and at the end of each the narrator reminds us, his voice trembling with noble passion, how terrible it would be if all these treasures were to be destroyed along with the great civilization that produced them. And on other channels, we are treated to documentary after documentary about nuclear explosions and the consequences of radiation. After such relentless programming, naturally public-opinion polls show a sudden increase in the number of those who believe that nuclear war is imminent.

Then there is the catchy new idea that "Our deterrent does not deter anymore." Why? Has a nuclear war begun already? Have the Soviets attacked any NATO country? Or is it simply because those who like to say the deterrent no longer deters have seen their full quota of televised nuclear explosions?

It is so easy to start a panic. The question is: who is served by this panic? The Soviet-controlled World Peace Council declared in 1980 (and the whole European peace movement repeats it as if under a hypnotic spell): "The people of the world are alarmed. Never before has there been so great a danger of a world nuclear holocaust. The nuclear arms build-up, the accumulation of deadly arsenals, has reached a critical point. Further escalation in the arms build-up could create a most dangerous situation, facing humanity with the threat of annihilation."

Never before. But was not the world in as much danger a year earlier? The leaders of the European peace movement themselves claim that the nuclear potential accumulated on both sides is sufficient for them to destroy one another ten times. Is there any technical reason why "twenty times" is more dangerous than, say, "five times"? Or is it that, like a nuclear charge itself, the accumulation must reach a "critical mass" in order to explode?

Somehow, in the midst of all this nuclear hysteria it seems to be totally forgotten that bombs themselves are quite harmless, unless somebody wishes to drop them. So why are we suddenly alarmed by the stockpile of hardware and not by the Soviet military move toward the Persian Gulf?

Again, quite suddenly, voices begin to cry out in a huge chorus, "Nuclear weapons are immoral!" Wait a minute. Did these weapons just become immoral? Are conventional weapons moral? Why should this idea come all at once into the minds of so many people? Take as another example the question of the new missiles to be deployed in Europe. Why is it more dangerous to replace the old missiles with the new ones than to leave the old ones where they are? Are not the old ones equipped with nuclear warheads as well? To be sure, the new missiles are more accurate. So what? We can thank God that they are on our side. They may make life more difficult for the Kremlin adventurers, but why should millions of people in the West perceive that as a tragedy and danger?

Deep in their hearts most of these terrified people have a very simple answer to all these "whys." They know that the only real source of danger is the Soviet Union and that anything which might make the Soviets angry is dangerous for that very reason. But fear is a paralyzing and deranging force. So deranging as to lead some people to advocate the abolition of the police because the criminals are becoming too aggressive.

Misplacing the Threat of War

Indeed, the most amazing aspect of the present antiwar hysteria—aside from the fact that it has arisen at a time so remarkably favorable for Moscow—is the direction of the campaign. Millions of people in Great Britain, Germany, Holland, Belgium, France, and Italy, supposedly of sound mind and with no evidence of the influence of LSD, march about claiming that the threat of war comes from . . . their own governments and the government of the United States.

The facts are too obvious to discuss here. One may like or dislike President Reagan or Chancellor Schmidt, but unlike comrade Brezhnev, they were elected by the majority of their respective populations and are fully accountable in their actions to the parliaments and to the people. They simply cannot declare a war on their own. Besides, it is quite enough to look around to see the real source of aggression. Was it American or Soviet troops who occupied half of Germany and built a wall in Berlin? Is it not the Soviets who still occupy Hungary, Czechoslovakia, the Baltic states, not to mention Afghanistan, very much against the wishes of the people in these countries? Was it East or West German troops who took part in the occupation of Czechoslovakia and who are prepared to invade Poland?

Everything in the West is done quite openly—one might say, far too openly. But what do we know about the decisions made by fourteen old fools in the Politburo whom nobody ever elected to make these decisions and whom nobody can call to account? No press is allowed to criticize them, no demonstrations to protest against their dictate. Anyone refusing to obey their secret orders would instantly disappear forever. There is in fact very little difference between the Soviet system and that of Nazi Germany. Is there anyone who supposes that he should have trusted Hitler more than the democracies?

After the experience of speaking several times with members of the current European peace movement, however, I know only too well how futile is the recourse to rational argument. They announce unabashedly that there is no Soviet military superiority. It is all, they say, CIA propaganda; the only reliable source of information as far as they are concerned seems to be the KGB.

But this is just a trifle. More seriously, our peace-lovers—repeating word for word an old *Pravda* cliché—maintain that the "crazy American generals" are so trigger-happy as to push the button just for the fun of it. I have never been able to understand why generals must invariably be crazy—American generals, of course, not the Soviet kind, who seem to have some innate immunity from craziness—and if they are crazy, why they did not push the damned button long ago. In any case, it is hard to imagine that the generals, who at least have some technical education, are less equipped to understand nuclear problems than the primary-school teachers who are so heavily represented in the peace movement.

Experimenting With Suicide

Some of the "peacemakers" sincerely believe that as soon as the West disarms itself, the Soviets will follow suit, and with an almost literally incredible naïveté they urge us to "try" this suicidal experiment. Others, far more sophisticated, know perfectly well that their Soviet comrades need to gain time so as to enjoy a more advantageous posture in future negotiations with the Americans. What they urge is that the West start negotiations first and improve the Western position later. Still others are more candidly selfish and object only to the deployment of nuclear weapons near their own village, so to speak—as if being protected is more dangerous than not being protected. Or better still, as if any single village, city, or country could maintain neutrality during a nuclear war. "Let the Americans fight the Russians," they say, implying that the entire problem of the modern world grows out of some stupid far-off quarrel between "Americans and Russians," who are apparently in some kind of conspiracy to destroy the poor Europeans. Surely if comrade Brezhnev promised to respect the "nuclear-free zones" in case of war, people could heave a sigh of relief and go to sleep untroubled. If Brezhnev says so, there will be no nuclear-armed submarines off your shores. After all, has comrade Brezhnev ever broken his word? Of course not. He is an honest man. He is so honest he can even guarantee you in what direction the contaminated clouds will move and locate for you the radioactive fallout. "Why should the Russians attack us, if we are disarmed?" Why indeed? Ask the Afghan peasants; they would probably know the answer.

There is no sense in rehearsing all the various "peace arguments," so contradictory and even incompatible that one wonders how those who make them manage to get along together in the same movement. Only one thing these various strands have in common: panic, and a readiness to capitulate to the Soviet threat even before such capitulation is demanded. Better red than dead. That is why current Soviet propaganda has so quickly become so remarkably successful.

Indeed, it is difficult to imagine a more openly pro-Soviet line than that of the European peace movement. It is even more pro-Soviet than that of the local Communist parties, who after all at least have to camouflage themselves with a cover of independence from Moscow. Nothing is more obvious, for example, than that the present increase in international tension was brought about by the

Soviet invasion of Afghanistan. There is hardly a country, a political party (including some Communist parties), or an international organization that did not condemn the Soviet aggression unequivocally. The only public movement in Western Europe that never condemned the invasion, paradoxically, is the one that calls itself the "peace movement." No such condemnation has ever been pronounced at a peace-movement rally in Western Europe, or passed as a resolution, or published in one of the movement's major publications, or circulated as a mass petition. Perhaps you will imagine that the peace groups condemned the invasion in their hearts? On the contrary, the evidence is far more convincing that they simply justify this international crime.

Not long ago I myself was publicly charged by the leaders of the British Campaign for Nuclear Disarmament (CND) with having distorted their position on Afghanistan. Therefore I find it particularly useful to quote from an official CND booklet, *Why We Need Action, Not Words,* by Betty England: "The intervention in Afghanistan may well have been caused partly by the Soviet Union's fear of its growing encirclement. The fear cannot be called unreasonable after Sir Neil Cameron's statement in Peking . . ." (p. 12). In other words, the poor Russians whom Sir Neil, Marshal of the Royal Air Force, so frightened with a speech critical of them, must have good reason for what they do. By this logic, we ought to be imposing strict censorship on anti-Soviet speeches lest we be faced with Soviet occupation of the entire world. But the implications are even more important. The idea buried in Miss England's passage is that the only way to keep the peace is gradually to accept the Soviet system and Soviet demands.

Even more outspoken than the CND is the World Peace Council. Its booklet, *Program of Action 1981,* contains a direct instruction to support the present puppet government of Afghanistan (p. 25). This program was *unanimously* adopted in 1980 by a gathering in Sofia, Bulgaria, of representatives of most of the peace groups (about this gathering, more later). After this it comes as no surprise that at the recent International Peace Conference in Denmark it was decided to convene the next meeting in Kabul, the capital of Afghanistan, within six months.

It is obvious that a Soviet invasion of Poland would bring us closer to world war, or, to be more precise, would make any real relaxation of international tension quite impossible for ten or fifteen years. And once again, the only public movement that has never condemned the continuous Soviet threat to Poland (and is still uncertain about its reaction to the Soviet-dictated imposition of martial law) is the peace movement. The leaders of the biggest British peace group, CND, went even further, publicly praising themselves for not "overreacting" to the events in Poland (B. Kent, letter to the London *Times,* December 9, 1981) only a few days before the imposition of martial law, and displaying their "impartiality" by equating the Polish crisis with that in East Timor. Perhaps the leaders of the movement seeking to promote peace in Europe should be reminded that in 1975 the thirty-five countries of Europe, together with Canada and the United States, solemnly recognized an inseparable link between security in Europe and respect for human rights in the participating countries. Should we assume that the CND leadership refuses to accept the Helsinki agreement, or are we to conclude that it is indifferent to the question of European security?

At least about Poland not all in the movement can be accused of indifference. I have, for instance, never heard of a case in which a representative of the Chilean or Argentinean government was invited to expound his government's views before any international peace conference. But for some strange reason, an exception was recently made for a representative of the Polish junta, who was invited by the World Peace Council to address the International Peace Conference in Denmark. His vicious lies about Solidarity and personal slanders against Lech Walesa (see the *Guardian,* January 11, 1982) were greeted with hearty applause by the peace-lovers (BBC report).

Unilateralism in the Peace Movement

It is simple common sense to try to restrain both sides of any would-be conflict if one wishes to preserve peace. But the European peace movement is so remarkably unilateral that it seems barely conscious of "the other side." It cries shame on the Americans for as yet nonexistent weapons like the neutron bomb, or the not-yet-deployed cruise and Pershing missiles, but speaks only in whispers, if that, of the hundreds of Soviet SS-20s already aimed at Europe.

Since, again, I have provoked an angry reaction from the CND leaders for pointing out this particular instance of extreme uni-lateralism (London *Times*, December 9, 1981), I looked through the major CND publications once more. The booklet by Betty England quoted above does not contain a single mention of the SS-20s, though it is virtually saturated with the names of American missiles. Nor does a widely distributed report on the CND annual conference of 1981 (the latest to my knowledge), nor the official CND leaflet, *Nuclear War and You,* dropped into my mailbox by some caring hand. Only recently I have learned that a decision to mention the SS-20 was finally taken by CND after many heated debates and very much against the wishes of the CND leadership, many of whom are also members of the British Communist party.

Oddly enough, there are many in the European peace movement who have worked (some still do) with Amnesty International in support of prisoners of conscience in the Communist countries. Unfortunately, this by itself does not seem to prevent one from making dangerous political mistakes, nor, to judge from the results, does it guarantee any moderating influence on the movement's leadership. Be that as it may, the fact is that the European peace movement (including its large constituent organizations) has never said a word in support of the thousands of people in the U.S.S.R. who are imprisoned for opposing aggressive Soviet policies, for refusing to serve in the army on errands of aggression, or to shoot civilians in Afghanistan. During all the time that hundreds of thousands of "peace-lovers" were noisily expressing their one-sided feelings on the streets of London, Bonn, Amsterdam, and Brussels, not one word was said about Sakharov, still in exile and on a hunger strike—Sakharov, who has done more than anyone in the world to halt nuclear testing. These peaceful souls would happily throw stones at General Haig, but they would welcome Marshal Brezhnev with servile smiles.

This is not to deny that there are plenty of well-intentioned, and genuinely concerned and frightened people in the movement's ranks. I am certain that the overwhelming majority of them are. Just as it did in the 1950s, the peace movement today probably consists of an odd mixture of Communists, fellow-travelers, muddleheaded intellectuals, hypocrites seeking popularity, professional political speculators, frightened bourgeois, and youths eager to rebel just for the sake of rebelling. There are also the inevitable Catholic priests with a "mission" and other religious people who believe that God has chosen them to make peace on earth right now. But there is also not the slightest doubt that this motley crowd is manipulated by a handful of scoundrels instructed directly from Moscow.

Communist Manipulation in Bonn

John Vinocur reported in the New York *Times* (April 6, 1982) "the first public substantiation from inside the anti-nuclear movement . . . that the West German Communist party, at the direction of the Soviet Union, has attempted to co-opt public sentiment against nuclear weapons." The environmentalist party known as the Greens "charged that the West German Communist party, which is aligned with Moscow, dominated and manipulated a meeting [in Bonn] Sunday [April 4] in which representatives of thirty-seven groups, describing themselves as elements of the anti-missile movement, planned a major demonstration against President Reagan when he visits Bonn . . . June 10." The Greens, who participated in the meeting, acknowledge that they themselves have cooperated with the Communists "on certain local issues," but what happened in Bonn was "scandalous" even to them. "The Communists dominated the meeting completely. It took place under seemingly democratic rules, but that was a joke. We could barely get a word in." The meeting—at which were represented such groups as the German Student Federation, the Evangelical Student Committee, the Federation of German Youth Groups, and the German Peace Society—rejected resolutions condemning Soviet interference in Poland and Soviet intervention in Afghanistan, and the delegates refused to express support for Solidarity. "They adopted, however, by a large majority, a motion condemning United States actions in Central America, the Middle East, southern Africa, and other regions."

Earlier, as I was in the process of writing this essay, news came that one of the Danish leaders of the movement, Arne Petersen, was arrested along with his wife for channeling Soviet money into the funds of the peace movement. His master, the Second Secretary of the Soviet embassy in Copenhagen, was expelled from the country. Now and then we hear about subsidized trips taken by peace activists to the best Soviet resorts where they are wined and dined royally—and, of course, shown kindergartens, schools, and hospitals (no munitions factories).

The majority of the European peace movement is undoubtedly not aware of these facts. Probably they will ignore the charges of the Greens, just as they missed the reports of Mr. Petersen's activities, which involved placing paid advertisements (out of Soviet donations) for the Danish peace movement in the Danish papers, ads signed by a number of prominent Danish intellectuals (who for sure knew nothing about it). And even our angry CND leaders "know nothing of the subsidized trips to Soviet resorts" (London *Times,* December 9, 1981). Well, sometimes it is very comfortable—even for professional intellectuals—not to know things. . . .

For those, however, who do wish to know, let us track down the origin of the current revival of the "struggle for peace." Anyone who has read thus far will not be surprised to hear that the earliest traces of this revival are to be found in Soviet publications, quite clear for those who know how to read them:

> The first bright colors of autumn have already touched the emerald green parks of Sofia. The golden leaves of maples and aspens are trembling on the breeze. And everywhere the tender-blue streamers bearing the insignia of the World Peace Council. Sofia is expecting an important event: the World Parliament of the Peoples for Peace will be working here from 23 to 27 September. It is the biggest and the most representative meeting of the world's peace forces convened in the last years by the World Peace Council [*Izvestia*, September 23, 1980].

The same day *Pravda* referred to "the biggest gathering in history of the fighters for peace." Indeed, the most peaceful and independent country of the world, Bulgaria, played host during those September days to 2,260 peace-lovers from 137 countries, claiming to represent 330 political parties, 100 international and over 3,000 national non-governmental organizations. To be sure, this was no ordinary meeting of the international Communist movement. The political spectrum of those represented was exceptionally wide: 200 members of different national parliaments, 200 trade-union leaders, 129 leading Social Democrats (33 of them members of their respective national executive bodies), 150 writers and poets, 33 representatives of different liberation movements (including the Association in Defense of Civil Rights from Northern Ireland), women's organizations (like the National Assembly of British Women), youth organizations, the World Council of Churches and other religious organizations, 18 representatives of different U.N. specialized committees and commissions, representatives of the Organization of African Unity and of OPEC, ex-military people, some of them generals, and representatives of 83 Communist parties (*Pravda,* September 23, 24, 25, 26, 27, 28, 29, November 5, 1980; *Izvestia,* September 23, 24, 27, 28, 1980).

Why Moscow Reactivated the Peace Movement

It had all started about a year earlier, as we are informed by a talkative Bulgarian, the chairman of the Organizational Bureau, responsible for the "practical preparation" for this show (*Pravda,* September 23, 1980). They had expected, you see, only 1,500 delegates, but 2,200 came.

Yet a year earlier—in 1979—none of the conditions now cited to explain the current miraculous resurrection of the peace movement existed. There was no so-called "new strategy of the Pentagon," the famous presidential directive 59; there was no new escalation of the arms race; there was no neutron bomb. The Vienna summit meeting had just been successfully concluded with the signing of SALT II. September 1979 was a time of universal happiness, the sky was cloudless. Only one significant thing happened in September 1979: a sudden wave of mass arrests in the Soviet Union and, as we have learned now, a decision to reactivate the peace movement. Who could have predicted in September 1979 that within a year the cold war would be back—who else but those involved in "practical preparations" for the invasion of Afghanistan? Given the nature of the Soviet planned economy, with its fabulously inflexible, slow, and inefficient workings, the Soviets must prepare everything well in advance. Why should they have allocated such a large sum of money to hold a Bulgarian peace show in the middle of happy times, if not in anticipation of grave political trouble ahead?

Furthermore, we learn from comrade Zhivkov, the Bulgarian Communist leader who opened the meeting with a long speech, about an appropriate decision taken by the Political Consultative Committee of the Warsaw Bloc countries in May 1980 (*Pravda*, September 24, 1980), as well as an appropriate resolution of the Plenary Session of the Central Committee in June 1980 (*Pravda*, September 29, 1980). Comrade Zhivkov was simply revealing the way decisions and resolutions first travel through the Communist bureaucratic machinery on their way to rubberstamping by a "representative" body—in this case, the Sofia "Parliament" in September.

Replaying the Stalin Scenario

Indeed, the whole show was depressingly familiar to anyone acquainted with the methods the Kremlin producers applied to the same scenario in the time of Stalin. Even the *dramatis personae* were the same. There was the same World Peace Council with its immortal President Ramesh Chandra; there was the same chief conductor, Boris Ponomarev, former official of the Comintern (now responsible in the Politburo for contacts with fraternal Communist parties as well as for intelligence). Even the slogan adopted for the occasion, "The people have the power to preserve peace—their basic right," was remarkably similar to the unforgettable words of comrade Stalin in 1952.

Only this time the personal message that comrade Ponomarev

brought to those convened was from comrade Brezhnev, not comrade Stalin. The latter, of course, would never have tolerated even the mention of the term "rights"—basic or any other—in his slogans. Well, the times have changed after all. Still, those damned "human rights" had gotten out of hand. Hence, better to find something like "basic rights."

The first to speak, as I said, was comrade Zhivkov, and he spilled the beans about the Soviets' real concern (*Pravda,* September 24, 1980). The aggressive circles in America, he said, refuse to accept the present balance of forces in the world. They don't wish to submit to their historically predestined defeat. They have become so arrogant as to reject all of the recent Soviet peace proposals. They have decided to replace détente with a policy based on a "position of strength." They don't observe agreements on cooperation; they interrupt political and economic contacts; they interfere with cultural and scientific exchange; they dissolve sporting and tourist connections (in other words, the grain embargo, the Olympic boycott, the scientific boycott, etc., responses to the invasion of Afghanistan and the persecution of scientists in the U.S.S.R.).

This theme was taken up by most of the speakers with only minor variations. The main speaker, comrade Ponomarev, suggested a whole program of action intended to bring America's aggressive circles into compliance. He appealed for unity among all those concerned with preservation of peace, irrespective of their political views. "The time has come for action, not words," he said. (Wait a minute, have we not met this sentiment somewhere already? Surely not in the CND official booklet?)

The show proceeded smoothly, exhibiting the whole gallery of monsters, from the greatest peace-lover of our time, Yasir Arafat, to a "representative" of Afghanistan.

How did all these 2,260 representatives of Social Democrats, trade unions, youth, women, and religious organizations react? Did they rush out in disgust? Did they demand the withdrawal of the Soviet troops from Afghanistan in order to remove the main obstacle to détente? Did they express concern about the massive Soviet arms build-up and the deployment of SS-20s? By no means.

This self-appointed World Parliament issued an Appeal in which the main ideas of comrade Ponomarev's speech were repeated. Thus, the "Parliament" is opposed "to the vast machine and arms build-up of the most aggressive forces of imperialism which seek to take the world toward a nuclear abyss; to the falsehoods and lies of the propaganda in favor of the arms build-up, which are disseminated through imperialist-controlled mass media."

Translated from party jargon, this constitutes a clear directive to work against the armament programs of the Western countries (first of all, of course, the United States—the "most aggressive forces of imperialism"), and to reject any "lies" of the mass media about the Soviet arms build-up.

Beyond this, the "parliamentarians" set "the new tasks and duties . . . for action of the peoples of all continents" and worked out the Charter of the Peoples for Peace which was adopted unanimously (!) together with the Peoples' Program for Peace for the 1980s. The year 1981 was chosen to be "the springboard of the eighties, a year of a decisive offensive of the peace forces to achieve a breakthrough in curbing the arms build-up."

Most of the program was carried out, the mass demonstrations of October 1981 in the European capitals having been planned within a framework of what is called in the Soviet program "U.N. Disarmament Week (October 24-31)." How on earth could the Soviets have known in 1980 about events that would take place at the end of 1981, unless they were running the whole show?

My pointing out this strange coincidence, which I did in an article in the London *Times* (December 4, 1981), was bound to provoke heated denials; and did so. The Soviets in *Literaturnaya Gazetta* (December 23, 1981), as well as the CND leaders in the London *Times* (December 9, 1981), made much of the fact that U.N. Disarmament Week had originally been designated as an annual observance by the U.N. General Assembly as early as June 1978. Now, the U.N. flag may seem to many to be a perfect cover. One must ask, however, why virtually nothing happened during that all-important week in 1978 or 1979—even the Sofia meeting was scheduled in September, not October, of 1980—until details for its observance were specified by the Soviet-inspired program?

Moreover, if one looks through the *Final Document of the Assembly Session on Disarmament (May 23 –July 1, 1978),* issued by the U.N., one can find hundreds of designated weeks, months, years, and decades, all totally ignored by our peace-lovers, whereas the suggestion singled out by the Soviets was the one, the *only* one, to gather thousands in the streets. For example, was anyone aware that the decade 1969 to 1979 was solemnly declared by the United Nations to be "The Decade of Disarmament"? If there were any huge rallies or vigorous campaigns during these ten years, they seem to have escaped notice.

The Soviet 'Peace' Program

But let us return to this remarkable program, unanimously adopted by the international community of peace-lovers. (It is published by the World Peace Council in Helsinki, as already noted, and is available in English under the title *Program of Action 1981.)*

This program includes such items as the "elimination of all artificial barriers to world trade," an amazingly frank recognition of the Soviet need for Western goods and technology and its desire to be granted the status of most-favored-nation. But what this has to do with the problem of peace and why all peace-loving people should fight for it tooth and nail is hardly made clear.

As could be expected, the program contains a clear definition of "just" and "unjust" wars: "The policy of destabilization of *progressive regimes* in developing countries actually constitutes an aggression, waged by psychological, economic, political, and other means, including armed intervention." However, similar acts against "racist and fascist" regimes are quite justified because the mere existence of non-progressive regimes "is abhorrent to the conscience of humankind." Accordingly, the sale of arms to these "abhorrent" countries should be banned, but nothing need restrain the peace-loving from selling arms to "progressive" regimes and to "liberation movements."

And, of course, there are directives to the mass media, which "must serve the cause of peace and not the military-industrial

complex by confusing public opinion with lies and disinformation."
(In other words, the media should not report on the Soviet arms
build-up.) A similar directive is issued to those "who bear responsibility for educating a new generation."

The program further specifies precisely which events and campaigns to undertake, and designates weeks for the collection of
signatures on various petitions all around the world. It constantly
emphasizes the urgent need for "further intensification of actions
against the deployment of the new U.S. weapons of mass annihilation in Western Europe" and plans for "strengthening and
broadening of national movements into a worldwide network of
peace organizations."

It is not possible here to discuss all the details of this remarkable
document. It simply introduces each and every aspect of Soviet
foreign policy wrapped around with the phraseology of peace. Not
surprisingly, therefore, it includes Afghanistan under the guise of a
"week of solidarity, with special emphasis on support for a political
settlement as proposed by the Afghan government." For Ethiopia
it proposes "a week of solidarity with the Ethiopian revolution"
and "support for the struggle of the Ethiopian people against
imperialist and reactionary conspiracies and plans in the Horn of
Africa." For Kampuchea there should be an "international campaign of solidarity with the government and people of Kampuchea
led by the National United Front for National Salvation and an
international campaign for recognition of the People's Revolutionary Council of Kampuchea and the seating of its representatives in the U.N.; exposure of the conspiracies of the Peking
hegemonists who are working in collusion with the U.S. imperialists against Kampuchea." For Israel: "Support for the peace
forces in Israel in their struggle for the complete withdrawal of
Israel from the occupied territories and for the realization of the
inalienable national rights of the Palestinian people." Whereas for
the Middle East in general: a "campaign of solidarity with the Arab
peoples in their struggle to liquidate the political and military
consequences of the Camp David and Washington accords; solidarity actions with Libya against the threats of aggression by the
Egyptian regime and U.S. imperialism." As for the United States,

even in so totally pro-Soviet a document as this the instruction to
campaign for the "release of political prisoners in the United States
of America" reads like a bad joke. Clearly, the love of peace dulls
the sense of humor. The only countries where violations of human
rights are recognized by the unanimous vote of 2,260 delegates
from 137 countries are: Bolivia, Chile, El Salvador, Guatemala,
Haiti, Israel, Paraguay, Uruguay, Indonesia, South Korea, Northern Ireland, and the United States. Has the world not undergone a
remarkable improvement?

After the successful adoption of this program, what followed
was simple. Returning from Sofia, the enthusiastic delegates threw
themselves into a hectic round of implementing the program,
pressing for appropriate resolutions, actions, and commitments in
each of their respective organizations (*Pravda*, November 5,
1980). An additional impetus was given to the campaign by an
endorsement from the World Council of Churches at its meeting in
Dresden (East Germany) on August 28, 1981, thus committing a
huge number of adherents of the various Christian denominations
to following the Soviet line. And in no time hundreds of thousands
in the West came honestly to believe that they were out to save
world peace.

Moscow's 'Useful Idiots'

Well, is there any further need to explain why the Soviet Union is
so interested in the peace movement? There is a term in party
jargon coined by Lenin himself: "a useful idiot." Now, despite all
their blunders, senseless adventures, economic disasters, the
Polish crisis and the stubborn resistance of the Afghan peasants,
Reagan's rearmament plan, and U.N. resolutions, the Soviet rulers
have scored a spectacular victory: they have recruited millions of
useful idiots to implement their bankrupt foreign policy. They are
no longer isolated, and there is still a big question as to whether the
Americans will be allowed to place missiles in Europe.

True enough, the American economy is vastly more productive
and efficient than the Soviet, but the Americans don't have a
weapon like the "struggle for peace." True again, this peace

movement will be expensive for the Soviet people (the meeting in Bulgaria alone must have cost them millions, to say nothing of subsidizing all peace activists on those jaunts to the best Soviet resorts; the cost of running this worldwide campaign must be simply astronomical). Still, it is cheaper than another round of the arms race, let alone the cost of maintaining a priceless military superiority. And the results will be long-lasting.

Mind you, we are into only the second year of a planned ten-year "struggle for peace." Within a few years, the whole earth will be trembling under the marching feet of the useful idiots, for their resources are inexhaustible.

I remember in the fifties, when the previous peace campaign was still in full swing, there was a popular joke which people in the Soviet Union whispered to each other: "A Jew came to his rabbi and asked: 'Rabbi, you are a very wise man. Tell me, is there going to be a war?' 'There will be no war,' replied the rabbi, 'but there will be such a struggle for peace that no stone will be left standing.' "

One of the most serious mistakes of the Western peace movement and of its ideologists is the obdurate refusal to understand the nature of the Soviet regime, and the concomitant effort to lift the question of peace out of the context of the broader problem of East-West relations. After several decades of listening to what they believe to be "anti-Communist propaganda," they have simply got "fed up with it." They ascribe everything they hear about the East to a "cold-war-type brainwashing," and make no attempt to distinguish what is true from what is not. This attitude, which I can only describe as a combination of ignorance and arrogance, makes them an easy target for any pseudo-theory (or outright Soviet propaganda) that happens to be fashionable at any given moment. Besides, baffled by endless and contradictory arguments among the "specialists" about the nature of the Soviet system, the leaders of the peace movement believe they have found a "new approach" which makes the entire problem irrelevant.

A few months ago in England, I attended a public debate on the problem of unilateral disarmament. The leader of a big peace group opened his speech by saying that from his standpoint, it is irrelevant who is the aggressor and who the victim. He said: "It is like when two boys have a fight in the churchyard. It is impossible to find out who started the fight, nor is there any need to do so. What we should do is to stop them."

Who Is the Aggressor?

This metaphor reflects very well the prevailing attitude among peace-movement members. They believe they have gotten around a baffling problem, whereas they have in fact inadvertently adopted the concept of the "normal opponent." From the "churchyard" standpoint, the present conflict seems very ordinary: two bullies have become so embittered by their prolonged quarrel—in which anyway the essence of the disagreement has been lost or forgotten—that they are quite prepared to kill each other and everybody else around. They are temporarily insane, mad, but are basically normal human beings. Pride and fury will not permit them to come to their senses, unless we, the sane people around them, are prepared to intervene. Let us make them talk to one another, let us pin down their hands, let us distract them from their quarrel. We cannot, to be sure, pin down the hands of one of them. Then, in the best Christian tradition, let us make the other repent, in all good Christian humility. Let us disarm him to convince his adversary of his peaceful intentions. Let us turn the other cheek. Sooner or later the other will come to feel ashamed.

This view sums up exactly what I mean by a combination of ignorance and arrogance. Indeed, if we look upon the world from the "churchyard" standpoint, there probably is no need to find out who is the aggressor and who the victim. There is no need for police or armed forces. All we can see is a row of graves with the dead lying orderly in them and a couple of children quarreling with each other. Unfortunately, outside the church walls there is a bigger and far more dangerous world with gangsters, murderers, rapists, and other perverse characters.

Needless to say, this churchyard model simply does not merit serious consideration. Unfortunately, it is a widespread belief (and not only within the peace movement) that the Soviet government, like any other government, is preoccupied with the well-being of its people, and will therefore be eager to reduce military expenditures. This notion comes so naturally to our peacemakers that they just do not notice they have taken on a view of the Soviet system which is both very old and unquestionably wrong. If they only took the trouble to study a little Soviet history, they would know immediately how misleading this seemingly natural view is. Not only are the Soviet rulers indifferent to the living condition of their populace, they *deliberately* keep it low; on the other hand, disarmament (irrespective of the problem of well-being) would lead very rapidly to the collapse of the Soviet empire.

But let us take an example relevant to the present discussion. Let us take the key question: why is the Soviet Union so aggressive, so eager to expand? We see how many schools of thought there are among those studying the problem (and we see, too, how all of them are wrong).

Soviet Expansionism as 'Colonialism'

There are some people who believe that the present Soviet expansionism is just a continuation of the Russian pre-revolutionary colonial policy. In other words, it is a bad legacy. Indeed, this notion about Soviet expansionism was the dominant one for a very long time—and still is in some quarters. In line with it, there have been repeated attempts to offer the Soviets a division of the world into spheres of influence. We owe to it the Yalta agreement, the Potsdam agreement, and assorted other disasters. Each time the Soviets have accepted the division into spheres of influence, and each time they have violated it. Is this because they need more mineral resources, more territory, a wider market for their goods? No. Their own territory is undeveloped, their own mineral resources are in the earth, they do not have enough goods for their own internal market. There are no useful mineral deposits in Cuba or Afghanistan. There is no Russian national interest in Angola or Vietnam. In fact, these new "colonies" cost the Soviet people many millions of dollars a day apiece. So, Soviet policy is no classical case of colonialism.

Then there is another theory, far more pernicious because much more widely accepted and because to reject it one needs a real knowledge of Soviet life. I mean the theory according to which Soviet aggressiveness is the result of the fear of hostile encirclement. The proponents of this theory argue that Russian history, particularly the history of repeated invasions of Russian territory within the last century, has made the Russian people almost paranoid about an external threat.

This theory sounds very scientific because many facts may be cited to back it up. Still, it is no more than a shrewd combination of obvious lies, wrong interpretations, and very perfunctory knowledge. It is mainly based on an overestimation of the importance of history for any given nation and on an oversimplification of the Soviet system.

To begin with, there is an obvious lie in this theory—that is, a deliberate confusion between the people and the government in the U.S.S.R. Those who know the Soviet system only moderately well may still need to be reminded that the people have no privilege of representation in the government—that is, have no free elections. Thus, the government does not reflect the feelings of the population. So if we are to believe that the population is frightened by the long history of invasions, the government has no reason to share these fears. The Soviet government, with its vast and omnipresent intelligence system, is extremely well informed about every move and every smallest intention of the West (anyway not very difficult to achieve in view of the remarkable openness of Western societies). By 1978-79, when their arms build-up was at a high pitch, whom were they supposed to be so afraid of? Their great friend, the French President Giscard? Or their even better friend in West Germany, Willy Brandt? Britain, with its puny armed forces (and ongoing discussion on unilateral disarmament), or perhaps Nixon and Carter, who between them shelved all the major armament programs? Japan, which has no army at all?

Clearly the Soviet government had no reason to be frightened. In fact, the theory of Soviet paranoia does not imply a frightened government, but rather a frightened *nation*. In a "normal" country this might drive the government to become aggressive. But in the

Soviet Union the people mean nothing and have no way of pressuring their government to do anything. They would not be allowed to voice any fears. So, who is so frightened in the Soviet Union? Besides, as far as the rulers are concerned, their own experience of war, World War II, could not frighten them for a very simple reason: they won the war. Can you show me any victorious general who is so afraid of war as to become paranoid? The psychology of Soviet rulers is in any case totally different.

One need only look at a map of the world to see how ridiculous this theory is. Can we honestly believe that the poor Communists in the Kremlin are so frightened that they must protect themselves by sending their troops to Cuba and Cuban troops to Angola? By sending military equipment and advisers to Ethiopia and Vietnam and then by sending Vietnamese troops to Kampuchea? Take another look at that map: it is not at all obvious that the U.S.S.R. is encircled by hostile powers. Rather the other way around: it is the Western world that is encircled by the hostile hordes of the Communists. Well, if their paranoia can be satisfied only by surrendering the whole world to their control, what difference can it make to us whether they act out of fear or out of endemic aggressiveness?

Finally, and most importantly for an understanding of this pernicious theory, is the fact that it was invented by the Kremlin propaganda experts. It was very successfully exploited in the years of détente, when Western governments, acting under its influence, deliberately permitted the Soviets to achieve military superiority. They would probably deny it now, but I remember very well the discussions of that period. The argument of the ideologists of détente was that once the Soviets caught up, they would relax; this would in turn lead to the internal as well as external relaxation of the Communist regime, i.e., to *liberalization*. The results of this brilliant experiment we can see now.

The Soviet population, too, has been subjected, day after day for sixty-five years, to an intense propaganda campaign about this putative "hostile encirclement." The Communist rulers unscrupulously exploit the tragedy of the Soviet people in World War II for the purpose of justifying both their oppressive regime and their monstrous military spending. They try their best to instill into the people a pathological fear of the "capitalist world." Fortunately, the people are sane enough to laugh at the very idea. Thus, contrary to this theory, there is no paranoid population demanding to be protected in the Soviet Union, despite the best efforts of a perfectly sober and cruel government.

What Motivates Moscow

No, it is not the fear of invasion or a World War II hangover that has driven the Soviet rulers to wage an undeclared war against the whole world for half a century now. It is their commitment—repeated quite openly every five years at each Party Congress since the beginning of this century—to support the "forces of progress and socialism," to support "liberation movements," everywhere.

Are we then to assume that the Soviet leadership consists of fanatics aiming at global control? Even such a model, crazy as it might sound, still imputes too much "normality" to the Soviet leaders. Or, more precisely, it is too big a simplification. This theory, too—fortunately for us—does not fit a number of the facts. Paradoxically, none of the present Communist leaders believes any longer in Communist doctrine. Fortunately, because no real fanatic would ever tolerate the destruction of the object of his obsession. He would rather witness the destruction of the entire world.

The Soviet rulers are a totally cynical lot, much more preoccupied with their own privileges and pleasures than with Marxist ideas. They probably hate Communist dogma more than any Western capitalist. Moreover, the majority of the Soviet people are as cynical as their leaders. There are many more sincere Communists to be found in the West than in the U.S.S.R.

But this fact has also created false hopes among Western politicians and the public. The same false hopes encouraged by the theory of encirclement—that it will be possible to treat the Soviets as normal partners at last, that it will be possible to negotiate, to cooperate, and to relax. Both theories lead equally to the same mistaken policy.

So what is the truth about the damned Soviet system?

Certainly, there was a period when the Soviet leaders were Communist fanatics, ready to sacrifice the whole world to their faith. There was a period, too, when at least some part of the population was prepared to greet this new idea with considerable enthusiasm. The people of my country, I suppose, could be excused for their delusion, because Communism was indeed a new idea and one that might be thought by the inexperienced to appeal to the best qualities in human nature. Is it after all not a worthy purpose, to secure unalloyed happiness for all future generations, to liberate and unite the whole of mankind? Naturally, such a thing will not be easy, but it is worth a great deal of sacrifice to achieve. Just as naturally there will be many selfish people to oppose it and we should learn to be ruthless with them. Only millions of individual wills fused into a single invincible "we," united by the iron fist of a Leader, can achieve so difficult an end.

This period of ecstasy, however, was very short-lived. One by one, the various elements of the Soviet population cooled down, sobered up, and then could not believe in their own former enthusiasm. The besieged minority reacted to this desertion of the public by becoming even more ruthless and single-minded: "We will make them happy against their will; their children will be grateful to us." I will not describe the mass slaughter that resulted from this great determination. It has been described many times. A terrorized majority obeyed with sham enthusiasm, because it was a crime to look gloomy. But underneath there was a silent, passive resistance. The minority of "believers" over time became simply a ruling clique which had lost its ideals in the constant fight for survival, in corruption, and in its abuses of power and its privileges. The ensuing political situation can best be described as a latent civil war in which a kind of balance has been maintained by political terror.

In this way the Soviet Union reached a condition in which absolute power was exercised by absolutely cynical people over absolutely cynical people, each side vociferously assuring the other that they were all still sincerely building an ideal future society. But the ideology exists now almost as in a work of science fiction: it has separated itself from its substratum and has petrified in the structure of the society. It has become an institution in which nobody (not even the top executive) is allowed verbally to deviate from the dead dogma. The will of millions is still being taken from them and welded into the iron fist of abstraction.

There is practically no free human being inside the entire country. The state—the only employer—will not allow anyone to be financially independent—as indeed no independence of any kind will be tolerated. Everybody must be carrying out a useful task, performing a needed function. Several nationwide networks of security and secret police spy first on each other and then together on everybody else. Such a system has created a new type of man, who thinks one thing, publicly expresses another, and does a third.

The enormous inertia of this system is not surprising. There is no internal "class enemy"any more; there is no need to terrorize so many millions. Still, there are huge concentration camps, because they have become an integral part of the country's economic, political, and spiritual life. Nobody believes now in the ultimate victory of Communism in the world, but the policy of external subversion and the promotion of "socialist forces" everywhere has become an integral part of the state machinery. The system rules the people.

Beyond inertia, there is something else, something even more decisive: the instinct of self-preservation of the ruling clique. Once you are riding a tiger, it is difficult to jump off. Any attempt at internal liberalization might prove fatal. If the central power were to weaken, the sheer amount of hatred accumulated within the population for these sixty-five years of the socialist experiment would be so dangerous, the results of any reform so unpredictable—and, above all, the power, the fabulous privileges, the very physical survival of the ruling clique would become so tenuous—that one would be mad to expect the Soviet leaders to play with liberal ideas. Only the imminent threat of total collapse might force them to introduce internal reforms.

The Link Between Oppression and Aggression

The two sides of the Soviet regime—internal oppression and external aggression—are inseparably interlocked, creating a sort of vicious circle. The more the regime becomes rotten inside, the more pains are taken by its leaders to present a formidable façade to the outside world. They need international tension as a thief needs the darkness of the night. In the political climate of latent civil war, given the enormous and senseless sacrifices of the last fifty years, the constant economic difficulties, and the lack of basic rights—not to mention, again, the extraordinary privileges enjoyed by the ruling clique—the only hope for stability lies in the need to cope with an external threat: "hostile encirclement" and the subversive activity of "world imperialism." In this artificially created state of war, the worker's demand for a better deal, or a captive nation's demand for its independence, can then be treated as an act of subversion, "playing into the hands of the enemy."

Nor is it enough to create a devil in order to maintain one's religious zeal. This imaginary enemy must be defeated over and over again or there will be the risk that he will seduce you. American "imperialism" must be defeated at any cost, and the liberation of proletarians in the capitalist countries must be promoted by all means. The failure to support a "friendly government," to establish Communist rule in a new country, will immediately be perceived as a weakening of Soviet power, and therefore an encouragement to the sullen and embittered population at home. Any failure of the Soviet international adventure may thus trigger a chain reaction leading to the ultimate collapse of the Soviet rulers. This is why they cannot allow a popular uprising in Hungary, a "Prague Spring" in Czechoslovakia, an anti-Communist "Holy War" in Afghanistan, or an independent alternative center of power in Poland. Immediate repercussions would be felt in all the other countries of the socialist camp as well as in the Ukraine, the Baltic states, Central Asia, and other occupied territories. The scenario of aggression is depressingly uniform. First, the Soviets undermine a democratic state, helping the friendly "progressive forces" come to power. Next, they have to save their bankrupt "progressive" friends, when the resistance of the population threatens to overthrow them.

Are they frightened to the point of aggressiveness? Yes, but not by your piles of hardware, not by your clumsy attempts at defense. They are frightened by their own people, because they know the end is inevitable. That is why they must score victory after victory over the "hostile encirclement." Behind every victory is a very simple message addressed to their own enslaved population: "Look, we are still very strong and nobody dares to challenges our might."

If they are afraid of you, it is because they are afraid of your freedom and your prosperity. They cannot tolerate a democratic state close to their borders (and then, close to the borders of their buffer-states), because a bad example of thriving democracy so close at hand might prove to be too provocative.

The Peril of Unilateral Disarmament

Knowing all this, let us ask ourselves a question: what would happen if the West were to disarm unilaterally? Could the Soviets follow suit? Certainly not. It would mean the rapid disintegration of their empire and a general collapse of their power. Does this mean they will simply roll over the now defenseless Western countries? Again, the answer is: no. They don't need your territory, which would be difficult to hold anyway. Above all, where would they acquire goods, technology, credits, grain, and the like, if they were to impose on you their inefficient economic system? They need you in the way China needs Hong Kong. *But from that very moment you will gradually begin to lose your freedom, being exposed to constant and unrestrained Soviet blackmail.*

You may like or dislike your trade unions, but would you like them to have to consider a possibility of foreign invasion every time they wanted to declare a strike—as Solidarity had to do in Poland for eighteen months? You make like or dislike your mass media, but would you like to see the self-censorship of your press in order to avoid an angry reaction by a powerful neighbor—as in Finland? You may like or dislike your system of representation, but at least you are free to elect those whom you choose without considering the desires of a foreign power. Nobody threatens to come into your country and impose a government of its choosing—as in Afghanistan. The nature of the Soviet system is such that it can never be satisfied until you are similar to them and are under their control.

So, we come to a very important conclusion: the issue now is not "peace versus war," but rather "freedom versus slavery." Peace and freedom appear to be inseparable, and the old formula "Better red than dead" is simply fatuous. Those who live by it will be both red *and* dead. Whether we like it or not, there will be no peace in our world, no relaxation of international tension, no fruitful cooperation between East and West, until the Soviet internal system changes drastically.

Has this simple and self-evident truth ever been understood by Western decision-makers? I doubt it. In a way, I can share some of the concern of the peace movement. Because for the West to react stereotypically by increasing military spending and stockpiling new hardware every time the Soviet instability-aggression complex manifests itself is simply to miss the target. At any rate, it is not enough. It is not going to change the Soviet system. It is not going to prevent Soviet expansion, especially in the Third World. Soviet ideological warfare is far shrewder than a big nuclear bludgeon. Would we, for instance, consider a nuclear bombardment if tomorrow there were to be a revolt of various tribes in Pakistan, instigated by Moscow? Or a Communist takeover in Iran?

There are plenty of "natural" troubles in the world, brought on by local conditions. But the influence of Moscow immediately turns them into major strategic problems. It would be senseless to try to solve all such problems by military means all over the globe. Simple logic suggests that we must deal first of all with the *source* of the world's major trouble—i.e., the Soviet system. We must find an effective way to help the Soviet population in its struggle for change. After all, they are our biggest ally.

Unfortunately, this has so far never been appreciated by the West, which has instead been continuously strengthening the Soviet system by credits, trade, technology. Why should the Soviets bother to introduce any internal reforms if their inefficient economy is periodically saved by the West? The West is still rich enough to help them out, and Siberia is also rich enough in turn to sell natural gas, gold, diamonds.

We may shake with indignation whenever we hear about the Soviet invasion of yet another country. We hate these little obedient soldiers, ever ready to do whatever they are told. Are they robots? But what do we propose that they should do? Do we honestly expect them to rebel and face a firing squad, while the entire world continues to provide their executioners with goods, credits, and modern technology? Don't we demand of them much more than we demand of ourselves? Somewhere, somehow, this vicious circle must be broken, if we are to survive as human beings. Why not start where it is easier?

There are 90,000 of these "robots" trapped in Afghanistan at this very moment. They cannot rebel because they will be shot down. Even so, there are occasional rebellions (and executions). They cannot desert, because they will either be killed in the process or, if they are lucky and manage to reach Pakistan, the Pakistani authorities will return them to the Soviet command (that is, again, to the firing squad). Does any government try to help them? No. Instead, several European governments have decided to buy Soviet natural gas, perhaps the very same gas that is being pumped out of Afghanistan by the Soviet occupation authorities as compensation for "liberating" Afghanistan.

There is a lot of noise about Poland right now. A lot of noise, and a lot of smoke screens. But does any government sacrifice anything? After issuing thunderous condemnations, the European governments decide not to apply economic sanctions against the Eastern bloc, because sanctions would "harm us, probably, more than them." Why should you establish the kind of relations that only make you more vulnerable than the enemy? Why do you continue to sign new agreements of the same type (natural gas, for example)? The American banks recently decided to cover the huge Polish deficit because the "bankruptcy of Poland would undermine the world financial system." What would happen, I wonder, if tomorrow the Soviet-bloc countries were to refuse to pay their debts and to suspend all trade?

This is what the struggle for peace and freedom boils down to: the people in the East should sacrifice their lives, but you should not sacrifice your profits. Small wonder that the Polish army does not rebel.

In fact, the imposition of economic sanctions on the Polish military junta and on their Soviet masters is not just a possible step; it is the actual *obligation* of the Western countries under the terms of the Helsinki agreement. A direct link among security, economic cooperation, and the observance of human rights is the very essence of this agreement. If that is forgotten now, of what point is all the noise lately heard from Madrid?

To tell the truth, I do not believe that any of it has been forgotten. Neither do I believe that the Western banks, industrialists, and governments are so "stupid" as to tie themselves to the Eastern chariot wheels by mistake. It is their deliberate policy, overtly articulated in the time of détente, and covertly now. Moreover, it is their philosophy. They love stability, these bankers and businessmen. And they are much against any resistance movement in the Communist countries, very much against any prospect of liberation for the enslaved nations of the East. They are the greatest peace-lovers of all, far more powerful than all those crowds on the streets of the European capitals. Thanks to them, we descend slowly into the Age of Darkness.

This article is not addressed to the bankers, or to the governments. I do not expect any help from them. In spite of all the harsh words used in it, I wish it to be read by sincere people who are seriously concerned with the problems of peace and freedom. They will probably dislike many of the things I have said here. I hope, however, that they will understand its main point: that peace has never been preserved by a hysterical desire to survive at any price. Nor has it ever been promoted by catchy phrases and cheap slogans. There are 400 million people in the East whose freedom was stolen from them and whose existence is miserable. It so happens that peace is impossible while they remain enslaved, and only with them (not with their executioners) should you work to secure real peace in our world.

Your recent mass peace demonstrations were disastrous, because in them you identified yourselves, willingly or unwillingly, with the rulers of the Eastern countries. To make broad alliances with any public (or governmental) forces just for the sake of power is a tremendous mistake. This mistake must be corrected if we are to live in peace and freedom. We should know who are our friends and who are our enemies. The fate of Solidarity should open our eyes.

13. Moscow's Response to U.S. 'Saber-Rattling'

By BORIS PONOMAREV

Focus
Boris Ponomarev is a member of the Soviet Politburo who is responsible for contacts with foreign Communist parties as well as for Soviet intelligence. He was formerly an official in the old Comintern, the Soviet-dominated council of fraternal Communist parties. In the article from which this selection is taken, Ponomarev describes the international significance of the Twenty-sixth Congress of the Soviet Communist party (held in 1981).

Ponomarev asserts that the Western peace movement is a result of "saber-rattling" by the U.S. government: "the turbid stream of militarist hysteria has become increasingly acute in line with the escalation of the aggressive speeches and actions of those who oppose détente." American militarism and madness contrast sharply with the "calm, assured, balanced nature" of the Soviet Communist party and its "concrete platform for the defense of peace corresponding to the interests and cherished hopes of all mankind," according to Ponomarev.

"The foreign policy initiatives of the Twenty-sixth Congress," he says, "imparted a powerful stimulus to the upsurge of the activity of peace-loving forces worldwide. The struggle over foreign policy questions between different political parties in the West and within these parties has been stepped up." Ponomarev goes on to boast about successful Soviet efforts in the British Labor party and among certain leaders of the German Social Democratic party.

He concludes that "the entire package of the U.S.S.R.'s peace-loving proposals" has served as a "convincing refutation of the false fable of the 'Soviet military threat.'" Ponomarev's article confirms much of what Barron (selection 10), the Isaacs (selection 11), and Bukovsky (selection 12) have said.

Boris Ponomarev is secretary of the Central Committee of the Communist Party of the Soviet Union and a member of the Politburo.

A S A COUNTERWEIGHT TO the destructive, negative concepts and actions of the forces pursuing a "Second Cold War" policy, the Twenty-sixth Congress put forth a concrete platform for the defense of peace corresponding to the interests and cherished hopes of all mankind. "There is currently no more important task on the international plane for our party, our people, and all the peoples of the world than the defense of peace." . . .

What are the special features of the Twenty-sixth Congress's foreign policy initiatives that have made them the center of present-day international life?

First, their timeliness and their suitability to the requirements ensuing from the evolved situation and their complete conformity with the demands of the moment. The objective need for the creation of a powerful barrier in the way of the turbid stream of militarist hysteria has become increasingly acute in line with the escalation of the aggressive speeches and actions of those who oppose détente. . . .

The calm, assured, balanced nature of the Communist Party of the Soviet Union (CPSU) Central Committee report made a particularly striking and positive impression against the background of the saber-rattling in Washington and NATO. And if the Soviet Union's peace-loving program caused confusion, as eyewitnesses report, in the camp of the aggressive forces, all peace-loving circles and realistic figures experienced—in their own words—a feeling of relief apropos of the fate of peace. . . .

Second, the world community is noting the unshakable, consistent resolve of the CPSU to do everything possible to lead the peoples away from the threat of nuclear war and to preserve peace in the world. "There is a desire to impress upon people that a nuclear war can be limited and to reconcile them to the idea of the

Reprinted by permission from the Summer 1981 issue of *Strategic Review* (published by the United States Strategic Institute).

permissibility of such a war," Comrade L. I. Brezhnev's report says. "But this is an out-and-out deception of the peoples! For a 'limited' nuclear war, according to American concepts, in, say, Europe, would mean at the very outset the sure destruction of European civilization. And the United States itself, of course, would not be able to remain untouched by the flames of war."

The CPSU combines emphatic condemnation of the plans to unleash a nuclear war with the categorical condemnation of attempts to achieve military superiority. "Attempting to outdo each other in an arms race and counting on victory in a nuclear war are a dangerous madness," Comrade L. I. Brezhnev said. Such an assessment is shared by all honest people who aspire to peace in the world, including those who are far from a Communist philosophy of life.

The foreign policy initiatives of the Twenty-sixth Congress imparted a powerful stimulus to the upsurge of the activity of peace-loving forces worldwide. The struggle over foreign policy questions between different political parties in the West and within these parties has been stepped up. The impressive arguments expressed at the Congress buttress the positions of those who, guided by the interests of national security and the preservation of peace, oppose the deployment of new American missiles and neutron weapons in the West European countries. . . .

A number of personalities in the social democratic parties observe that the peace initiatives put forward by the Twenty-sixth CPSU Congress are contributing to the struggle against the conservative, militarist forces inspired by the new U.S. administration. Members of the British Labor party adopted a special resolution in support of the new peace initiatives of the Soviet Union. A considerable proportion of Social Democrats and certain Social Democratic Party (SPD) personalities in the Federal Republic of Germany (FRG) expressed a positive view of the Soviet proposals. SPD Chairman Willy Brandt observed that the reaction to L. I. Brezhnev's report refutes the viewpoint of those who, in past months, have constantly claimed that a new stage in the arms race between East and West is absolutely inevitable.

"Modern social democracy," Comrade L. I. Brezhnev's report said, "has considerable political weight. It could do more to defend the people's vital interests and primarily to strengthen peace, improve the international situation and repulse fascism and racism and reaction's offensive against the working people's political rights." The propositions expressed from the high tribune of the Congress concerning the role of social democracy are undoubtedly a subject for serious contemplation by both the leading personalities and ordinary members of the social democratic parties. Both the great possibilities of social democracy and its great historical responsibility for the cause of peace and the people's security were again emphasized. Once again, this century's Communists extend their hands to social democrats in a joint struggle to save mankind from new wars of destruction and to save peace.

Third, it is important to note that the Soviet Union is displaying maximum flexibility in the search for ways and means of solving the problem of preventing nuclear war. . . .

The readiness for a dialogue with the United States expressed in the CPSU Central Committee report and the proposition that meetings at the highest level are the decisive element here drew a very broad response. The U.S.S.R.'s peace-loving proposals and the world public movement in support of them pose a dilemma for America's ruling circles: either to approach these proposals positively or show to the whole world their disregard for the people's cherished hopes and to appear as warmongers. . . .

Anti-war sentiment in the West European countries has increased. Circles advocating a policy of détente . . . have come to life in the United States itself. A number of prominent figures have vigorously supported the idea of a Soviet-American dialogue. . . .

The entire package of the Soviet Union's peace-loving proposals serves as a convincing refutation of the false fable of the "Soviet military threat." In fact, a country which has such a far-reaching program of peaceful construction, economic growth, and increased well-being for the people, a country which puts forward important proposals to consolidate peace and halt the arms race, and which actively struggles for these proposals, such a country cannot fail to want peace. It needs neither an arms race nor international tension, and it is interested in mutually profitable and broad cooperation with other states, and not in expansion and armed confrontation. . . .

The Twenty-sixth CPSU Congress confirmed our party's invariable adherence to the cause of the people's social and national liberation and its solidarity with the liberation movement.

This solidarity of friends is helping the Soviet people tackle the tasks of building Communism and peace-loving foreign policy. The representatives of the Communist and other progressive parties emphatically repudiated anti-Sovietism, which is particularly important in the present conditions of the exacerbation of the confrontation of the two systems. Their speeches pursued an entirely correct idea, namely, that repudiation of anti-Sovietism is the fundamental criterion of a class, internationalist position. On the basis of specific examples, many speakers showed the dangerous nature of Beijing's intrigues aimed at subverting the Communist and entire revolutionary-liberation movement.

The twenty-sixth CPSU Congress showed once again how baseless is the talk of proletarianism being "outdated" and of the need to replace it with some "new" internationalism. The entire work of the Congress and the speeches of the representatives of the fraternal parties and the delegations of revolutionary-democratic and other progressive parties and movements are striking testimony to the vitality of proletarian internationalism, its constant enrichment and development, and its capacity for "absorbing" and embracing increasingly new social forces actively involved in the revolutionary transformation of the world.

14. Why Peace Movements Fail

By JAMES CLOTFELTER

Focus Drawing on the history of peace movements since 1900, the author (who is sympathetic to them) says there are several unavoidable reasons and seven "possibly avoidable" reasons why such movements fail to achieve their objectives.

The seven "possibly avoidable" reasons for failure are: (1) Peace movements are not seen as reflecting the basic values of a society. (2) They identify with such widely approved national symbols and themes that they deny themselves a clear identity. (3) They focus on the past, the present, or the distant future, rather than on the immediate future. (4) They are unable or unwilling to convince people that wars hurt economies. (5) They fail to bridge class or ideological divisions. (6) They become identified with threatening symbols unrelated to peace. (7) They become identified with the appeasement of national adversaries.

Other essays in this volume suggest that reasons 1, 6, and 7 may explain why the peace movement of 1981-82 has been able to attract only a small minority of the population in the United States or Western Europe, though its influence has clearly been broader than the numbers directly involved.

Another more subjective reason why peace crusades fail, Clotfelter says, is their tendency to dwell on fear rather than hope. Here he strikes at the heart of the case developed by Jonathan Schell (selection 15) and others motivated by an essentially apocalyptic premise. Focusing on the consequences of nuclear war "tends to stimulate anxiety without providing a constructive release for that anxiety."

James Clotfelter is professor of political science at the University of North Carolina at Greensboro.

PEACE MOVEMENTS OF the twentieth century generally have been unable to achieve their immediate objectives, and have had even less impact on long-term public policy. Wars ultimately end, but rarely because of the work of peace movements. These movements in the United States and Europe have failed because they lack numbers, influence, and access to power, or because they lack the programs to hold both popular and elite support. Why is this so?

Some problems facing national peace movements, I would argue, are unavoidable and thus not worth much attention. One is their inability to reconcile the fact that they are asking a *nation* for action with the fact that the action has *international* dimensions. There is no way around this problem, but it confronts proponents of military solutions as well. A second inevitable weakness of peace movements is their factionalism. I see no cure for this ill; it must be endured where it is troublesome, and exploited where it is helpful. Third, it is claimed that the peace movement is all heart and no head, that it is weak on realistic analysis. Peace activists should avoid the purely sentimental and the wildly hyperbolic. Regardless of their efforts at rigor, however, peace activists will ultimately call on people to make decisions with their hearts as well as their heads.

A look at seven possibly avoidable causes for the failure of peace movements might suggest new approaches for the future. The first two are the extremes of the continuum of consonance with national values. The third is the time perspective. The last four relate to appeals and symbols used by or forced on the movement.

1. *Peace movements fail because they are not seen as reflecting the basic values of a society.* This was the case with the pre-1914 movement in Germany, widely identified as foreign in its spirit and impetus. This hazard can never be entirely eliminated, because

Reprinted with adaptations by permission from the July 21-28, 1982, issue of *The Christian Century* (© 1982 by the Christian Century Foundation).

peacemaking *is* foreign to some values of all nations. There are indigenous peace themes in the history of the English-speaking countries that did not exist in Germany, but the American and English themes are those of a tolerated minority rather than of the dominant culture.

2. *Peace movements fail because they identify with such widely approved national symbols and themes as to deny themselves a clear identity.* This situation describes the pre-1914 peace movement in the United States. Presidents Taft and Wilson and five secretaries of state between 1905 and 1914 were members of peace societies. Yet in 1917, when the United States entered the European war, only a small number of socialists, social reformers, and religious pacifists maintained that a peace movement must of necessity oppose war.

3. *Peace movements fail because they focus on the past, the present, or the distant future, rather than the intermediate future.* Each time perspective has its own hazards. But I am asserting, without benefit here of evidence, that the focus should be on the intermediate future: later than next year, sooner than the withering away of the state.

Leaders of peace organizations, like military generals, often prepare to fight the previous war. The American peace movement of the 1930s benefited from a retrospective distaste for the Great War of 1914-18. William Allen White spoke for many Americans in the thirties when he warned: "The next war will see the same hurrah and the same bowwow of the big dogs to get the little dogs to go out and follow the blood scent and get their entrails tangled in the barbed wire." Yet, even as the movement restated the evils of the Great War, some peace elements came to feel that they were irrelevant to the European situation of the late 1930s, while others found themselves uncomfortably allied with isolationists at home. The peace testimony of the churches was muted. Soon the war effort was attracting many a William Allen White.

Movements with immediate goals sometimes achieve those goals. American opposition to atmospheric nuclear testing helped make possible the 1963 partial test-ban treaty. So much of the energy of the movement had focused on that immediate goal, however, that when the treaty was ratified, public support could not be mobilized for a next step. Immediate goals often are modest ones, and the linkage with larger goals may not be clear.

Furthermore, linkages with immediate and intermediate goals may not be clear when a peace movement's focus is on the distant future, as in the pre-1914 European socialists' opposition to "capitalists' wars." The European socialists had not sufficiently considered the power of nationalism, nor had they built mechanisms able to withstand that power. The opposition to war evaporated in 1914, and soon French proletarians were killing German proletarians and vice versa.

4. *Peace movements fail because they are unable, or unwilling, to convince people that wars hurt economies.* "Business pacifism" was part of pre-1914 peace sentiment in the United States and Western Europe. Norman Angell, in *The Great Illusion,* argued that wars destroy prosperity, even for the victor. As the president of the National Association of Manufacturers (U.S.) commented, "Dead men buy no clothes." After World War II, which stimulated the American economy and created jobs, "business pacifism" was almost obliterated in America, and President Eisenhower's identification of a "military-industrial complex" seemed to confirm that war is good for business. Yet the Vietnam war severely damaged the American economy, and by 1968 radical proposals on Vietnam were appearing in *Forbes* and the *Wall Street Journal.* Peace activists of the 1960s were slow to argue that war, although it benefits some, has a negative net effect on the economy. Perhaps they were reluctant to appeal to people's self-interest, or perhaps they were slow to believe that economic self-interest *could* work against war.

5. *Peace movements fail because they fail to bridge class and ideological divisions.* The class and ideological characteristics of peace activists are well known. Activists usually are from the middle class; in the United States they tend to be white, from the Northeast, or from large cities in the West and Midwest; women, college students, and "modernist" Protestant clergy have been conspicuously represented. In political ideology (except for pre-1914 America), peace movements have drawn disproportionately

from the radical left. None of these characteristics is inevitably associated with peacemaking. All are cause and effect of the minority status of peace movements.

6. *Peace movements fail because they become identified with threatening symbols unrelated to peace.* By 1967 the anti-war movement in America had become stereotyped as a band of long-haired, profane, pot-smoking kids in revolt against the older generation and its institutions. Whereas participants in the civil rights movement a few years earlier had combed their hair and curbed their tongues to present a positive public image, the anti-war activists sought to shock and in some cases to offend. The result was that while the Vietnam war was unpopular, the anti-war movement was even less popular—and the style of some activists may have deterred working-class and rural Americans from moving to an anti-war stance.

7. *Peace movements fail because they become identified with appeasement of national adversaries.* This charge often is made unjustly, but it remains a difficult one for peace activists to deal with. The pre-1914 German peace movement, when it was noticed at all, was attacked as a stooge for the English. The appeasement charge was particularly unjust at the time of World War II, for American peace activists had been outspoken critics of Hitler and of the Munich agreement. But if it was unjust to link peace work and appeasement in the forties, the suspicion was more understandable in the sixties, when some American anti-war activists made no effort to conceal their sympathies for an authoritarian regime in North Vietnam.

So much for what may be empirically verifiable. Other flaws in peace movements can be evaluated only subjectively. I am identifying two that frequently concern peace advocates. To the extent that these flaws exist, they are, I suggest, the most serious ones; however, they are now widely recognized. My first assertion below is conventional wisdom in 1982 in some circles, and the second reflects one of the oldest articles of Christian faith.

1. *Peace movements fail because they work for a "peace" too narrowly defined.* Too often in the past, peace has been defined as

order—as the absence of conflict, even as the absence of change. Given the inevitability and in some instances the desirability of conflict and change, this concept of peace fails on both empirical and normative grounds. The pre-1914 French, German, and American peace movements all possessed an unduly legalistic notion of what peace involved. The same could be said of the more respectable elements of the post-1945 movement in the United States. A better concept would be some variation of "peace with justice" (amply discussed in available literature).

2. *Peace movements fail because they dwell on fear rather than hope.* Just as peace movements need both optimism and pessimism to thrive, it is inevitable that in their appeals fear will be mixed with hope. But introducing fear in popular appeals is like introducing poison gas to a battlefield on a gusty day. Fear produces unstable and unpredictable results. In America between 1938 and 1941, for example, fear of war generated support for such disparate goals as peace, isolation, and military involvement.

The recent discovery of nuclear war by television and mass-circulation magazines, and efforts to publicize the consequences of nuclear war through Ground Zero and university teach-ins, have brought war concerns to a wider audience. The risk is that this attention will encourage fear without giving grounds for hope, that it will stimulate anxiety without providing a constructive release for that anxiety.

The fact that peace movements persist despite their failures is a tribute to the capacity of peace activists to sustain hope. Nonetheless, a study of the history of peace movements challenges one's ability to be optimistic. This review, loosely in the tradition of Lasswell's Garrison State and Dicken's Ghost of Christmas Future, uses historical trends to suggest the future that awaits us if we do not mend our ways.

I do not believe that we are in a unique era in which the past is irrelevant. The argument has been made that, just as the nuclear age has transformed the ways in which weapons can be used in pursuit of national interests, so it has altered the prospects for peace movements. However, nuclear weapons have not yet transformed our way of thinking about weapons, and so I doubt that peace movements can use this reason to ignore their past.

The tasks remain the same as always. People still need to be reached, still need to be convinced, to be moved. Worldwide vulnerability due to nuclear weapons does not in itself reach, convince, or move people. Such efforts are the tasks of peace movements.

PART THREE

The Apocalyptic Premise

15. *The Fate of the Earth*

By JONATHAN SCHELL

Focus   In his widely publicized book *The Fate of the Earth*, Jonathan Schell elaborates a simple thesis: the unleashing of the atom that made possible nuclear weapons now threatens planetary doom; salvation requires a new man and a new politics. His apocalyptic vision of nuclear catastrophe leads him to a utopian vision of a new world. Nuclear arms, violence, and the nation-state itself must be abolished.

Schell writes as though he alone has seen the light. "In our present-day world, in the councils where the decisions are made there is no one to speak for man and for the earth, although both are threatened with annihilation," he says. "As citizens and statesmen we go on living in a pre-nuclear world.... We try to make do with a Newtonian politics in an Einsteinian world."

The only genuine national defense, Schell asserts, is "for all nations to give up violence together." This requires "revolutionizing the politics of the earth.... We must lay down our arms, relinquish sovereignty, and found a political system for the peaceful settlement of international disputes. ... The task is nothing less than to reinvent politics; to reinvent the world."

How do we make this leap from the present to utopia? The very first step is a "freeze on the further deployment of nuclear weapons" and a 50 per cent reduction in the arsenals of the superpowers. Most of all we need a spirit of non-violence,

Schell maintains, quoting Gandhi: "In the dictionary of non-violent action, there is no such thing as
an 'external enemy.'"

Jonathan Schell is a staff writer for *The New
Yorker*. Among his other works are *The Village of
Ben Suc, The Time of Illusion,* and *The Military
Half.*

THE SELF-EXTINCTION OF our species is not an act that anyone describes as sane or sensible; nevertheless, it is an act that, without quite admitting it to ourselves, we plan in certain circumstances to commit. Being impossible as a fully intentional act, unless the perpetrator has lost his mind, it can come about only through a kind of inadvertence—as a "side effect" of some action that we do intend, such as the defense of our nation, or the defense of liberty, or the defense of socialism, or the defense of whatever else we happen to believe in.

To that extent, our failure to acknowledge the magnitude and significance of the peril is a necessary condition for doing the deed. We can do it only if we don't quite know what we're doing. If we did acknowledge the full dimensions of the peril, admitting clearly and without reservation that any use of nuclear arms is likely to touch off a holocaust in which the continuance of all human life would be put at risk, extinction would at that moment become not only "unthinkable" but also undoable. What is needed to make extinction possible, therefore, is some way of thinking about it that at least partly deflects our attention from what it is. And this way of thinking is supplied to us, unfortunately, by our political and military traditions, which, with the weight of almost all historical experience behind them, teach us that it is the way of the world for the earth to be divided up into independent, sovereign states, and for these states to employ war as the final arbiter for settling the disputes that arise among them.

This arrangement of the political affairs of the world was not intentional. No one wrote a book proposing it; no parliament sat down to debate its merits and then voted it into existence. It was simply there, at the beginning of recorded history; and until the

Reprinted by permission of Alfred A. Knopf, Incorporated, from *The Fate of the Earth* by Jonathan Schell (© 1982 by Jonathan Schell). This material originally appeared in *The New Yorker*.

invention of nuclear weapons it remained there, with virtually no fundamental changes. Unplanned though this arrangement was, it had many remarkably durable features, and certain describable advantages and disadvantages; therefore, I shall refer to it as a "system"—the system of sovereignty.

Perhaps the leading feature of this system, and certainly the most important one in the context of the nuclear predicament, was the apparently indissoluble connection between sovereignty and war. For without sovereignty, it appeared, peoples were not able to organize and launch wars against other peoples, and without war they were unable to preserve their sovereignty from destruction by armed enemies. (By "war" I here mean only international war, not revolutionary war, which I shall not discuss.) Indeed, the connection between sovereignty and war is almost a definitional one—a sovereign state being a state that enjoys the right and the power to go to war in defense or pursuit of its interests.

It was into the sovereignty system that nuclear bombs were born, as "weapons" for "war." As the years have passed, it has seemed less and less plausible that they have anything to do with war; they seem to break through its bounds. Nevertheless, they have gone on being fitted into military categories of thinking. One might say that they appeared in the world in a military disguise, for it has been traditional military thinking, itself an inseparable part of the traditional political thinking that belonged to the system of sovereignty, that has provided those intentional goals—namely, national interests—in the pursuit of which extinction may now be brought about unintentionally, or semi-intentionally, as a "side effect." The system of sovereignty is now to the earth and mankind what a polluting factory is to its local environment. The machine produces certain things that its users want—in this case, national sovereignty—and as an unhappy side effect extinguishes the species.

The ambivalence resulting from the attempt to force nuclear weapons into the pre-existing military and political system has led to a situation in which, in the words of Einstein—who was farseeing in his political as well as in his scientific thought—"the unleashed power of the atom has changed everything save our modes of thinking, and we thus drift toward unparalleled catastrophes." As Einstein's observation suggests, the nuclear revolution has gone quite far but has not been completed. The question we have to answer is whether the completion will be extinction or a global political revolution—whether the "babies" that the scientists at Alamogordo brought forth will put an end to us or we will put an end to them. For it is not only our thoughts but also our actions and our institutions—our global political arrangements in their entirety—that we have failed to change.

We live with one foot in each of two worlds. As scientists and technicians, we live in the nuclear world, in which, whether we choose to acknowledge the fact or not, we possess instruments of violence that make it possible for us to extinguish ourselves as a species. But as citizens and statesmen we go on living in the pre-nuclear world, as though extinction were not possible and sovereign nations could still employ the instruments of violence as instruments of policy—as "a continuation of politics by other means," in the famous phrase of Karl von Clausewitz, the great philosopher of war. In effect, we try to make do with a Newtonian politics in an Einsteinian world. The combination is the source of our immediate peril. For governments, still acting within a system of independent nation-states, and formally representing no one but the people of their separate, sovereign nations, are driven to try to defend merely national interests with means of destruction that threaten not only international but intergenerational and planetary doom. In our present-day world, in the councils where the decisions are made there is no one to speak for man and for the earth, although both are threatened with annihilation. . . .

War Is Obsolete

By effectively removing the limits on human access to the forces of nature, the invention of nuclear weapons ruined war, which depended for its results, and therefore for its usefulness, on the exhaustion of the forces of one of the adversaries. War depended, above all, on the weakness of human powers, and when human powers came to exceed human and other earthly endurance—

when man as master of nature grew mightier than man as a vulnerable, mortal part of nature—war was ruined. Since war was the means by which violence was fashioned into an instrument that was useful in political affairs, the ruin of war by nuclear weapons has brought about a divorce between violence and politics. I submit that this divorce, being based on irreversible progress in scientific knowledge, not only is final but must ultimately extend across the full range of political affairs, and that the task facing the species is to shape a world politics that does not rely on violence.

This task falls into two parts—two aims. The first is to save the world from extinction by eliminating nuclear weapons from the earth. Just recently, on the occasion of his retirement, Admiral Hyman Rickover, who devoted a good part of his life to overseeing the development and construction of nuclear-powered, nuclear-missile-bearing submarines for the United States Navy, told a congressional committee that in his belief mankind was going to destroy itself with nuclear arms. He also said of his part in the nuclear build-up that he was "not proud" of it, and added that he would like to "sink" the ships that he had poured so much of his life into. And, indeed, what everyone is now called on to do is to sink all the ships, and also ground all the planes, and fill in all the missile silos, and dismantle all the warheads. The second aim, which alone can provide a sure foundation for the first, is to create a political means by which the world can arrive at the decisions that sovereign states previously arrived at through war.

These two aims, which correspond to the aims mentioned earlier of preserving the existence of life and pursuing the various ends of life, are intimately connected. If, on the one hand, disarmament is not accompanied by a political solution, then every clash of will between nations will tempt them to pick up the instruments of violence again, and so lead the world back toward extinction. If, on the other hand, a political solution is not accompanied by complete disarmament, then the political decisions that are made will not be binding, for they will be subject to challenge by force. And if, as in our present world, there is neither a political solution nor disarmament, then the world will be held perpetually at the edge of doom, and every clash between nuclear powers will threaten to push it over the edge. . . .

In the pre-nuclear world, the threat of war, backed up by the frequent practice of war, served as a deterrent to aggression. Today, the threat of extinction, unsupported, for obvious reasons, by practice but backed up by the existence of nuclear arms and the threat to use them, serves as the ultimate deterrent. Thus, in today's system the actual weapons have already retired halfway from their traditional military role. They are "psychological" weapons, whose purpose is not to be employed but to maintain a permanent state of mind—terror—in the adversary. Their target is someone's mind, and their end, if the system works, is to rust into powder in their silos. And our generals are already psychological soldiers—masters of the war game and of the computer terminal but not, fortunately, of the battlefield. In this cerebral world, strategy confronts strategy and scenario battles scenario, the better to keep any of them from ever actually unfolding. But we need to carry this trend further. We need to make the weapons *wholly* cerebral—not things that sit in a silo ready to be fired but merely a thought in our minds. We need to destroy them. Only then will the logical fallacy now at the heart of the deterrence doctrine be removed, for only then will the fear of extinction by nuclear arms be used for the sole purpose of preventing extinction, and not also for the pursuit of national political aims.

Deterred by Knowledge

In a perfected nuclear deterrence, the knowledge in a disarmed world that rearmament potentially means extinction would become the deterrent. Now, however, it would be not that each nuclear-armed country would deter its nuclear-armed adversary but that awareness of the peril of extinction would deter all mankind from reembarking on nuclear armament. All human beings would join in a defensive alliance, with nuclear weapons as their common enemy. But since that enemy could spring only from our own midst, deterrer and deterred would be one.

We thus arrive at the basic strategic principle of life in a world in which the nuclear predicament has been resolved: *Knowledge is the deterrent*. The nuclear peril was born out of knowledge, and it must abide in knowledge. The knowledge in question would be, in the first place, the unlosable scientific knowledge that enables us to build the weapons and condemns us to live forever in a nuclear world. This knowledge is the inexpungible minimum presence that the nuclear peril will always have in the life of the world, no matter what measures we adopt. In the second place, the knowledge would be the full emotional, intellectual, spiritual, and visceral understanding of the meaning of extinction—above all, the meaning of the unborn generations to the living. Because extinction is the end of mankind, it can never be anything more than "knowledge" for us; we can never "experience" extinction. It is *this* knowledge—this horror at a murderous action taken against generations yet unborn, which exerts pressure at the center of our existence, and which is the whole reality of extinction insofar as it is given to us to experience it—that must become the deterrent.

In a disarmed world, we would not have eliminated the peril of human extinction from the human scene—it is not in our power to do so—but we would at least have pitted our whole strength against it. The inconsistency of threatening to perpetrate extinction in order to escape extinction would be removed. The nuclei of atoms would still contain vast energy, and we would still know how to extinguish ourselves by releasing that energy in chain reactions, but we would not be lifting a finger to do it. There would be no complicity in mass murder, no billions of dollars spent on the machinery of annihilation, no preparations to snuff out the future generations, no hair-raising lunges toward the abyss.

Realism and Idealism

The "realistic" school of political thinking, on which the present system of deterrence is based, teaches that men, on the whole, pursue their own interests and act according to a law of fear. The "idealistic" school looks on the human ability to show regard for others as fundamental, and is based on what Gandhi called the law of love. (Whereas the difference between traditional military thinking and nuclear strategic thinking lies in the different factual premises that they start from, the difference between the "realistic" and the "idealistic" schools of political philosophy lies in different judgments regarding human nature.) Historically, a belief in the necessity of violence has been the hallmark of the credo of the "realist"; however, if one consistently and thoroughly applies the law of fear in nuclear times one is driven not to rely on violence but to banish it altogether. This comes about as the result not of any idealistic assumption but of a rigorous application to our times of the strictly "military" logic of traditional war. For today the only way to achieve genuine national defense for any nation is for all nations to give up violence together.

However, if we had begun with Gandhi's law of love we would have arrived at exactly the same arrangement. For to one who believed in nonviolence in a pre-nuclear setting, the peril of extinction obviously adds one more reason—and a tremendous one, transcending all others—for giving up violence. Moreover, in at least one respect the law of love proves to fit the facts of this peril better than the law of fear. The law of fear relies on the love of self. Through deterrence—in which anyone's pursuit of self-interest at the expense of others will touch off general ruin that will destroy him, too—this self-love is made use of to protect everyone. However, self-love—a narrow, though intense, love—cannot, as we have seen, extend its protection to the future generations, or even get them in view. They still do not have any selves whose fear of death could be pooled in the common fund of fear, and yet their lives are at stake in extinction. The deterrence doctrine is a transaction that is limited to living people—it leaves out of account the helpless, speechless unborn (while we can launch a first strike against them, they have no forces with which to retaliate)—and yet the fate of the future generations is at the heart of extinction, for their cancellation is what extinction is. Their lives are at stake, but their vote is not counted. Love, however, can reach them—can enable them to be. Love, a spiritual energy that the human heart can pit against the physical energy released from the heart of matter, can create, cherish, and safeguard what extinction would destroy and shut up in nothingness. But in fact there is no need, at least on the practical level, to choose between the law of fear and the law of love, because ultimately they lead to the same destination. It is no more realistic than it is idealistic to destroy the world. . . .

The task we face is to find a means of political action that will permit human beings to pursue any end for the rest of time. We are asked to replace the mechanism by which political decisions, whatever they may be, are reached. In sum, the task is nothing less than to reinvent politics: to reinvent the world. However, extinction will not wait for us to reinvent the world. Evolution was slow to produce us, but our extinction will be swift; it will literally be over before we know it. We have to match swiftness with swiftness. Because everything we do and everything we are is in jeopardy, and because the peril is immediate and unremitting, every person is the right person to act and every moment is the right moment to begin, starting with the present moment. For nothing underscores our common humanity as strongly as the peril of extinction does; in fact, on a practical and political plane it establishes that common humanity. The purpose of action, though, is not to replace life with politics. The point is not to turn life into a scene of protest; life is the point.

A Rebellion Against Extinction

Whatever the eventual shape of a world that has been reinvented for the sake of survival, the first, urgent, immediate step, which requires no deep thought or long reflection, is for each person to make known, visibly and unmistakably, his desire that the species survive. Extinction, being in its nature outside human experience, is invisible. No one will ever witness extinction, so we must bear witness to it before the fact. And the place for the rebellion to start is in our daily lives. We can each perform a turnabout right where we are—let our daily business drop from our hands for a while, so that we can turn our attention to securing the foundation of all life, out of which our daily business grows and in which it finds its justification. This disruption of our lives will be a preventive disruption, for we will be hoping through the temporary suspension of our daily life to ward off the eternal suspension of it in extinction. And this turnabout in the first instance can be as simple as a phone call to a friend, a meeting in the community.

However, even as the first steps are taken, the broad ultimate requirements of survival must be recognized and stated clearly. If they are not, we might sink into self-deception, imagining that inadequate measures would suffice to save us. I would suggest that the ultimate requirements are in essence the two that I have mentioned: global disarmament, both nuclear and conventional, and the invention of political means by which the world can peacefully settle the issues that throughout history it has settled by war. Thus, the first steps and the ultimate requirements are clear. If a busload of people is speeding down a mountainside toward a cliff, the passengers do not convene a seminar to investigate the nature of their predicament; they see to it that the driver applies the brakes. Therefore, at a minimum, a freeze on the further deployment of nuclear weapons, participated in both by countries that now have them and by countries that do not yet have them, is called for. Even better would be a reduction in nuclear arms—for example, by cutting the arsenals of superpowers in half, as George Kennan suggested recently.

Simultaneously with disarmament, political steps of many kinds could be taken. For example, talks could be started among the nuclear powers with the aim of making sure that the world did not simply blunder into extinction by mistake; technical and political arrangements could be drawn up to reduce the likelihood of mechanical mistakes and misjudgments of the other side's intentions or actions in a time of crisis, and these would somewhat increase the world's security while the predicament was being tackled at a more fundamental level.

For both superpowers—and, indeed, for all other powers—avoiding extinction is a common interest than which none can be greater. And since the existence of a common interest is the best foundation for negotiation, negotiations should have some chance of success. However, the existence of negotiations to reduce the nuclear peril would provide no reason for abandoning the pursuit of other things that one believed in, even those which might be at variance with the beliefs of one's negotiating partner. Thus, to give one contemporary example, there is no need, or excuse, for the United States not to take strong measures to oppose Soviet-sponsored repression in Poland just because it is engaged in disarmament talks with the Soviet Union. The world will not end if we suspend shipments of wheat to the Soviet Union. On the other hand, to break off those talks in an effort to help the Poles, who will be as extinct as anyone else if a holocaust comes about, would be self-defeating. To seek to "punish" the other side by breaking off those negotiations would be in reality self-punishment. All the limited aims of negotiation can be pursued in the short term without danger if only the ultimate goal is kept unswervingly in mind. But ordinary citizens must insist that all these things be done, or they will not be.

Principles for a Vital Endeavor

If action should be concerted, as it eventually must be, in a common political endeavor, reaching across national boundaries, then, just as the aim of the endeavor would be to hold the gates of life open to the future generations, so its method would be to hold its own gates open to every living person. But it should be borne in mind that even if every person in the world were to enlist, the endeavor would include only an infinitesimal fraction of the people of the dead and the unborn generations, and so it would need to act with the circumspection and modesty of a small minority. From its mission to preserve all generations, it would not seek to derive any rights to dictate to the generations on hand. It would not bend or break the rules of conduct essential to a decent political life, for it would recognize that once one started breaking rules in the name of survival no rule would go unbroken. Intellectually and philosophically, it would carry the principle of tolerance to the utmost extreme. It would attempt to be as open to new thoughts and feelings as it would be to the new generations that would think those thoughts and feel those feelings. Its underlying supposition about creeds and ideologies would be that whereas without mankind none can exist, with mankind all can exist. For while the events that might trigger a holocaust would probably be political, the consequences would be deeper than any politics or political aims, bringing ruin to the hopes and plans of capitalists and socialists, rightists and leftists, conservatives and liberals alike. Having as the source of its strength only the spontaneously offered support of the people of the earth, it would, in turn, respect each person's will, which is to say his liberty. Eventually, the popular will that it marshalled might be deployed as a check on the power of whatever political institutions were invented to replace war.

Since the goal would be a nonviolent world, the actions of this endeavor would be nonviolent. What Gandhi once said of the spirit of nonviolent action in general would be especially important to the spirit of these particular actions: "In the dictionary of nonviolent action, there is no such thing as an 'external enemy.' " With the world itself at stake, all differences would by definition be "internal" differences, to be resolved on the basis of respect for those with whom one disagreed. If our aim is to save humanity, we must respect the humanity of every person. For who would be the enemy? Certainly not the world's political leaders, who, though they now menace the earth with nuclear weapons, do so only with our permission, and even at our bidding. At least, this is true for the democracies. We do not know what the peoples of the totalitarian states, including the people of the Soviet Union, may want. They are locked in silence by their government. In these circumstances, public opinion in the free countries would have to represent public opinion in all countries, and would have to bring its pressure to bear, as best it could, on all governments.

At present, most of us do nothing. We look away. We remain calm. We are silent. We take refuge in the hope that the holocaust won't happen, and turn back to our individual concerns. We deny the truth that is all around us. Indifferent to the future of our kind, we grow indifferent to one another. We drift apart. We grow cold. We drowse our way toward the end of the world. But if once we shook off our lethargy and fatigue and began to act, the climate would change. Just as inertia produces despair—a despair often so deep that it does not even know itself as despair—arousal and action would give us access to hope, and life would start to mend: not just life in its entirety but daily life, every individual life. At that point, we would begin to withdraw from our role as both the victims and the perpetrators of mass murder. We would no longer be the destroyers of mankind but, rather, the gateway through which the future generations would enter the world. Then the passion and will that we need to save ourselves would flood into our lives. Then the walls of indifference, inertia, and coldness that now isolate each of us from others, and all of us from the past and future generations, would melt, like snow in spring.

E. M. Forster told us, "Only connect!" Let us connect. Auden told us, "We must love one another or die." Let us love one another—in the present and across the divides of death and birth. Christ said, "I come not to judge the world but to save the world." Let us, also, not judge the world but save the world. By restoring our severed links with life, we will restore our own lives. Instead of stopping the course of time and cutting off the human future, we would make it possible for the future generations to be born. Their inestimable gift to us, passed back from the future into the present, would be the wholeness and meaning of life.

Two paths lie before us. One leads to death, the other to life. If we choose the first path—if we numbly refuse to acknowledge the nearness of extinction, all the while increasing our preparations to bring it about—then we in effect become the allies of death, and in everything we do our attachment to life will weaken: our vision, blinded to the abyss that has opened at our feet, will dim and grow confused; our will, discouraged by the thought of trying to build on such a precarious foundation anything that is meant to last, will slacken; and we will sink into stupefaction, as though we were gradually weaning ourselves from life in preparation for the end.

On the other hand, if we reject our doom, and bend our efforts toward survival—if we arouse ourselves to the peril and act to forestall it, making ourselves the allies of life—then the anesthetic fog will lift: our vision, no longer straining not to see the obvious, will sharpen; our will, finding secure ground to build on, will be restored; and we will take full and clear possession of life again. One day—and it is hard to believe that it will not be soon—we will make our choice. Either we will sink into the final coma and end it all or, as I trust and believe, we will awaken to the truth of our peril, a truth as great as life itself, and, like a person who has swallowed a lethal poison but shakes off his stupor at the last moment and vomits the poison up, we will break through the layers of our denials, put aside our fainthearted excuses, and rise up to cleanse the earth of nuclear weapons.

16. *Apocalyptic Panic Is No Help*

By HERMAN KAHN

Focus For thirty years Herman Kahn, a physicist and futurist, has been "thinking about the unthinkable." However, he is considerably less pessimistic than Jonathan Schell, whose *Fate of the Earth* (see selection 15) Kahn considers simplistic, naïve, vastly overrated, and dangerous. If the West undertook policies based on Schell's apocalyptic vision, says Kahn, it would move far down the road of "unilateral disarmament, appeasement, even surrender."

Kahn asserts that Schell overestimates the probability of nuclear war, "focuses almost exclusively on an implausible 'worst-case scenario'—nuclear holocaust and global annihilation," and comes up with a "morally uninspiring and politically naïve" solution. Schell's assertion that the multiplication of nuclear weapons multiplies the chances of nuclear war by accident, says Kahn, is simply not true. In fact, in many important ways the chances of accidental war have substantially diminished as stockpiles have grown.

Schell also vastly exaggerates the destructiveness of nuclear weapons, according to Kahn. There is no evidence to suggest that a nuclear war will lead to the extinction of humanity. A nuclear war may well be limited. Even in an unlimited war "a wide variety of outcomes are possible, but the side with more and better weapons would have a clear advantage."

235

236

Furthermore, "civil-defense measures can significantly reduce casualties," and "deterrence is most apt to work when it is backed by solid war-fighting capabilities in both the conventional and nuclear spheres." "The ultimate flaw in the Schell book," says Kahn, "is that it does not explain what we should do if deterrence fails."

Herman Kahn is chairman and director of research at the Hudson Institute, which he founded in 1961. He has written *On Thermonuclear War* (1961), *Thinking About the Unthinkable* (1962), and *The Coming Boom* (1982), among other works.

JONATHAN SCHELL'S BEST-SELLING *The Fate of the Earth* has been hailed as the publishing event of the year. The acclaim accorded the book reflects in part extraordinarily good timing, publication having coincided with an explosion of anti-nuclear sentiment. And because the book is undeniably moving and passionate, and a lot of thought has gone into it, many reviewers have uncritically accepted it as a profound statement. They appear not to understand how far Schell is willing to go down the road of unilateral disarmament, appeasement, even surrender, if that is what it takes to lessen the probability of nuclear war.

A prose stylist with an apocalyptic vision is hard to talk back to, and there may also be something like the religious-art syndrome at work here—one doesn't criticize a painting of Christ because the subject itself is above criticism. In the present atmosphere, many reviewers sense that it would be unseemly and impolitic to criticize an anti-nuclear book.

However, the book has three major problems. (1) While we do not know how to measure the likelihood of nuclear war, Schell almost certainly overstates it. (2) He focuses almost exclusively on an implausible "worst-case scenario"—nuclear holocaust and global annihilation. (3) His prescription for forestalling the holocaust is morally uninspiring and politically naïve.

Many passages in *The Fate of the Earth* reflect confusion about one critical idea—the idea that as one multiplies the number of nuclear weapons one multiplies the chances of accidental nuclear war. In some essentially unimportant ways this is true. In many important ways, however, the chances of accidental war have diminished considerably even while the nuclear stockpiles have been growing since the 1950s. Mechanical safeguards (coded

Reprinted with adaptations by permission from the June 28, 1982, issue of *Fortune* Magazine (© 1982 by Time, Incorporated).

"locks" on nuclear weapons), procedural checks and balances (the "two-man rule," under which no one can be alone with a nuclear weapon), improved tactical warning systems, and the diversification and pre-launch protection of the delivery systems carrying nuclear weapons—taken together, these probably make accidental nuclear war less likely today than ever in the past. Indeed, some knowledgeable officials are concerned that we have *too many* safeguards in place. One former deputy director of the Pentagon's Joint Strategic Target Planning Staff, which is charged with developing U.S. nuclear war plans, argues that these numerous precautions might actually leave the United States "unable to release and launch a nuclear weapon or weapons if it decided to do so, even with the civilian hierarchy intact, in full control of their faculties, and all communications systems in full working order." This view is by no means an isolated one. The evidence suggests that U.S. and Soviet leaders have been willing to increase the risk that their nuclear forces will not work well in wartime in order to reduce the risk that they will be used when they shouldn't be.

Perhaps the greatest danger of accidental war lies in a rash of proposals that I would view as totally mindless if so many of my friends weren't recommending them. In particular, the concept of "launch on warning" is almost certainly accident-prone. One of the most important, and constructive, events of the fifties was the realization by both American and Soviet planners that neither side could be trigger-happy. This agreement was not arrived at by treaty, but flowed from greater awareness of the ways in which war might break out accidentally, and it resulted in the development of strategic forces that could survive a first strike and retaliate after deliberation. Now, however, our forces are once again vulnerable to various kinds of first strikes, because we have allowed the Russians to deploy a panoply of nuclear weapon systems (especially, large numbers of ICBMs with highly accurate warheads) without taking measures to restore the invulnerability of our own forces. And many defense analysts are seriously proposing to deal with this new vulnerability via hair-trigger arrangements in which our missiles would be launched the instant we knew a Soviet attack was under way.

Why have we allowed this destabilizing situation to arise? One reason, ironically, is that there are so many thinkers like Jonathan Schell, who believe that we needn't worry about "military details" because we already have boundless "overkill" and every war would be a holocaust anyway. If this reasoning is valid, then our concerns about vulnerability to a first strike are indeed academic. But the reasoning is not valid: there could be intense crises in which both sides, while preferring not to go to war, would be under great pressure to strike first because doing so looked less dangerous than letting the crisis carry them into unknown territory. A first strike would be particularly likely when the other side's forces looked both threatening and vulnerable. It's clearly desirable that we not be in any such situation. Yet Schell's frame of reference, with its insistent emphasis on "overkill," predisposes people to complacency about the emergence of such vulnerabilities. Categorical opposition to defense can make one's situation more dangerous (but what's new about that?).

Nuclear War May Well Be Limited

There is no reason to assume that a nuclear war will lead to the extinction of all, or almost all, humanity. In fact, those who have worked hardest at analyzing scenarios involving nuclear weapons believe that nuclear wars may well be limited; that they can come in many shapes and sizes; that even in unlimited wars a wide variety of outcomes are possible, but that the side with more and better weapons would have a clear advantage; that civil-defense measures can significantly reduce casualties; and that deterrence is most apt to work when it is backed by solid war-fighting capabilities in both the conventional and the nuclear sphere.

To support many of his extreme statements about the effects of nuclear war, Schell refers to two studies: *Long-Term Worldwide Effects of Multiple Nuclear-Weapons Detonations,* issued in 1975 by the National Academy of Sciences (NAS), and *The Effects of Nuclear War,* prepared in 1979 by the congressional Office of Technology Assessment (OTA). However, Schell excerpts from these studies only that which supports his vision of global holocaust. Any evidence that includes the possibility of a "spectrum" of wars is left out. For example, the NAS report emphasizes—contrary to Schell—that nuclear war would *not* cause the extinction of the human race. The letter of transmittal by the NAS president, reprinted at the front of the published report, includes these words: "If I may restate the principal question as, 'Would the biosphere and the species, *Homo sapiens,* survive?' the response by our committee is 'yes.' "

Preparing to Deter, Fight, Survive

In criticizing Schell for focusing only on the worst-case scenarios, I do not mean to imply that non-worst-case scenarios would involve small costs. One twenty-kiloton bomb at Nagasaki killed about 75,000 people, and some bombs today are about a thousand times more devastating. (It seems, however, that the explosive power per unit of weight has now about reached the limits set by the laws of physics.) In addition, there are many more nuclear weapons around. Still, it is essential for planners to contemplate a range of contingencies. And one trouble with the Schell perspective, which equates any nuclear war with the destruction of mankind, is that it strongly discourages any preparation for survival. If we knew for certain that no one would survive, we could spare ourselves the costs of arming. But we know no such thing. Under the circumstances, I believe it is immoral—an abdication of our responsibility to generations as yet unborn, not to mention our own—and dangerous not to take reasonable precautions to (a) deter, (b) fight, and (c) survive and recuperate from a nuclear war.

Without doubt, even a very limited attack on the United States—one that concentrated more or less exclusively on our strategic forces—would involve catastrophic human and material losses. Yet these would still be considerably less than those associated with strikes on a wide range of civilian and military targets. An illustration of this critical distinction can be found in the OTA study Schell frequently cites. After reviewing analyses of hypothetical nuclear attacks on the United States and the Soviet Union, OTA concluded that the range of immediate U.S. fatalities in an attack limited to "counterforce targets" (a term that mainly refers to our ICBMs and B-52s) would be 1 million to 20 million. In contrast, the range in a comprehensive attack on military and civilian targets would be 20 million to 160 million. These differences are significant, to put it mildly.

What seems to me especially counter-productive is the current pressure for a nuclear "freeze." The freeze movement is another manifestation of mindless commitment to the idea of overkill. At a moment when the Russians seem to possess a margin of strategic superiority, a freeze would leave current systems intact; furthermore, it would maintain the vulnerabilities of forces on both sides.

So long as the weapons remain—and even most of the anti-nuclear groups aren't yet talking about large-scale unilateral disarmament—it is irresponsible not to consider what might happen in the event that they are used. The simple assertion that nuclear war is unacceptable doesn't get us anywhere. We may be forced to accept one. Consider, for example, the damage inflicted on Russia in the Napoleonic and the First and Second World Wars. The damage was clearly "unacceptable," even by modern standards. But the country survived, and each time emerged stronger than before. Schell's supporters tend to overlook the possibility that people are sometimes forced to accept unacceptable events.

The ultimate flaw in the Schell book is that it does not explain what we should do if deterrence fails. My own view is that the kind of thinking put forward in *The Fate of the Earth* represents a real danger—that is, by increasing the fears of nuclear war to an almost intolerable degree, while offering no guide to policy, it *increases* the probability of nuclear war. The state of mind Schell wants Americans to be in would permit the Russians to manipulate the threat of nuclear holocaust as a cover for new and dangerous aggressions.

At one point in the book, Schell quotes me as having "rightly" said that "it will do no good to inveigh against theorists; in this field everyone is a theorist." Fortunately, that comment, made in 1962, is still true. But I'd like to update it by adding that some theorists are more realistic than others, and they are the ones who are more likely to inherit the earth and less likely to surrender it.

17. *Nuclear Holocaust in Perspective*

By MICHAEL KINSLEY

Focus
Like Herman Kahn, Michael Kinsley finds Jonathan Schell (selection 15) confused and arrogant. He calls Schell's book *The Fate of the Earth* "one of the most pretentious things I've ever read." Kinsley is appalled both by its apocalyptic vision and by its "hothouse reasoning ... protected from the slightest chill of common sense." We do not need to be persuaded that nuclear war is undesirable, says Kinsley; our challenge is to make it less likely and, if deterrence fails, less destructive. On this key question both the peace movement and Schell are virtually silent.

Schell and his fellow romantics are simply unrealistic. "The basic balance of terror cannot be dismantled without perfect trust between the world's greatest enemies—an unlikely development," says Kinsley. The West could attempt to "replace nuclear arms with conventional defense," but this idea is "utterly alien to the mentality of most anti-nuclear activists. Is the horror of nuclear weapons *sui generis*, or is the goal abolition of all weapons and war? Are there practical steps that can be taken, or must we await a transformation of human nature? Jonathan Schell's essay well illustrates the confusion of the anti-nuclear movement."

Kinsley focuses on the anti-nuclear utopians and does not address the practical questions of state policy, but his analysis suggests that he would not be in basic disagreement with Herman Kahn or the arguments advanced in selections 2, 4, and 6.

Michael Kinsley is the editor of *Harper's* magazine. He has been the managing editor of *The New Republic* and *The Washington Monthly* and is the author of *Outer Space and Inner Sanctums*.

IT WOULD BE VERY SAD if the world were destroyed in a nuclear holocaust. Jonathan Schell may well feel this sadness more profoundly than I do. His acclaimed three-part series in *The New Yorker,* "The Fate of the Earth," now rushed into book form by Knopf, is mostly a meditation on how sad it would be. He demands "the full emotional, intellectual, spiritual, and visceral understanding of the meaning of extinction." He asserts that even now "The peril of extinction surrounds . . . love with doubt." And "Politics, as it now exists, is . . . thoroughly compromised." And "Works of art, history, and thought . . . are undermined at their foundations. . . ." Schell cites scientific evidence against any complaisant hope that human life, once destroyed in a nuclear war, might evolve again in a few million years. And don't suppose that humanity might escape nuclear war by fleeing the earth in a spaceship. Schell points out that this would be not only "an injustice to our birthplace and habitat," but futile: "[T]he fact is that wherever human beings went, there also would go the knowledge of how to build nuclear weapons, and, with it, the peril of extinction." I confess that this spaceship business had never occurred to me. But, really, I think a nuclear holocaust would be very, very sad.

That said, where do we stand?

We stand where we've stood for three decades, with East and West in a nuclear stalemate that could turn at any moment into mutual annihilation. In addition, we stand with nuclear weapons as the only genuine deterrent to a Soviet invasion of Europe (and of the Middle East, a threat implicitly invoked in the Carter Doctrine). Third, we stand at the edge of a large expansion of the nuclear club, with unpredictable consequences.

Over the past few months a mass political movement—the first in years—has sprouted in the United States and Europe, demanding that something be done about this. Something, but what? On this, the movement is vaguer, because it's hard to think what the Western governments can do to prevent a nuclear war. On the third point, they might stop competing with one another to sell nuclear equipment to the third world, but it's already a little late for that. On the first point, they might show a bit more enthusiasm for a strategic arms limitation treaty. But this would be primarily a matter of saving money and reducing the risk of a disastrous accident. The basic balance of terror cannot be dismantled without perfect trust between the world's greatest enemies—an unlikely development.

The West really could do something about problem number two, the dependence on nuclear weapons to protect Europe. That something would be to replace nuclear arms with conventional defense. John Keegan assesses our conventional defense of Europe in this issue of *Harper's* [May 1982]. But a conventional defense strong enough to justify forswearing first use of nuclear weapons would require massively increased military spending for the other NATO countries, and probably a draft for the United States.

The thought of increasing conventional military strength to replace nuclear bombs (like the thought that a successful nuclear ban would increase the chance of conventional warfare) is utterly alien to the mentality of most anti-nuclear activists. Is the horror of nuclear weapons *sui generis,* or is the goal abolition of all weapons and war? Are there practical steps that can be taken, or must we await a transformation of human nature? Jonathan Schell's essay well illustrates the confusion of the anti-nuclear movement.

Perhaps it is *lèse majesté* to call a major three-part series in *The New Yorker* "pretentious," but "The Fate of the Earth" is one of the most pretentious things I've ever read, from the title through the grand finale (which begins, "Four and a half billion years ago, the earth was formed"). "Gosh, is this profound," is about all that many sonorous passages convey:

> [T]he limitless complexity [of nuclear war] sometimes seems to be as great as that of life itself. But if these effects should lead to human extinction, then all the complexity will give way to the utmost simplicity—the simplicity of nothingness.

Like the thought "I do not exist," the thought "Humanity is now extinct" is an impossible one for a rational person, because as soon as *it* is, we are not.

Even funnier are the pompous generalities that come attached to *New Yorker*-style cautionary notes:

Human beings have a worth—a worth that is sacred. But it is *for* human beings that they have that sacred worth, and for them that the other things in the creation have their worth (although it is a reminder of our indissoluble connection with the rest of life that many of our needs and desires are also felt by animals).

Hannah Arendt "never addressed the issue of nuclear arms," Schell tells us, but of course she is dragged in. "I have discovered her thinking to be an indispensable foundation for reflection on this question." Evil, you know. What is really indispensable is her graphic descriptions of Nazi death camps. They pop up here to illustrate the point (both unenlightening and untrue, on recent evidence) that you can't deny horrors that have already happened. Himmler appears a little later, expressing his desire to make Europe "Jew-free." Schell observes, "His remark applies equally well to a nuclear holocaust, which might render the earth 'human-free.'" In fact, Hannah and Himmler are here for aesthetic rather than pedagogical purposes. This is simply how you decorate apocalyptic bigthink.

Despite a lot of wacky judiciousness ("From the foregoing, it follows that there can be no justification for extinguishing mankind"), Schell's method is basically bullying rather than argument. The pomp is intended to intimidate, and the moral solemnity is a form of blackmail. Unless you feel as anguished about nuclear war as Jonathan Schell, unless you worry about it *all the time* like him (allegedly), your complacency disqualifies you from objecting. In fact, you are suffering "a kind of sickness" or "a sort of mass insanity." So shut up.

Much of Schell's essay does take the form of argument, but it tends to be hothouse reasoning: huge and exotic blossoms of ratiocination that could grow only in an environment protected from the slightest chill of common sense. For example, here he is arguing that we should not have an experimental nuclear war in order to see what would happen:

We cannot run experiments with the earth, because we have only one earth, on which we depend for our survival; we are not in possession of any spare earths that we might blow up in some universal laboratory in order to discover their tolerance of nuclear holocausts. Hence, our knowledge of the resiliency of the earth in the face of nuclear attack is limited by our fear of bringing about just the event—human extinction—whose likelihood we are chiefly interested in finding out.

Now we welcome please "The famous uncertainty principle, formulated by the German physicist Werner Heisenberg," which makes a brief star turn at this point in the argument. Its role is to escort "an opposite but [not very] related uncertainty principle: our knowledge of extinction is limited because the experiments with which we would carry out our observations interfere with us, the observers, and, in fact, might put an end to us."

The argument is crowned with a portentous aphorism: "the demand for certainty is the path toward death." Then, just to show that he's thought of everything, Schell considers and rejects the idea of holding an experimental nuclear war on another planet, ". . . for if we have no extra, dispensable earths to experiment with, neither are we in possession of any planets bearing life of some different sort." The reader is left convinced that an experimental nuclear war is a bad idea, and that Jonathan Schell posseses either an absurdly swelled head, or a "philosophical synthesis" that is "profoundly new" (—Eliot Fremont-Smith, the *Village Voice*).

Schell prefaces his discussion of the consequences of nuclear war with a discussion of the difficulty of imagining it. Some of the alleged obstacles are of this sort: "when we strain to picture what the scene would be like after a holocaust we tend to forget that for most people, and perhaps for all, it wouldn't be *like* anything, because they would be dead."

But the main set of obstacles involves a supposed reluctance of people to hear about it. Schell pleads with his readers to make this sacrifice: "it may be only by descending into this hell in imagination now that we can hope to escape descending into it in reality at some later time." He promises to protect their delicate sensibilities: "I hope in this article to proceed with the utmost possible respect for all forms of refusal to accept the unnatural and horrifying prospect of a nuclear holocaust." He flatters their "investigative modesty" as "itself . . . a token of our reluctance to extinguish ourselves." And thence to pages of the usual gruesome description. The horror is lightened only by some *New Yorker*y punctiliousness, as when, having killed off millions in a one-megaton bomb over Manhattan, he adds that newspapers and dry leaves would ignite "in all five boroughs (though in only a small part of Staten Island)."

Schell's posture of reluctant scientific inquiry will be familiar to aficionados of pornographic movies. And there *is* something pornographic about the emphasis on grisly details that is the distinguishing feature of the anti-nuclear movement in its latest manifestation. Perhaps Jonathan Schell is so sensitive that he really does find these disaster scenarios painful to contemplate, and probably we all do withhold true visceral understanding of what it would be like. But others will find such disaster scenarios grimly fascinating (certainly the most interesting part of Schell's book). Is that sick? If so, it is a sickness that is widespread, and one that the anti-nuclear movement both shares and exploits. The coy posture is annoying.

'First Strike' Against the Unborn

But destruction of civilization, or even the agonizing death of everybody in the whole world, would be, to Schell, just a minor aspect of the tragedy of a nuclear holocaust. The greatest crime would be against "the helpless, speechless unborn." Schell brandishes this notion of the unborn as his trump card, in case anyone still thinks nuclear war is a good idea. By "the unborn," he does not merely mean fetuses (though by his analysis—liberals please note—abortion is unthinkably immoral). Nor does he mean the future human race as an entity. He does not even mean future people who might inherit a nuclear-wrecked civilization and environment. He means individual people who will *never be born* if there is no one left to conceive them. "While we can launch a first strike against them," Schell inimitably points out, "they have no forces with which to retaliate."

Schell concedes "the metaphysical-seeming perplexities involved in pondering the possible cancellation of people who do not yet exist—an apparently extreme effort of the imagination, which seems to require one first to summon before the mind's eye the countless possible people of the future generations and then to consign these incorporeal multitudes to a more profound nothingness. . . ." But he's up to the challenge:

> Death cuts off life: extinction cuts off birth. Death dispatches into the nothingness after life each person who has been born; extinction in one stroke locks up in the nothingness before life all the people who have not yet been born. For we are finite beings at both ends of our existence—natal as well as mortal—and it is the natality of our kind that extinction threatens. We have always been able to send people to their death, but only now has it become possible to prevent all birth and so doom all future human beings to uncreation.

And so on and on. Schell is *very strict* about what might be called "alive-ism." Having waxed eloquent for pages about the unborn as repositories for our hopes and dreams, he stops to warn that we should not treat them merely "as auxiliaries to *our* needs," because "no human being, living or unborn, should be regarded as an auxiliary." The unborn, he scolds, "are not to be seen as beasts of burden. . . ."

Well, my goodness. Do we really have a moral obligation not to deny birth to everyone who, with a bit of help, might enjoy the "opportunity to be glad that they were born instead of having been prenatally severed from existence by us"? I shudder to think how I've failed. For that matter, I shudder for Jonathan Schell—for every moment he's spent banging away on his typewriter, instead of banging away elsewhere.

An End to Sovereignty

In solving the problem of nuclear war, Schell cautions, we must "act with the circumspection and modesty of a small minority," since "even if every person in the world were to enlist, the endeavor would include only an infinitesimal fraction of the people of the dead and unborn generations." Yes, the dead count too. So he proposes "a worldwide program of action," involving an "organization for the preservation of mankind." We must "delve to the bottom of the world" and then "take the world on our shoulders." He writes, "Our present system and the institutions that make it up are the debris of history. They have become inimical to life, and must be swept away." What he proposes, in short, is that the nations of the world abjure all future violence—nuclear *and* conventional warfare—and give up their sovereignty to some central organization.

This idea will win no prizes for circumspection and modesty. Other problems come to mind, too. Like, how shall we arrange all this? Schell writes:

> I have not sought to define a political solution to the nuclear predicament—either to embark on the full-scale examination of the foundations of political thought which must be undertaken . . . or to work out the practical steps. . . . I have left to others those awesome, urgent tasks.

Good heavens. This sudden abandonment, on page 219, puts Schell's hyperventilated rhetoric in an odd light. Is he just going to head off on a book tour and leave us stranded?

Schell is convinced, though, like the rest of the anti-nuclear movement, that the main task is education—convincing people of how bad a nuclear war would be. "If we did acknowledge the full dimension of the peril . . . extinction would at that moment become not only 'unthinkable' but also undoable." The key word here is "we." But there is no "we." There are individual actors who cannot completely know or trust one another. That's life. Even if everyone in the world shared Schell's overwrought feelings about nuclear war, the basic dilemma would not disappear: the best defense against an enemy's use or threat to use nuclear weapons is the threat to use them back.

Schell correctly points out the weakness in deterrence theory: since nuclear wars are unwinnable, it's hard to make a potential aggressor believe you would actually strike back once your country was in ruins. "[O]ne cannot credibly deter a first strike with a second strike whose *raison d'etre* dissolves the moment the first strike arrives." This may be "a monumental logical mistake," as Schell asserts, but it has prevented anyone from using a nuclear weapon, or even overtly threatening to use one first, for thirty-five years. And in any event, pending his proposed outburst of "love, a spiritual energy that the human heart can pit against the physical energy released from the heart of matter," it's all we've got.

So the first problem with Schell's solution is that you can't get there from here. The second problem is what "there" could be like. Speaking, if I may, for the unborn, I wonder if they might not prefer the risk of not being born at all to the certainty of being born into the world Schell is prepared to will them.

The supreme silliness of "The Fate of the Earth," and of much of the anti-nuclear movement, is the insistence that any kind of perspective on nuclear war is immoral. Schell complains, "It is as though life itself were one huge distraction, diverting our attention from the peril to life." And to Schell, apparently, all considerations apart from the danger of nuclear war *are* mere distractions. He repeatedly asks, What could be worse than the total annihilation of the earth and everything and everyone on it forever and ever? He demands that "this possibility must be dealt with morally and politically as though it were a certainty." We can opt for "human survival," or for "our transient aims and fallible convictions" and "our political and military traditions":

> On the one side stand human life and the terrestrial creation. On the other side stands a particular organization of human life— the system of independent, sovereign nation-states.

Gee, I just can't decide. Can you?

If the choice were "survival" versus "distractions," it would be easy, and Schell wants to make it seem easy (though I have to wonder whether he really lives his own life at the peak of obsessive hysteria posited in his writing). In fact, that's not the choice. The choice is between the chance, not the certainty, of a disaster of uncertain magnitude, versus institutional and social arrangements that have some real charm.

Schell suggests at one point that "say, liberty" and other "benefits of life" are relatively unimportant in his scheme of things, because

> to speak of sacrificing the species for the sake of one of these benefits involves one in the absurdity of wanting to destroy something in order to preserve one of its parts.

But it's clear that he imagines his post-nuclear world as a delightful lion-and-lamb affair, no nation-states, no war, free *hors d'oeuvres* at the Algonquin bar, a place anyone would prefer even apart from the nuclear dilemma. Some of his admirers know better. In a recent column, Eliot Fremont-Smith of the *Village Voice* expressed the general dazzlement "The Fate of the Earth" has induced in the New York literary scene. He called on Knopf to cancel the rest of its spring list in deference to Schell's vital message. But Fremont-Smith did indicate some passing regret for what might have to be given up when Schell's world organization replaces national sovereignty. His list includes "freedom, liberties, social justice"—but he is willing to kiss these trinkets away in the name of "a higher and longer-viewed morality." Others may demur.

Actually, if Schell and his admirers really believe that the nuclear peril outweighs all other considerations, they are making unnecessary work for themselves by proposing to convince all the leaders of the world to lay down their weapons. Schell concedes that the people of the Soviet Union don't have much influence over their government, and suggests, rather lamely, that "public opinion in the free countries would have to . . . bring its pressure to bear, as best it could, on all governments." But why not avoid this problem by concentrating on our own governments? Schell is right: the doctrine of deterrence is only necessary for nation-states that wish to preserve themselves as political entities. Nothing would reduce the peril of nuclear war more quickly and dramatically than for the free and open societies of the West to renounce the use of nuclear weapons unilaterally. That would solve the flaw Schell sees in deterrence theory by making the Soviet threat to use them thoroughly credible, and therefore making their use unnecessary. More creatively, we might offer the Soviets a deal: you forswear nuclear weapons, and we'll forswear *all* weapons, nuclear and conventional. They might find this very tempting. So, by his own logic ("the nuclear powers put a higher value on national sovereignty than they do on human survival"), would Jonathan Schell.

In practice, the anti-nuclear movement *is* concentrating on the free governments of the West, for the obvious reason that these are the only governments susceptible to being influenced. I do not think most anti-nuclear protesters want unilateral disarmament. But the suspicion that they do is widespread among the political leaders they must attempt to persuade, and is hampering their basically worthy efforts. The glorious muddle of their thinking is hampering those efforts even more. What *do* they want?

18. *Recovery From Nuclear Attack*

By JACK C. GREENE

Focus   In this essay written in 1979, during the Carter administration, a specialist from the U.S. Defense Civil Preparedness Agency addresses what many people regard as an "unthinkable" question: Can we survive a full-scale nuclear attack? His short answer is yes. His long answer, from which this selection was excerpted, is based on more than three decades of government and private research here and abroad. It will surprise those who are convinced that nuclear war will inevitably mean the end of the United States, civilization, or the human race.

Greene introduces some technical language to trace the effects of a nuclear attack and its aftermath on people in and outside the target areas, on food supplies, on ecology, and on the economy. He considers in turn blast, radiation, and genetic effects.

Greene acknowledges that the scenario he describes is filled with uncertainties, but he concludes that 50 per cent of the American population would survive a general Soviet attack against U.S. military targets and cities. A post-attack census, he says, would count slightly over 100 million people, approximately the population of 1921. About 50 per cent of the industrial plant would be destroyed and an additional 20 per cent damaged. There would be many other dire consequences. Depending on the adequacy of pre-war civil defense preparations and

256

the quality of post-war recovery arrangements, most of the immediate survivors would continue to have a tolerable and productive existence. The chances of dying from late radiation effects in a single year would be 2 in 10,000. Genetic damage would not be so great as to "threaten the survival of society or seriously impede the progress of recovery."

Greene's belief that the country could survive a nuclear attack is shared by Herman Kahn (see selection 16) and most other American specialists on nuclear war.

Jack C. Greene, now retired, served as director of post-attack research (1963-73) and deputy assistant director of research (1973-74) for the U.S. Defense Civil Preparedness Agency.

O N DECEMBER 5, 1945, just four months after the news burst on the world that an atomic bomb had been developed by the United States and had been dropped on Japan, Dr. Hans Bethe, one of the designers of the bomb, was asked to appear before the Special Committee on Atomic Energy of the U.S. Senate. The committee was concerned that an atomic explosion might "ignite" the earth's atmosphere or start some sort of chain reaction in the air or in the ocean.

Although these fears are no longer taken seriously, fears of other almost equally catastrophic occurrences have arisen to take their place. These include:

—triggering a new ice age;

—upsetting the delicate balance of nature, leading to disastrous changes in the ecology;

—creation of vast radioactive wastelands that would be uninhabitable for generations;

—great increases in the incidence of leukemia and other malignancies among the survivors;

—vast increases in the number of congenital defects due to gene mutations, lasting for many generations;

—depletion of the ozone layer in the stratosphere, thus decreasing the protection from ultraviolet radiation and causing proliferation of skin cancers, killing wild and domestic animals, and making it difficult, if not impossible, to grow many of the crops that provide our food and fiber.

The underlying motive behind these negative hypotheses may be psychological. If everyone "knew" that nuclear war either directly or indirectly would trigger a mechanism for annihilating the human species, somehow the world would appear more secure. No sane person would initiate a series of events that would lead to everyone's death, including his own. Thus to many people the idea of assured destruction contains elements of reassurance.

257

Why has the argument that "recovery from a nuclear war would be impossible" been so persuasive in limiting U.S. civil defense? Leaving aside the psychological element, it may be the way in which the question has been stated. Those who argue for a civil defense program have been challenged to prove beyond a reasonable doubt that the United States *could* recover from a nuclear attack.

On the other hand, what if those who oppose civil defense had to prove beyond a reasonable doubt that the United States *could not* recover from a nuclear attack? Both present extremely difficult, if not impossible, tasks. At today's level of knowledge, no such degree of proof exists for either proposition. Although the search is certainly not over, a great deal of research effort has been expended looking for an "Achilles heel" that would preclude recovery. In years of research, no insuperable barrier to recovery has been found.

The chances of surviving the immediate effects of the bombs caused by high overpressures and thermal radiation—effects that killed most of the victims of the atomic bombs in Japan—are about two in three. There is about one chance in two of surviving the fallout radiation effects as well. In all, the chances are about one in three of *not* receiving a radiation, blast, or burn injury.

In short, the prospects are:

—one in three of being killed outright by blast or thermal effects;

—one in six of being killed by fallout radiation;

—one in six of being injured, but non-fatally, by blast, thermal, or fallout radiation;

—one in three of being uninjured.

These are gross estimates, of course. They would vary considerably, depending upon such factors as type of attack (whether a counterforce attack or an industry attack, for example) and weight of attack. The amount of warning and the status of civil defense preparedness would also have an important influence on the number of casualties. The estimates above are based on the assumption that civil defense at the time of attack is essentially the same as it is at the time of writing (1979), and that the attack is a full-scale strike against both counterforce and industrial targets.

The estimates would also vary depending on how the casualty calculations are made. The "damage functions" used in the computer programs for the calculations represent a less-than-perfect understanding of how the bomb-produced blast, thermal, and ionizing radiation phenomena interact with structures and with people. However, damage functions that are reflected in the numbers given above represent many years of research, and major improvements or changes are unlikely.

Now picture the United States one or two weeks after a full-scale attack against major military targets and population centers. Approximately 50 per cent of the population would have survived. Certain assumptions, based on years of research, can be made about the composition of the surviving population:

1. The next census will show a United States population of a little over 100 million—approximately the same as in 1921.

2. The population is no longer predominantly urban, for a considerably higher percentage of the rural population survived.

3. The male-female ratio remains about the same, but the age distribution is different. There are considerably fewer of the very old or very young.

4. The life expectancy of the average person is shortened, perhaps by as much as four to five years.

5. Proportionally there are fewer doctors and hospitals, corporate headquarters and executives, petroleum-refining and pharmaceutical-production plants, and public administrators.

6. Many of the males in the surviving population are or will soon be temporarily sterile.

7. There is an increase in the percentage of orphans and other dependents as well as an increase in broken families.

8. There are other changes in the composition of the labor force, both geographically and in terms of skills.

9. About 50 per cent of the manufacturing capacity of the nation has been destroyed and an additional 20 per cent damaged. Of the remaining 30 per cent, some will not be accessible until radiation levels decay or decontamination has been performed.

10. Many domestic and wild animals and crops have been killed or severely damaged; compared to people, a higher percentage have survived.

11. People are learning how to avoid or minimize the consumption of contaminated food and water and how to ration carefully their exposure to external sources of radiation.

12. The general behavior pattern among the survivors is adaptive rather than maladaptive. By and large, people can be counted on to participate constructively in future efforts to achieve national recovery as long as there appears to be a leadership that has a plan and knows what it is doing.

Survivors of the direct blast and early fallout effects still face an uncertain future. Serious additional hazards and obstacles must be overcome before the society to which they now belong returns to a semblance of its pre-attack status. Some of the hazards will have to be faced immediately, while others will not become important until months or even years later.

Of course, before recovery can start, individuals must survive the blast and thermal effects, fallout, and the prospect of being trapped without rescue or medical help. Even after the immediate post-attack period (roughly the first week), there would still be many obstacles to overcome, beginning with the possibility of insufficient life-support requisites such as food, water, and shelter.

The major elements in this "obstacle course to recovery" and the times during which they will be most important are:

Attack Effect	Time After Attack
Blast and thermal	1–2 days
Fallout	2–20 days
Trapped; no medical treatment	2–7 days
Life-support inadequacies	5–50 days
Epidemics and diseases	2 weeks–1 year
Economic breakdown	1–2 years
Late radiation effects	5–20 years
Ecological effects	10–50 years
Genetic damage	2 –several generations

These obstacles are not necessarily independent of one another, and of course the times indicated are not precise.

Life-Support Inadequacies

People who have to remain in fallout shelters because of continuing high fallout-radiation levels in the outside environment may run out of food and water. Unless adequate supplies of water for drinking are maintained, severe consequences will be experienced within a very short time. People either will leave the shelter in search of water, thereby exposing themselves to excessive radiation, or will become ill from dehydration. If water is completely denied, deaths will begin to occur in a few days.

Food supplies are less critical. Most people could survive for several weeks on a severely limited amount of nourishment. The most important consequences could be hunger-motivated pressure to emerge prematurely from shelter in search of food.

As with almost any kind of severe stress, the early victims would be those who are least resilient—the very young, the very old, and the infirm.

The food and water problem is one of distribution, not of insufficient resources. Although water distribution systems could be damaged and water service interrupted, analysis has shown that in most cases enough water for drinking would be available—trapped in the plumbing, in hot water heaters, in the flush tanks of toilets, and the like. Proportionally far more food would survive than people to consume it. The problem is getting the food to the people who need it.

In some localities, and under some conditions, the shortages could be severe. Extremely hot or cold weather and disrupted transportation and communications systems could have a serious impact.

Radiological contamination of food and water would not be a serious complicating factor. With simple precautions people could avoid use of food and water with excessive contamination levels. Most people would not be affected to any significant extent.

In summary: there is no intrinsic reason why life-support requirements for the survivors of a nuclear attack should not be met. The basic problem is one of distributing the surviving supplies.

Epidemics and Diseases

Among the potential contributors to an increase of epidemics and diseases in a post-nuclear-war society are these factors:

a. Many sanitation facilities and waterworks could be either destroyed, damaged, or disrupted.

b. Public health organizations could be disrupted and lose personnel.

c. There could be inadequate supplies of prophylactic and therapeutic chemicals—vaccines, anti-toxins, antibiotics, and other necessities for disease control.

d. The higher-than-normal radiation exposures to which the survivors of nuclear war have been subjected may increase susceptibility to infection and disease.

Counterbalancing factors that would serve to prevent or limit the development of epidemics or increase of debilitating diseases include:

a. Most of the diseases that caused great epidemics in the past—cholera, smallpox, typhus, and yellow fever—no longer exist in the United States or in most other societies.

b. Sources of broad-spectrum antibiotics which would have been severely depleted by the attack could be quickly created or augmented. Veterinary-grade antibiotics, which today are produced in copious quantities, could be used for human beings in an emergency. The fermentation vats used to produce enzyme-additives for detergents could be readily converted to produce penicillin. Surviving production facilities could concentrate on a few generic broad-spectrum antibiotics rather than making numerous specialized varieties.

c. Perhaps *knowledge* is the single most important factor that would serve to mitigate the effects of epidemics and diseases. Knowledge cannot be destroyed by a nuclear attack. The great discoveries of Pasteur and Lister do not need to be repeated.

Even under the worst circumstances imaginable, there is no danger of a repetition of the bubonic plague that devastated Europe in the mid-fourteenth century, or other types of catastrophic epidemics.

Modest expenditures, primarily for developing detailed plans to augment supplies of broad-spectrum antibiotics quickly, could have a significant payoff in the event of a nuclear attack upon the United States.

In sum, the specter of pestilence and disease stalking the land in the aftermath of nuclear war is probably just that—a specter, not a realistic probability. It need not, and probably would not, occur.

Economic Breakdown

The post-attack economic problem may be thought of in two parts—the physical component and the need for management. Would the physical constituents of the economy—land with acceptably low radiation levels, seeds, fertilizers and pesticides, industrial plants, energy, raw materials, transportation, a skilled labor force—be available where needed in sufficient amounts so that, if used in an optimal way, the goods and services required by the survivors could be produced? If not, economic recovery could not occur, and the question of management becomes academic.

Do we have confidence in our ability to forecast the kinds and degrees of damage that could result to U.S. industry and its production capacity in the event of nuclear war?

The answer is yes. But it is a qualified yes.

Limitations in the ability to predict levels of damage to the various industrial sectors probably lie mostly in the uncertainties about the type of attack (targeting) an enemy would undertake, and the number and explosive power of the weapons that would be used.

Given a particular pattern and weight of attack, prediction of damage to a certain industrial sector (say, oil refineries) or a certain agricultural zone (say, the wheat and corn fields of the middle west) probably can be quite realistic. The prediction of physical damage to an individual industrial plant or the fallout level at a specific location, however, are highly uncertain. In a sense, this is analogous to the military commander who may quite accurately estimate the number of casualties to be expected in a certain military operation, but who cannot predict who the actual individuals will be.

Studies indicate that an attack intended to damage particular elements of the economy by targeting selected industries could succeed in reducing their capacity to small percentages of their pre-attack levels. Petroleum refining, iron and steel plants, drugs, engines and turbines, and the measuring devices for industrial processes are particularly vulnerable. However, because of dispersal and because of the difficulty a foreign nation would have learning the exact location of each and every U.S. facility, such attacks do not destroy the final few per cent of productive capacity of any industrial sector.

It should be kept in mind that weapons aimed at specific industries because of their importance for recovery could otherwise be aimed at missile sites or other military targets. Therefore, the weapons that one side aimed at industry would not reduce effectively the other side's ability to strike back. A philosophy of targeting specific industries in effect trades greater damage to the homeland for an attempt to make the enemy's path to recovery more difficult. Under the weapon limitations proposed in the SALT II agreement, this would continue to be the case. With an unlimited supply of weapons, of course, it would not.

Even without a deliberate attempt to create them, industrial imbalances inevitably would occur. Some economic sectors are more vulnerable than others (1) because they are concentrated in different locations—for example, agriculture in rural areas and manufacturing in urban areas; and (2) because of differences in physical vulnerability—refineries, for example, are more easily damaged than coal mines. Also, there are differences in sensitivity to the various nuclear effects. People can withstand considerably higher direct blast pressures than buildings (although people in buildings that are destroyed by blasts may die as a result of building collapse). Fallout radiation may damage living things such as people, livestock, and crops but would produce no damage to inanimate objects such as buildings and production machinery.

Common sense indicates that this country could continue to grow the food and fiber necessary to sustain its citizens after nuclear attack. The United States has a highly efficient agricultural industry. Less than 4 per cent of the total population is all that is required not only to meet the needs of the nation but also to provide huge surpluses for export. This industry is almost immune to significant damage in a nuclear attack. Farm machinery would be scarcely affected at all, and the farm workers themselves are not very vulnerable providing they take simple precautions against fallout. Priority allocation of fuel for the farm machinery and of fertilizers and other farm inputs is all that is necessary to bring the agricultural industry substantially back to its pre-attack rate.

The studies that give us information about the physical component of the economic recovery problem assume that there will be effective management and that human factors such as worker productivity and morale will be favorable—at least as favorable as they are today. These non-physical elements are the most difficult part of the problem to predict, and the one least studied.

In the event of a massive nuclear exchange between the United States and the Soviet Union, some obviously top-priority actions for management would be to:

—maintain communications;

—get essential transportation systems functioning;

—keep the agricultural industry going;

—avoid further deterioration of damaged or idle production equipment or facilities;

—proscribe non-essential activities (at least those that would "waste" material in critically short supply); and

—mobilize manpower (in particular, assure that people with those specialized skills needed in the recovery effort are used effectively).

There are important questions about decentralization. The economist Sidney Winter, while at the Rand Corporation, expressed his belief that more economic decision-making, both public and private, would need to be decentralized than is the practice in our present peacetime economy.

Dr. Winter further suggested that four of the major tasks for the federal government would be to reestablish:

1. private property rights;

2. the use of money (to prevent the inefficiency of a barter economy);

3. price expectations, possibly by operating a futures market and by a limited set of price supports; and

4. the traditional government operations in providing important public goods and services.

Should the need arise, the plans and procedures for carrying out
these tasks would have to be developed on an ad hoc basis. They do
not exist today. Unless more creative and imaginative study is
applied to develop better strategies for managing the post-attack
economy, this barrier to recovery could turn out to be the most
difficult of all.

Late Radiation Effects

Longer-term radiation effects would include thyroid damage,
bone cancer, leukemia, and other forms of cancer of the types that
occur today. Radiation does not induce new forms of cancer; it
increases the frequency of occurrence of those that result from
other causes. A physician examining cancer patients in the post-
war world would not be able to discriminate between cancers
caused by the fallout radiation and those that would have occurred
anyway. Radiation exposure would increase the incidence of various types of cancer so that the net effect would be observable on a
statistical basis. There is no danger that the increased incidence
would be great enough to pose a threat to the survival of the
society.

During a symposium held in 1969, the chairman of the National
Academy of Sciences' Division of Medical Science summarized
such long-term biological effects of a nuclear attack by stating:

> Twenty thousand additional cases per year of leukemia during
> the first fifteen to twenty years post-attack followed by an equal
> number of miscellaneous cancers, added to the normal incidence
> in the population for the next thirty to fifty years, constitute the
> upper limiting case. They would be an *unimportant* social, eco-
> nomic, and psychological burden on the surviving population.

Perspective is provided by a comparison of the death expectancy
from late radiation effects among the survivors with the death
expectancy from various causes in today's society. In the comparison, it is assumed all the fallout-radiation-induced leukemia and
other cancers among the survivors will result in death, which of
course is extreme and not to be expected.

If 20,000 people die each year from leukemia and other cancers following a nuclear attack in a society of 100 million population, the chance of dying from these causes in a single year is 2 in 10,000. This same risk of death is faced by the average person in today's society who travels 80,000 miles by commercial air, or travels 24,000 miles by car, or spends five hours rock climbing, or lives three days after his sixtieth birthday.

Perhaps it is more meaningful to compare post-attack radiation effects with the dangers of cigarette smoking, since both take their toll over time. According to the U.S. Public Health Service, 340,000 people die annually from causes attributed to cigarette smoking. If the smoking habits of the surviving population were to be similar to those of our existing population, the chance of dying from smoking would be seven times greater than that of dying from post-attack radiation effects.

This estimate assumes 100 million survivors with an average exposure of 100 roentgens—a realistic possibility.

If, because of depletion of the ozone in the stratosphere, increased amounts of ultraviolet radiation should reach the earth, there could be an increased incidence of skin cancers. The number would depend on the intensity of the ultraviolet radiation and the extent to which the survivors protect themselves.

Whether there actually would be an ozone problem is uncertain. Limited observations following nuclear tests have failed to support this hypothesis. In 1961-62, both the United States and the Soviet Union tested atomic devices in the atmosphere. The yield was in excess of 300 megatons. A worldwide network of stations that since 1960 has published daily ozone concentrations detected no evidence of an ozone decrease during the months following these test explosions. The Northern Hemisphere seemed to show, if anything, a steady rise in ozone content.

In any case, further research and study are needed to evaluate more fully the extent of this potential hazard.

Ecological Effects

There is still uncertainty concerning the probable ecological consequences of nuclear war. Some fairly extensive study programs were undertaken during the 1960s but had to be abandoned because of lack of funds. Nevertheless, they produced some important results.

A 1963 report of a study by a committee of the National Academy of Sciences states, "Ecological imbalances that would make normal life impossible are not to be expected." A 1969 update, conducted under the auspices of the Oak Ridge National Laboratory, says it is "a reasonable conclusion" that "the long-term ecological effects would not be severe enough to prohibit or seriously delay recovery."

The various ecological catastrophes postulated to follow a nuclear war—fire, erosion, flooding, pest outbreaks, epidemic diseases, and balance-of-nature disturbances—have been individually examined in terms of their probable importance. The objective of the scientist who conducted this research, Dr. Robert Ayres, formerly of the Hudson Institute, was to "take seriously and examine in their own terms all of the supposed mechanisms leading to catastrophe which have been subjects of speculation in recent years." He summarized by saying, "We have not found any of these mechanisms to be plausible in terms of any reasonable definition of catastrophe."

Dr. Ayres made his study before the ozone-depletion hypothesis—which, as we saw earlier, needs careful analysis—came into prominence. In the future, other hypotheses for post-attack catastrophe will no doubt be developed. Those that seem to have any basis in fact should be taken seriously and subjected to scientific scrutiny.

In thinking about post-attack ecology, it is useful to keep in mind that nature may not be so delicately balanced after all. No logical weight of nuclear attack could induce gross changes in the balance of nature that approach in type or degree the ones that human civilization has already produced. This includes cutting most of the original forests, tilling the prairies, irrigating the deserts, damming and polluting the streams, eliminating certain species and introducing others, overgrazing hillsides, flooding valleys, and even preventing forest fires. Man has radically changed the face of this continent, but should he leave the scene it seems overwhelmingly probable that the continent would gradually return to a state very like its original one, rather than fluctuate violently or continue to change to a new state of equilibrium.

Genetic Damage

In common with late-radiation and ecological effects of nuclear war, the genetic effects of radiation are widely misunderstood and, consequently, feared. The specter of a vast increase in the incidence of congenital defects among our descendants is awesome. Perspective is hard to develop, partly because any threat to our children is laden with emotion.

But a great deal is now known about the genetic effects of radiation. Dr. H. J. Muller, Nobel Prize-winning American geneticist, established that gene mutations produced by ionizing radiation are not different in their effect from the mutations produced by other agents. Therefore, any nuclear-war-produced genetic damage would not be manifested in unfamiliar ways, such as the birth of two-headed monsters. Rather, there would be a statistical increase in cases of the various types of genetic-related diseases and disabilities that occur in today's world.

Extensive laboratory and field studies are under way. The latter include studies of people given radiation for therapeutic and diagnostic purposes, people involved in nuclear accidents, and the survivors of Hiroshima and Nagasaki.

During a 1967 symposium, the chairman of the National Academy of Sciences' Division of Medical Sciences summarized the post-attack genetic problem as follows: "The genetic effects would be lost, as at Hiroshima and Nagasaki, in all the other 'background noise.'"

Whether the expected genetic consequences of nuclear war are currently overstated or understated, the discrepancy probably is small. Even though the radiation-induced genetic consequences of a nuclear war may add some degree of suffering to the attack survivors and their offspring, these consequences will not be of sufficient magnitude to threaten the survival of the society or seriously impede recovery.

Conclusion

On the question of whether the United States would recover following a massive nuclear attack, the jury is still out—and most probably always will be. Everyone hopes and most people believe the question will always remain in the abstract. The probability of nuclear war seems very remote, and we will never know for sure whether recovery is possible unless nuclear war actually occurs.

No nation can realistically hope to be better off after a nuclear exchange than it was before. One might inflict more damage on the other than it itself sustained, but any such "victory" would be a Pyrrhic one.

The argument that a nuclear war could eliminate the human species or bring an end to civilization as we know it has not stood up to the light of objective and scientific examination. New hypotheses for doom and disaster will arise, and they must be examined and evaluated. But no prudent society will allow unproved hypotheses to exert a paralyzing influence on its preparedness programs.

PART FOUR

The Churches and Nuclear Arms

19. *Nuclear Morality*

By GEORGE F. WILL

Focus Political commentator George Will summarizes in advance much of the argument to follow in Part Four. In criticizing Catholic clergy who urge a nuclear freeze or who admonish American Catholics not to pay taxes for national defense, Will quotes St. Thomas Aquinas, who said that rulers must "defend the state against external war weapons." Mentioning the bishop of Amarillo, who urged workers at a nuclear arms plant to seek other jobs, Will asks: "If a bishop desires a free Europe and America, and also desires unilateral disarmament, can he say how he thinks his desires are compatible?"

Will acknowledges important political and moral differences between traditional arms and weapons of mass destruction, but he insists that the latter may be "tolerated if the unilateral renunciation of them would bring on an intolerable evil (such as subjugation to an evil regime), and if the nation strives to reduce and end reliance on them." Will's positions are similar in practical terms to those in selections 2, 4, and 6, and in moral terms to selections later in this section that affirm the necessity for the United States to maintain a nuclear deterrent.

He warns against sentimental and superficial statements on nuclear arms: "Unless the bishops, including the Bishop of Rome [see selection 24], think and speak about this clearly and soon, the Church's reputation for rigorousness in moral rea-

274

soning will be jeopardized, and they will forfeit
their rightfully important role in the Western
world's debate about practical policy options."

George F. Will is a nationally syndicated colum-
nist and TV commentator. He is the author of *The
Pursuit of Virtue and Other Tory Notions* and *The
Pursuit of Happiness and Other Sobering Thoughts*.

A MONG THE SUNDRY and manifold changes in the world (the words are from the prayer book) is a political message from portions of the clergy, especially the Roman Catholic clergy. The bishop of Corpus Christi protested the naming of a submarine for that city. This drew from the Navy Secretary (a Catholic) a starchy letter rejecting the implication that "naval ships and even military service are somehow profane." He says church teachings recognize the need for deterrent systems for the virtuous task of peace-keeping. "To maintain peace within the natural order of men," Augustine said, "rulers require the power and decision to declare war." They must, Aquinas said, "defend the state against external war weapons."

Do nuclear weapons invalidate that? When an Indianapolis parish votes to protest nuclear-arms spending by withholding half the $50 tax on its yearly phone bill, it is just confusing right-mindedness with moral seriousness. But when the bishop of Amarillo urges workers at a nuclear-weapons assembly plant to consider seeking other jobs, is he saying that deterrence is possible without nuclear weapons? That deterrence is not a great enough good to justify involvement with nuclear weapons because they are inherently immoral? It is morally incoherent to will an end without willing the means to that end. If the bishop desires a free Europe and America, and also desires unilateral nuclear disarmament, can he say how he thinks his desires are compatible?

Seattle's archbishop urges people to consider refusing to pay half their federal taxes to protest spending on nuclear arms. (Such spending accounts for about two cents of every tax dollar.) He says: "We have to refuse to give our incense—in our day, tax dollars— to the nuclear idol. Some would call what I am urging 'civil dis-obedience.' I prefer to see it as obedience to God." The archbishop is hardly the first person to put his political objectives above the law and to think he hears God's applause for doing so. He says, "When crimes are being prepared in our name, we must speak plainly." Moralists, especially, must speak carefully, which the archbishop is not doing when he uses words like "idol" and "crimes."

A coherent position, consistent with traditional church teaching, can turn on the distinction between what is tolerated and what is approved. Instruments of mass destruction, which for reasons of accuracy or controllability cannot be or are not apt to be used in ways that discriminate between military and civilian targets, cannot be approved. But they can be tolerated if the unilateral renunciation of them would bring on an intolerable evil (such as subjugation to an evil regime), and if the nation strives to reduce and end reliance on them.

Unless the bishops, including the Bishop of Rome, think and speak about this, clearly and soon, the Church's reputation for rigorousness in moral reasoning will be jeopardized, and they will forfeit their rightfully important role in the Western world's debate about practical policy options. Already a growing number of clergymen assert that any use of nuclear forces, against any target, even in response to a Soviet use, is immoral, and so is the threat to use them under certain conditions, which is the basis of deterrence. As a practical matter in today's world, this amounts to asserting a moral duty to eschew effective resistance to a gross evil, Soviet tyranny.

Any of the wide variety of possible uses of nuclear weapons would be dreadful. However, it is reckless to decree that any use, even any possession for deterrence purposes, is necessarily a larger evil than the long night of centuries that would follow the extinguishing of Western cultural values by armed totalitarianism.

The idea that nuclear weapons require such radical revision of all rules about the use of force derives, in part, from the idea that those weapons make possible devastation on a scale hitherto unimaginable. But it is well to remember that wolves roamed through deserted villages at the end of the Thirty Years War, when weapons were primitive. In the 1950s John Courtney Murray wrote that "the whole concept of force has undergone a rapid and radical transformation, right in the midst of history's most acute political crisis."

The technology of nuclear weapons and delivery systems has driven us to a deterrence policy based on a practice that was once universally condemned: holding enemy civilian populations as hostages. But even before August 6, 1945, injuries inflicted on noncombatants were not just unintended collateral effects of war; they were deliberate results, on a vast scale, of tactics tailored to conventional weapons.

What was done to Dresden and other cities does not make the use of nuclear weapons any less dreadful. But our thinking should not be controlled by the mistaken notion that any use of a nuclear weapon, of any size, would involve violence vaster and less discriminating than anything mankind has experienced.

The tone of this century (as it has been experienced by Cambodians, Biafrans, Russian Kulaks, European Jews, among others) was set by the Turkish massacres of Armenians (1914-15), which followed the Bulgarian massacres of Armenians (1894-95). They did not require sophisticated technology. Sixty thousand people died in a single day in the First World War, half a million died at Verdun, without the use of missiles, nuclear weapons, or even bombing.

Between 1914 and 1918 not a single photograph of a corpse appeared in a French, German, or British newspaper. Perhaps that is one reason why the carnage continued so long that our civilization suffered wounds that may yet prove terminal. Clearly, societies should face facts, and the facts about nuclear weapons are so appalling they can numb any imagination not already numbed by modern history, and can provoke unreasonable responses. That is why when the subject is nuclear weapons, everyone, and especially persons propounding radical and dubious new religious duties inimical to deterrence, should remember the duty to be clear in their own minds about where their logic leads, and to be candid with others about the probable real-world consequences of the behavior they favor.

20. The Case for Nuclear Pacifism

By BISHOP ROGER MAHONY

Focus In a widely publicized pastoral letter published in December 1981, Bishop Roger Mahony of Stockton, California, called upon his fellow Catholics to embrace nuclear pacifism. Making no distinction between the power and intentions of the Soviet Union and of the United States, he asserted that the "arms race" has "long exceeded the bounds of justice and moral legitimacy" and "makes it impossible effectively to end the urgent crisis of world hunger. It can no longer be tolerated."

Any use of nuclear arms and "any intention to use them," says the bishop, "is always morally—and gravely—a serious evil. No Catholic can ever support or cooperate with the planning or executing of policies to use . . . nuclear weapons even in a defensive posture. . . ."

He quotes with approval Richard Barnet of the Institute for Policy Studies: "Once the nuclear force is regarded as a 'flexible' instrument for achieving purposes beyond the crude one of deterring a nuclear attack with the threat of an all-out counterattack on Soviet society, the arms race becomes a never-ending, infinitely escalating contest." The idea that a nuclear war could be either "winnable" or "limited" is, says Mahony, a "moral monstrosity."

Bishop Mahony implies that the United States is largely responsible for the "nuclear arms race."

"With each new American acquisition the Soviets rushed to catch up and vice versa. Now we are making an unprecedented leap in arms expenditures as a pre-condition for any arms-limitation talks with the Soviets. . . ." Americans need a "radical change of our hearts and attitudes," he says, "a new awareness of our calling to be a people dedicated to peace."

The Most Reverend **Roger Mahony** is the Roman Catholic bishop of Stockton, California, and a leading peace advocate in the National Conference of Catholic Bishops.

THE ROMAN CATHOLIC CHURCH, as is well known, has never held a position of absolute pacifism. It accepts the premise that one can legitimately resist evil by force in justified self-defense. It has espoused a complex moral reasoning about the right to declare and engage in warfare known as the "just-war theory." Nevertheless, in recent years more and more Catholics—our popes, bishops in this country and elsewhere, theologians and other scholars, and conscientious priests, religious, and lay Catholics throughout the world—have increasingly asked: How can we become, truly, advocates of peace?

Today I add my voice to the growing chorus of Catholic protests against the arms race because I believe the current arms policy of our nation, as well as of the Soviet Union, has long since exceeded the bounds of justice and moral legitimacy. Moreover, the arms race makes it impossible effectively to end the urgent crisis of world hunger. It can no longer be tolerated.

Each day we permit it to continue without protest it perpetuates itself by becoming embedded in our everyday habits and attitudes. What is needed instead is a radical change of our hearts and our attitudes—a new awareness of our calling to be a people dedicated to peace.

I have said that the Roman Catholic Church is not a pacifist church, but this needs some qualification. The bishops of the world at the Second Vatican Council asserted their strong support for those individual Catholics who adopt a position of absolute pacifism. Their words bear repeating here: "We cannot fail to praise those who renounce the use of violence in the vindication of their rights and who resort to methods of defense which are otherwise available to weaker parties too, provided that this can be done without injury to the rights and duties of others or of the community itself."[1]

The same Vatican Council document also states: "It seems right that laws make humane provisions for the case of those who for

Excerpted from "Becoming a Church of Peace Advocacy," December 30, 1981.

reasons of conscience refuse to bear arms, provided however, that they accept some other form of service to the human community."[2]

We American bishops extended the range of this principle by supporting the right to "conscientious objection" of Catholics who conclude in conscience, following the reasoning of the just-war theory, that some particular war of their nation is unjust, even if they are not opposed to all wars in principle. We advocated that American law recognize the right to selective conscientious objection as the legitimate extension of our First Amendment rights to free exercise of religious conscience.[3]

It is even more important to recall that the moral reasoning involved in classic just-war theory led the bishops at the Second Vatican Council to declare that a form of nuclear pacifism is a weighty and unexceptional obligation of Christians. This means that any use of nuclear weapons, and by implication, any intention to use them, is always morally—and gravely—a serious evil. No Catholic can ever support or cooperate with the planning or executing of policies to use, or which by implication intend to use, nuclear weapons even in a defensive posture, let alone in a "first strike" against another nation.

This Catholic version of nuclear pacifism follows directly from just-war premises. According to this tradition of moral reasoning, aggressive or "first-strike" wars are always immoral. The legitimacy of a defensive use of force depends on certain conditions. One such condition is that there be specific, limited objectives in going to war. Others include: the immunity of noncombatants from direct attack, and the proportionality of specific tactics and weapons to the purpose of the war. Since nuclear weapons involve indiscriminate and massive violence committed against civilian populations, their employment or contemplated use can never be morally permitted. Indeed, the closest thing to an anathema in all of the Second Vatican Council documents are the plain words of "The Church in the Modern World" which enjoin a form of nuclear pacifism on the Catholic conscience: "Any act of war aimed indiscriminately at the destruction of entire cities or of extensive areas along with their population is a crime against God and man himself. It merits unequivocal and unhesitating condemnation."[4]

The bishops were not inventing a new position in this regard, but following the consistent and repeated teaching of the Church since the beginning of the atomic age. On the basis of the just-war theory, during World War II leading Catholic moral theologians in our own country condemned the use of atomic weapons in Hiroshima and Nagasaki, as well as the obliteration bombings of Dresden and Tokyo.

The majority of American Catholic journals too, in dissent from the wider American public, but decidedly in continuity with Catholic moral thinking, condemned the use of atomic weapons in Japan. The prominent Catholic layman Thomas E. Murray, a member of the Atomic Energy Commission, pronounced three practices of the Allies during World War II immoral and barbaric by the standards of Catholic moral teaching: obliteration bombing, the demand for unconditional surrender, and the atomic bombing of Hiroshima and Nagasaki.[5] This Catholic position on nuclear pacifism has been repeated over and over by Popes John XXIII, Paul VI, and John Paul II. It was affirmed again by the 1974 world Synod of Bishops. In 1976, we American bishops confirmed it once again in our collective pastoral letter entitled *To Live in Christ Jesus.*[6]

Nor is this nuclear pacifism—this conviction that any use of nuclear weapons or, by implication, intention to actually use them is morally indefensible—a uniquely Catholic position. The World Council of Churches at its New Delhi assembly in 1961 uttered words similar to those of the Second Vatican Council: "Christians must also maintain that the use of nuclear weapons or other forms of major violence against centers of population is in no circumstances reconcilable with the demands of the Christian Gospel."[7]

Now, more than three decades and 50,000 nuclear weapons later, the question of whether the use of nuclear weapons can be justified on any ethical grounds is rarely heard in our national debates and almost never in formal arms negotiations. All attention is riveted on questions such as how to put a ceiling on the further growth in numbers of weapons, for example, by limiting the number of warheads to no more than ten per ICBM or fourteen per sea-launched ballistic missile.

It is the absence of this moral dimension in our public policy discussions and a growing moral callousness which permit some government officials to speak publicly and rashly of "limited" and "winnable" nuclear wars. This has impelled me to add my voice to the growing number of American bishops who are calling for a fundamental about-face in the arms race.

Is Nuclear Deterrence Permissible?

For some time many Christian moralists have held that the possession of nuclear weapons as a deterrent—but never their use or the intention to actually use them—is morally permissible.

They have reasoned that the threat of nuclear retaliation may in fact be preventing the use of nuclear weapons. Moreover, they have argued that condemning the possession of nuclear weapons as a deterrent without suggesting a practical political and military alternative is, at best, politically inadequate, and at worst dangerously naïve.

Just as the right to legitimate defense is not a justification for unleashing any and every form of destruction, so moral arguments for the possession of nuclear weapons for deterrence do not constitute support for every national arms policy that is advanced in the name of deterrence.

The only possible Catholic support for a national nuclear-deterrence policy depends on three related moral judgments: first, that the primary moral imperative is to prevent any use of nuclear weapons under any circumstances; second, that the possession of nuclear weapons is always an evil which could at best be tolerated, but only if the deterrence strategy is used in order to make progress on arms limitation and reductions; and third, that the ultimate goal of what remains at best an interim deterrence policy is the eventual elimination of nuclear arms and of the threat of mutual assured destruction.[8]

We need to look, then, at the facts of the arms race to see whether: (1) ours is truly an interim deterrence policy aimed at reducing the risks of any use of nuclear weapons; (2) the framework of deterrence is actually used to reduce arms; and (3) our goal is really a world free of nuclear threats and terror. It is my judgment that the present U.S. and Soviet arms policy does not meet the demands of any of these three premises.

Since the first use of the atomic bomb in 1945, the risk of actually using nuclear weapons has escalated in a staggering way. Today we can explode the equivalent of 1.5 million Hiroshima bombs. In the past three years alone we have increased the destructive power of our nuclear arsenal by 50 per cent. Now we are about to embark on the largest single arms build-up in our national history. Having spent more than $1 trillion on defense in the past ten years, we now plan to spend $1 trillion more in the coming four years and another $1 trillion in the three years after that.[9] Long ago, it would seem, we have ceased looking at deterrence as an interim policy aimed at genuine arms reduction.

Secretary of Defense Robert McNamara estimated that a force of 100 nuclear weapons with explosive yields of no more than fifty kilotons each would suffice as a "deterrent," because it would be capable of destroying 25 per cent of the Soviet population, some 65 million people, as well as 50 per cent of all Soviet industrial capacity. A more cautious estimate assumes that 400 "warheads would constitute a more than adequate deterrence capability."[10] Merely two of our thirty-one Poseidon submarines would, on this basis, be sufficient to guarantee this capability—if deterrence were our real goal.

Instead of 400 warheads, we currently have a total of 11,893, and we plan to build another 18,500 by 1990.[11]

Furthermore, the deterrence envisioned by the tenuous Catholic moral toleration of possession of nuclear weapons as a permissible evil is aimed at deterring the use of other nuclear weapons against us. It is not morally permissible to use nuclear weapons to deter mere conventional warfare. Yet the United States possesses 22,000 tactical nuclear weapons designed for the purpose of use in conventional wars. The neutron bomb, for example, is designed mainly to deter Soviet tanks, not other nuclear bombs. In fact, our nation has either threatened to use or actually planned to use nuclear weapons against conventional forces on at least nine occasions.[12] Richard Ellis of the U.S. Strategic Air Command testified recently that "deterrence can no longer be neatly divided into subgroups such as nuclear and conventional. It must be viewed as an interrelated single entity."[13]

Clearly we have moved beyond true deterrence to the production and use of nuclear weapons as an assertion of our national superiority. We are being urged to use our nuclear arsenal as bargaining chips for diplomatic and political adventures far beyond questions of deterrence. "Bargaining chips" is the language used by the defense establishment, which also speaks of "a menu of flexible nuclear options." As Richard Barnet has recently asserted: "Once the nuclear force is regarded as a 'flexible' instrument for achieving purposes beyond the crude one of deterring a nuclear attack with the threat of an all-out counterattack on Soviet society, the arms race becomes a never-ending, infinitely escalating contest."[14]

The moral justification for an interim deterrence policy flows from the right of a nation and its people to security. But no nation or people has any right to total supremacy or superiority in "bargaining chips," or any of the other goals of the new "flexible" nuclear policy. By seeking for something other than a legitimate right to security through limited deterrence capability, we have actually been escalating the risks of nuclear war and undermining the real security of our own nation and the rest of the world.

The Shift to a First-Strike Strategy

Since President Carter's Presidential Directive 59, announced in August of 1980, we have also shifted away from a policy of deterrence to a "counterforce" first-strike strategy which does not and cannot make us or anyone else more secure. Now we are constructing weapons such as the cruise missile which would elude any verification. These new weapons in principle impede any possible arms limitation agreements between the United States and the Soviet Union. We are designing weapons unneeded for deterrence, which will make it more difficult to achieve genuine bilateral reductions in arms.

The very use of the term "deterrence" in moral argument has become very dangerous because of its ambiguities. We now need to distinguish between legitimate deterrence strategies and the rhetoric of a spurious "deterrence" within which hawks on each side of the East-West divide compete to increase arms and provocations, envision fictitious gaps and windows of vulnerability, enter unending inconclusive negotiations which do not really stop the arms race, and accelerate our drift toward nuclear collision.

Recently we have heard public officials speak foolishly and imprudently of "limited" and "winnable" nuclear wars, as if to prepare us to accept and to accustom ourselves to such moral monstrosity. We have all become so numbed, so used to the nuclear umbrella, that we forget that less than a decade ago no responsible statesman on either side ever spoke of actually using nuclear weapons. With the present escalation in the arms race there has also been an escalation in the rhetoric of threats and expectations and conceivable risks. The attitude that it is possible to "win" a nuclear war assumes that there is no longer any such thing as an unacceptable level of population loss. Any level of loss is apparently acceptable so long as our side "wins." In the face of such arrogance, such aridity of feeling and moral bankruptcy, we must not remain silent. This has never been and is not now a position that Catholics can in any way endorse or even merely tolerate or leave unchallenged.

With the one exception of the Nuclear Test Ban Treaty, which outlawed all above-ground nuclear detonations, there has not really been any reduction in the arms race. Even the SALT I agreement in 1972, which placed some limits on the quantity of American and Soviet ICBMs and sea-launched ballistic missiles, in no way placed limits on new improvements in the precision, reliability, or explosive yield of those weapons already permitted. Neither did it prevent other qualitative "improvements" such as the development of the cruise missile and the neutron bomb. The arms race, in fact, continued to escalate after SALT I. As is well known, the United States did not ratify the SALT II agreement.

On a number of occasions since the end of World War II, the American public has been systematically misled into believing in a fictitious strategic bomber "gap" (1948), a strategic "gap" (1956), and a missile "gap" (1960). Subsequent evidence showed that no such gaps ever existed.[15] In the meantime the arms race continued to escalate. With each new American acquisition the Soviets rushed to catch up and vice versa. Now we are making an unprecedented leap in arms expenditure a precondition for any arms-limitation talks with the Soviets.

This is not deterrence, nor is it aimed at a genuine reduction of existing arms. At best it envisions a higher plateau of "deputed" security from which alone we might enter guarded and highly limited arms negotiations. Although the language of deterrence is still used, it is curious how each new "gap" allows the introduction of weapons that were in any case designed and executed for production before anyone had noticed the "gap"! This is not the kind of deterrence which can be morally permitted. It escalates rather than reduces the arms race.

Many of those who are now urging American arms increases are looking to an American "military superiority" beyond mere deterrence capability—one which will give us a psychological advantage and somehow impress the Soviet leadership with our willingness to risk catastrophe. It looks to a show of superior power and the will to use it, the aim of which is not genuine security, but extended space for diplomatic and political adventures in the world. These people, of course, call themselves "realists." They speak of a "flexible" nuclear policy and "limited" nuclear wars, but in doing so they both ignore the dangers of escalation—with its terrible risk of the actual use of nuclear weapons—and contribute significantly to this very danger. It is more realistic, in my judgment, to devote ourselves to creating the conditions of possibility for peace and disarmament. Those who minimize this danger and believe that the escalation of violence can be controlled in warfare are the ones who have lost touch with reality.

Loss of a Secure Moral Basis

Since I believe the American arms policy has exceeded the moral limits of deterrence and has eroded our real security, and since there has been up until now no serious connection between American arms policy and a serious attempt to reduce arms worldwide, it is my conviction that Catholics no longer have a secure moral basis to support actively or cooperate passively in the current U.S. arms policy and escalating arms race.

Not only does our present arms policy force us to neglect our own poor and the disparate poverty and hunger of other nations, but there is good reason to believe that it will destroy our own economy. In a recent contribution to the *Bulletin of the Atomic Scientists,* one noted economist argues that our military expenditures have directly contributed to our industrial decline. He concludes that "the arms race has a deeply damaging effect on the free-enterprise economy," and also asserts that "the arms race as it now proceeds does not strengthen free institutions or free enterprise."[16] Another policy analyst asserts that "the war economy has brought us inflation, technological backwardness, maldistribution of wealth, a sinking dollar, and unemployment."[17] Still another economic historian refers to "the baroque arsenal" which helps erode our national economy by erecting a perverse hierarchy of values.

In whose interest could our present war economy possibly be? It is not in the interest of all the millions of ordinary men, women, and children in this country and in the Soviet Union at whose homes and cities these insane weapons are now aimed. We should not forget the warning of President Dwight D. Eisenhower when he urged us Americans to be wary of "the acquisition of unwarranted influence, whether sought or unsought, by the military-industrial complex. The potential for the disastrous rise of misplaced power exists and will persist. We should take nothing for granted."

The evidence for this "unwarranted influence" of an industrial-military complex is even more obvious today than it was twenty years ago when he made that statement. Of the fifty largest U.S. industrial companies, thirty-two make or export arms. Half of the nation's engineers or scientists work directly or indirectly for the Pentagon.

Many of the technical experts on arms in fact constitute the very group whose interest is served by arms escalation. We must be suspicious of the "expertise" of those who sell and manufacture weapons. Because self-serving interests often lie behind the claims of this military-industrial complex, we must not allow the larger questions of public policy, especially the inescapable moral questions, to be decided by the so-called experts.

We are all aware, of course, that the United States is not a single actor in this nuclear terror. The Soviet Union does represent a real threat to our national interests and security. Clearly we have a right to genuine security. An industrial-military complex similar to our own exists also in the Soviet Union.

The Goal Is Disarmament

I am not, therefore, advocating unilateral disarmament or an unqualified pacifism. But unilateral disarmament is something quite different from serious, persistent, even unilateral, initiatives toward bilateral disarmament. The goal must be disarmament, arms reduction, not merely a ceiling on new, even more monstrous weapons.

The arms race also cripples the Soviet economy and places severe strains on Soviet institutions. It is in their interest as well as ours to withdraw resources from these sterile contests of arms production to other and urgent social issues. The Soviets, including their leaders, like us have children and grandchildren, cities and landscapes which they love, desires and hopes for a better future. We must not evade the real danger posed by Soviet policy, but we must refuse to "demonize" them and caricature their views and aspirations. As Christians called to love even our enemies, we must at least concede their essential humanity and search tirelessly and with all our energy for grounds of mutual understanding and accord with them.

I am proposing that we search together for ways to become a peace-advocate church. We American Catholics will need to become more aware of all the true facts and issues concerning the arms race. We will need to make new efforts to continue to educate ourselves about all the relevant factors.

But first of all we must pray for a conversion of heart to become the kind of peacemakers spoken of in the Gospel. As peace advocates, Catholics will collaborate with the various existing groups and movements already active in the cause of peace.

We must use every political resource, including support for peace lobbies and pressure on our congressional representatives, to ensure that the United States returns to a minimal deterrence policy and initiate serious comprehensive proposals for arms limitation and reduction based on parity. Successful collective bargaining initiatives always respect parity; arms limitation should attempt to guarantee security on both sides, include clear economic benefits for both sides, and be as comprehensive as possible. Real parity must be the goal in step-by-step reduction of arms.

A reduction of current armaments by one-half on both sides would still guarantee a mutual capability of totally destroying the other country several times over. It would furthermore entail a significant program of industrial-technological conversion to peacetime uses. Such a reduction would require the leaders of both nations to confront powerful interests that have a bureaucratic and ideological commitment to the arms race. Their ability to do this successfully would represent the best test of their sincerity in moving toward deterrence as an interim strategy.

Short of an actual reduction, many are now urging a three-year bilateral freeze by the United States and the Soviet Union on all research, construction, or testing of nuclear weapons systems. In my judgment, nothing short of these two proposals—a reduction in half or a freeze—will be adequate strategies for the present situation. We Catholics must bear witness to the conviction voiced by Pope John Paul II in his stirring appeal at the memorial of the dead in Hiroshima last year: "Our future on this planet, exposed as it is to nuclear annihilation, depends on one single factor. Humanity must make a moral about-face."

As an American bishop, I deeply respect our nation's tradition of separation of church and state. I would deplore, however, any attempt to turn this legitimate separation into a separation of church from society or into a privatization of religion that would divorce our faith and hope from public concerns and crucial moral questions that face us all as citizens. I would deplore any attempt to discuss the arms race merely as a "technical" issue—for example, of comparative nuclear engineering—devoid of ethical considerations or religious significance. We must all decide what consti-

tutes the true relationship between religious faith and social justice, and I would deplore any attempt by politicians and government officials to claim for themselves some special competence to
define this relationship.

As your bishop I depend on your freedom of conscience and
your Christian imaginations in becoming more effective advocates
of peace. I want to avoid at this time making more specific recommendations about the steps we must now take. I have reminded
you, as I have reminded myself, of what the Catholic teaching is
and has been concerning nuclear weapons. I ask you to help one
another and to help me to find new approaches for combating this
great evil. The survival with dignity of the whole human race is at
stake and the terrible urgency of threatened starvation for millions
of people. Can anyone really believe these are not profoundly
religious concerns? Now we must find the way to allow these
passionate concerns to become effective action.

NOTES

1. "The Church in the Modern World," 78, in David O'Brien and Thomas
Shannon, eds., *Renewing the Earth: Catholic Documents on Peace, Justice and
Liberation*, New York: Doubleday, 1977.

2. Ibid., 79.

3. Cf. the U.S. Catholic Conference, "Declaration on Conscientious Objection and Selective Conscientious Objection," October 21, 1971.

4. "The Church in the Modern World," 80.

5. Thomas E. Murray, "Morality and Security: The Forgotten Equation," in
William Nagle, ed., *Morality and Modern Warfare: The State of the Question*,
Baltimore, 1960, pp. 58-68.

6. "To Live in Christ Jesus," National Conference of Catholic Bishops,
November 11, 1976.

7. Cf. "The New Delhi Report 1961," London, 1962, par. 64, p. 108. Cf. also
the collective pastoral letter of the House of Bishops of the Protestant Episcopal
Church, U.S.A., against nuclear proliferation, "Apocalypse and Hope," Oct. 9,
1981.

8. This statement of the moral premises for deterrence is available in Archbishop Joseph Bernardin's report of the ad hoc committee on war and peace to the
National Conference of Catholic Bishops, November 1981. It is also the argument
contained in the Vatican Declaration on Disarmament to the United Nations,
May 7, 1976.

9. Cf. Tom Gervasi, *Arsenal of Democracy II,* New York, 1981, p. 2.

10. Robert Aldridge, an aeronautical engineer, cited in Gervasi, p. 24.

11. Cf. Ruth Leger Sivard, *World Military and Social Expenditures, 1981.*

12. Gervasi, p. 29. Cf. also for this assertion and the evidence, *A Matter of Faith: A Study for Churches on the Nuclear Arms Race,* Washington, D.C.: Sojourners, 1981, pp. 6-13.

13. Cited in Gervasi, p. 28.

14. Richard Barnet, *Real Security: Restoring American Power in a Dangerous Decade,* New York, 1981, p. 26.

15. Robert Aldridge, "The Deadly Race," in Gervasi, p. 13. Significantly, all the alleged "gaps" took place in presidential election years. Nuclear policy is allowed to become a political ploy.

16. John Kenneth Galbraith, "The Economics of the Arms Race—and After," in *The Bulletin of the Atomic Scientists,* June-July 1981, pp. 13-16.

17. Barnet, p. 97.

21. The Church's Views on Nuclear Arms

By BISHOP JOHN J. O'CONNOR

Focus Though written well before Bishop Mahony's letter (selection 20), this essay on the Catholic doctrine of the "just war" provides a comprehensive answer to Mahony's position. Noting that the nuclear arms discussion is "laden with extreme emotion" and that the professional moralists have not provided analytical writing in this area similar to that "in medical ethics or other fields," Bishop O'Connor systematically examines the positions of each pope of the atomic age, the Second Vatican Council, and the U.S. National Conference of Catholic Bishops. His well-documented conclusions are quoted here in full:

"1. The Church condemns war of aggression, unlimited war, acts of war 'directed to the indiscriminate destruction of whole cities or vast areas with their inhabitants,' the use of weapons of mass destruction.

"2. The Church does not condemn defensive war, limited war, acts of war directed to the destruction of military targets, the manufacture or possession of nuclear weapons, the use of weapons of limited destruction.

"3. The Church seriously questions the strategy of nuclear deterrence, abhors the arms race, considering it a treacherous trap for humanity, potentially destructive of all life, and draining resources critically needed to feed the hungry and generally advance civilization.

"4. The Church calls for the eventual goal of banning nuclear weapons, urging that in the meanwhile, there be continuing, balanced, mutual, progressive reductions in nuclear weapons 'backed up by authentic and workable safeguards,' and urging negotiations and treaties that will help reduce risks of nuclear war."

These conclusions are a far cry from Catholic calls for a nuclear freeze, unilateral disarmament, or a no-first-use pledge by the United States.

The Most Reverend **John J. O'Connor,** a bishop who holds the rank of rear admiral, USN (ret.), is vicar general of the Military Vicariate of the Roman Catholic Church in the United States.

EACH POPE OF THE ATOMIC AGE has addressed the subject of nuclear weapons as a radically new and horrifying dimension among destructive forces confronting the world. So with Vatican II and with the National Conference of Catholic Bishops of the United States. But since of its very nature the subject is both extraordinarily technical and laden with extreme emotion, one must examine with special care both what is said and what is not said, if a fair sense of church teaching is to be gleaned. Again it is worth recalling that even though nuclear weaponry has been publicly known for some thirty-five years, professional moralists have still not provided the analyses or the body of literature similar to that available in medical ethics or other fields. Further, technical developments have been so rapid and complex, and so much remains classified by governments and unavailable to the theologian, that few can speak knowledgeably, and perhaps none definitively.

Pope Pius XII was deeply concerned, as heir to Hiroshima and Nagasaki. His anticipation of what would happen should such powerful nuclear weapons be used is sobering.

> This is the spectacle offered to the terrified gaze as a result of such uses: entire cities, even the largest and the richest in art and history, wiped out; a pall of death over pulverized ruins, covering countless victims with limbs burnt, twisted and scattered while others groan in their death agony. Meanwhile, the specter of a radioactive cloud hinders survivors from giving any help and inexorably advances to snuff out any remaining life. There will be no song of victory, only the inconsolable weeping of humanity, which in desolation will gaze upon the catastrophe brought on by its own folly.

Yet Pius XII did not seem to feel the need to outlaw the use of the atomic bomb, as he knew it, under all possible circumstances. Con-

Reprinted by permission of the author and publisher from *In Defense of Life* (© 1981 by the Daughters of St. Paul Press).

ceivably atomic warfare could be used, he suggested, in response to "an obvious, extremely serious, and otherwise unavoidable injustice." But the restriction he then imposes is all important, both as a major factor that must henceforth be considered critical as a condition of the just war, and as a harbinger of the controversy that would arise as successive generations of nuclear weapons appeared, each with its own sophisticated refinements and claims for "safety" in use.

> Even then, however, one must strive to avoid it by all possible means through international understanding or to impose limits on its use that are so clear and rigorous that its effects remain restricted to the strict demands of defense. When, moreover, putting this method to use involves such an extension of the evil that it *entirely escapes from the control of man,* its use must be rejected as immoral. Here there would be no longer a question of "defense" against injustice or a necessary "safeguarding" of legitimate possessions, but the pure and simple annihilation of all human life within the radius of action. This is not permitted for any reason whatsoever [emphasis added].

This is a critically important statement that goes beyond the demand for what is usually called "proportionality"—that war is never justified if the means used, the cost, and the consequences seriously outweigh the anticipated gain, redress of wrong, or whatever. Here the Pope goes directly to the heart of the crucial question about nuclear weapons, the question of *predictability.*

John XXIII and his successors, the Council, and the bishops worry a great deal, and justifiably, about the cost of such weapons systems, at the expense of feeding the poor and advancing civilization, and are anxious about various other aspects of nuclear weapons. But the expressions of horror and revulsion found in the judgments passed by these churchmen, relating to development, stockpiling, deployment as deterrents, or use of nuclear weapons, always relate to the awesome fears generated by the *unpredictability* of such weapons. So fearsome is that unknown, that from John XXIII to John Paul II, the dread of the "what if" is expressed repeatedly, in urgent tones.

So John XXIII warns in *Pacem in Terris:*

... people live in constant fear lest the storm that every moment threatens should break upon them with dreadful violence. And with good reason, for the arms of war are ready at hand. Even though it is difficult to believe that anyone would dare bring upon himself the appalling destruction and sorrow that war would bring in its train, it cannot be denied that the conflagration can be set off by some unexpected and unpremeditated act. And one must bear in mind that, even though the monstrous power of modern weapons acts as a deterrent, there is nevertheless reason to fear that the mere continuance of nuclear tests, undertaken with war in mind, can seriously jeopardize various kinds of life on earth.

Paul VI echoes the theme, briefly but starkly, in his Day of Peace message on January 1, 1977.

... if, in defiance of logic, peace and life can in practice be dissociated, there looms on the horizon of the future a catastrophe that in our days could be immeasurable and irreparable for both peace and life. Hiroshima is a terribly eloquent proof and a frighteningly prophetic example of this. In the reprehensible hypothesis that peace were thought of in unnatural separation from its relationship with life, peace could be imposed as the sad triumph of death. The words of Tacitus come to mind: "They make a desert and call it peace."

Pope John Paul II strikes the same note in *Redemptor Hominis.*

Man ... lives increasingly in fear. He is afraid that what he produces ... can become the means and instrument for an unimaginable self-destruction, compared with which all the cataclysms and catastrophes of history known to us seem to fade away.

And in his October 1979 address to the United Nations:

We are troubled also by reports of the development of weaponry exceeding in quality and size the means of war and destruction ever known before. In this field also we applaud the decisions and agreements aimed at reducing the arms race. Nevertheless, the life of humanity today is seriously endangered by the threat of destruction and by the risk arising even from accepting certain "tranquilizing" reports. And the resistance to actual concrete proposals of real disarmament, such as those called for by this assembly in a special session last year, shows that together with the will for peace that all profess and that most desire there is also in existence—perhaps in latent or conditional form but nonetheless real—the contrary and the negation of this will. The continual preparation for war demonstrated by the production of ever more numerous, powerful, and sophisticated weapons in various countries shows that there is a desire to be ready for war, and being ready means being able to start it; it also means taking the risk that sometime, somewhere, somehow, someone can set in motion the terrible mechanism of general destruction.

The warning expressed in Vatican II's *Gaudium et Spes* carries a special sense of urgency related to the unpredictability or uncontrollability of destruction possible.

The development of armaments by modern science has immeasurably magnified the horrors and wickedness of war. Warfare conducted with these weapons can inflict immense and indiscriminate havoc which goes far beyond the bounds of legitimate defense. Indeed if the kind of weapons now stocked in the arsenals of the great powers were to be employed to the fullest, the result would only be the almost complete reciprocal slaughter of one side by the other, not to speak of the widespread devastation that would follow in the world and the deadly after-effects resulting from the use of such arms.

The bishops of the United States express themselves in similar fashion in pastoral letters issued in 1968 and 1976. In the earlier, *Human Life in Our Day,* one reads:

It is in nuclear warfare, even in its "cold" phase or form, that mankind confronts the moral issue of modern war in its extreme case. This has become a situation in which two adversaries possess and deploy weapons which, if used against each other, could annihilate their respective civilizations and even threaten the survival of the human race. Nothing more dramatically suggests the anti-life direction of technological warfare than the neutron bomb; one philosopher declares that the manner in which it would leave entire cities intact, but totally without life, makes it, perhaps, the symbol of our civilization. It would be perverse indeed if the Christian conscience were to be unconcerned or mute in the face of the multiple moral aspects of these awesome prospects.

To Live in Christ Jesus puts the same thought in equally sober words. This pastoral warns about the immediate impact of warfare today and its potential for future harm, for example to the human gene pool, an unpredictable potential, indeed. The pastoral then continues:

> With respect to nuclear weapons, at least those with massive destructive capability, the first imperative is to prevent their use. As possessors of a vast nuclear arsenal, we must also be aware that not only is it wrong to attack civilian populations but it is also wrong to threaten to attack them as part of a strategy of deterrence. We urge the continued development and implementation of policies which seek to bring these weapons more securely under control, progressively reduce their presence in the world, and ultimately remove them entirely.

Finally, the September 6, 1979, testimony of His Eminence, John Cardinal Krol, concerning SALT II repeats and makes its own the dread of nuclear weapons expressed by successive popes, the Council, and the United States bishops.

It is time to ask again what has been said by the Church, what left unsaid, concerning nuclear weapons.

What the Popes Have Said

Pope John XXIII certainly expressed his own conviction in the words "Justice, right reason, and humanity . . . urgently demand . . . that nuclear weapons should be banned. . . ." By whom? Presumably by the governments of the world. Is this equivalent to a papal anathema on individuals employed in building or generally handling nuclear weapons, such as military personnel? Could the Holy Father enjoin "that the stockpiles which exist in various countries should be reduced equally and simultaneously by the parties concerned" if *possession* of such weapons is in itself sinful? An evil means cannot be justified however good the end. If simply to build or to possess nuclear weapons is evil, why are they not condemned outright, regardless of questions about self-defense? Why are Catholics not told officially: You must destroy all nuclear weapons you possess and cease building others, regardless of what your prospective enemies do? The fact is that strong and unconditional as was his abhorrence of the arms *race* and his warnings about its consequences, one cannot look to Pope John XXIII or to his predecessor, Pius XII, for such a statement as this one made by a priest in a national Catholic magazine: "It is a sin to build a nuclear weapon."

What can be said of the positions of Pope John XXIII's two successors?

In his Day of Peace message of January 1, 1977, Pope Paul VI expresses strong disagreement with the "fallacious" formula of the kind of deterrence which amounts to "a perpetual threat of life."

> The policy of massive armament is immediately called into question. The ancient saying, which has taught politics and still does so—"if you want peace, prepare for war" *(si vis pacem, para bellum)*—is not acceptable without radical reservation (cf. Lk. 14:31). With the forthright boldness of our principles, we thus denounce the false and dangerous program of the "arms race," of the secret rivalry between peoples for military superiority. Even if through a surviving remnant of happy wisdom, or through a silent yet tremendous contest in the balance of hostile deadly powers, war (and what a war it would be!) does not break out, how can we fail to lament the incalculable outpouring of economic resources and human energies expended in order to preserve for each individual state its shield of ever more costly, ever more efficient weapons, and this to the detriment of resources for schools, culture, agriculture, health, and civic welfare. Peace and life support enormous and incalculable burdens in order to maintain a peace founded on a perpetual threat to life, as also to defend life by means of a constant threat to peace. People will say: it is inevitable. This can be true within a concept of civilization that is still so imperfect. But let us at least recognize that this constitutional challenge which the arms race sets up between life and peace is a formula that is fallacious in itself and which must be corrected and superseded. We therefore praise the effort already begun to reduce and finally to eliminate this senseless cold war resulting from the progressive increase of the military potential of the various nations, as if these nations should necessarily be enemies of each other, as if they were incapable of realizing that such a concept of international relations must one day be resolved in the ruination of peace and of countless human lives.

The indictment of the Cold War is unmistakable, as is Pope Paul VI's unquestionable aversion to a strategy developed in the name of deterrence that could ignite a "hot" war at any moment. Does he, then, issue an outright condemnation of the building, possession, or strategic positioning of nuclear weapons for purposes of deterrence? He simply does not.

After repeating a similar warning against the ancient maxim *Si vis pacem, para bellum,* Pope John Paul II in his address before the U.N. expresses skepticism of weapons superiority as a deterrent.

> But can our age still really believe that the breathtaking spiral of armaments is at the service of world peace? In alleging the threat of a potential enemy, is it really not rather an intention to keep for oneself a means of threat, in order to get the upper hand with the aid of one's own arsenal of destruction? Here, too, it is the human dimension of peace that tends to vanish *in favor of ever new possible forms of imperialism.*

And with what appear to be similar implications he says in his message for the World Day of Peace on January 1, 1979:

> . . . fear of a precarious peace, military and political imperatives, and economic and commercial interests lead to the establishment of arms stockpiles or to the sale of weapons capable of appalling destruction. The arms race then prevails over the great tasks of peace, which ought to invite peoples in new solidarity; it fosters sporadic but murderous conflicts and builds up the gravest threats.

As in the various other instances cited, the revulsion the Holy Father experiences toward all the horrors of war is manifest. But once again it would be distorting the text and indulging in assumptions to translate these sentiments, however intensely expressed, into the conclusion: "The Church, as represented by Pope John Paul II, morally censures those who manufacture, possess, or deploy nuclear weapons as part of a strategy of deterrence."

What Vatican II Said

Surprising though it may seem, given the vehemence of feeling expressed by the Council, the Fathers of Vatican II did not condemn manufacture and possession of nuclear weapons. Again, the sentiments of horror and revulsion concerning the multiplication and potential use of "scientific weapons" are unmistakable, but *Gaudium et Spes* stopped short of what some might have expected, and gave its reasons for doing so quite explicitly.

Scientific weapons, to be sure, are not amassed solely for use in war. The defensive strength of any nation is considered to be dependent upon its capacity for immediate retaliation against an adversary. Hence this accumulation of arms, which increases each year, also serves, in a way heretofore unknown, as a deterrence to possible enemy attack. Many regard this state of affairs as the most effective way by which peace of a sort can be maintained between nations at the present time.

So Vatican II did not outlaw the manufacture, possession, or deployment of nuclear weapons as a deterrent to war. As noted previously, the Council leaves open a judgment on the validity of the strategy of deterrence.

What the Bishops Have Said

In *Human Life in Our Day* the bishops of the United States commented extensively on the Vatican Council's decision to condemn "the use of weapons of mass destruction" but to abstain from condemning "the *possession* of such weapons" to deter "possible enemy attack." And noting that the Council did not call for unilateral disarmament, but "for reciprocal or collective disarmament" proceeding at an equal pace according to agreement and backed up by authentic and workable safeguards, "the bishops saw hopeful signs that such a formula may be strengthened by the Partial Test Ban Treaty" and that the commitment under the Non-Proliferation Treaty to begin negotiating a balanced reduction of nuclear weapons and simultaneously extending the use of nuclear power for peaceful development of needy nations "may provide a positive, sane pattern for the future."

The bishops then begin to express a number of significant reservations about certain aspects of a strategy of nuclear deterrence and nuclear superiority, reservations to be reflected, in part, eight years later in *To Live in Christ Jesus,* and forcefully in the testimony of Cardinal Krol on SALT II in 1979. Their comments deserve extensive citing, particularly because of the clear trend they advance. After expressing their hopes, as noted above, they go on to say:

Meanwhile, it is greatly to be desired that such prospects not be dashed by irrational resolves to keep ahead in "assured destruction" capability. Rather it is to be hoped that the early ratification by the Senate of the Non-Proliferation Treaty—which in essence is a treaty between the U.S.S.R. and the United States and other nations—will hasten discussion of across-the-board reductions by the big powers. Despite, and even because of, the provocations in Eastern Europe and elsewhere, the United States should continue steps to create a better climate for these discussions, such as taking the lead in inviting the U.N. Atomic Energy Commission and other organizations and foreign states to visit its nuclear facilities, and scrupulously reviewing all commitments for the sale, loan, or lease of armaments.

The Council's position on the arms race is clear. To recall it: "Therefore, we declare once again: the arms race is an utterly treacherous trap for humanity. . . . It is much to be feared that if this race persists, it will eventually spawn all the lethal ruin whose path it is now making ready."

Nonetheless, the nuclear race goes on. The latest act in the continuing nuclear arms race is no doubt the U.S. decision to build a thin anti-ballistic-missile system to defend against possible nuclear attack by another world power. This decision has been widely interpreted as the prelude to a thick ABM system to defend against possible nuclear attack.

In themselves, such anti-ballistic missiles are purely defensive, designed to limit the damage to the United States from nuclear attack. Nevertheless, by upsetting the present strategic balance, the so-called balance of terror, there is grave danger that a United States ABM system will incite other nations to increase their offensive nuclear forces with the seeming excuse of a need to restore the balance.

Despite the danger of triggering an expanded escalation of the arms race, the pressures for a thick ABM deployment persist. We seriously question whether the present policy of maintaining nuclear superiority is meaningful for security. There is no advantage to be gained by nuclear superiority, however it is computed, when each side is admittedly capable of inflicting overwhelming damage on the other hand, even after being attacked first. Such effective parity has been operative for some years. Any effort to achieve superiority only leads to ever higher levels of armaments as it forces the side with the lesser capability to seek to maintain its superiority. In the wake of this action-reaction phenomenon comes a decrease in both stability and security.

Since the entire section on peace and war is very brief in *To Live in Christ Jesus,* it is not surprising that the later pastoral makes but brief reference to those issues, particularly the matter of nuclear deterrence, which so preoccupied the bishops in *Human Life in Our Day.* The pertinent passage has been quoted above, but its brevity permits repetition here.

With respect to nuclear weapons, at least those with massive destructive capability, the first imperative is to prevent their use. As possessors of a vast nuclear arsenal, we must also be aware that not only is it wrong to attack civilian populations but it is also wrong to threaten to attack them as part of a strategy of deterrence. We urge the continued development and implementation of policies which seek to bring these weapons more securely under control, progressively reduce their presence in the world, and ultimately remove them entirely.

As previously observed, the overtones of the concerns expressed by Vatican II and spelled out at some length in *Human Life in Our Day* are advanced still further in Cardinal Krol's testimony on SALT II. The cardinal calls nuclear deterence a paradox and a moral dilemma, and notes this as one reason for giving only qualified support to the proposed treaty. He goes on to say:

The moral paradox of deterrence is that its purpose is to prevent the use of nuclear weapons, but it does so by an expressed threat to attack the civilian population of one's adversary. Such a threat runs directly counter to the central moral affirmation of the Christian teaching on war: that innocent lives are not open to direct attack. The complexity of the moral dilemma is reflected in the statement on deterrence of the American bishops in 1976. [The cardinal then quotes the passage from *Human Life in Our Day* cited immediately above in this paper.]

Then, after quoting from *Human Life in Our Day* the statement cited immediately above about "threatening" attacks, the cardinal says:

The moral judgment of this statement is that not only the use of strategic nuclear weapons, but also the *declared intent* to use them involved in our deterrence policy, is wrong. This explains the Catholic dissatisfaction with nuclear deterrence and the urgency of the Catholic demand that the nuclear arms race be reversed. It is of the utmost importance that negotiations proceed to meaningful and continuing reductions in nuclear stockpiles, and eventually, to the phasing out altogether of nuclear deterrence and the threat of mutual assured destruction.

As long as there is hope of this occurring, Catholic moral teaching is willing, while negotiations proceed, to tolerate the possession of nuclear weapons for deterrence as the lesser of two evils. If that hope were to disappear, the moral attitude of the Catholic Church would almost certainly have to shift to one of uncompromising condemnation of both use *and* possession of such weapons. With this in mind, the Catholic bishops of this country ask the Senate of the United States to ratify this treaty because the negotiations which produced it, and the further round of negotiations which it permits, offer the promise of escape from danger of a nuclear holocaust and from the ethical dilemma of nuclear deterrence.

What We Can Conclude

The foregoing has been an effort to discern the basic position of the Church as of 1980, in the persons of four popes, the Vatican Council, and the body of bishops of the United States. That the position is completely unambiguous would be arguable. That it seems to be still evolving might be a fair appraisal. To return to the question raised above, admittedly at risk of oversimplification—What does the Church say and leave unsaid about nuclear weapons?—it seems fair to assert the following:

a. The Church condemns war of aggression, unlimited war, acts of war "directed to the indiscriminate destruction of whole cities or vast areas with their inhabitants," the use of weapons of mass destruction.

b. The Church does not condemn defensive war, limited war, acts of war directed to the destruction of military targets, the manufacture or possession of nuclear weapons, the use of weapons of limited destruction.

c. The Church seriously questions the strategy of nuclear deterrence, abhors the arms race, considering it a treacherous trap for humanity, potentially destructive of all life, and draining resources critically needed to feed the hungry and generally advance civilization.

d. The Church calls for the eventual goal of banning nuclear weapons, urging that in the meanwhile, there be continuing, balanced, mutual, progressive reductions in nuclear weapons "backed up by authentic and workable safeguards," and urging negotiations and treaties that will help reduce risks of nuclear war.

To deduce from official statements of popes, Vatican II, or the National Conference of Catholic Bishops that the "Church" has *condemned* more than is noted above would appear to be precisely that—an act of deduction. To discern less in what the Church says would appear to be an act of short-sightedness.

22. *The Peace Bishops*

By MICHAEL NOVAK

Focus   Michael Novak, a Catholic lay theologian, here addresses the moral and political errors of the "peace bishops" and other clerics. His essay, written after Bishop O'Connor's (selection 21), is in a sense an elaboration of the bishop's conclusions.

Novak insists that the bishops who have "denounced the American strategy of nuclear deterrence and in its stead recommended a policy whose ultimate logic will demand unilateral nuclear disarmament" have misread the popes and the Second Vatican Council. Such bishops, he says, "have not shrunk even from the view that military defeat and surrender to superior Soviet power are morally preferable to the possession of nuclear weapons for the sake of deterrence." "It is not 'better to be dead than red,'" says Novak; "it is better to be neither. As the history of our time amply demonstrates, some choosing the latter have not avoided the former."

Novak examines the key paragraphs on war and weapons in the documents of Vatican II. Then, comparing these with congressional testimony and a White House sermon by John Cardinal Krol of Philadelphia and with statements by Father Francis X. Winters, S.J., of Georgetown University, he finds these two clerics seriously out of step with Vatican II.

The "nuclear pacifists," says Novak, use essentially secular arguments but at the same time ig-

310

nore the impressive evidence of "lay Catholics
whose entire adult life has been spent studying such
perplexities."

Novak defends the U.S. military build-up essential to nuclear deterrence. He quotes Terence Cardinal Cooke to support his view: "It is legitimate to
develop and maintain weapons systems to try to
prevent war by 'deterring' another nation from attacking."

Michael Novak is a resident scholar in religion
and public policy at the American Enterprise Institute. Among his books are *The Experience of Nothingness* (1970) and *The Spirit of Democratic
Capitalism* (1982).

A NEW AND STARTLING development has taken place in the thinking of the American Catholic hierarchy on questions of war and peace. In the name of Catholic morality, and on the alleged authority of Vatican Council II, influential bishops have publicly denounced the American strategy of nuclear deterrence and have in its stead recommended a policy whose ultimate logic will demand unilateral nuclear disarmament. Such bishops have not shrunk even from the view that military defeat and surrender to superior Soviet power are morally preferable to the possession of nuclear weapons for the sake of deterrence. In the words of one Jesuit enthusiast of this new trend of thought, the position of these bishops represents a "stark and radical realism." He calls it "an olive branch all fresh and unexpected," and foresees the day when government officials who happen to be Catholic will have to resign their positions if they are to follow the new church doctrine on nuclear warfare.

How has this extraordinary development come about? Its theological root lies in three key passages in the documents of Vatican II, relatively overlooked at the time; in a collective pastoral letter of the American hierarchy, *Human Life in Our Day*, issued November 15, 1968; and in its sequel, *To Live in Christ Jesus*, issued November 11, 1976. The most decisive document of all, however, is the Senate testimony in support of SALT II offered by John Cardinal Krol on September 6, 1979, and his sermon at the White House almost one week later. Finally, in early November 1981, Archbishop John Roach, president of the Catholic bishops, brought these issues to prominence in his annual address to the National Conference of Catholic Bishops.

Of the sixteen key documents issued by Vatican II, one, "The Church in the Modern World" *(Gaudium et Spes),* includes a chapter on peace and war. The three passages important for the later discussion are the following:

1. Any act of war aimed indiscriminately at the destruction of entire cities or of extensive areas along with their population is a crime against God and man himself. It merits unequivocal and unhesitating condemnation [from section 80].

2. Scientific weapons, to be sure, are not amassed solely for use in war. The defensive strength of any nation is considered to be dependent upon its capacity for immediate retaliation against an adversary. Hence this accumulation of arms, which increases each year, also serves, in a way heretofore unknown, as a deterrent to possible enemy attack. Many regard this state of affairs as the most effective way by which peace of a sort can be maintained between nations at the present time.

Whatever be the case with this method of deterrence, men should be convinced that the arms race in which so many countries are engaged is not a safe way to preserve a steady peace [from section 81].

3. Therefore, it must be said again: the arms race is an utterly treacherous trap for humanity, and one which injures the poor to an intolerable degree. It is much to be feared that if this race persists, it will eventually spawn all the lethal ruin whose path it is now making ready [from section 81].

These three passages are, in a sense, traditional enough, and perhaps that is why initially they were not widely noted. Yet they are preceded by a curious phrase, whose ambiguity opened a Pandora's box. Speaking of "the horror and perversity of war . . . [which have been] immensely magnified by the multiplication of scientific weapons," section 80 announces: "All these considerations compel us to undertake an evaluation of war *with an entirely new attitude*" (emphasis added).

Earlier, Pope John XXIII in *Pacem in Terris* (1963) had likewise employed an ambiguous sentence: "Thus, in this age which boasts of its atomic power, it no longer makes sense to maintain that war is a fit instrument with which to repair the violation of justice." (Other published translations read: ". . . it is hardly possible to imagine that in an atomic era war could be used as an instrument of justice." Again: ". . . it is irrational to think that war is a proper way to obtain justice for violated rights.")

Some have used this passage, and also Pope John's failure to mention the right of a people to defend itself, to argue that the Church has abandoned its teaching on just war in the case of atomic power. But it is not credible that after fifteen centuries, the Church would simply discard its teaching on just war without saying so explicitly and clearly. Indeed, the Vatican II documents, despite the ambiguity noted above, are in general clear on this point: "As long as the danger of war remains and there is no competent and sufficiently powerful authority at the international level, governments cannot be denied the right to legitimate defense once every means of settlement has been exhausted" (section 79).

Moreover, the search for the new, precisely *qua* new, is a departure from traditional Catholic realism. From that point of view, the "new" is a dangerous criterion. Nevertheless, by 1968 the U.S. Catholic bishops were calling upon "American Catholics to evaluate war with that 'entirely new attitude' for which the Council appealed." To be sure, they recognized "the right of legitimate self-defense and, in a world society still unorganized, the necessity for recourse to armed defense and to collective security action." They regarded members of the armed forces as "agents of security and freedom on behalf of their people." But they also included a curious paragraph that was a portent of things to come:

> Nothing more dramatically suggests the anti-life direction of technological warfare than the neutron bomb; one philosopher declares that the manner in which it would leave entire cities intact, but totally without life, makes it, perhaps, the symbol of our civilization.

The bishops duly noted that "the Council did not call for unilateral disarmament; Christian morality is not lacking in realism." They did, however, support the Non-Proliferation Treaty then before the Senate, "despite, and even because of, the provocations in Eastern Europe and elsewhere," their phrase for the Soviet invasion of Czechoslovakia that summer. Furthermore, they opposed the anti-ballistic-missile system, and they made the following sweeping assertion:

> We seriously question whether the present policy of maintaining nuclear superiority is meaningful for security. There is no advantage to be gained by nuclear superiority, however it is computed, when each side is admittedly capable of inflicting overwhelming damage on the other, even after being attacked first. Such effective parity has been operative for some years.

It is important to recall that this statement was issued in 1968, just after Robert McNamara had frozen the U.S. ICBM force at 1,054 and had begun sustained reductions in the B-52 bomber fleet and the interceptor fighter fleet, which eventually were to reduce the former from 1,364 in 1964 to 316 by 1980 and the latter from 1,800 to 312.

Eight years later, in *To Live in Christ Jesus* (1976), the bishops were already thinking "with an entirely new attitude." They began by raising a question:

> The Church has traditionally recognized that, under stringent conditions, engaging in war can be a form of legitimate defense. But modern warfare, both in its technology and in its execution, is so savage that one must ask whether war as it is actually waged today can be morally justified.

They went on to limit the right to self-defense:

> The right of legitimate defense is not a moral justification for unleashing every form of destruction. For example, acts of war deliberately directed against innocent noncombatants are gravely wrong, and no one may participate in such an act.

They then advanced a prohibition against the threat—that is, the intention—of deterrence. This was to become the wedge of future developments:

> With respect to nuclear weapons, at least those with massive destructive capability, the first imperative is to prevent their use. As possessors of a vast nuclear arsenal, we must also be aware that not only is it wrong to attack civilian populations but it is also wrong to threaten to attack them as part of a strategy of deterrence.

The stage was now set for Cardinal Krol's dramatic testimony before the Senate Foreign Relations Committee on September 6, 1979, critical of the opponents of SALT II and strongly in favor of the agreement. The choice of Cardinal Krol, an ecclesiastical conservative and close associate of Pope John Paul II, was itself significant, and his testimony is widely regarded as a breakthrough. Father Francis X. Winters, the Jesuit professor at Georgetown whose words I quoted at the beginning of this article, says it "may come in time to be counted among the most prophetic and courageous words spoken by any religious leader in the twentieth century" ("The Bow or The Cloud," *America*, July 25, 1981).

Cardinal Krol made a number of important qualifications at the beginning of his testimony. Citing the principles of Vatican II, he properly observed the gap between them and the specific legislation on which he was testifying. Next he confessed that this gap "admits a divergence of views." Finally, he was careful to say that his position was "not a unanimous position within the conference of bishops nor is it the unanimous position of all Catholics in the United States." Still, it did represent "the official policy of the U.S. Catholic Conference, and in expressing it, we bishops seek to fulfill a role of responsible citizenship as well as religious leadership."

The particular perspective shaping Cardinal Krol's testimony, he said, "judges that some forms of war can be morally legitimate, but judges that nuclear war surpasses the boundaries of legitimate self-defense." Then he came to the heart of his new doctrine, which rests on the Catholic teaching concerning intention. Catholics consider it immoral not only to perform an evil act but even to mean to perform it: deliberately and willfully to form such an intention, even in one's heart. The evil of murder, for example, occurs not only in the deed but even in the premeditated resolve to do it. The Cardinal applied this principle to the strategy of deterrence:

> The moral judgment of this statement is that not only the use of strategic nuclear weapons, but also *the declared intent to use them involved in our deterrence policy is wrong*. This explains the Catholic dissatisfaction with nuclear deterrence and the urgency of the Catholic demand that the nuclear arms race be reversed. It is of the utmost importance that negotiations proceed to meaningful and continuing reductions in nuclear stockpiles, and eventually, to the phasing out altogether of nuclear deterrence and the threat of mutual-assured destruction [emphasis added].

Only the "hope" of phasing out nuclear arms permits Catholics, "while negotiations proceed, to tolerate the possession of nuclear weapons for deterrence as the lesser of two evils." Absent that hope, the Cardinal would condemn "both use *and* possession of such weapons."

The Cardinal was not yet ready to demand unilateral nuclear disarmament. Since weapons don't fire themselves, their mere possession, he conceded, is morally neutral. He did not allow, however, any *intention* to use them. This prohibition leads logically to having no deterrent at all, i.e., to unilateral nuclear disarmament. It also completely undercuts the moral basis of official U.S. deterrence policy.

That the Cardinal both did and did not face the ultimate logic of his premises was shown by the sermon he preached at the White House six days later, pondering the prospect of military defeat for a United States that had renounced the use and the threat of deterrence:

> This does not mean we accept as inevitable the conquest of the world by a totalitarian system. . . . History goes on and political systems are subject to change. As long as life exists there is hope, hope that God's grace will enable suffering and oppressed peoples to endure.

Father Winters, at any rate, was ready to draw out approvingly the implications of Cardinal Krol's sermon:

> Our security is not compatible, he argues, with the use of nuclear weapons. It is compatible, though arduously so, with military defeat. . . . Security depends on restraint, the unilateral renunciation of the intention to light the fuse that links the superpowers. Security may dictate surrender.

Individual bishops have gone further than Cardinal Krol in advocating steps to be taken in line with the "new attitude." Archbishop Hunthausen of Seattle urged Catholics in his diocese to withhold from the Internal Revenue Service the 50 per cent of their taxes which, by his calculations, goes into the arms build-up. Bishop Matthiesen of Amarillo urged Catholics working in a nuclear-arms plant in his diocese to quit their jobs. With a sudden rush, nearly 60 of the 350 U.S. bishops joined Pax Christi, an international Catholic disarmament movement. A large number of bishops and priests demanded that the U.S. Navy rename the nuclear submarine *Corpus Christi,* named for the city in Texas, thinking it "almost sacrilegious" so to use the name of Christ. As for Father Winters, he applauds the bishops for having

> formulated a position that imposes on Catholic officials of our government the burden of choosing between their consciences, as illuminated by church teachings, and their professional careers and commitments.

Among those "thrust into the dilemma of choosing between politics and religion . . . their constitutional responsibilities and their conscience," Father Winters lists the President and executive-branch officials, the military chain of command, the present Secretary of State, the Speaker of the House, and "approximately 30 per cent of the U.S. Army personnel" who are Catholic.

All sane persons have as their first priority no use of nuclear weapons. There is no real debate about that goal. Yet in their enthusiasm for evaluating war "with an entirely new attitude," the reasoning of the bishops becomes less religious than political, and partisan in a secular way. By stating the issue the way they have, they are virtually certain to bring about a real schism in the Church—and between the Church and other portions of U.S. society.

The Bishops' Dangerous Power

When secular critics reach the same conclusions as the bishops, on similar secular grounds, one may argue with them fact for fact, concept for concept, and one may also take the issue to citizens at the polls. The bishops, in their strategy for "peace," are subject to no such checks and balances. They can claim, as others scarcely can, to speak for the Church and to bar dissenters under pain of sin from the sacraments. This is a dangerous power, invoking sacred authority for a position to which others have strong and reasoned objections.

Even on theological grounds it is an error for the bishops to believe that they compose the part of the Church most competent and most directly called by God to illuminate what human beings, living under nuclear threat, ought to do to maintain peace. There are many lay Catholics whose entire adult lives have been spent studying such perplexities. It is entirely possible that the most devout believer, sharing every one of the bishops' theological principles, might, nonetheless, perceive facts differently and make sharply divergent analyses at any number of crucial turning points, and arrive at a diametrically opposed strategy for peace.

Take, for example, the question of "intention" and "threat to use" raised by Cardinal Krol. Suppose that a U.S. President were to follow the Cardinal's prescription and announce publicly that, even though the United States maintained a nuclear deterrent, he had no intention of ever using it under any conditions. It is unlikely that Soviet leaders would believe such words. But they might be inclined, little by little, to test them. Would that not induce a war of nerves far more dangerous than anything yet experienced?

One must distinguish, as well, between objective and subjective intentions. In order to maintain a nuclear force, a carefully constructed plan must be coordinated, a type of "architectonic" which, for Aristotle, is a classic form of political intention. This intention would be present even if leaders in any one administration privately and subjectively decided never to use or to threaten the use of nuclear weapons. Then too, the degree of intention required for deterrence depends upon the actions of the adversary to be deterred. Absent a Soviet threat, U.S. deterrence could operate at a very low level indeed. Thus, the relative nuclear decline of the U.S. between 1968 and 1980, had it been imitated by the Soviets, would have diminished the role of nuclear arms in the present period. Yet it does not seem that a strategy of weakness deters the U.S.S.R.

That Cardinal Krol's view of these matters is not the only possible Catholic response is clear from the fact that a contrary view was voiced only recently by Terence Cardinal Cooke of New York, who is responsible as Military Vicar for pastoral care of all Catholics in military service. In that capacity he sent a letter to chaplains on December 7, 1981, the fortieth anniversary of Pearl Harbor.

Cardinal Cooke began by recalling that "the Church has traditionally taught and continues to teach that a government has both the right and the duty to protect its people against unjust aggression. This means that it is legitimate to develop and maintain weapons systems to try to prevent war by 'deterring' another nation from attacking. Very simply put, police carry guns for the same reason." He went on:

> Although the Church urges nations to design better ways— ideally, nonviolent ways—of maintaining peace, it recognizes that as long as we have good reason to believe that another nation would be tempted to attack us if we could not retaliate, we have the right to deter attack by making it clear that we could retaliate. In very simple terms, this is the "strategy of deterrence" we hear so much about. It is not a desirable strategy. It

can be terribly dangerous. Government leaders and peoples of all nations have a grave moral obligation to come up with alternatives. But as long as our nation is sincerely trying to work with other nations to find a better way, the Church considers the strategy of nuclear deterrence morally tolerable; not satisfactory, but tolerable. As a matter of fact, millions of people may be alive in the world today precisely because government leaders in various nations know that if they attacked other nations, at least on a large scale, they, themselves, could suffer tremendous losses of human life or even be destroyed. . . .

The Church does not require, nor have the Popes of the nuclear age or the Second Vatican Council recommended, unilateral disarmament.

Within forty-eight hours after his letter became public, Cardinal Cooke was scathingly attacked by some clergy and laity who claimed he was out of step with the Church. Even Archbishop Roach, interviewed by the press, averred that Cardinal Cooke had not made all the new distinctions current since 1976. Still, as the example of Cardinal Cooke indicates, the bishops' understanding of Vatican II does not go unchallenged even within their own ranks. Bishop John J. O'Connor, Vicar General of the Military Vicariate, has written a book, *In Defense of Life,* showing that the Church has not abandoned its traditional just-war theory, its resistance to unilateral disarmament, or its toleration of deterrence as a necessary evil. And James V. Schall, a Jesuit professor of government at Georgetown, has gone through all the papal and conciliar teachings on war and peace and reported similar conclusions.

From a theological and moral point of view, the most questionable maneuver of the bishops is to write and speak as if they possess an Olympian view and inhabit a neutral zone. Although Archbishop Bernardin recognizes that "the enormous build-up of nuclear and conventional arms procured by the Soviet Union in recent years has done more than its share to heighten the peril of the present moment," he concludes from this that the "duty of responsible moral action falls equally on both superpowers."

In their "neutrality" as between the United States and the U.S.S.R., the bishops also distance themselves from the concept of American national security. Thus Cardinal Krol in his White House sermon:

. . . should we not, as Christians, reject the actual use of such weapons, whatever the consequences? At the point of such decisions, I submit, our political and military authorities are responsible to a higher set of values; no longer are they defending "the national security," they are defending human values, the survival and future welfare of the whole human race.

Cardinal Krol seems to imagine here that national security has nothing to do with "liberty and justice for all," and that human values have an existence so separate from the security of the United States that even with the collapse of American power these values would not be threatened.

Let us suppose, for a moment, that the human race were to come under the tutelage of the U.S.S.R. and, further, that rival factions in the socialist world threatened one another with nuclear arms. In that case, the "neutrality" of the bishops would not have succeeded even in banishing the specter of nuclear destruction, only in surrendering the fate of humanity into Soviet hands.

Peace Through Deterrence, Not Surrender

The bishops speak in the name of peace, and claim, with their "entirely new attitude," to have developed a strategy for peace. Yet the peace of the world has never been purchased through surrender. Cardinal Krol cites "the history of certain countries occupied during World War II" to show that there are "other means of resistance" than nuclear arms—forgetting the annihilation of 16 million persons under that "resistance." Throughout the post-war era, it is the American deterrent that has kept the nuclear peace. Renouncing that deterrent would be as sure a way of bringing about war as one could devise. Such a consequence cannot be moral.

Already the imbalance in nuclear power that has developed in recent years through the unprecedented Soviet build-up of nuclear arms has created an atmosphere of peril. General Andrew J. Goodpaster has recently remarked that the Soviet SS-20s now ringing Europe are the most effective weapons he has seen in his lifetime. Without ever being expended, without ever requiring a single loss to Soviet equipment or life, they have terrorized Europe, plunged NATO into crisis, and led Western churchmen and others to plead for further weakness.

The bishops seem to be willing, with Archbishop Bernardin, "to have our own principles, to be prepared to live by them and, in faith, to accept the consequences of doing so." Or, in the sermon of Cardinal Krol, to accept submission, as Eastern Europe has done since World War II. This they demand in the name of "faith" and "citizenship." Yet this cannot be the demand of Catholic faith or of the American experiment in liberty. Such a strategy will not guarantee escape from future nuclear disaster, but leave it solely at the discretion of totalitarian leaders. It will certainly imperil the liberty we have, through the grace of God, inherited. Perhaps the Church is ready to live under totalitarian conditions, but a free people sworn to defend free institutions cannot.

The point of deterrence is to deter. Weapons do not fire themselves; neither do they deter by themselves. Where the will is lacking, deterrence is absent. Blackmail is potent. To deter nuclear disaster and the spread of totalitarian power is not a pleasant business. It is not a form of cheap grace. It demands of us extremes of self-discipline and self-sacrifice. "National security" is not separable from the defense of free institutions, built at the cost of so much intellectual diligence, sweat, and blood. Freedoms of religion, thought, association, speech, and heart have their existence only within institutions and under governments of certain sorts. To treat these cavalierly as dispensable is an outrage to civilization itself.

Those who choose deterrence do not choose less than the highest human values; they choose the only state of development within which humans would freely choose to live. It is not "better to be dead than red"; it is better to be neither. As the history of our time amply demonstrates, some choosing the latter have not avoided the former. Avoidance of both sickening alternatives is the moral good which deterrence, and deterrence alone, effects.

The bishops hold the American system cheap, in that they would be willing to surrender it in order to have clean hands. They use the freedom purchased for them by the strategy of deterrence they decry to look down upon those who keep them free. Insofar as they claim to speak not solely for themselves but for all Catholics, their political views need to be questioned and their appeals to "faith" exposed for the wishfulness that they are. Insofar as they seek a role as citizens, their words carry no special moral or spiritual weight, but need to be tested against the plainly expressed will of the American people, who have chosen to preserve their institutions through deterring both nuclear war and totalitarian night. That is a moral, religious, and political good worth the sacrifice of one's life and energies, if anything in history has ever been.

23. *Military Balance Is Essential to Peace*

By the CENTRAL COMMITTEE OF GERMAN CATHOLICS

Focus Readers accustomed to the emotional tone and thin factual basis of many church statements on nuclear arms will find this essay a refreshing relief. It begins where any responsible discussion of Western military defense must begin—with the nature of the threat. The West German committee notes that Moscow is now using military superiority gained over the past decade to attain political objectives in Afghanistan and elsewhere in Asia, as well as in Africa and Latin America. "One of its main objectives continues to be the achievement of hegemony over Europe."

The committee supports the NATO two-track approach of simultaneously upgrading its arms and negotiating for verifiable nuclear arms constraints on both sides. Critics of this approach have a duty to propose alternatives that would "establish and maintain" a stable balance. The options suggested by the nuclear pacifists and unilateral disarmers would invite war, appeasement, or nuclear blackmail. An individual may choose to be a martyr, the statement says, but he has no right to inflict this fate upon "countless others" who do not share his views.

"Political reason and ethical responsibility for the common good require us to establish and maintain a balance of forces . . . the prerequisite for any sensible efforts to achieve arms control." Imbalance is a dangerous condition.

In making this prudent and clear statement, West German Catholics stand in sharp contrast to their American counterparts, for whom the question of nuclear arms is a source of division and continuing conflict. The statement is in general agreement with the views of the four German political leaders published in *Foreign Affairs* (selection 2).

The **Central Committee of German Catholics,** a body of West German Catholic clerical and lay delegates, meets annually to consider matters affecting the Church. It has no episcopal authority but works closely with the West German hierarchy; its statements generally represent the views of the West German Catholic leadership.

THROUGH ITS TREMENDOUS EFFORTS in the arms field over the last ten years, the Soviet Union has tipped the scales decisively in its favor. On the basis of the military superiority thus achieved it is now seeking to reach its political objectives, as borne out by the invasion of Afghanistan and a number of operations in Asia, Africa, and South America. One of its main objectives continues to be the achievement of hegemony over Europe.

This policy has a destabilizing impact on the international situation. If the Western states simply watch these developments without taking any action of their own, there is an increasing danger that the Soviet Union will be tempted to make demands and take initiatives that the West would ultimately be able to accept only at the price of submission. Should the West decide at that point to offer resistance, the Soviet Union might yield to the temptation to pursue its objectives by using force as well. This would inevitably give rise to very serious conflicts and, in the worst scenario, lead to war. We must not forget that similar developments preceded the outbreak of the Second World War.

If peace is to be preserved, therefore, it is absolutely vital to work for and restore a balance of forces. Only from such a position of military balance do we stand a chance of reducing the level of armaments through a process of give-and-take without endangering anyone's security. As a result, major efforts are required, in the fields of both foreign policy and arms policy and in arrangements for safeguarding peace by military means.

The member states of the North Atlantic Alliance have clearly recognized this, and, by adopting the "two-track" decision of December 1979, they have taken a course in line with the peace policy the West has been pursuing to date. This decision includes an offer for negotiations that, in accordance with the principle of

Excerpted from a statement adopted by the Plenary Assembly of the Central Committee of German Catholics in November 1981; its title was "On the Current Peace Discussion."

325

reciprocity, is aimed at the restoration of balance. It clearly involves advance concessions in order to build confidence; for another three years, it tolerates the existing imbalance and puts off the necessary force modernization in the hope of reaching an agreement on the restoration of balance at the lowest possible level within those three years. Finally, it leaves no doubt as to what the member states of NATO will do if that time limit passes without the concluding of an agreement; this makes the policy of the West a calculable one.

NATO's two-track decision is a policy that aims at a reduction in armaments, détente, and peace by choosing the path of military balance. Those who consider such a policy to be inadequate or even harmful have a duty to reveal the means by which they would establish and maintain that balance.

There is a current tendency not to consider individual aspects of the peace policy but rather to call into question the established principles for dealing with tension and conflicts as a whole; frequently these principles are alleged to be morally questionable and to add fuel to such conflicts.

A Dangerous Simplification

Here a radical ethic of conviction and the moral condemnation of today's weapons technology combine with the hope that it is possible, through unilateral disarmament, to give a signal that would convince the Soviet Union to follow suit. In view of the geopolitical situation of Western Europe in general and that of the Federal Republic of Germany in particular, as well as the existing potential for destruction, doubts are often expressed as to whether defense is still possible at all. Some people consequently call for the dissolution of the defense alliance. They assume that Western Europe, or the Federal Republic alone, could thus gain a neutral position between the superpowers and keep out of what, in a dangerous simplification, is considered to be a rivalry between those two. And, finally, there are those who—along the lines of the slogan "better red than dead"— are willing to accept Soviet conditions and, should worse come to worst, to capitulate militarily and politically. The latter view in particular stems from complex emotions and ideas. There is the idea of a martyr's role, which one is not only willing to accept for oneself but also prepared to see inflicted upon countless others. There is also something of the longing, repeatedly frustrated but always reasserting itself, for "socialism with a human face," as well as the hope that following a possible conquest through force there might still be the opportunity to offer what is termed "social resistance."

The proposed alternatives to a peace policy based on a balance of forces are unconvincing. They play down the frightening consistency of totalitarian thinking; they fail to grasp the special situation in which Germany and especially Berlin find themselves with regard to security; and they jeopardize the commitments and the trust placed in us by allies who have for many decades given us protection and aid. In many cases these alternatives reflect a tendency to apply private standards to the realm of politics, which makes them unpolitical.

In the final analysis, these alternatives promote a kind of thinking that ultimately leads to the destruction of political stability in freedom. People who think that way fail to realize that political stability in freedom does not merely provide us with a pleasant environment but is the very prerequisite for a life of human dignity. Whenever a nation fails to visualize the extent to which life under a totalitarian system is devoid of human dignity, it becomes a breeding ground for active minorities that use the word peace and the longing for peace as a vehicle for asserting their own totalitarian or anarchistic goals—goals that are opposed to freedom. Where the fatal tendency to disregard history is combined with political ignorance, an insufficiently developed ability to make ethical distinctions, and the reluctance to fight for our common order, such minorities can gain an influence that far transcends their real importance.

Political reason and ethical responsibility for the common good require us to establish and maintain a balance of forces. That balance is the prerequisite for any sensible efforts to achieve arms control, disarmament, and hence political peace; such efforts are sensible because they take into account the interests and the power of those involved. The necessary efforts and the risks constitute less heavy a burden than the efforts and hazards that would result from a perpetuation, or even aggravation, of the existing imbalance. Furthermore, a policy conducted along such lines offers the best chance of arriving at an international community that, starting at the roots, might prove capable of resolving the dangerous dilemma of making peace secure in a long-term process of change. This objective must be pursued energetically and through credible means.

In this connection, the urgently needed cooperation between East and West takes on added significance because of our relations with the countries of the Third World. The greater the success of that cooperation, the greater its contribution towards stabilizing international peace will be. The more political tensions in the East-West conflict are eliminated or at least reduced, resulting in a corresponding controlled reduction in arms expenditure, the greater the chances of channeling additional funds to the developing world. The present situation, in which the Eastern-bloc countries taken together spend less on development aid than the Federal Republic of Germany alone, not least because of their disproportionate arms efforts, is unacceptable and gives rise to new conflicts that pose a threat to peace. Peace research, too, should help to clarify these facts and contribute to long-term changes in international relations.

The West German Peace Policy

The Federal Republic of Germany has, from the very beginning, committed itself to this comprehensive peace policy aimed at maintaining freedom and the rule of law, as well as at the development of a worldwide solidarity among all states without exception; and it has made its position clear in numerous agreements and statements. This is evidenced by the unconditional ban on any preparations for a war of aggression, laid down in Article 26 of the Basic Law; the Federal Republic's entry into the European Community; its integration into the North Atlantic Alliance, whose purely defensive character is borne out by its concept, structure, and capabilities; its commitment to the renunciation of the use of force;

its renunciation of nuclear, biological, and chemical weapons as set down twenty-seven years ago; and its untiring efforts to achieve détente and arms limitation. Nor should it be forgotten that to have integrated millions of expellees [from the East] in a manner that did not transform them into a reservoir of revenge and violence—which would have created a factor of permanent instability in Europe—constitutes a considerable achievement toward peace.

Thus the Federal Republic of Germany, together with its allies, has laid an important foundation for a stable peace in Europe and has become an indispensable component of the Western order of peace in freedom. For many years governments and parliamentarians have time and again grappled with the principles underlying this peace order and the resultant consequences. They have taken their decisions to the best of their ability and in accordance with their consciences, working for the good of the free part of Germany and protecting it from harm. The citizens of our country have repeatedly affirmed these decisions in free elections.

24. *Deterrence Is Morally Acceptable*

By POPE JOHN PAUL II

Focus
Pope John Paul II has not issued a systematic and comprehensive pronouncement on the problem of nuclear arms, but his views clearly reflect the general thrust of statements made by his predecessors and the Second Vatican Council. (For interpretations of these see selections 21 and 22.)

This selection is drawn from two addresses by John Paul II; the first six paragraphs are from his World Day of Peace Message, released December 21, 1981, and the rest of the selection is from his address to the Second Special Session on Disarmament of the U.N. General Assembly, read by his secretary of state on June 11, 1982.

Rejecting secular and religious utopian schemes, the Pope says that Christians should approach the task of preventing war with "realism and humility." They must recognize that drives for aggression and domination lurk in the human heart, and they should not be deceived by the "false peace of totalitarian regimes." Christian citizens "have a right and even a duty to protect their existence and freedom by proportionate means against an unjust aggression."

John Paul II says that current peace movements reflect a "sincere desire for peace" but warns that they "often lend themselves to political exploitation." Deterrence "based on balance" and as a step toward arms control is a "morally acceptable" strategy.

Pope John Paul II, bishop of Rome, was formerly cardinal archbishop of Cracow, Poland. Long a major Catholic philosopher, he is the author of *The Acting Person* and many other works.

CHRISTIAN OPTIMISM BASED on the glorious cross of Christ and the outpouring of the Holy Spirit is no excuse for self-deception. For Christians, peace on earth is always a challenge because of the presence of sin in man's heart.

Motivated by their faith and hope, Christians therefore apply themselves to promoting a more just society; they fight hunger, deprivation, and disease; they are concerned about what happens to migrants, prisoners, and outcasts (cf. Mt. 25:35-36). But they know that while all these undertakings express something of the mercy and perfection of God (cf. Lk. 6:36., Mt. 4:48), they are always limited in their range, precarious in their results, and ambiguous in their inspiration. Only God the giver of life, when he unites all things in Christ (cf. Eph. 1:10), will fulfill our ardent hope by himself bringing to accomplishment everything that he has undertaken in history according to his Spirit in the matter of justice and peace.

Although Christians put all their best energies into preventing war or stopping it, they do not deceive themselves about their ability to cause peace to triumph, nor about the effect of their efforts to this end. They therefore concern themselves with all human initiatives in favor of peace and very often take part in them, but they regard them with realism and humility. One could almost say that they relativize them in two senses: they relate them both to the self-deception of humanity and to God's saving plan.

In the first place, Christians are aware that plans based on aggression, domination, and the manipulation of others lurk in human hearts, and sometimes even secretly nourish human intentions in spite of certain declarations or manifestations of a pacifist

---

"Beyond Nuclear Terror: Dialogue, 1982 World Day of Peace Message," was issued December 21, 1981; "Message of His Holiness Pope John Paul II Delivered by His Eminence Agostino Cardinal Casaroli, Secretary of State, on the Occasion of the Second Special Session of the General Assembly Devoted to Disarmament," was delivered June 11, 1982.

nature. For Christians know that in this world a totally and permanently peaceful human society is unfortunately a utopia, and that ideologies that hold up that prospect as easily attainable are based on hopes that cannot be realized, whatever the reason behind them.

It is a question of a mistaken view of the human condition, a lack of application in considering the question as a whole; or it may be a case of evasion in order to calm fear, or in still other cases a matter of calculated self-interest. Christians are convinced, if only because they have learned from personal experience, that these deceptive hopes lead straight to the false peace of totalitarian regimes. But this realistic view in no way prevents Christians from working for peace; instead, it stirs up their ardor, for they also know that Christ's victory over deception, hate, and death gives those in love with peace a more decisive motive for action than what the most generous theories about man have to offer; Christ's victory likewise gives a hope more surely based than any hope held out by the most audacious dreams.

This is why Christians, even as they strive to resist and prevent every form of warfare, have no hesitation in recalling that, in the name of an elementary requirement of justice, peoples have a right and even a duty to protect their existence and freedom by proportionate means against an unjust aggressor (cf. *Gaudium et Spes,* 79). However, in view of the difference between classical warfare and nuclear or bacteriological war—a difference, so to speak, of nature—and in view of the scandal of the arms race seen against the background of the needs of the Third World, this right, which is very real in principle, only underlies the urgency for world society to equip itself with effective means of negotiation.

SINCE THE END OF THE Second World War and the beginning of the "atomic age," the attitude of the Holy See and the Catholic Church has been clear. The Church has continually sought to contribute to peace and to build a world that would not have recourse to war to solve disputes. It has encouraged the maintenance of an international climate of mutual trust and cooperation. It has supported those structures that would help ensure peace. It has called attention to the disastrous effects of war. With the growth of new and more lethal means of destruction, it has pointed to the dangers involved and, going beyond the immediate perils, it has indicated what values to develop in order to foster cooperation, mutual trust, fraternity, and peace.

My predecessor Pius XII, as early as 1946, referred to "the might of new instruments of destruction," which "brought the problems of disarmament into the center of international discussions under completely new aspects" (Address to the College of Cardinals, 24 December 1946).

Each successive Pope and the Second Vatican Council continued to express their convictions, introducing them into the changing and developing situation of armaments and arms control. If men would bend to the task with good will and with the goal of peace in their hearts and in their plans, then adequate measures could be found, appropriate structures erected, to ensure the legitimate security of every people in mutual respect and peace; thus the need for these grand arsenals of fear and the threat of death would become superfluous.

Clear and Consistent Church Teaching

The teaching of the Catholic Church in this area has been clear and consistent. It has deplored the arms race and called for mutual, progressive, and verifiable reduction of armaments as well as greater safeguards against possible misuse of these weapons. It has done so while urging that the independence, freedom, and legitimate security of each and every nation be respected.

I wish to reassure you that the constant concern and consistent efforts of the Catholic Church will not cease until there is a general verifiable disarmament, until the hearts of all are won over to those ethical choices that will guarantee a lasting peace.

In turning to the current debate that concerns you, and to the subject at hand, we must recognize that no element in international affairs stands alone and isolated from the many-faceted interests of nations. However, it is one thing to recognize the interdependence of questions; it is another to exploit them in order to gain advantage. Armaments, nuclear weapons, and disarmament are too important in themselves and for the world ever to be made part of a strategy that would exploit their intrinsic importance in favor of politics or other interests.

Therefore it is important and right that every serious proposal that would contribute to real disarmament and that would create a better climate be given the prudent and objective consideration it deserves. Even small steps can have a value that would go beyond their material or technical aspects. Whatever the area under consideration, we need today freshness of perspective and a capacity to listen respectfully and carefully to the honest suggestions of every responsible party in this matter.

No Room for Rhetoric

In this context, there is what I would call the phenomenon of rhetoric. In an area already tense and fraught with unavoidable dangers, there is no place for exaggerated speech or threatening stances. Indulgence in rhetoric, in inflamed and impassioned vocabulary, in veiled threat and scare tactics, can only exacerbate a problem that needs sober and diligent examination.

On the other hand, governments and their leaders cannot carry on the affairs of state independent of the wishes of their peoples. The history of civilization gives us stark examples of what happens when that is tried. Currently the fear and preoccupation of so many groups in various parts of the world reveal that people are more and more frightened about what would happen if irresponsible parties unleash a nuclear war.

In fact, peace movements have been developing just about everywhere. In several countries, these movements, which have become very popular, are being supported by an increasing sector of the citizenry from various social levels and from different age groups and backgrounds, but especially by youth. The ideological bases of these movements are multiple. Their projects, proposals, and policies vary greatly and can often lend themselves to political exploitation. However, all these differences of form and shape manifest a profound and sincere desire for peace.

May I also join myself to the spirit of your draft appeal to public opinion for the birth of a truly universal consciousness of the terrible risks of war. May that consciousness in its turn lead to a general spirit of peace.

In current conditions, "deterrence" based on balance, certainly not as an end in itself but as a step on the way toward a progressive disarmament, may still be judged morally acceptable. Nonetheless, in order to ensure peace, it is indispensable not to be satisfied with this minimum, which is always susceptible to the real danger of explosion.

The Power of Negotiation

What then can be done? In the absence of a supranational authority of the type Pope John XXIII sought in his encyclical *Pacem in Terris,* one that one would have hoped to find in the United Nations organization, the only realistic response to the threat of war still is *negotiation.* Here I would like to remind you of an expression of Saint Augustine that I have already cited in another context: "Destroy war by the words of negotiations but do not destroy men by the sword." Today once again before you all I reaffirm my confidence in the power of true negotiations to arrive at just and equitable solutions. Such negotiations demand patience and diligence and must notably lead to a reduction of armaments that is balanced, simultaneous, and internationally controlled.

To be even more precise: The development of armaments seems to lead to the increasing interdependence of kinds of armaments. In these conditions, how can one countenance a balanced reduction if negotiations do not include the whole gamut of arms? To that end the continuation of the study of the "Complete Program of Disarmament" that your organization has already undertaken could facilitate the needed coordination of different forums and bring to their results greater truth, equity, and efficacy. . . .

May I close with one last consideration. The production and the possession of armaments are a consequence of an ethical crisis that

is disrupting society in all its political, social, and economic dimensions. Peace, as I have already said several times, is the result of
respect for ethical principles. True disarmament, that which will
actually guarantee peace among peoples, will come about only
with the resolution of this ethical crisis. To the extent that the
efforts at arms reduction and then at total disarmament are not
matched by parallel ethical renewal, they are doomed in advance
to failure.

25. *The Moral Imperative of Nuclear Disarmament*

By FOUR AMERICAN PROTESTANT BODIES

Focus The Catholic debate on nuclear arms on both sides of the Atlantic has been characterized by considerable depth and breadth. The same cannot be said for the discussion in mainline American Protestant churches. This is striking, because two decades earlier, both Protestant and Catholic leaders—Reinhold Niebuhr, John Courtney Murray, S.J., John C. Bennett, Paul Ramsey, A. J. Muste, William V. O'Brien, and Gordon Zahn, among others—made significant contributions to the American debate. Contemporary religious leaders in Western Europe have spoken more carefully and wisely than their American counterparts, perhaps because Europeans now feel closer to the nuclear threat than Americans do. In the 1960s, the Europeans assumed they were protected by the U.S. nuclear umbrella, and the Americans felt more vulnerable.

This selection contains excerpts from nuclear arms pronouncements made by four mainline Protestant bodies: the United Presbyterian Church, the Episcopal Church, the United Methodist Church, and the National Council of Churches. All four take a position similar to that of Jonathan Schell (selection 15). They speak of the madness of the "arms race," which, if unchecked, will lead to catastrophe for the human race, and they advocate an immediate, mutual, and verifiable nuclear freeze and a deep cut in the numbers and deployment of nuclear arms on both sides. Several endorse the Kennedy-Hatfield nuclear freeze resolution (selection 5) and appear to support the nuclear pacifism of Sidney Lens (selection 8). There is little evidence to suggest that these official Protestant views represent the majority opinion among Presbyterians, Methodists, Episcopalians, and the millions of other members of the National Council's constituent denominations.

None of the pronouncements addresses the actual alternatives facing statesmen in Western Europe or the United States. None comes to grips with the value or requirements of deterrence. Hence these Protestant voices contradict the views of Pope John Paul II and other Catholic leaders in this section.

The **Episcopal House of Bishops** includes all bishops of the Episcopal Church in the United States; it issues statements in its own name. The **Council of Bishops** of the **United Methodist Church** is composed of all bishops in the United States (plus those in Europe and non-autonomous Africa); it issues statements in its own name. The **Program Agency** of the **United Presbyterian Church,** which circulates the statement printed below, is a staff organization under the authority of the General Assembly, the ranking deliberative body of the church. The **National Council of the Churches of Christ in the U.S.A.** is an ecumenical body composed of 32 of the 219 Protestant and Orthodox religious denominations in the United States.

A. United Presbyterian Church

The "Call to Halt the Nuclear Arms Race," approved in May 1981 by the General Assembly of the United Presbyterian Church in the U.S.A., supports a nuclear freeze, a drastic reduction in nuclear arms, and a reallocation of resources to help the poor in the Third World. It is reprinted here in full.

To improve national and international security, the United States and the Soviet Union should stop the nuclear arms race. Specifically, they should adopt a mutual freeze on the testing, production, and deployment of nuclear weapons and of missiles and new aircraft designed primarily to deliver nuclear weapons. This is an essential, verifiable first step toward lessening the risk of nuclear war and reducing the nuclear arsenals.

The horror of a nuclear holocaust is universally acknowledged. Today, the United States and the Soviet Union possess 50,000 nuclear weapons. In half an hour, a fraction of these weapons can destroy all cities in the northern hemisphere. Yet over the next decade, the United States and the U.S.S.R. plan to build over 20,000 more nuclear warheads, along with a new generation of nuclear missiles and aircraft.

The weapon programs of the next decade, if not stopped, will pull the nuclear tripwire tighter. Counterforce and other "nuclear warfighting" systems will improve the ability of the United States and the U.S.S.R. to attack the opponent's nuclear forces and other military targets. This will increase the pressure on both sides to use their nuclear weapons in a crisis, rather than risk losing them in a first strike.

Such developments will increase hairtrigger readiness for massive nuclear exchange at a time when economic difficulties, political dissension, revolution, and competition for energy supplies may be rising worldwide. At the same time, more countries may acquire nuclear weapons. Unless we change this combination of trends, the danger of nuclear war will be greater in the late 1980s and 1990s than ever before.

Rather than permit this dangerous future to evolve, the United States and the Soviet Union should stop the nuclear arms race.

A freeze on nuclear missiles and aircraft can be verified by existing national means. A total freeze can be verified more easily than the complex SALT I and II agreements. The freeze on warhead production could be verified by the Safeguards of the International Atomic Energy Agency. Stopping the production of nuclear weapons and weapon-grade material and applying the Safeguards to U.S. and Soviet nuclear programs would increase the incentive of other countries to adhere to the Nonproliferation Treaty, renouncing acquisition of their own nuclear weapons, and to accept the same Safeguards.

A freeze would hold constant the existing nuclear parity between the United States and Soviet Union. By precluding production of counterforce weaponry on either side, it would eliminate excuses for further arming on both sides. Later, following the immediate adoption of the freeze, its terms should be negotiated into the more durable form of a treaty.

A nuclear weapons freeze, accompanied by government-aided conversion of nuclear industries, would save at least $100 billion each in U.S. and Soviet military spending (at today's prices) in 1981-1990. This would reduce inflation. The savings could be applied to balance the budget, reduce taxes, improve services, subsidize renewable energy, or increase aid to poverty-stricken Third World regions. By shifting personnel to more labor-intensive civilian jobs, a nuclear weapons freeze could also raise employment.

Stopping the U.S.-Soviet nuclear arms race is the single most useful step that can be taken now to reduce the likelihood of nuclear war and to prevent the spread of nuclear weapons to more countries. This step is a necessary prelude to creating international conditions in which:

- further steps can be taken toward a stable, peaceful international order;
- the threat of first use of nuclear weaponry can be ended;
- the freeze can be extended to other nations; and
- the nuclear arsenals on all sides can be drastically reduced or eliminated, making the world truly safe from nuclear destruction.

B. Episcopal Church

In a pastoral letter entitled "Identity, Pilgrimage, and Peace," the Episcopal House of Bishops in September 1982 calls the "arms race" a "strange insanity that grips the governments of the great nations." The bishops say that a U.S. "policy of deterrence that intends the use of nuclear weapons in a massive first strike against whole cities" is evil, that U.S. spending on nuclear arms is "an act of aggression" against starving children, and that the "American fever to match the Soviet Union weapon for weapon appears to be damaging the personality structure of a whole generation." A major portion of the "Peace" section of the letter follows.

YOUR BISHOPS PERCEIVE the nuclear arms race as the most compelling issue in the world public order. The arms race summons all morally serious people to action. Christians and Jews and all religious people are joined by multitudes of no religious allegiance.

Thus the voice we raise in this Pastoral Letter mingles with a chorus across the earth, in and out of the churches. The chorus mounts each precious day of life on the planet, warning against the strange insanity that grips the governments of the great nations.

We take seriously the lament of the former American ambassador to the Soviet Union, George Kennan, who writes, "We are losing rational control of weapons. . . . We are becoming victims of the monster we have created. I see it taking possession of our imagination and behavior, becoming a force in its own right, detaching itself from the political differences that inspired it, and leading both parties inexorably to the war they no longer know how to avoid."

Most of the passion for arms in America appears to rise from fear of a predatory power. If Russia would slow down, we would slow down. If Russia would stop, we would stop. Who is free? Who is hostage to whom? From whence shall come the moral freedom to break the spiraling thrall of seeking security in instruments that only purchase a diminished safety for both countries and a mounting insecurity for the entire world?

Does any Episcopalian seriously wish at this perilous moment for a muted Church, unready to risk the corrective clarity of a heavenly citizenship? This citizenship transcends in prophetic judgment all political systems. All human freedom finally depends on the value of human life and the freedom from paralyzing fear that a transcendent allegiance bestows.

We urge upon our people the detachment of penitence and forgiveness. Such detachment quiets our worldly fevers. It reveals our true identity. We are pilgrims with first fealty to the crucified and risen Christ. Holding that identity clearly and firmly, Christians may still disagree on the means of peace. We need not disagree, however, on our need for a dedicated military. We recognize that devoted Christians serve in our armed forces, which forces we need lest the United States signal irresolution. Still, we assert that a morally serious people must consider three aspects of American policy.

First, it is our understanding that the United States has never disavowed a policy of deterrence that intends the use of nuclear weapons in a massive first-strike against whole cities and land areas should it serve the national interest in warfare. Two hundred population centers are now targeted for such a strike. We ask, how can this policy be squared with a free nation's commitment to justice when it intends the calculated killing of millions of human beings who themselves are not on trial? We hold such an intention to be evil.

Second, the undiminished production and deployment of nuclear weapons, even if never used, consume economic, technical, and natural resources of astronomically rising proportions. The squandering of such resources constitutes an act of aggression against the thirty children who die every sixty seconds of starvation in the world. It is a callous act of indifference to the 500 million people of the world who are underfed. We declare this to be immoral and unjust.

Third, American fever to match the Soviet Union weapon for weapon appears to be damaging the personality structure of a whole generation. Current studies show that our children are growing up with a pervasive sense of fear, menace, cynicism, sadness, and helplessness. The effect of these eroding inner sensations is to impair the ability to form stable values, a sense of continuity and purpose, and a readiness for responsibility. Insofar as a belligerent nuclear arms policy distorts the spiritual and moral formation of children, such a policy defeats the free nations from within. The decadence that marks our culture may be of our own making. We believe it can only worsen without a tide of peacemaking witness, especially the steady protest of Christian people who claim their first allegiance, declare their true identity, and recover the bravery of pilgrim people.

We believe it to be the responsibility of the United States to take the bold initiative in nuclear disarmament, and to keep on taking it. The United States was the first to possess a nuclear weapon. The United States is the only nation to have used the weapon in war. If it comes to pass that these weapons, which the United States continues to refine and aim and stockpile, are used in war again, it is difficult to believe that any history a surviving neutral nation might record would fail to fix the blame on the United States.

C. United Methodist Church

The "Pastoral Letter to a People Called United Methodist" approved by the United Methodist Council of Bishops in May 1982 deals in part with nuclear arms. Like the Presbyterian call, it supports a nuclear freeze, deep cuts in nuclear stockpiles, and a reallocation of resources for civilian purposes. It refers to the U.S.–U.S.S.R. "arms race" as "madness." Portions of the letter are reprinted here.

IN 1945 TWO ATOMIC BOMBS initiated our current nightmarish dilemma. Today there are 50,000 nuclear weapons deployed or stockpiled. Thousands of these weapons have more than fifty times the lethal power of the bombs dropped on Hiroshima and Nagasaki. Even arguments concerning parity have become irrelevant because of the frightening overkill capacities of both the United States and the Soviet Union.

With military budgets skyrocketing and Cold War rhetoric escalating, the possibility of a nuclear holocaust becomes more and more real. The people of the world, both East and West, are awakening to the fact that we are on the verge of blowing ourselves up. The leaders of the superpowers, with the push of a button, could provide a "final solution" to the human story. Hundreds of millions of people would be burned to death or blown away or reduced to subhuman levels of existence. Networks of transportation and communication would be destroyed. The fabric of the social order would be torn to shreds. Life as we know it would cease to exist. It would be "annihilation without representation."

Because the threat of nuclear destruction looms ever larger and is qualitatively different from any other challenge confronting the human family, the Council of Bishops of the United Methodist Church endorses the Joint Resolution on Nuclear Freeze and Arms Reduction, now sponsored by more than 190 U.S. Senators and members of the House of Representatives. Governments must stop manufacturing nuclear weapons. Deployed weapons must be removed. Stockpiles must be reduced and dismantled. Verification procedures must be agreed upon. Eventual nuclear disarmament is necessary if the human race, as we know it, is to survive.

The Nuclear Freeze Resolution does not call for unilateral disarmament. Rather, it calls upon both the U.S.S.R. and the U.S.A. to halt the manufacture of nuclear weapons, reduce current supplies of nuclear arms, and agree upon verification procedures. Realizing that the superpowers do not trust one another, the serious negotiations called for should be based on mutual self-interest and a commitment to a global future.

Your Council of Bishops calls upon every United Methodist to pray for and work for peace with justice and freedom. Let your voice be heard in your own community. Let your convictions be shared with your state and national lawmakers. Write the President of the United States. We urge United Methodists outside the United States to work in their own communities and with their leaders and governments, as we join together in seeking an end to the arms race.

We must reverse the madness of our present course for the sake of your children, grandchildren, and generations yet unborn.

D. NATIONAL COUNCIL OF CHURCHES

The National Council of Churches of Christ in the U.S.A. is composed of some thirty Protestant and Orthodox denominations, including most of America's mainline bodies. Reprinted below are the "Resolution on a Nuclear Weapons Freeze" adopted by the Governing Board of the Council in May 1981 and portions of the Board's "Swords Into Plowshares" resolution passed in May 1982.

The 1981 statement urges "the United States and the Soviet Union to halt the nuclear arms race now by adopting promptly a mutual freeze on all further testing, production, and deployment of weapons and aircraft designed primarily to deliver nuclear weapons." It also supports unilateral initiatives on either side to make such a freeze more likely.

The 1982 statement reaffirms the Governing Board's commitment to a nuclear freeze and calls for a no-first-use pledge by the United States. It also urges American Protestants to "work to change those institutions in our society which are obstacles to peace," though it does not specify what these institutions are. It views with "satisfaction" the many manifestations of disarmament sentiment in America and Western Europe.

The 1981 Statement

Whereas, the Strategic Arms Limitation Talks (SALT) between the Soviet Union and the United States are in abeyance as a result of events of the last two years; and

Whereas, heightened international tension is leading to sharp increases in the armament programs of the Soviet Union and the United States as well as other nations with a consequent increase in the danger of war; and

Whereas, the National Council of Churches has long held that all the earth's resources are gifts of God, the Lord of Creation, and that men and women have a responsibility to preserve and enhance the created order, not to abuse and destroy it; and

Whereas, the National Council of Churches has consistently stressed the value of human life and God's activity in creation through the reconciling act in Christ whereby we are called to be agents of reconciliation, and

Whereas, representatives of the Orthodox and Protestant Churches of the Soviet Union and of the National Council of Churches, in a joint statement on March 27-29, 1979, entitled "Choose Life," "confessed that seeking our security through arms is, in fact, a false and idolatrous hope, and that true security can be found only in relationships of trust";

Therefore be it resolved that the Governing Board of the National Council of the Churches of Christ in the United States of America:

1. Urges both the United States and the Soviet Union to halt the nuclear arms race now by adopting promptly a mutual freeze on all further testing, production, and deployment of weapons and aircraft designed primarily to deliver nuclear weapons;

2. Until such time as a nuclear freeze by the United States and the Soviet Union may be agreed upon, supports initiatives by either or both that would demonstrate good faith and make it easier for the other to take similar steps; and

3. Encourages all program units of the National Council of Churches to examine their responsibilities and opportunities in providing educational materials and other resources regarding the nuclear freeze to constituent communions; and

4. Calls upon affiliated denominations, their judicatories and congregations, and related councils of churches to consider supporting this call for a nuclear freeze by:

a. Making available to their membership speeches, printed resources, and audio-visual materials that inform Christians about the reasons for and the importance of such a freeze;

b. Supporting financially and by direct involvement the movement for a nuclear freeze;

c. Calling upon their senators and representatives to provide congressional support for implementing such a freeze; and

d. Urging the President and the Department of State to pursue initiatives leading toward a mutual freeze on the testing, production, and deployment of all nuclear weapons and delivery vehicles.

The 1982 Statement

The Governing Board:

• *Calls for new initiatives* by the United States at the Second Special Session [on Disarmament of the United Nations General Assembly], including (a) a declaration of no first use of nuclear weapons, (b) a willingness to place a freeze on the production and deployment of strategic nuclear weapons, (c) a declaration of its willingness to proceed rapidly to the ratification of a Comprehensive Test Ban Treaty;

• *Calls upon the member communions,* in the light of our Christian vocation as peacemakers, to commit ourselves anew to the biblical vision of *shalom* by allocating more human and financial resources to education and action for peace and disarmament, by increasing our efforts to work to change the institutions in our society which are obstacles to peace, and by urging our people to turn away from an attitude of reliance on nuclear weapons as the chief source of our national security and to turn to the task of developing more effective political means to resolve international conflicts without the threat or use of armed force;

• *Views* with satisfaction the many new initiatives for peace and disarmament taken within and by the member communions and by the public in general in the United States and in many other countries of the world, most notably of late in Western Europe, and hopes that the Special Session will find ways to meet the desires for disarmament which have been so widely and massively expressed in recent months; and

• *Communicates* to churches in other nations, notably nations in Eastern Europe and other parts of the Soviet bloc, its readiness to join with them in common pursuit of the goal of disarmament, to unite with them and with people of all faiths in prayerful concern and support for the Second Special Session of the United Nations General Assembly, and to cooperate actively with them in continuing efforts to create a just, peaceful, and disarmed world.

26. An Ethic of Purity vs. An Ethic of Responsibility

By WOLFHART PANNENBERG

Focus   Professor Pannenberg, a Protestant theologian in West Germany, sympathizes with current anti-war sentiment but says it is naïve in the face of the "ugly reality" of the massive Soviet military build-up during a period of declining U.S. power and influence.

He criticizes earlier U.S. support of an unrealistic version of détente and notes a certain unevenness in U.S. policy. "Certainly, the United States is no longer looked upon as the sublime symbol of the democratic ideal in its moral purity." But the peace movement is "not . . . simply anti-American." Although Western Europeans no longer rely as fully on U.S. initiatives as they used to, they must continue to join with Americans in a common defense against a common adversary.

Professor Pannenberg identifies two schools of moral thinking among German religious leaders: "an ethics of conviction that adheres to the purity of moral principles, and an ethics of responsibility that feels obliged to consider the consequences that might follow from the decision embraced." These two approaches have been in conflict throughout the Christian era, though the ethic of responsibility has usually prevailed both in the teachings of theologians and in the behavior of statesmen. Pannenberg admonishes contemporary adherents of both schools to respect each other, but he clearly sides with the "Christian realism" of the German Catholic statement (selection 23) over the "utopian idealism" of some of his fellow Protestants.

Wolfhart Pannenberg is a noted Protestant theologian who teaches systematic theology at the University of Munich.

T HE PEACE MOVEMENT STARTED in the Netherlands (in the late 1970s) and has spread throughout Europe. In 1981, many of the major European cities saw demonstrations with participants numbering in the hundreds of thousands. Slogans like "living without armament" and "achieving peace without weapons" became major issues of the German Protestant *Kirchentag* at Hamburg last year. This was not simply the product of Eastern propaganda, although the Communist governments are not so foolish as to miss the opportunity of influencing such a mass movement to support their policies against the NATO decision of stepping up Western nuclear defense. That the issue was an ambiguous one to exploit for Eastern propaganda became obvious, however, when the dynamics of the peace movement crossed the Iron Curtain, and its concern was articulated, if more cautiously, in some of the Eastern countries themselves, especially in East Germany. The Western peace movement has not been simply anti-American either. When its participants call on their governments to go ahead with unilateral nuclear disarmament, it is because they think that one has to start where one is. The expectation, however, is that the other side will follow as soon as the socialist countries are relieved of their anxieties over nuclear destruction.

This reasoning sounds naïve after the sobering experience of Soviet exploitation of the détente mentality in the West during the seventies. But it was the Western governments and Western public opinion that until fairly recently encouraged the spirit of détente. They aroused the hopes for peaceful coexistence on a basis of mutual trust that the people now are reluctant to dismiss as delusive. It took a number of dramatic experiences to alert the Western governments to the ugly realities of Soviet imperialism. Many people could not adapt to that drastic change in political outlook. Europeans, especially, are somewhat slow to do so, because they

Reprinted by permission from the July-August 1982 issue of *Freedom at Issue*.

had been particularly pleased by the relaxation of East-West tensions. After all, Europeans, and especially the Germans, had been those who felt most directly the burden of the earlier confrontation. Afterwards, they were told that such confrontation was unnecessary, a device of poor politics. Now many don't understand why they are asked to fall back upon an attitude that they had learned to overcome. Little wonder that some of them suspect sinister machinations behind the sudden change of the scenario.

It is easy to respond that in recent years the West has had to learn certain lessons the hard way and that we must be more realistic now than most of the Western governments were for more than a decade. Yet, if until recently Western governments were so fundamentally mistaken in their evaluation of the situation, who guarantees that their present outlook is correct? And above all: the people are tired of confrontation. They are tired of living under the continuous threat of nuclear destruction for so many decades.

Moreover, it is not a question of a realistic assessment of the situation which seems to be subject to conflicting interpretations. It is a matter of emotional attitude. It is the need to breathe freely. An intelligent observer pointed to the peculiar fact that those involved in the movement talk as if there were no Soviet military threat. This is precisely the point. There are strong inducements for turning away from that ugly reality. Anything allowing such a turning away will be welcome. That it provides a rationale for doing so is part of the satisfaction the peace movement has to offer, and the more so the closer one lives to the Iron Curtain.

Decline of American Power

There is another side to the story. When in the fifties Europeans, and especially West Germans, accepted the ideological and political confrontation between liberal democracy and Communist totalitarianism, they were not without hope that the West could prevail. These days, however, the odds seem much less promising. Instead of a turning of the tide of Soviet expansionism, as John Foster Dulles promised, there has been a steady decline of Western and especially of U.S. power and influence all over the world, and at the same time a remarkable build-up by the other side. After so many agonizing occasions when the Western powers did not interfere with Soviet repressive action—from Prague in 1948, to East Germany in 1953, to Budapest in 1956, to Berlin in 1961, to Prague in 1968, to Warsaw in 1981—it seems unlikely that Western policies could bring about any significant change inside the Soviet bloc. And when we are told to expect internal changes toward some form of liberalization within the Communist power structures, why not act upon that premise now by avoiding the kind of confrontation that tends to harden the authoritarian forms of government on the other side?

It is this reasoning based on détente policies that continues to be persuasive within the peace movement. But behind this reasoning, there is the long-repeated experience of American political weakness against the Communist bloc and its political strategies. It seems to be the awareness of the weakness of the American position that finally explains the unwillingness of many Europeans to live up to the realities of the Communist threat in Europe. If seen against the background of such real or supposed American weakness, the almost desperate effort of the present U.S. administration to restore American military strength at this late hour of postwar history can be felt to be dangerously provocative in eliciting incalculable reactions from the other side.

Furthermore, in this situation Europeans have developed a new sensitivity to living in that part of the world that in all likelihood would become a major battlefield in any future war between the superpowers. The feeling was different, especially on this side of the Iron Curtain, as long as one could count on the secure superiority of the United States. Such superiority reduced the risk of war itself to a remote possibility. But this no longer seems to be the situation. And the concern is greatly increased in view of the Western strategic tendency in recent years to rely increasingly on nuclear deterrence against the superiority of the Warsaw Pact in conventional warfare. This Western strategy explains why so many Europeans are afraid of the U.S. nuclear weapons that are supposed to protect them.

The situation might be different if there were a stronger emphasis on conventional defense. This has been advocated by such a knowledgeable and brilliant mind as C. F. v. Weizsäcker, and certainly the development of a stronger conventional defense within the Western strategy—not to speak of a more balanced variety of military response—could ease the emotional stress felt by many Europeans.

The Question of Western Unity

It is perfectly understandable that many Americans feel puzzled by some of the new European sensitivities and especially by some of the ways of expressing them publicly. At times it may seem that Europeans are playing hazard with the loyalties of the Atlantic alliance, and some surely are. In general, however, the situation is more complex. Certainly, the United States is no longer looked upon as the sublime symbol of the democratic ideal in its moral purity. The last U.S. politician to arouse that kind of response in Europe, and especially in Germany, was John F. Kennedy, and it is hard to imagine that this enthusiasm could be easily restored after Vietnam. But there is a more realistic and thus perhaps a more secure basis for mutual trust and continuing alliance—a sense of sharing in a common tradition of cultural and political values. It is this awareness that keeps the alliance together beyond all occasional quarrels and frustrations. In this perspective, each defeat of U.S. politics in recent years was felt as a defeat of the European cause too, and if Europeans are afraid of what they suspect to be dangerous or mistaken directions in U.S. foreign and/or military politics, it is because they know the common cause to be at stake.

Within the framework of that common cause, there emerge particular concerns of a regional character. These need not occasion especial alarm. If the Atlantic alliance could survive only at the expense of the more peculiar interests of the European nations, it would already be dead. In the present situation, most Europeans feel that the U.S. position of power is no longer such that they can entrust their own national interests completely to the lead of the U.S. government—they must also look after themselves. France discovered this many years ago; other countries followed more recently.

This more pluralistic situation within the alliance undeniably creates difficulties for common action. A case in point is the recent disagreement over economic sanctions in response to Soviet military repression in Poland. The European nations felt it necessary to follow their own line in this matter, not only because of their interest in continuing political ties with Eastern governments, but also with a view to their own economic difficulties, which in turn reflect the high interest rate of the U.S. dollar. It seems to be understood now that this is not the issue for pushing the question of loyalty to the alliance to the breaking point.

One might think that questions like these had little to do with the peace movement. But in fact they are part of the larger picture that explains the movement's momentum. It springs from the aforesaid widespread feeling that Europeans cannot leave everything to U.S. strategic decisions, but must act for themselves. The peace movement is one manifestation of that mood. There are occasional anti-U.S. overtones and suspicions, but it would be unwise to overestimate their importance. By doing so one would only promote alienation between the two parts of the Western world. If anything, it is such an alienation that could present a real danger to the Atlantic alliance. There is no reason for dramatizing the situation.

European concern with the dangers of nuclear armament and strategy is not new. Although its present form is new, the concern itself has been expressed in popular movements and demonstrations since the fifties. At first it opposed nuclear weapons as such. It waned during the period of détente, but it is not surprising that it is again on the rise at the end of that period and in the face of new advances in the technology and numbers of nuclear weapons.

From the beginning, the European churches have been deeply involved, and the continuity of the issue can be seen most easily by studying the discussions carried on within those churches throughout the last three decades. The question of peace, after all, was always a fundamental and natural concern of Christian participation in the responsibility for social life. In the fifties, conflicting opinions about how the churches should respond to the new threat of nuclear weapons to the survival of humankind almost jeopardized the unity of some churches, including the German Evangelical Church (EKD). The conflict occurred, as it does now, between two different ethical attitudes: an ethics of conviction that adheres to the purity of moral principles, and an ethics of responsibility that feels obliged to consider the consequences that might follow from the decision embraced. In 1958, the synod of the EKD resolved that the two parties, while the conflict of their opinions could not be overcome, should respect each other in their Christian integrity as representing complementary courses toward the same end, the attainment of peace.

More recently, the question has been raised whether such a position is still sufficient after a quarter of a century. It had been understood as a provisional solution in a temporary phase of political crisis, and the period of détente created the feeling that the crisis and its danger had been overcome. Now it has become clear that the crisis is still with us and that the danger has increased rather than lessened. Some Christians, therefore, feel that they cannot go on recognizing the politics of securing peace by atomic weapons and increased armament as a genuinely Christian possibility. The Reformed Church of the Netherlands recently came to the conclusion that it can no longer consider participation in nuclear defense as a Christian option, and called on that nation to go ahead with unilateral nuclear disarmament.

The German Evangelical Church (EKD), on the other hand, reemphasized in its recent memorandum "on securing, promoting, and renewing peace" (1981) the position of the late fifties that Christians of opposite persuasion concerning the course for securing peace should continue to respect each other's Christian integrity. In this view, reconciliation must begin in the Christian community itself. Only thus does the church remain credible in its call for the replacement of military confrontation by political cooperation.

Peace Still Needs Protection

This is the vision of the memorandum. The sad truth, of course, is that precisely this was the political vision of the détente strategy that now seems to have failed, because Western hopes for cooperation, and Western restraint, have not been honored by the other side, but have been exploited for achieving political gains as well as for stepping up Eastern armaments. This experience does not mean that the vision of replacing military confrontation by political cooperation was wrong in itself. To the contrary, it enshrines the only hope for lasting peace. But apparently it takes more patience and must be followed through with more realism than idealistic enthusiasm sometimes expected. The sobering effect of the recent demonstrations of Soviet *Realpolitik* is more clearly expressed in a statement of the Central Committee of German Catholics, issued in November 1981 [see selection 23]. But the peace memorandum of the German Evangelical Church, also, warns that "serving peace without weapons" should not be turned into an absolute and uncompromising principle, as if we lived in a world that were no longer in need of protecting the peace we seek.

In addressing the question of peace, there is an element of utopian idealism in the Christian community that is basically a healthy reminder of the radicalism of Christian eschatological hope. In the context of the psychological warfare that accompanies the political struggle between the world powers, such utopian vision is easily misused. Many are concerned that this may happen or has already happened to the Christians participating in the larger peace movement. Nevertheless, it is good to hear their voice, while also sobering their enthusiasm by means of Christian realism. For that realism—concerning the power of sin in human societies and in their political conflicts—has characterized the Christian outlook on the world of politics from the beginning.

The kingdom of peace is not yet at hand, except in faith, and yet the Christian Church is there to witness to it. Perhaps the twofold witness of the churches—to the peace of God's kingdom promised to humanity, as well as to the realities of human sinfulness—can contribute to a continuous preservation of the precarious peace we enjoy these years. Certainly it should be taken into account so as to avoid unnecessary tensions and prejudices between the two parts of the Western world.

PART FIVE

Official Views

27. *Peace, Tyranny, and Arms Control*

By RONALD REAGAN

Focus   President Reagan delivered a major address on nuclear arms and arms control before the U.N. General Assembly on June 17, 1982. It is printed here in a slightly shortened version.

President Reagan places the nuclear problem in its historical and strategic context, briefly noting America's contribution to peace and stability since World War II. He recalls the record of Soviet tyranny and expansion—"violations of the Yalta agreements leading to the domination of Eastern Europe, symbolized by the Berlin Wall"; the takeovers of Czechoslovakia, of Hungary, and of Afghanistan; the repression of Poland; Soviet-sponsored terrorists in Central and South America, Africa, the Middle East, and Europe; and "Communist atrocities in Southeast Asia." He also protests the Soviet Union's illegal and brutal use of chemical and toxin weapons in Asia and Afghanistan.

"The decade of so-called détente witnessed the most massive Soviet build-up of military power in history," says the President. "They increased their defense spending by 40 per cent while American defense actually declined...." Because "the scourge of tyranny cannot be stopped by words alone," we have "embarked on an effort to renew our strength...."

The President says the United States has led in "serious disarmament and arms control proposals"

363

since 1945. He summarizes his four major proposals for reducing the risk of war: the elimination of land-based, intermediate-range missiles in Europe; a one-third reduction in strategic missile warheads on both sides; a substantial reduction in NATO and Warsaw Pact ground and air forces; and new safeguards to reduce the risk of accidental war. He stresses the need for effective verification safeguards. Calling his four proposals "an agenda for peace," he says: "We urge the Soviet Union to join with us in this quest."

D AG HAMMARSKJÖLD SAID twenty-four years ago this month, "We meet in a time of peace, which is no peace." His words are as true today as they were then. More than a hundred disputes have disturbed the peace among nations since World War II, and today the threat of nuclear disaster hangs over the lives of all our people. The Bible tells us there will be a time for peace, but so far this century mankind has failed to find it.

The record of history is clear: Citizens of the United States resort to force reluctantly and only when they must. Our foreign policy, as President Eisenhower once said, "is not difficult to state. We are for peace first, last, and always for very simple reasons." We know that only in a peaceful atmosphere, a peace with justice, one in which we can be confident, can America prosper as we have known prosperity in the past, he said.

At the end of World War II, we were the only undamaged industrial power in the world. Our military supremacy was unquestioned. We had harnessed the atom and had the ability to unleash its destructive force anywhere in the world. In short, we could have achieved world domination, but that was contrary to the character of our people. Instead, we wrote a new chapter in the history of mankind.

We used our power and wealth to rebuild the war-ravaged economies of the world, both East and West, including those nations who had been our enemies. We took the initiative in creating such international institutions as this United Nations, where leaders of good will could come together to build bridges for peace and prosperity.

America has no territorial ambitions. We occupy no countries, and we have built no walls to lock our people in. Our commitment

"Remarks Before the General Assembly, June 17, 1982," in *Weekly Compilation of Presidential Documents*, June 21, 1982.

to self-determination, freedom, and peace is the very soul of America. That commitment is as strong today as it ever was.

We look around the world and see rampant conflict and agression. There are many sources of this conflict—expansionist ambitions, local rivalries, the striving to obtain justice and security. We must all work to resolve such discords by peaceful means and to prevent them from escalation.

In the nuclear era, the major powers bear a special responsibility to ease these sources of conflict and to refrain from aggression. And that's why we're so deeply concerned by Soviet conduct. Since World War II, the record of tyranny has included Soviet violation of the Yalta agreements leading to domination of Eastern Europe, symbolized by the Berlin Wall—a grim, gray monument to repression that I visited just a week ago. It includes the takeovers of Czechoslovakia, Hungary, and Afghanistan; and the ruthless repression of the proud people of Poland. Soviet-sponsored guerrillas and terrorists are at work in Central and South America, in Africa, the Middle East, in the Caribbean, and in Europe, violating human rights and unnerving the world with violence. Communist atrocities in Southeast Asia, Afghanistan, and elsewhere continue to shock the free world as refugees escape to tell of their horror.

The decade of so-called détente witnessed the most massive Soviet build-up of military power in history. They increased their defense spending by 40 per cent while American defense actually declined in the same real terms. Soviet aggression and support for violence around the world have eroded the confidence needed for arms negotiations. While we exercised unilateral restraint, they forged ahead and today possess nuclear and conventional forces far in excess of an adequate deterrent capability.

Soviet oppression is not limited to the countries they invade. At the very time the Soviet Union is trying to manipulate the peace movement in the West, it is stifling a budding peace movement at home. In Moscow, banners are scuttled, buttons are snatched, and demonstrators are arrested when even a few people dare to speak about their fears.

Eleanor Roosevelt, one of our first ambassadors to this body, reminded us that the high-sounding words of tyrants stand in bleak contradiction to their deeds. "Their promises," she said, "are in deep contrast to their performances."

My country learned a bitter lesson in this century: The scourge of tyranny cannot be stopped with words alone. So we have embarked on an effort to renew our strength that had fallen dangerously low. We refuse to become weaker while potential adversaries remain committed to their imperialist adventures.

U.S. Leadership in Disarmament Proposals

Since the end of World War II, the United States has been the leader in serious disarmament and arms control proposals. In 1946, in what became known as the Baruch plan, the United States submitted a proposal for control of nuclear weapons and nuclear energy by an international authority. The Soviets rejected this plan. In 1955 President Eisenhower made his "Open Skies" proposal, under which the United States and the Soviet Union would have exchanged blueprints of military establishments and provided for aerial reconnaissance. The Soviets rejected this plan.

In 1963 the Limited Test Ban Treaty came into force. This treaty ended nuclear weapons testing in the atmosphere, outer space, or under water by participating nations. In 1970 the Treaty on the Non-Proliferation of Nuclear Weapons took effect. The United States played a major role in this key effort to prevent the spread of nuclear explosives and to provide for international safeguards on civil nuclear activities.

My country remains deeply committed to those objectives today, and to strengthening the non-proliferation framework. This is essential to international security. In the early 1970s, again at U.S. urging, agreements were reached between the United States and the U.S.S.R. providing for ceilings on some categories of weapons. They could have been more meaningful if Soviet actions had shown restraint and commitment to stability at lower levels of force.

The United Nations designated the 1970s as the First Disarmament Decade. But good intentions were not enough. In reality that ten-year period included an unprecedented build-up in military weapons and the flaring of aggression and use of force in almost every region of the world. We are now in the Second Disarmament Decade. The task at hand is to assure civilized behavior among nations, to unite behind an agenda of peace.

Over the past seven months, the United States has put forward a broad-based, comprehensive series of proposals to reduce the risk of war. We have proposed four major points as an agenda for peace: elimination of land-based, intermediate-range missiles; a one-third reduction in strategic ballistic missile warheads; a substantial reduction in NATO and Warsaw Pact ground and air forces; and new safeguards to reduce the risk of accidental war. We urge the Soviet Union today to join with us in this quest. We must act not for ourselves alone, but for all mankind.

On November 18 [1981], I announced U.S. objectives in arms control agreements. They must be equitable and militarily significant. They must stabilize forces at lower levels, and they must be verifiable. The United States and its allies have made specific, reasonable, and equitable proposals.

In February, our negotiating team in Geneva offered the Soviet Union a draft treaty on intermediate-range nuclear forces. We offered to cancel deployment of our Pershing II ballistic missiles and ground-launched cruise missiles in exchange for Soviet elimination of the SS-20, SS-4, and SS-5 missiles. This proposal would eliminate with one stroke those systems about which both sides have expressed the greatest concern.

On May 9 [1982] I announced a phased approach to the reduction of strategic arms. In a first phase, the number of ballistic missile warheads on each side would be reduced to about 5,000. No more than half the remaining warheads would be on land-based missiles. All ballistic missiles would be reduced to an equal level, at about one-half the current United States number. In the second phase, we would reduce each side's overall destructive power to equal levels, including a mutual ceiling on ballistic missile throw-weight below the current U.S. level. We are also prepared to discuss other elements of the strategic balance.

Before I returned from Europe last week, I met in Bonn with the leaders of the North Atlantic Treaty Organization. We agreed to introduce a major new Western initiative for the Vienna negotia-

tions on Mutual Balanced Force Reductions. Our approach calls
for common, collective ceilings for both NATO and the Warsaw
Treaty Organization. After seven years, there would be a total of
700,000 ground forces and 900,000 ground and air force personnel combined. It also includes a package of associated measures to
encourage cooperation and verify compliance.

We urge the Soviet Union and members of the Warsaw Pact to
view our Western proposal as a means to reach agreement in
Vienna after nine long years of inconclusive talks. We also urge
them to implement the 1975 Helsinki agreement on security and
cooperation in Europe.

Need for Effective Verification

Let me stress that for agreements to work, both sides must be
able to verify compliance. The building of mutual confidence in
compliance can be achieved only through greater openness. I
encourage the special session on disarmament to endorse the importance of these principles in arms control agreements. I have
instructed our representatives at the forty-nation Committee on
Disarmament to renew emphasis on verification and compliance.
Based on a U.S. proposal, a committee has been formed to examine these issues as they relate to restrictions on nuclear testing.

We are also pressing the need for effective verification
provisions in agreements banning chemical weapons. The use of
chemical and biological weapons has long been viewed with revulsion by civilized nations. No peacemaking institution can ignore
the use of those dread weapons and still live up to its mission. The
need for a truly effective and verifiable chemical weapons agreement has been highlighted by recent events. The Soviet Union and
its allies are violating the Geneva Protocol of 1925, related rules of
international law, and the 1972 Biological Weapons Convention.
There is conclusive evidence that the Soviets have provided toxins
for use in Laos and Kampuchea, and are themselves using chemical
weapons against freedom-fighters in Afghanistan.

We have repeatedly protested to the Soviet government, as well
as to the governments of Laos and Vietnam, their use of chemical

and toxin weapons. We call upon them now to grant full and free access to their countries or to territories they control so that United Nations experts can conduct an effective, independent investigation to verify cessation of these horrors.

Evidence of noncompliance with existing arms control agreements underscores the need to approach negotiation of any new agreements with care. The democracies of the West are open societies. Information on our defenses is available to our citizens, our elected officials, and the world. We do not hesitate to inform potential adversaries of our military forces and ask in return for the same information concerning theirs.

The amount and type of military spending by a country is important for the world to know, as a measure of its intentions and the threat that country may pose to its neighbors. The Soviet Union and other closed societies go to extraordinary lengths to hide their true military spending, not only from other nations but from their own people. This practice contributes to distrust and fear about their intentions.

Today, the United States proposes an international conference on military expenditures to build on the work of this body in developing a common system for accounting and reporting. We urge the Soviet Union, in particular, to join this effort in good faith, to revise the universally discredited official figures it publishes, and to join with us in giving the world a true account of the resources we allocate to our armed forces.

We will approach the Soviet Union with proposals for reciprocal exchanges in such areas as advance notification of major strategic exercises that otherwise might be misinterpreted; advance notification of ICBM launches within, as well as beyond, national boundaries; and an expanded exchange of strategic forces data.

While substantial information on U.S. activities and forces in these areas already is provided, I believe that jointly and regularly sharing information would represent a qualitative improvement in the strategic nuclear environment and would help reduce the chance of misunderstandings. I call upon the Soviet Union to join the United States in exploring these possibilities to build confidence, and I ask for your support of our efforts.

America urges you to support the agenda for peace that I have outlined today. We ask you to reinforce the bilateral and multilateral arms control negotiations between members of NATO and the Warsaw Pact and to rededicate yourselves to maintaining international peace and security, and removing threats to peace.

We who have signed the U.N. Charter have pledged to refrain from the threat or use of force against the territory or independence of any state. In these times when more and more lawless acts are going unpunished—as some members of this very body show a growing disregard for the U.N. Charter—the peace-loving nations of the world must condemn aggression and pledge again to act in a way that is worthy of the ideals that we have endorsed. Let us finally make the Charter live.

Let no nation abuse this common longing to be free of fear. We must not manipulate our people by playing upon their nightmares. We must serve mankind through genuine disarmament. With God's help we can secure life and freedom for generations to come.

28. *Strategy, Deterrence, and Arms Control*

By CASPAR W. WEINBERGER

Focus
During the summer of 1982, Secretary of Defense Caspar Weinberger and other senior administration officials became increasingly concerned with sensational and distorted accounts in both the American and the foreign press about the U.S. policy of nuclear deterrence. Many American and European scholars and others outside government shared this concern. To set the record straight, Secretary Weinberger took the unusual step of sending a letter to all American newspapers with a circulation of 500,000 or more. Since this is one of the clearest statements on deterrence made by a U.S. official, it is regrettable that only a handful of papers carried it in full.

Weinberger indirectly responds to the advocates of a nuclear freeze and a no-first-use pledge as well as to critics who say the United States is seeking a "first-strike capability." Emphasizing that the primary U.S. objective is to prevent nuclear war, he says that our strategy of deterrence, though "difficult for some to grasp because it is based on a paradox," is basically quite simple: "to make the cost of nuclear war much higher than any possible benefit to the country starting it. If the Soviets know in advance that a nuclear attack on the United States would bring swift nuclear retaliation, they would never attack in the first place."

For U.S. deterrence to continue to be successful, says Weinberger, "we must take steps to offset the

Soviet military build-up. If we do not modernize our arsenal now, as the Soviets have been doing for more than twenty years, we will, within a few years, no longer have the ability to retaliate." Retaliatory power is essential to avoid Soviet nuclear blackmail and to continue to deter Moscow from launching a first strike against us or our European allies.

Secretary Weinberger's views are in full harmony with President Reagan's arms control proposals.

I AM INCREASINGLY concerned with news accounts that portray this administration as planning to wage protracted nuclear war, or seeking to acquire a nuclear "war-fighting" capability. This is completely inaccurate, and these stories misrepresent the Administration's policies to the American public and to our allies and adversaries abroad. It is the first and foremost goal of this administration to take every step to ensure that nuclear weapons are never used again, for we do not believe there could be any "winners" in a nuclear war.

Our entire strategy aims to deter war of all kinds, but most particularly to deter nuclear war. To accomplish this objective, our forces must be able to respond in a measured and prudent manner to the threat posed by the Soviet Union.

That will require the improvements in our strategic forces that the President has proposed. But it does not mean that we endorse the concept of protracted nuclear war, or nuclear "war-fighting."

It is the Soviet Union that appears to be building forces for a "protracted" conflict (the doctrine of *zatyazhnaya voyna).*

The policy of deterrence is difficult for some to grasp because it is based on a paradox. But this is quite simple: to make the cost of nuclear war much higher than any possible "benefit" to the country starting it.

If the Soviets know in advance that a nuclear attack on the United States could and would bring swift nuclear retaliation, they would never attack in the first place. They would be "deterred" from ever beginning a nuclear war.

There is nothing new about our policy. Since the awful age of nuclear weapons began, the United States has sought to prevent nuclear war through a policy of deterrence. This policy has been

"Letter to Editors of Major Newspapers"; this text is from the *Los Angeles Times*, August 25, 1982.

approved, through the political processes of the democratic nations it protects, since at least 1950.

More important, it works. It has worked in the face of major international tensions involving the great powers, and it has worked in the face of war itself.

But for deterrence to continue to be successful in the future we must take steps to offset the Soviet military build-up. If we do not modernize our arsenal now, as the Soviets have been doing for more than twenty years, we will, within a few years, no longer have the ability to retaliate.

The Soviet Union would then be in a position to threaten or actually to attack us with the knowledge that we would be incapable of responding. We have seen in Poland, in Afghanistan, in Eastern Europe, and elsewhere that the Soviet Union does not hesitate to take advantage of a weaker adversary. We cannot allow the Soviet Union to think it could begin a nuclear war with us and win.

This is not just idle speculation. The Soviet Union has engaged in a frenzied military build-up, in spite of its economic difficulties.

The Soviets have continued to build greater numbers of nuclear weapons far beyond those necessary for deterrence. They now have over 5,000 nuclear warheads on ICBMs compared to about 2,000 only five years ago.

They have modified the design of these weapons and their launchers so that many of their land-based missiles are now more accurate, more survivable, and more powerful than our own.

They have also developed a refiring capability that will allow them to reload their delivery systems several times. They have elaborate plans for civil defense and air defense against any retaliation we might attempt.

And finally, their writings and military doctrine emphasize a nuclear war-fighting scenario. Whatever they claim their intentions to be, the fact remains that they are designing their weapons in such a way and in sufficient numbers to indicate to us that they think they could begin, and win, a nuclear war.

In the face of all this, it is my responsibility and duty as secretary of defense to make every effort to modernize our nuclear forces in such a way that the United States retains the capability to deter the Soviet Union from ever beginning a nuclear war. We must take the steps necessary to match the Soviet Union's greatly improved nuclear capability.

That is exactly why we must have a *capability* for a survivable and enduring response—to demonstrate that our strategic forces *could* survive Soviet strikes over an extended period. Thus we believe we could deter any attack.

Otherwise we would be tempting them to employ nuclear weapons or try to blackmail us. In short, we cannot afford to place ourselves in the position where the survivability of our deterrent would force the President to choose between using our strategic forces before they were destroyed or surrendering.

Those who object to a policy that would strengthen our deterrent, then, would force us into a more dangerous, hair-triggered posture. Forces that must be used in the very first instant of any enemy attack are not the tools of a prudent strategy. A posture that encourages Soviet nuclear adventurism is not the basis of an effective deterrent.

Our entire strategic program, including the development of a response capability that has been so maligned in the press recently, has been developed with the express intention of assuring that nuclear war will never be fought.

I know this doctrine of deterrence is a difficult paradox to understand. It is an uncomfortable way to keep the peace. We understand deterrence and accept the fact that we must do much more in order to continue to keep the peace.

It is my fervent hope that all can understand and accept this so that we can avoid the sort of sensationalist treatment of every mention of the word "nuclear" that only serves to distort our policy and to frighten people all over the world. Our policy is peace, and we deeply believe that the best and surest road to peace is to secure and maintain an effective and credible deterrent.

The purpose of U.S. policy remains to prevent aggression through an effective policy of deterrence, the very goal which prompted the formation of the North Atlantic Alliance, an alliance which is as vital today as it was the day it was formed.

29. Highlights of U.S. Arms Control Policy

By the DEPARTMENT OF STATE

Focus
The United States government, the most complex democratic organization in history, produces a gargantuan flow of words, from presidential speeches and other high-level pronouncements to countless statements by lesser officials and unnamed bureaucrats, many of them in the turgid and jargon-laden style known as "governmentese." The outlines of policy are hard to discern in all this. Little wonder that the American public, to say nothing of our friends abroad, is confused. And the press, for its part, has done a less than adequate job in making clear the essence of official domestic and foreign policy and proposals.

Defense Secretary Weinberger made a modest attempt to break through the maze with his lucid letter on nuclear deterrence (selection 28). Another noteworthy effort to clarify U.S. policy is the continuing series of two-page *Gist* memoranda put out by the State Department's Bureau of Public Affairs. *Gist* (whose editors emphasize that it is not an official statement) summarizes U.S. policy toward a particular country, region, or problem. Its summaries—despite their brevity—tend to be more coherent and complete than most of the official sources they draw upon.

This is true of the July 1982 *Gist* memorandum outlining U.S. arms control policy, reproduced here with slight editorial changes. It surveys U.S.

380

arms control efforts since World War II, the principles behind them, and the current initiatives of the Reagan administration, concluding with a section on verification and compliance. It further clarifies the President's address before the U.N. General Assembly in June 1982 (selection 27) and is probably the best brief exposition of where the United States stands on arms control.

SINCE THE END OF World War II, the United States has been the leader in serious disarmament and arms control proposals. Many of these have focused on controlling the spread of nuclear weapons. For example, in 1946 the United States submitted a proposal (the Baruch plan) for international control of nuclear weapons and nuclear energy. In 1955, President Eisenhower presented his "open skies" proposal, under which the United States and the U.S.S.R. would have exchanged blueprints of military establishments and provided for aerial reconnaissance. The Soviets rejected both plans.

Major arms control agreements to which we are a party include the Limited Test Ban Treaty (1963), which prohibits nuclear weapon tests in the atmosphere, in outer space, and under water; the Direct Communications Link or "hot line" agreement (1963), improved in 1971, for use by the United States and U.S.S.R. during international crises; the Outer Space Treaty (1967), which bans placing nuclear weapons or other weapons of mass destruction in outer space; the Non-Proliferation Treaty (1968), the purpose of which is to prevent the further spread of nuclear weapons; the Seabed Arms Control Treaty (1971), which prohibits the emplacement of nuclear weapons or weapons of mass destruction on the seabeds and ocean floor beyond a twelve-mile coastal zone; the Accidents Agreement (1971), which provides for U.S.-Soviet measures to reduce the likelihood of accidental nuclear war; the ABM Treaty (1972), which imposes limitations on defense against ballistic missile weapons; and the Interim Agreement on Strategic Offensive Arms (1972), which froze the number of strategic ballistic missile launchers on either side.

One of President Reagan's first official acts was to order an intense review of arms control policy, to learn the lessons of the

---

"U.S. Arms Control Policy," slightly edited from *Gist*, U.S. Department of State, Bureau of Public Affairs, July 1982.

381

past in order to achieve more lasting progress in the future. Four principles, which the Administration is working to implement, underlie the U.S. approach to arms control. We seek agreements that:

• Produce significant reductions in the arsenals of both sides;

• Result in equal levels of arms on both sides, since an unequal agreement, like an unequal balance of forces, can encourage coercion or aggression;

• Are verifiable, because when national security is at stake, agreements cannot be based upon trust alone; and

• Enhance U.S. and allied security and reduce the risk of war, because arms control is not an end in itself but rather a complement to defense preparations as an important means of underwriting peace and international stability.

On November 18, 1981, President Reagan offered to cancel deployments of the Pershing II and ground-launched cruise missile (GLCM) if the U.S.S.R. would eliminate its SS-20, SS-4, and SS-5 missiles. The United States is negotiating toward this end with the U.S.S.R. in Geneva.

On May 9 [1982] the President announced a two-phased approach to the Strategic Arms Reduction Talks (START), which began on June 29, aimed at the following objectives:

• In the first phase, we will seek to reduce the number of ballistic missile warheads on each side by one-third, to about 5,000. No more than half the remaining ballistic missile warheads will be on land-based missiles. We also will seek to cut the total number of all ballistic missiles to an equal level—about half the current U.S. level.

• In the second phase, we will seek further reductions in overall destructive power of each side's arsenal, including an equal ceiling on ballistic missile throw-weight below the current U.S. level.

The United States is party to the two existing international arms control agreements affecting chemical and biological weapons: The Geneva Protocol of 1925 prohibits the use in war of these weapons; the Biological Weapons Convention of 1972 prohibits the production, development, stockpiling, and transfer of biological and toxin weapons. Both agreements contain a common and fundamental flaw. Neither incorporates adequate means to verify compliance. Soviet compliance with both has been brought into sharp question by events in Southeast and Southwest Asia and in Sverdlovsk in the U.S.S.R. Because of this, it is clear that effective verification provisions are essential to future agreement in these fields. The United States is committed to achieving a complete and verifiable prohibition of chemical weapons development, production, stockpiling, and transfer, and, to that end, we participate in the forty-nation Committee on Disarmament in Geneva.

The Mutual and Balanced Force Reductions (MBFR) talks between NATO and the Warsaw Pact, under way in Vienna since 1973, are concerned with the reduction and limitation of conventional forces in Central Europe and with associated confidence-building, stabilization, and verification measures. On June 10, 1982, the President announced in Bonn the new NATO initiative to seek common collective ceilings in the reductions area (the Federal Republic of Germany, Belgium, the Netherlands, and Luxembourg in the West, and East Germany, Poland, and Czechoslovakia in the East) of about 700,000 ground forces and about 900,000 ground and air forces. The NATO initiative also includes measures to encourage cooperation and verify compliance.

Arms control agreements with a highly secretive adversary like the U.S.S.R. cannot be based simply on trust. We must have effective means of verification that enable us to know with confidence whether agreements are being honored. In practice, this means we must be able to monitor activities in the areas covered by such agreements in order to detect any violations; we must be able to do so early enough to permit us to assure Soviet compliance and take steps to offset the effects of any noncompliance. Agreements that cannot be effectively verified are not acceptable. In the past, we have relied primarily on national technical means (NTM) of verification—sophisticated data-collection methods (e.g., photographic, electronic, radar, seismic) operated unilaterally by the United States. As arms control agreements, the systems they cover, and the possibilities of concealment become more complex, it will be essential to supplement NTM with some form of "cooperative" verification measures. The Reagan administration has made clear that the United States will insist on verification procedures, including the possibility of measures beyond NTM, if necessary, to insure full compliance with any agreement.

30. The Soviet Approach to Arms Control

By LEONID BREZHNEV

Focus As George Orwell long contended, any official statement by a Soviet political leader must be translated from Marxist-Leninist jargon and interpreted in light of that ideology. Kremlin pronouncements on détente, arms control, or nuclear war may seem straightforward on the surface, but they are usually designed to accomplish a political purpose: to divide and weaken the West and to drive a wedge between the United States and its allies.

Other Soviet statements reveal Moscow's real intention more directly. In April 1980 the First Deputy Chief of the Main Political Administration of the Soviet Armed Forces, Colonel General G. V. Sredin, made such a statement (reprinted in the Fall 1980 *Strategic Review*, published by the United States Strategic Institute). Countering Western views that nuclear arms present the world with a radically different situation, General Sredin asserted that according to Marxist-Leninist precepts a nuclear war is "the continuation of politics by other, violent means" and that such a war would lead to "the inevitable demise" of the "entire imperialist system."

This argument has apparently convinced the Kremlin to prepare to fight a nuclear war with the expectation that it would speed the ultimate victory of Communism. Soviet troops on the European front, for example, are equipped to fight in and launch assaults through a radioactive environment.

General Sredin's views stand in sharp contrast to those of Leonid Brezhnev in this essay as well as those of Boris Ponomarev (selection 13). In the address printed below, which was read to the U.N. General Assembly on June 12, 1982, by Soviet Foreign Minister Andrei Gromyko, Brezhnev says, "Peace is the dominant feature of the Soviet Union's policy," and Moscow "solemnly" pledges not to be the first to use nuclear weapons. A nuclear war, he says, "could mean the destruction of human civilization and perhaps the end of life itself." He advocates an immediate nuclear freeze in Europe and asserts that the Soviet Union is the "convinced champion" of "the elimination of chemical weapons from the face of the earth."

Evidence suggests that Yuri Andropov, former KGB chief who succeeded Leonid Brezhnev on November 12, 1982, as the Soviet Communist party chairman, will continue with little change the policies of his predecessor. On the day of his election by the Central Committee, Andropov said: "We know full well that it is useless to beg peace from the imperialists. It can be upheld only by resting upon the invincible might of the Soviet armed forces."

CONCERN FOR PEACE is the dominant feature of the Soviet Union's policy. We are convinced that no contradictions between states or groups of states, no differences in social systems, ways of life, or ideologies, and no transient interests can eclipse the fundamental need common to all peoples—the need to safeguard peace and avert a nuclear war. Today, as never before, purposeful considered action is required of all states in order to achieve this lofty goal.

Guided by the desire to do all in its power to deliver the peoples from the threat of nuclear devastation and, ultimately, to exclude its very possibility from the life of mankind, the Soviet state solemnly declares: The Union of Soviet Socialist Republics assumes an obligation not to be the first to use nuclear weapons. This obligation shall become effective immediately, at the moment it is made public from the rostrum of the United Nations General Assembly.

Why is it that the Soviet Union is taking this step at a time when the nuclear powers participating in the North Atlantic Treaty Organization (NATO) grouping, including the United States, make no secret of the fact that not only does their military doctrine not rule out the possibility of the first use of nuclear weapons; it is actually based on this dangerous premise?

In taking this decision, the Soviet Union proceeds from the indisputable fact, which plays a determining role in the present-day international situation, that should a nuclear war start, it could mean the destruction of human civilization and perhaps the end of life itself on earth. Consequently, the supreme duty of leaders of states, conscious of their responsibility for the destinies of the world, is to exert every effort to ensure that nuclear weapons never be used.

The peoples of the world have the right to expect that the decision of the Soviet Union will be followed by reciprocal steps on

Excerpted from Chairman Brezhnev's message to the Second Special Session on Disarmament of the U.N. General Assembly, June 12, 1982, in the U.N. *Provisional Verbatim Record*, June 12, 1982.

the part of the other nuclear states. If the other nuclear powers assume an equally precise and clear obligation not to be the first to use nuclear weapons, that would be tantamount in practice to a ban on the use of nuclear weapons altogether, which is espoused by the overwhelming majority of the countries of the world.

In the conduct of its policy the Soviet Union will naturally continue to take into account how the other nuclear powers act, whether they heed the voice of reason and follow our good example or push the world downhill.

It is also the objective of the Soviet Union's initiative to raise the level of trust in relations between states, and that is particularly important in the present-day international situation, where trust has been gravely jeopardized by the efforts of those who are trying to upset the prevailing balance of forces, to gain military superiority over the Soviet Union and its allies, and to wreck everything positive which the policy of détente brings.

The military-political stereotypes inherited from the times of the one-time monopoly on the atom bomb have become outdated. The realities of today require a fundamentally different approach to the questions of war and peace. The present move of the Soviet Union makes it easier to take a different look at the entire complex of problems related to the limitation and reduction of armaments, especially nuclear arms, and furthers the cause of disarmament as a whole.

The vast achievements obtained by human creative and technological genius permit the peoples to open a new chapter in their history. Even now boundless opportunities exist for approaching the solution of such human problems of global magnitude as the struggle against hunger, disease, poverty, and many others; but that requires that scientific and technological progress be used exclusively to serve people's peaceful aspirations.

The Soviet Union is assuming an obligation not to be the first to use nuclear weapons, being confident in the power of sound judgment, and believing in mankind's ability to avoid self-annihilation and to ensure peace and progress for the present and coming generations.

In the search for measures which would actually halt the arms race, many political and public figures of various countries have recently turned to the idea of a freeze; in other words, of stopping a further build-up of nuclear potentials. The considerations advanced in this connection are not all in the same vein; still, on the whole, we believe they go in the right direction. We see in them the reflection of people's profound concern for their destinies. To use a figure of speech, people are voting for preserving the supreme value in the world, which is human life.

The idea of a mutual freeze of nuclear arsenals as a first step towards their reduction and, eventually, complete elimination is close to the Soviet point of view. Moreover, our country was the initiator of concrete proposals aimed at stopping the nuclear arms race in its quantitative and qualitative aspects.

And, finally, still another issue which the United Nations General Assembly, in our view, cannot disregard. Despite the obvious danger inherent in nuclear weapons, it is not to be forgotten that there are other means of mass destruction in the arsenals of states, including chemical weapons. The fact, however unthinkable, is that a few kilograms of poisonous agents from the tens of thousands of tons which are operational in the armies of certain countries are sufficient to kill several million people, and, in addition, new programs are being launched for the production of still more sophisticated lethal types of chemical weapons.

Everything should be done for the elimination of chemical weapons from the face of the earth. The Soviet Union is a convinced champion of this approach. We are prepared to agree without delay on the complete prohibition of chemical weapons and destruction of their stockpiles.

On the whole, the Soviet Union is in favor of moving ahead in all areas where opportunities exist for limiting and radically reducing armaments, be it nuclear weapons, other types of weapons of mass destruction, or conventional armaments. There is no type of weapon which the Soviet Union would not be prepared to limit or ban on the basis of reciprocity.

31. Peace With Freedom and Justice

By MARGARET THATCHER

Focus It is fitting to conclude this anthology of official and unofficial views on nuclear arms with a statement from the Prime Minister of Great Britain that for an official speech is unusually straightforward. Prime Minister Thatcher states her objective clearly: "peace with freedom and justice." Both arms and arms control must contribute to the achievement of these central aims of the West.

A strong advocate of nuclear deterrence, Mrs. Thatcher notes that "for thirty-seven years nuclear weapons *have* kept the peace between East and West"—a "priceless achievement." "Provided there is the will and good sense, deterrence can be maintained at substantially reduced levels of nuclear weapons."

"Nuclear war is indeed a terrible threat," she says, "but conventional war is a terrible reality." She points out that since Nagasaki there have been "something like 140 conflicts fought with conventional weapons, in which up to ten million people have died." Neither particular types of weapons nor the so-called arms race is the cause of war. "Aggressors do not start wars because an adversary has built up his own strength" but "because they believe they can gain more by going to war than by remaining at peace."

Mrs. Thatcher joins President Reagan (selection 27) in calling for a conventional and nuclear build-up by NATO to counter Soviet superiority and thus deter a Soviet first strike. This would be a position of strength from which the West could attempt to negotiate verifiable arms control and reduction agreements that would serve the true interests of all parties.

THE STATED PURPOSE of this Special Session is disarmament. The underlying and more important purpose is peace: not peace at any price, but peace with freedom and justice. As President Roosevelt commented during the last war, "We, born to freedom and believing in freedom, would rather die on our feet than live on our knees."

If arms control helps us to achieve those central aims more surely and at less cost, we must pursue it vigorously. But if it is carried out in a way that damages peace, we must resist it, recalling that there have been occasions when the known or perceived military weakness of an opponent has been at least as potent a cause of war as military strength. The true definition of disarmament should be the balanced and verifiable reduction of armaments in a manner that enhances peace and security.

Our generation faces a special responsibility, because the march of modern technology has made ever more deadly the weapons of war. We are most keenly aware of that in the case of nuclear weapons because of their terrifying destructive power, which my generation has witnessed and which none of us will ever forget. However alarmed we are by those weapons, we cannot disinvent them. The world cannot cancel the knowledge of how to make them. It is an irreversible fact.

Nuclear weapons must be seen as deterrents. They contribute to what Winston Churchill called "a balance of terror." There would be no victor in a nuclear exchange. Indeed, to start a war among nuclear powers is not a rational option. These weapons succeed insofar as they prevent war. And for thirty-seven years nuclear weapons *have* kept the peace between East and West.

The text (slightly abbreviated here) of Prime Minister Margaret Thatcher's statements before the Second Special Session on Disarmament of the U.N. General Assembly, June 23, 1982, is from British Information Services (New York), Policy Statements Series, Number 33, June 24, 1982.

393

That is a priceless achievement. Provided there is the will and good sense, deterrence can be maintained at substantially reduced levels of nuclear weapons. Of course we must look for a better system of preventing war than nuclear deterrence. But to suggest that between East and West there is such a system within reach at the present time would be a perilous pretense.

For us the task is to harness the existence of nuclear weapons to the service of peace, as we have done for half a lifetime. In that task, the duty of the nuclear powers is to show restraint and responsibility. The distinctive role of the non-nuclear countries, I suggest, is to recognize that proliferation of nuclear weapons cannot be the way to a safer world.

Since Nagasaki there have been no conflicts in which nuclear weapons have been used. But there have been something like 140 conflicts fought with conventional weapons, in which up to ten million people have died.

Nuclear war is indeed a terrible threat; but conventional war is a terrible reality. If we deplore the amount of military spending in a world where so many go hungry and so much else needs to be done, our criticism and our action should turn, above all, to conventional forces, which absorb up to 90 per cent of military spending worldwide.

We are all involved—we all have conventional forces. I am convinced that we need a deeper and wider effort throughout the non-nuclear field to see what we can do together to lighten the risks, the burdens, and the fears.

Aggression, Not Weapons, Causes War

But in a crucial sense we have not reached the root of the matter. For the fundamental risk to peace is not the existence of weapons of particular types. It is the disposition on the part of some states to impose change on others by resorting to force. This is where we require action and protection. And our key need is not for promises against first use of this or that kind of military weapon—such promises can never be dependable amid the stresses of war. We need a credible assurance, if such can ever be obtained, against starting military action at all. The leaders of the North Atlantic Alliance have just given a solemn collective undertaking to precisely that effect. They said: "None of our weapons will ever be used except in response to attack."

Let us face the reality. The springs of war lie in the readiness to resort to force against other nations, and not in "arms races," whether real or imaginary. Aggressors do not start wars because an adversary has built up his own strength. They start wars because they believe they can gain more by going to war than by remaining at peace. Few, if any, of the 140 conflicts since 1945 can be traced to an arms race. Nor was the World War of 1939-45 caused by any kind of arms race. On the contrary, it sprang from the belief of a tyrant that his neighbors lacked the means or the will to resist him effectively. Let us remember what Bismarck said, some seventy years earlier: "Do I want war? Of course not—I want victory." Hitler believed he could have victory without war, or with not very much or very difficult war. The cost to humanity of disproving that belief was immense; the cost of preventing him from forming it in the first place would have been infinitely less.

The causes that have produced war in the past have not disappeared today, as we know to our cost. The lesson is that disarmament and good intentions on their own do not ensure peace.

There is a natural revulsion in democratic societies against war, and we would much prefer to see arms build-ups prevented, by good sense or persuasion or agreement. But if that does not work, then the owners of these vast armories must not be allowed to imagine that they could use them with impunity.

But mere words, speeches, and resolutions will not prevent them. The security of our country and its friends can be ensured only by deterrence and by adequate strength—adequate when compared with that of a potential aggressor.

I have explained why in general I do not believe that armaments cause wars and why action on them alone will not prevent wars. It is not merely a mistaken analysis but an evasion of responsibility to suppose that we can prevent the horrors of war by focusing on its instruments. These are more often symptoms than causes.

But I have made these points not in any way to decry disarmament and arms control—I believe in them both—but to make quite clear what they can and cannot achieve. Excessive claims and demands have too often been not an aid to practical measures but a substitute for them. Arms control alone cannot remove the possibility of war. Nevertheless, the limitation and reduction of armaments can still do a great deal. They can reduce the economic burden of military preparation for legitimate self-defense. They can diminish the inhumanity of conflict. They can restrict the military use of advancing science and technology. They can ease tension between states and lessen the fears of people everywhere. To do these things, and to do them in a way that is balanced, verifiable, and dependable, is worth sustained and persistent endeavor.

Critics too often play down what has already been done through arms control agreements, whether formal or informal—such agreements as those on Outer Space, the Sea Bed, and Antarctica, the Partial Test Ban Treaty, the Non-Proliferation Treaty, and the various Geneva accords over the years.

My country was among the architects of some of these successes. Although a Comprehensive Test Ban Treaty has not been signed and the recent review of the Non-Proliferation Treaty was unproductive, there has been no additional nuclear weapon state since 1964.

We also contributed substantially to the banning of biological and toxin weapons in 1972.

We all wish that the achievements had been greater. But to suggest that what has been done so far is insignificant, is both inaccurate and unhelpful to further progress. We have a useful foundation upon which to build. Now we must go a stage further.

In the nuclear field, the hopes of the world lie in direct talks between the United States and the Soviet Union, the countries which have by far the largest arsenals. These could be greatly reduced in a way which would not endanger security. Decisive action is needed, not just declarations or freezes. I welcome the radical proposals made by the United States for substantially cutting strategic weapons, and for eliminating a whole class of intermediate-range systems (the zero option). The negotiations deserve the wholehearted support of us all.

We are also deeply concerned about the dangers of chemical warfare. When the world community decided in 1972 to ban the possession of biological and toxin weapons, we all looked forward to corresponding action next on chemical weapons. It has not happened. Moreover, there is reason to doubt whether every country that signed the 1972 Treaty is observing it. There have been disquieting and well-documented reports, which urgently need investigation, that chemical weapons and toxins have been used in some countries in Asia. The Committee on Disarmament needs to give renewed and determined impetus to a properly verifiable convention banning development and possession of such weapons.

Instability in the Warsaw Pact

The biggest concentration and confrontation of conventional forces anywhere in the world lies in Europe. But it is heavily weighted on the side of the Warsaw Pact. This situation is in itself a cause for concern. But there is the more fundamental question whether the Warsaw Pact can or wishes to sustain a stable relationship with the rest of the world. Do not the events in Poland and Afghanistan call this into question, the one by revealing deep disillusion within the Soviet empire, the second by demonstrating the Soviet propensity to extend its frontiers? Both are evidence of an underlying instability. Thus the need to secure a better balance in conventional arms becomes even more imperative.

For nine years we have patiently pursued talks in Vienna on Mutual and Balanced Force Reductions. Our diplomats involved in those talks must be the most patient of all, but they know that their work is of vital importance for peace. Fresh proposals are being made, and we hope that this time we shall see some progress.

Britain would also like to see a special effort made to agree on new mandatory confidence- and security-building measures in Europe. These could be a valuable complement to action in Vienna on force levels.

Through all these many negotiations there runs a crucial factor—verification. How can we be sure that what it is said will be done, will be done? Where national security is at stake we cannot take agreements on trust, especially when some states are so secretive and such closed societies. Agreements which cannot be verified can be worse than useless—they can be a new source of danger, fear, and mistrust. Verification is not an optional extra in disarmament and arms control. It is the heart of the matter.

Differences over verification have often proved a stumbling block in arms control negotiations. But we note that the Soviet Union is now prepared to open part of its civil nuclear installations to inspection by the International Atomic Energy Agency—a step that the United Kingdom took years ago. I note also that the Soviet Union now seems ready to accept the need for systematic on-site inspection in respect of a chemical weapons treaty. We need to redouble our efforts to bridge the gaps that still remain.

Britain's record over the years in work on disarmament and arms control stands up to any comparison. We wish to do more—not by rhetoric, still less by propaganda postures, but by steady, relevant work going step by step through these difficult and complex matters. This is a long, patient, and unspectacular business. There is no short cut if we are to retain security and peace.

The message I bring is practical and realistic. It is the message of a country determined to preserve and spread the values by which we live.

It contains nought of comfort to those who seek only a quiet life for themselves at the expense of the freedom of others, nor to those who wish to impose their will by force. Peace and security require unbroken effort.

- We believe that the human values of civilization must be defended.

- We believe that international law and the United Nations Charter must be upheld.

- We believe that wars are caused not by armaments but by the ambitions of aggressors and that what tempts them is the prospect of easy advantage and quick victory.

- We believe that the best safeguard of peace lies not only in a just cause but in secure defense.

- We believe in balanced and verifiable disarmament where it can be the servant of peace and freedom.

- We believe that the purpose of nuclear weapons should be to prevent war and that it can be achieved by smaller armories.
- We believe that a balanced reduction in conventional weapons could create greater stability.
- We believe we have a right and a duty to defend our own people whenever and wherever their liberty is challenged.

My country seeks the path of peace with freedom and justice. As Abraham Lincoln put it in his Second Inaugural Address: "With malice towards none, with charity for all, with firmness in the right ... let us strive on to finish the work we are in. . . ."

Bibliography

Much valuable and available material could not, for reasons of space, be listed here. The serious reader may want to consult some of the following sources:

Government Documents: U.S. Department of State, Bureau of Public Affairs: *Gist, Current Policy, Special Report,* and *Department of State Bulletin.*

Public Policy Analysis: *Commentary.* Committee on the Present Danger. *Foreign Affairs. Foreign Policy.* The Heritage Foundation: *Backgrounder, Issue Bulletin, National Security Record,* and *Policy Review. Strategic Review. Survival* (London). *The Washington Quarterly.*

Protestant Views: *The Christian Century. Christianity and Crisis. Christianity Today.* National Association of Evangelicals, Office of Information. National Council of Churches, Office of Information. Religious News Service.

Catholic Views: *America. Commonweal.* National Catholic News Service: *Origins* and *Catholic Trends. National Catholic Register. National Catholic Reporter.*

Part One: The Issues

BOOKS

Allen, Richard V.; Gray, Colin; Kalicki, Jan; Pfaltzgraff, Robert; and Scoville, Herbert. *A Heritage Roundtable: The Nuclear Freeze.* Washington: The Heritage Foundation, 1982.

Brennan, Donald G., ed. *Arms Control, Disarmament, and National Security.* New York: George Braziller, 1961.

Freedman, Lawrence D. *The Evolution of Nuclear Strategy.* New York: St. Martin's Press, 1981.

Graham, Daniel O. *Shall America Be Defended? SALT II and Beyond.* New Rochelle, N.Y.: Arlington House, 1979.

Hackett, Sir John. *The Third World War: The Untold Story.* New York: Macmillan, 1982.

Kahan, Jerome H. *Security in the Nuclear Age.* Washington: The Brookings Institution, 1975.

Kahn, Herman. *On Thermonuclear War.* Princeton, N.J.: Princeton University Press, 1960.

401

_____. *Thinking About the Unthinkable.* New York: Horizon Press, 1962.

Kennan, George F. *Russia, the Atom, and the West.* New York: Greenwood, 1974.

_____. *The Nuclear Delusion: Soviet-American Relations in the Atomic Age.* New York: Pantheon, 1982.

Kissinger, Henry A. *Nuclear Weapons and Foreign Policy.* New York: Anchor, 1958.

Lefever, Ernest W., ed. *Arms and Arms Control.* New York: Praeger, 1962.

Levine, Robert A. *The Arms Debate.* Cambridge, Mass.: Harvard University Press, 1963.

Osgood, Robert E. *Limited War Revisited.* Boulder, Colo.: Westview Press, 1979.

Stewart-Smith, Geoffrey, ed. *Global Collective Security in the 1980s.* London: Foreign Affairs Publishing Co., 1982.

Thompson, W. Scott, ed. *From Weakness to Strength.* San Francisco: Institute for Contemporary Studies, 1980.

ARTICLES

Adelman, Kenneth. "Beyond MAD-ness." *Policy Review* 17, Summer 1981.

Bahr, Egon. "No First Use." *The New York Times,* May 10, 1982.

Ball, Desmond. "Can Nuclear War Be Controlled?" *Adelphi Papers* No. 169, Autumn 1981.

Bethe, Hans A., and Long, Franklin A. "The Value of a Freeze." *The New York Times,* September 22, 1982.

Coats, Wendell John, Jr. "The Ideology of Arms Control." *Journal of Contemporary Studies,* Summer 1982.

Dean, Jonathan. "Beyond First Use." *Foreign Policy* 48, Fall 1982.

Gray, Colin S. "'Dangerous to Your Health': The Debate Over Nuclear Strategy and War." *Orbis,* Summer 1982.

Joffe, Josef. "Retain First Use." *The New York Times,* June 16, 1982.

Kahn, Herman. "Thinking About Nuclear Morality." *The New York Times Magazine,* June 13, 1982.

Kissinger, Henry A. "Strategy and the Atlantic Alliance." *Survival,* September/October 1982.

Lowe, George E. "Twentieth-Century Deterrents and Deterrence." *The Virginia Quarterly Review,* Winter 1970.

Pipes, Richard. "Why the Soviet Union Thinks It Could Fight and Win a Nuclear War." *Commentary,* July 1977.

Snyder, Jed. "Strengthening the NATO Alliance: Toward a Strategy for the 1980s." *Naval War College Review,* March-April 1981.

Walworth, Andrew, and Meslin, Brad. "Soviet Strategic Doctrine: A Reader's Guide." *Journal of Contemporary Studies,* Summer 1982.

Part Two: The Peace Movement

BOOKS

Adams, Ruth, and Cullen, Susan. *The Final Epidemic: Physicians and Scientists on Nuclear War.* Chicago: Educational Foundation for Nuclear Science, 1981.

Barron, John. *The KGB's Magical War for 'Peace.'* New York: Reader's Digest Press, forthcoming 1983.

Ground Zero. *Nuclear War: What's in It for You?* New York: Pocket Books, 1982.

Lens, Sidney. *The Bomb.* New York: Lodestar Books, 1982.

Taylor, Richard, and Pritchard, Colin. *The Protest Makers: The British Nuclear Disarmament Movement of 1958-1965, Twenty Years On.* New York: Pergamon Press, 1980.

ARTICLES

Butterfield, Fox. "Anatomy of the Nuclear Protest." *The New York Times Magazine,* July 11, 1982.

Flannery, Christopher. "Vox Populi." *Journal of Contemporary Studies,* Summer 1982.

Hornung, Klaus. "Die Friedensbewegung und der Staat ohne letzte Verantwortung." *Criticon* 68, November/December 1981.

Kissinger, Henry A. "Nuclear Weapons and the Peace Movement." *The Washington Quarterly,* Summer 1982.

Kittlaus, Paul. "German Protestantism and the Peace Movement." *The Christian Century,* December 23, 1981.

Sincere, Richard E. "Ground Zero: What's in It for You?" *Journal of Civil Defense,* June 1982.

Sobran, Joseph. "Rainbow in Central Park." *National Review,* July 9, 1982.

Voorhoeve, Joris J. C. "Pacifism in the Netherlands." *Freedom at Issue,* July/August 1982.

Voorst, L. Bruce van. "The Critical Masses." *Foreign Policy* 48, Fall 1982.

Part Three: The Apocalyptic Premise

GOVERNMENT DOCUMENTS

Brown, William M. *The Nuclear Crisis of 1979.* Washington: Defense Civil Preparedness Agency, 1975.

Chester, C. V., and Kearny, C. H., eds. *Chinese Civil Defense* (excerpts from *Basic Military Knowledge,* Shanghai, 1975). Oak Ridge, Tenn.: Oak Ridge National Laboratory, 1977.

Civil Defense (Hearings of January 8, 1979). Washington: Senate Committee on Banking, Housing, and Urban Affairs, 1979.

Civil Defense and Limited Nuclear War (Hearings of April 28, 1976). Washington: Joint Committee on Defense Production, 1976.

Deterrence and Survival in the Nuclear Age (The 'Gaither Report' of 1957). Washington: Joint Committee on Defense Production, 1976.

Glasstone, Samuel, and Dolan, Philip J., eds. *The Effects of Nuclear Weapons.* 3rd edition. Washington: United States Department of Defense and the Energy Research and Development Administration, 1977.

In Time of Emergency. Washington: Defense Civil Preparedness Agency, 1977.

Protection in the Nuclear Age. Washington: Defense Civil Preparedness Agency, 1977.

Swedish Civil Defence Administration. *Facts About the Civil Defence . . . to Protect and Save Lives.* Karlstad, Sweden, 1978.

Titov, M. N.; Yegorov, P. T.; Gayko, B. A.; et al. *Civil Defense* (1974 edition). Moscow: Publishing House for Higher Education, 1974. Translation edited by G. A. Cristy. Oak Ridge, Tenn.: Oak Ridge National Laboratory, July 1975. (The 1969 and 1970 editions have also been published by the Oak Ridge National Laboratory.)

Zivilschutz heute: für den Bürger—mit dem Bürger. Bonn: Der Bundesminister des Innern, 1979.

BOOKS

Calder, Nigel. *Nuclear Nightmares: An Investigation Into Possible Wars.* New York: Penguin Books, 1981.

Kahn, Herman. *Thinking About the Unthinkable.* New York: Horizon Press, 1962.

Kearny, Cresson H. *Nuclear War Survival Skills.* Boston, Va.: American Security Council Foundation, 1979.

Royal United Services Institute. *Survival in the Nuclear Age: A Symposium.* New York: Pergamon Press, 1982.

405

Scheer, Robert. *With Enough Shovels: Reagan, Bush, and Nuclear War.* New York: Random House, 1982.

Schell, Jonathan. *The Fate of the Earth.* New York: Knopf, 1982.

ARTICLES

Clayton, Bruce Douglas. "Planning for the Day After Doomsday." *The Bulletin of the Atomic Scientists,* September 1977.

Devaney, John F. "Shute and Schell: Nuclear Pollution." *Journal of Civil Defense,* August 1982.

Glynn, Patrick. "Nuclear Polemics." *Journal of Contemporary Studies,* Vol. V, No. 3, Summer 1982.

Hampsch, George H. "On Preventing Nuclear Genocide: The Moral Dilemma of Nuclear Deterrence." *Vital Speeches of the Day,* September 1, 1982.

Lardner, James. "Fear and the Bomb." *The Washington Post,* April 16, 1982.

Lerner, Max. "Visions of the Apocalypse." *The New Republic,* April 28, 1982.

Silber, John R. "Of True and False Apocalypses: A Dialectic." *Bostonia,* February 1982. Reprinted in *Public Opinion,* August/September 1982.

Sincere, Richard E. "Concept of Nuclear War Survival Defended." *United Methodist Reporter,* October 8, 1982.

Thaxton, Richard. "The Logic of Nuclear Escalation." *The Progressive,* February 1982.

Zuckerman, Ed. "Hiding From the Bomb—Again." *Harper's,* August 1979.

————. "How Would the U.S. Survive a Nuclear War?" *Esquire,* March 1982.

Part Four: The Churches

BOOKS

Abbott, Walter M., S.J., and Gallagher, Joseph, eds. *The Documents of Vatican II.* New York: America Press, Association Press, 1966.

Allers, Ulrich S., and O'Brien, William V., eds. *Christian Ethics and Nuclear Warfare.* Washington: Institute of World Policy, Georgetown University, 1961.

Before It's Too Late: Report of the Public Hearing on Nuclear Weapons and Disarmament. Geneva: World Council of Churches, 1982.

Benestad, J. Brian. *The Pursuit of a Just Social Order: Policy Statements of the U.S. Catholic Bishops, 1966-80.* Washington: Ethics and Public Policy Center, 1982.

Bonhoeffer, Dietrich. *Ethics.* New York: Macmillan, 1955.

Church and the Bomb, The: Nuclear Weapons and the Christian Conscience. London: CIO Press, 1982.

Durnbaugh, Donald F., ed. *On Earth Peace.* Elgin, Ill.: The Brethren Press, 1978.

Goodwin, Geoffrey, ed. *Ethics and Nuclear Deterrence.* New York: St. Martin's Press, 1982.

Johnson, James T. *Just War Tradition and the Restraint of War: A Moral and Historical Inquiry.* Princeton, N.J.: Princeton University Press, 1981.

Kaplan, Morton A., ed. *Strategic Thinking and Its Moral Implications.* Chicago: University of Chicago Press, 1973.

Lawler, Philip F. *The Bishops and the Bomb: The Morality of Nuclear Deterrence.* Washington: The Heritage Foundation, 1982.

Lefever, Ernest W. *Ethics and United States Foreign Policy.* New York: Meridian Press, 1957.

————, ed. *Ethics and World Politics.* Baltimore: Johns Hopkins University Press, 1972.

McSorley, Richard, S.J. *Kill? For Peace?* Washington: Center for Peace Studies, 1977.

Moral Dilemma of Nuclear Weapons, The. New York: Council on Religion and International Affairs, 1961.

Nagle, William J., ed. *Morality and Modern Warfare.* Baltimore: Helicon Press, 1960.

Niebuhr, Reinhold. *The World Crisis and American Responsibility.* Edited by Ernest W. Lefever. New York: Association Press, 1958.

O'Brien, William V. *The Conduct of Just and Limited War.* New York: Praeger, 1981.

O'Connor, John J. *In Defense of Life.* Boston: St. Paul Editions, 1981.

Peace and Disarmament: Documents of the World Council of Churches and the Roman Catholic Church. Geneva and Rome: Commission of the Churches on International Affairs and the Pontifical Commission *Iustitia et Pax,* 1982.

Ramsey, Paul. *The Just War: Force and Political Responsibility.* New York: Scribner's, 1968.

Walzer, Michael. *Just and Unjust Wars.* New York: Basic Books, 1977.

Weigel, George. *The Peace Bishops and the Arms Race: Can Religious Leadership Help in Preventing War?* Chicago: World Without War Council, 1982.

ARTICLES

Fialka, John J. "Atom-Weapons Issue Stirs Divisive Debate in the Catholic Church." *The Wall Street Journal,* June 9, 1982.

Graham, Billy. "Graham's Mission to Moscow." *Christianity Today*, June 18, 1982.

Hall, Terry. "Of Myth and Reality: The Arms Race." *The Presbyterian Layman*, September/October 1982.

Hehir, J. Bryan. "The New Nuclear Debate: Political and Ethical Considerations." In *American Society of Christian Ethics: Selected Papers*. Missoula, Montana: Scholars Press, 1975.

Lefever, Ernest W. "The Just War Doctrine: Is It Relevant to the Nuclear Age?" *Worldview*, October 1961.

Lyles, Jean Caffrey. "Canons for Postnuclear Christians." *The Christian Century*, October 6, 1982.

Murray, John Courtney, S.J. "Morality and Foreign Policy." *America*, March 19 and March 26, 1960. Reprinted in *Worldview*, May 1960.

————. "Morality and Modern War." *Worldview*, December 1958.

————. "The Issue of 'Survival.'" *Worldview*, August 1958.

Niebuhr, Reinhold. "Nuclear War and the Christian Dilemma." *Theology Today*, January 1959.

Novak, Michael. "Mahonyism." *National Review*, July 9, 1982.

O'Brien, Conor Cruise. "Ethics, the Church, and the Bomb." *The Observer* (London), October 24, 1982.

O'Brien, William V. "The Moral Problem of Force." *Worldview*, December 1960.

————. "The Peace Debate and American Catholics." *The Washington Quarterly*, Spring 1982.

Pézéril, Daniel. "L'épiscopat catholique des Etats-Unis et le défi atomique." *Le Monde* (Paris), August 25, 1982.

Preus, David W. "The Need to Be Evenhanded." *Freedom at Issue*, July/August 1982.

"Proposal to Tilt the Balance of Terror, A." *Christianity Today*, April 9, 1982.

Ramsey, Paul. "The Politics of Fear." *Worldview*, March 1960.

Schall, James V., S.J. "Ecclesiastical Wars Over Peace." *National Review*, June 25, 1982.

————. "Religion and National Security." *International Security Review*, Summer 1982.

Sincere, Richard E. "Repugnant Moralism: Churches and Nuclear Weapons." *Journal of Civil Defense*, October 1982.

Spaeth, Robert L. "Disarmament and the Catholic Bishops." *This World*, Summer 1982.

Stanmeyer, William. "Toward a Moral Nuclear Strategy." *Policy Review* 21, Summer 1982.

Von Hoffman, Nicholas. "Bombing Out." *The New Republic,* June 9, 1982.

Winters, Francis X., S.J. "The Bow or the Cloud? American Bishops Challenge the Arms Race." *America,* July 25, 1981.

————. "Nuclear Deterrence Morality: Atlantic Community Bishops in Tension." *Theological Studies,* September 1982.

Part Five: Official Views

GOVERNMENT DOCUMENTS

Arms Control and Disarmament Agreements. U.S. Arms Control and Disarmament Agency, 1980.

"Arms Control and the Nuclear Freeze Proposal." U.S. Department of State, Bureau of Public Affairs, April 1982.

Haig, Alexander M. "Arms Control and Strategic Nuclear Forces." *Current Policy* No. 339, U.S. Department of State, Bureau of Public Affairs, November 4, 1981.

————. "Peace and Deterrence." *Current Policy* No. 383, U.S. Department of State, Bureau of Public Affairs, April 6, 1982.

Reagan, Ronald. "Arms Control and the Future of East-West Relations." *Current Policy* No. 387, U.S. Department of State, Bureau of Public Affairs, May 9, 1982.

————. "Promoting Democracy and Peace" (Speech before the British Parliament). *Current Policy* No. 399, U.S. Department of State, Bureau of Public Affairs, June 8, 1982.

ARTICLES

"Brezhnev's Statement and Excerpts from Gromyko's Speech." *The New York Times,* June 16, 1982.

"Excerpts from Mrs. Thatcher's Talk." *The New York Times,* June 24, 1982.

Feulner, Edwin, Jr. "The Critical Questions of War and Peace." *Vital Speeches of the Day,* September 1, 1982.

Nitze, Paul H. "A-Arms and NATO." *The New York Times,* April 13, 1982.

Reagan, Ronald; Rostow, Eugene; Brezhnev, Leonid; and *Pravda.* "Nuclear Weapons and Arms Control." *Survival,* September/October 1982.

Index of Names

Waldheim, Kurt, 124
Walesa, Lech, 181
Wall Street Journal, 97, 142, 215
War Resisters League, 93, 95, 142,
 145-46, 152-54, 159-60, 164
Warsaw, 155, 355
Warsaw Pact, 14, 24, 29, 31, 41, 47, 52,
 78, 355, 364, 368-69, 371, 383, 397
Washington, D.C., 15-16, 93, 97, 103,
 112, 119, 124, 129-30, 136-37, 149-50,
 154, 156, 190, 207
Washington Post, 110, 125
Weather Underground, 134
Weinberger, Caspar, 101, 374, 380
Weiss, Cora, 133-34, 161
Weiss, Ted, 131
Weizsäcker, C. F. von, 355
Westmoreland, William, 155
White House, 130, 309, 311, 316, 319
White, William Allen, 214
Why We Need Action, Not Words
 (England), 180
Wilson, Woodrow, 214
Winter, Sidney, 265
Winters, Francis X., S.J., 309, 314,
 316-17
Wisconsin, 96, 153
Wisconsin, University of, 134
Women's International League for Peace

and Freedom, 142-43, 150, 152,
 159-61
Women Strike for Peace, 132-33, 139,
 146, 149-50, 152, 158-59
Woodward, Joanne, 161
Woolsey, James, 74
World Bank, 4
World Council of Churches, 185, 191, 283
World Peace Council (WPC), 105, 107,
 117-19, 122, 124, 127-29, 131-32,
 134-35, 139, 147-50, 152-56, 158,
 160-61, 163, 165-66, 170, 176, 180-81,
 184, 186, 189
World War I, 43, 142, 167, 214, 241, 277
World War II, 43, 85, 87, 110, 114, 123,
 125, 145-47, 155, 157, 163, 168*n.,* 169,
 196-97, 215-16, 241, 283, 287, 320-21,
 325, 334, 364-67, 380-81, 395

Yalta, 194, 364, 366
Yemen, 118
Yugoslavia, 4

Zahn, Gordon, 339
Zhivkov, Todor, 186-87
Zhurkin, Vitaly, 137
Zia-ul-Haq, Mohammed, 77
Zuckerman, Sir Solly, 102

Ethics and Public Policy Reprints

Reprints are $1 each. Postpaid if payment accompanies order.
Orders of $20 or more, 10 per cent discount.